Interpersonal Communication

Relating to Others

Steven A. Beebe
Texas State University

Susan J. Beebe
Texas State University

Mark V. Redmond
Iowa State University

Lisa Salem-Wiseman
Humber College

Pearson

EDITORIAL DIRECTOR: Claudine O'Donnell
ACQUISITIONS EDITOR: Jennifer Sutton
MARKETING MANAGER: Euan White
PROGRAM MANAGER: Emily Dill and Kamilah Reid-Burrell
PROJECT MANAGER: Colleen Wormald
MANAGER OF CONTENT DEVELOPMENT: Suzanne Schaan
DEVELOPMENTAL EDITOR: Christine Langone
MEDIA EDITOR: Christine Langone
MEDIA DEVELOPER: Bogdan Kosenko

PRODUCTION SERVICES: Cenveo® Publisher Services
PERMISSIONS PROJECT MANAGER: Shruti Jamadagni
PHOTO AND TEXT PERMISSIONS RESEARCH:
    Integra Publishing Services
INTERIOR AND COVER DESIGNER: Anthony Leung
COVER IMAGE: Rawpixel.com/Shutterstock
VICE-PRESIDENT, CROSS MEDIA AND PUBLISHING
    SERVICES: Gary Bennett

Pearson Canada Inc., 26 Prince Andrew Place, Don Mills, Ontario M3C 2T8.

ISBN: 978-0-13-427664-9

3   17

Library and Archives Canada Cataloguing in Publication

Beebe, Steven A., 1950-, author
   Interpersonal communication : relating to others/Steven A. Beebe, Susan J. Beebe, Mark V. Redmond, and Lisa Salem-Wiseman.—Seventh Canadian edition.

Includes bibliographical references and index.
ISBN 978-0-13-427664-9 (hardback)

   1. Interpersonal communication—Textbooks. I. Beebe, Susan J., author II. Redmond, Mark V., 1949-, author III. Salem-Wiseman, Lisa, author IV. Title.

BF637.C45I68 2017   153.6   C2016-905312-1

DEDICATED TO OUR FAMILIES

Mark and Matthew Beebe

Peggy, Nicholas, and Eric Redmond, and Beth Maroney

Rachel and Jonathan Salem-Wiseman

Contents

PART TWO
Interpersonal Communication Skills 99

7 Nonverbal Communication Skills 152

8 Conflict Management Skills 179

PART THREE
Interpersonal Communication in Relationships 210

Special Features

ADAPTING TO DIFFERENCES: Understanding Others

CANADIAN CONNECTIONS

BUILDING YOUR SKILLS

E-CONNECTIONS: RELATING TO OTHERS

Preface

The world does not revolve around you. While that may seem obvious, we believe that this observation has profound implications for the study of interpersonal communication because at the heart of quality interpersonal relationships is an emphasis on others. A focus on others rather than on oneself has been the hallmark of most volunteer, community, and faith movements in the world for millennia. Yet this book is not about religion or philosophy. It's about how to enhance the quality of your interpersonal communication with others.

This book takes an other-oriented approach to interpersonal communications. Becoming other-oriented is not a single skill but rather a collection of skills and principles designed to increase your sensitivity to and understanding of others. Being other-oriented doesn't mean you abandon your own thoughts, ignore your feelings, and change your behaviour only to please others; that would not only be unethical, it would also be an ineffective approach to developing genuine, honest relationships with others. An other-oriented person is self-aware as well as aware of others. As we stress throughout the book, true empathy, emotional intelligence, and sensitivity are possible only when we feel secure about our own identities.

The importance of being other-oriented was the foundation of the first six Canadian editions of *Interpersonal Communication: Relating to Others,* and it continues as the central theme of the seventh Canadian edition.

Why You Need This New Edition

We have written this book for Canadian college and university students who are seeking to enhance their interpersonal communication and relationships. While retaining the strengths that readers seem to value most—an easily accessible style, an other-oriented approach, and a balance of theory and skills—this new edition gave us the opportunity to add fresh examples and research throughout and to fine-tune every feature, activity, and illustration. Here are five good reasons to give this new edition a close look:

1. **Further integration of learning objectives:** We have refined the learning objectives and coordinated them with each chapter's key topic headings. These pairings are highlighted in the opening section of each chapter.

2. **Increased emphasis on technology:** Our updated and expanded coverage now includes increased discussion of the role and function of new technologies in interpersonal communication. The revised feature *E-Connections: Relating to Others*, included in each chapter, explores the influence of new technologies on interpersonal communication and relationships.

3. **Increased emphasis on diversity:** Inherent in our other-oriented approach is the understanding that people differ in significant ways. It is because of these differences that we need skills and principles that allow us to develop links to other people and encourage us to establish meaningful interpersonal relationships with them.

   The updated *"Adapting to Differences: Understanding Others"* features in every chapter present research conclusions and communication strategies for understanding differences. In addition, through examples, illustrations, and research conclusions liberally woven throughout the book, we identify ways to become other-oriented despite differences we encounter in people of other genders or of other cultures or ideologies.

4. **New and updated discussions, research findings, and examples:** New material throughout the book covers such provocative topics as emotional intelligence and how to measure it, hate speech, listening in the 21st century, the dark side of the Internet, meta-messages and online communication, and networked families and co-workers.

5. **Increased and updated Canadian content:** This new edition continues to provide a Canadian context for understanding interpersonal communication to allow Canadian students to see themselves and their environment reflected in the text. This is achieved through the introduction of new and updated examples, photographs, statistics, and stories from contemporary Canadian society, as well as through the updated "*Canadian Connections*" feature, included in every chapter, which presents new information and research.

Our Partnership with Students and Instructors

As important as we think a textbook is, it is only one tool that facilitates teaching and learning. In the seventh Canadian edition of *Interpersonal Communication: Relating to Others*, we continue our tradition of offering a wide variety of instructional resources to help instructors teach and students learn principles and skills of interpersonal communication.

Built into the book is a vast array of pedagogical features:

- Chapter-opening sections highlight the one-to-one correspondence of the learning objectives and chapter outlines.
- Student-friendly Recap features periodically summarize key concepts and terms.
- *Building Your Skills* boxes throughout the text offer practical strategies for applying chapter content to help students improve their own communication skills and relationships.
- Key terms are defined in the margins and are included in a glossary at the end of the book.
- Our Study Guide feature at the end of each chapter gives students the opportunity to review, apply, and explore key chapter concepts through critical thinking questions, questions about ethics, and classroom activities.

Instructor Supplements

- An Instructor's Resource Manual includes teaching suggestions, suggested course syllabi, and guidelines for using the complete teaching–learning package.
- A Test Item File is available in Microsoft Word or in computerized format in MyTest for Windows® and Macintosh®.
- PowerPoint® Presentations can be used to enhance lectures and tutorial instruction.

Student Supplements

The Companion Website for *Interpersonal Communication: Relating to Others* will benefit students and instructors alike. For students, this website provides:

- Multiple choice self-assessment quizzes for practice testing
- Glossary flashcards relevant to the terms in the text

Acknowledgments

The authors are grateful to those colleagues who acted as reviewers for this seventh Canadian edition, including Natalie Chinsam, Centennial College; Mary Close, Canadore College; Christopher M. Gee, Northwest Community College; Kim Ann Laush, Mohawk College; Diana Fong Lee, Conestoga College; Jenny Quianzon, Centennial College; and Nathan Wilson, Durham College.

© Diego Cervo/Shutterstock

1

Introduction to Interpersonal Communication

66 The single biggest problem in communication is the illusion that it has taken place. **99** —George Bernard Shaw

1

Interpersonal communication is like breathing; it is a requirement for life, and, like breathing, it is inescapable. Unless you live in isolation, you communicate interpersonally every day, whether you're texting a friend, discussing vacation plans with your significant other, or emailing a professor to ask for an extension on an assgnment.

Even before we are born, we respond to movement and sound. With our first cry, we announce to others that we are here, and we continue to communicate until our last breath. Even before we can talk, we communicate our feelings, needs, and wants to others, and as we grow, even though many of our messages are not verbalized, we continually send messages to others through our facial expressions, body language, and gestures. Without interpersonal communication, a special form of human communication that occurs as we manage our relationships, people suffer and even die. For this reason, the United Nations has denounced the practice of long-term solitary confinement, as it is considered a form of torture.[1]

Human communication is at the core of our existence. Think of the number of times you communicate with people each day as you work, eat, study, shop, or go about your other daily activities. How many conversations did you have today? How many text messages did you send? How many emails did you exchange? How many times did you post on social media? We spend most of our waking hours engaging in some form of interpersonal communication, and it is through these exchanges that we develop relationships with others.

Because these relationships are so important in our lives, later chapters will focus on the communication skills and principles that explain and predict how we develop, sustain, and sometimes end relationships. We'll explore such questions as the following:

- Why do we like some people and not others?

- How can we interpret other people's unspoken messages with greater accuracy?

- Why do some relationships blossom and others die?

- How can we better manage disagreements with others?

- How can we better understand our relationships with our family, friends, and co-workers?

communication. The process of acting upon information.

In face-to-face encounters, we simultaneously exchange verbal and nonverbal messages that result in shared meanings. Through this kind of interrelation, we build relationships with others.

(© Monkey Business Images/Shutterstock)

This chapter charts the course ahead, addressing key questions about what interpersonal communication is and why it is important. We will begin by seeing how our understanding of the interpersonal communication process has evolved, and we will conclude by examining how we initiate and sustain relationships through interpersonal communication.

What Is Interpersonal Communication?

To understand interpersonal communication, we must begin by understanding how it relates to two broader categories: communication in general and human communication. For decades, scholars have attempted to arrive at a general definition of communication, and yet experts cannot agree on a single one. In the broadest sense, however, we can define **communication** as the process of acting on information.

One person does or says something, and others think or do something in response to the actions or words as they understand them.

To refine our broad definition, we can say that **human communication** is the process of making sense out of the world and sharing that sense with others by creating meaning through the use of verbal and nonverbal messages.[2] We learn about the world by listening, observing, tasting, touching, and smelling; then we share our conclusions with others. Human communication encompasses many media, including speeches, songs, letters, books, articles, poems, advertisements, radio and television broadcasts, email, online discussion groups, texts, and tweets.

Interpersonal communication is a distinctive, transactional form of human communication involving mutual influence, usually for the purpose of managing relationships. Three essential elements of this definition set the unique nature of interpersonal communication apart from other forms of human communication: interpersonal communication is (1) a distinctive form of communication, which (2) involves mutual influence between individuals and (3) helps us manage our relationships.

Interpersonal Communication Is a Distinctive Form of Communication

For years, many scholars defined interpersonal communication simply as communication that occurs when two people interact face to face. This limited definition suggests that if two people are interacting, then they are engaged in interpersonal communication. Today, interpersonal communication is defined not just by the number of people who communicate but also by the quality of the communication. Interpersonal communication occurs not when you simply interact with someone, but when you treat the other as a unique human being.[3]

Philosopher Martin Buber influenced our thinking about human communication when he presented the concept of true dialogue as the essence of authentic communication. He described communication as consisting of two different qualities of relationships. An "I–It" relationship, in Buber's terminology, is an impersonal one; the other person is viewed as an "It" rather than as an authentic, genuine person. Think of all human communication as ranging on a continuum from impersonal to interpersonal communication. **Impersonal communication** occurs when you treat people as objects, or when you respond to their roles rather than to who they are as unique individuals. When you ask a server in a restaurant for a glass of water or respond to a stranger's advertisement on Kijiji or Craigslist, you are interacting with the role, not necessarily with the person. You know nothing personal about this individual, and he or she knows nothing personal about you.

Interpersonal communication occurs when you interact with another person as a unique, authentic individual rather than as an object or "It." Buber calls this kind of relationship an "I–Thou" relationship. An "I–Thou" relationship involves true dialogue and is not self-centred. The communicators have developed an attitude toward each other that is honest, open, spontaneous, nonjudgmental, and based on equality rather than superiority.[4] When you chat with your neighbour over coffee, call your mother, or engage in a series of texts with your best friend, you are communicating interpersonally.

Although interpersonal communication is more intimate and reveals more about the people involved than does impersonal communication, not all interpersonal communication involves sharing closely guarded personal information. As we discuss later in the text, there are degrees of intimacy when interacting with others.

human communication. The process of making sense of the world and attempting to share that sense with others by creating meaning through the use of verbal and nonverbal messages.

interpersonal communication. A distinctive, transactional form of human communication involving mutual influence, usually for the purpose of managing relationships.

impersonal communication. Communication that occurs when we treat people as objects, or when we respond to their roles rather than to who they are as unique persons.

RECAP — The Continuum Between Interpersonal Communication and Impersonal Communication

Interpersonal Communication	Impersonal Communication
• People are treated as unique individuals.	• People are treated as objects.
• People communicate in an "I–Thou" relationship. Each person is treated as a unique individual.	• People communicate in an "I–It" relationship. Each person is reduced to his or her role.
• There is true dialogue and honest sharing of self with others.	• There is mechanical interaction rather than an honest sharing of feelings.
• Interpersonal communication often involves communicating with someone you care about and depend upon, such as a friend, family member, or co-worker.	• Impersonal communication involves communicating with people with whom you share no history and expect no future.

Interpersonal Communication Involves Mutual Influence Between Individuals

Mutual influence means that all partners are affected by the transaction. The degree of mutual influence varies a great deal from transaction to transaction. You probably would not be affected a great deal by a brief smile you receive from a stranger on a bus, but you would be greatly affected by hearing the words "I love you" for the first time from your romantic partner. Long-lasting interpersonal relationships are sustained by a spirit of mutual equality and respect. True dialogue, says researcher Daniel Yankelovich, involves a collaborative climate. It's not about winning or losing an argument. It's about being understood and accepted.[5]

Buber asserts that the quality of being fully "present" when communicating with another person is an essential part of an "I–Thou" relationship.[6] To be present is to give your full attention to the other person. The quality of interpersonal communication is enhanced when both you and your communication partner are simultaneously present and focused on each other.

Interpersonal Communication Helps Us Manage Our Relationships

A **relationship** is the ongoing connection you make with another person through interpersonal communication. When two individuals are in a relationship, everything that one person says or does influences the other person.

We initiate and form relationships by communicating with others whom we find appealing in some way. When we wish to develop a relationship with someone, we seek to increase our interactions with that person, and we use interpersonal communication continually to maintain the relationship. We also use interpersonal communication to redefine or end relationships.

- **Mass communication** occurs when someone communicates the same message to many people at once, but the creator of the message is usually not physically present, and listeners have virtually no opportunity to respond immediately to the speaker. Messages communicated via radio and TV are examples of mass communication.

- **Public communication** occurs when a speaker addresses a large audience in person.

- **Small-group communication** occurs when a group of, say, 3 to 15 people meet to interact with a common purpose and mutually influence one another. The purpose of the gathering could be to solve a problem, make a decision, learn, or just have fun. While communicating with others in a small group, it is also possible to communicate

relationship. An ongoing connection made with another person through interpersonal communication.

mass communication. Type of communication that occurs when one person issues the same message to many people at once; the creator of the message is usually not present and there is virtually no opportunity for listeners to respond to the speaker.

public communication. Type of communication that occurs when a speaker addresses a large audience in person.

small-group communication. Type of communication that occurs when a group of from 3 to 15 people meet to interact with a common purpose and mutually influence one another.

interpersonally, that is, to communicate in order to manage a relationship with one or more individuals in the group.

- Finally, **intrapersonal communication** is communication with oneself. Thinking is perhaps the best example of intrapersonal communication. In our discussion of self and communication in Chapter 2, we discuss the relationships between one's thoughts and one's interpersonal communication with others.

▶ RECAP Comparing Key Definitions

Term	Definition
Communication	The process of acting on information
Human communication	The process of making sense of the world and sharing that sense with others
Interpersonal communication	A distinctive, transactional form of human communication involving mutual influence, usually for the purpose of managing relationships

Why Is Interpersonal Communication Important?

Why learn about interpersonal communication? Because it touches every aspect of your life. Developing quality interpersonal relationships with others is not only pleasant or desirable; it is vital for your well-being. Learning how to understand and improve interpersonal communication can improve relationships with family, loved ones, friends, classmates, and colleagues, and can enhance the quality of your physical and emotional health.

Improve Relationships with Family

Relating to family members can be a challenge. The divorce statistics in Canada document the difficulties that can occur when people live in relationships with each other: about half of all marriages end in divorce. While we don't claim that you will avoid all family conflicts if you learn the principles and skills of interpersonal communication, you will be more likely to develop creative, constructive solutions to family conflict if you understand what's happening and can promote true dialogue with your spouse, parent, sibling, or child. Furthermore, family relationships play a major role in determining how you interact with others. Author Virginia Satir calls family communication "the largest single factor determining the kinds of relationships [people make] with others."[7]

Improve Relationships with Friends and Lovers

How many friends do you have? Are you currently in love or have you been in love before? Developing friendships and falling in love can provide crucial sources of satisfaction and happiness in life. Conversely, the end of a relationship can cause a great deal of stress and can even lead to depression. Studying interpersonal communication may not unravel all the mysteries of romantic love and friendship, but it can offer insight into our behaviour and help us to improve our relationships.

Improve Relationships with Classmates and Colleagues

Although we choose our friends and lovers, we don't always have the same flexibility in choosing those with whom we work or attend classes, even though we may spend more time with them than with our family and friends. Understanding how relationships develop

intrapersonal communication. Communication with oneself; thinking.

at school and on the job can help us avoid conflict and stress and can increase our sense of satisfaction. Experts agree that relationships with peers have a significant impact on student success at the postsecondary level; in fact, one study concluded that "the student's peer group is the single most potent source of influence on growth and development during the undergraduate years."[8]

Moreover, success or failure in a job can often hinge on how well we get along with our supervisor and our peers. Recent studies have shown that training workers to relate and communicate as a team improves quality and productivity in many occupations, and so today more and more workplaces are adopting teamwork as a management strategy. In fact, as we discuss in the following *Canadian Connections* box, the Conference Board of Canada and its partners, including business organizations and training/education partners, have identified teamwork skills as one of the three main areas of essential employability skills.[9] These *Canadian Connections* boxes will highlight Canadian research and issues throughout the text.

It is impossible to avoid family conflicts altogether, but strong interpersonal communication skills can help you understand and manage them.

(© Jupiterimages/Thinkstock/Getty Images)

Improve Your Physical and Emotional Health

Research has shown that the lack or loss of a relationship can lead to ill health and even death. Physicians have long observed that patients who are widowed or divorced experience more medical problems, such as heart disease, cancer, pneumonia, and diabetes, than do married people.[10] One Canadian study even found that married retired couples reported happier relationships than older couples where one was retired and the other was still working.[11]

Research findings are similar for mental illness: widowed and divorced individuals are more likely to experience mental illness, especially depression, than those in ongoing relationships.[12] In fact, **depression** is the most commonly diagnosed mental illness.

depression. A widespread emotional disorder in which the person has problems with sadness, changes in appetite, difficulty sleeping, and a decrease in activities, interests, and energy.

Canadian Connections

Can Interpersonal Communication Skills Help My Career?

If your job search is going to be successful, from the beginning you need to know not just your own goals, but also what employers are looking for. Courses that teach interpersonal communication skills can help you improve your own skills and become a more attractive candidate. The Conference Board of Canada has published a brochure that outlines an Employability Skills Profile based on information gathered from hundreds of Canadian employers. This brochure can assist you in developing various skills.

The brochure summarizes the skills that are in demand under three headings: Academic Skills, Personal Management Skills, and Teamwork Skills. Under the Personal Management Skills heading, the brochure notes that employers look for those with self-esteem and confidence; who recognize and respect people's diversity and individual differences; who have a positive attitude toward learning, growth, and personal health; and who have the ability to identify and suggest new ideas to get a job done in a creative way. Under the Teamwork Skills heading, the brochure discusses such aspects as respecting the thoughts and opinions of others in the group, using conflict-management strategies to facilitate give-and-take and thereby achieve group results, planning and making decisions with others, and supporting those outcomes.

Although many may view these as "soft skills," there is no doubt that in an economic climate where getting a job can be challenging, interpersonal communication skills skills could be the ones that set you apart from other candidates.

In Chapter 11 you will find the Employability Skills presented in full.

Source: Mary Ann McLaughlin, ED399484 95 *Employability Skills Profile: What Are Employers Looking For?* (ERIC Publications). © Steven A. Beebe

The Canadian Mental Health Association has estimated that 15% of the population will have a major depressive episode at some point in their lives.[13] On the positive side, however, establishing a quality social support system can be a major factor in improving and maintaining your health.

All of these findings show that the stress of loneliness can make us sick, but if we have support from people who care about us, we can adjust to life's challenges and surprises. By learning more about effective communication, you are paving the way for closer, more satisfying relationships and a longer, healthier life.

The Communication Process

Interpersonal communication is a complex process of creating meaning in the context of an interpersonal relationship. This process can occur online as well as face to face. To better understand interpersonal communication as a distinct form of communication, it is useful to examine the basic communication process.

The most basic components of communication include the following elements: source, message, channel, receiver, noise, feedback, and context. Understanding each of these elements can help you analyze your own communication with others as you relate to them in interpersonal situations and other communication contexts. Let's explore these elements in greater detail.

Source. The **source** of a message is the originator of the ideas and feelings expressed. The source puts a message into a code, a process called **encoding**. You might see a friend and think to yourself "There's Mike. I want to say hello." You are the source, and you then encode that thought into words ("Hi Mike!") or gestures (a wave).

Message. **Messages** are the written, spoken, and unspoken elements of communication to which we assign meaning. You can send a message intentionally (talking to a professor before class) or unintentionally (falling asleep during class), verbally ("Hi. How are you?"), nonverbally (a smile), or in written form (a tweet, a text, or a handwritten note).

Channel. The **channel** is the means by which the message is expressed to the receiver. Most people receive messages through a variety of channels that include mediated channels such as text messaging, email, phone, video, or Facebook.

Receiver. The **receiver** of the message is the person who interprets the message and ultimately determines whether your message was understood. **Decoding**, the opposite of encoding, occurs when the words or unspoken signals are interpreted by the receiver.

Noise. **Noise** is anything that interferes with a message being interpreted as it was intended. If there were no noise, all of our messages would be interpreted accurately. But noise is always present. It can be literal—such as your smartphone beeping to signal an incoming email—or psychological—such as competing thoughts, worries, and feelings that distract us from the message.

Feedback. **Feedback** is the response to a message. We talk; someone listens and responds; we respond to their response; and so forth. Without feedback, communication is rarely effective. When you order a large cup of coffee with cream and sugar and the server says in response, "That's a large coffee with cream and sugar, right?" he or she has provided feedback to ensure that the message has been understood correctly. Like other messages,

source. The originator of a thought or emotion who puts it into a code that can be understood by a receiver.

encoding. The translation of ideas, feelings, and thoughts into a code.

messages. The written, spoken, and unspoken elements of communication to which people assign meaning.

channel. The pathway by which messages are sent.

receiver. The person who decodes a message and attempts to make sense out of what the source has encoded.

decoding. The interpretation of ideas, feelings, and thoughts that have been translated into a code.

noise. Information, either literal or psychological, that interferes with the accurate reception of the communication of the message.

feedback. The response to a message.

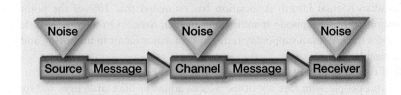

FIGURE 1.1

A Simple Model of Human Communication as Action

it can be intentional (your mother hugs you when you announce you're on the dean's list) or unintentional (you blush when someone you like pays you a compliment); verbal (your mother exclaims, "You're on the dean's list? That's wonderful!") or nonverbal (you smile in response to the compliment).

Context. **Context** is the physical and psychological environment for communication. All communication takes place in some context, whether you are chatting with a friend at your local coffee shop, emailing your mother, or expressing condolences to your neighbour at his father's funeral.

Models of the Communication Process

The elements of the communication process are typically arranged in one of three communication models, showing communication as an action, as an interaction, or as a transaction. Let's look at each model in more detail to see how expert thinking about communication has evolved.

Communication as Action: Message Transfer. The oldest and simplest model, shown in Figure 1.1, is communication as action—a transferring of meaning. The question "Did you get my message?" reflects this simple approach to human communication. Communication takes place when a message is sent and received. Period.

Communication as Interaction: Message Exchange. The perspective of communication as interaction adds two elements to the action model: feedback and context. As shown in Figure 1.2, the interaction model is more realistic than the action perspective, but it still has limitations. Although it emphasizes feedback and context, the interaction model still views communication as a linear, step-by-step process. As such, it does not quite capture the complexity of simultaneous human communication.

context. The physical and psychological communication environment.

FIGURE 1.2

A Model for Communication as Interaction

Interaction models of communication include feedback as a response to a message sent by the communication source and context as the environment for communication.

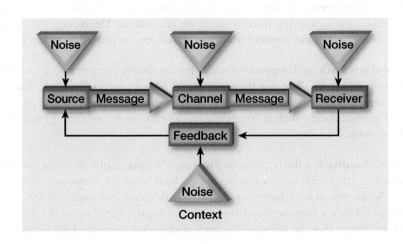

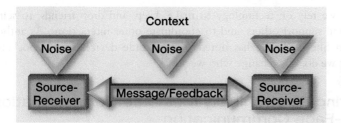

FIGURE 1.3

A Model for Communication as Mutual Transaction

In this model, the source and the receiver of a message experience communication simultaneously.

Communication as Transaction: Message Creation. Today, the most sophisticated and realistic model views communication as a transaction in which each element influences all of the other elements in the process at the same time. This perspective acknowledges that when you talk to another person face to face, you are constantly reacting to your partner's responses. In this model, all the components of the communication process are simultaneous. As Figure 1.3 indicates, even as you talk, you are also interpreting your partner's nonverbal and verbal responses.

The transactional approach to communication is based on **systems theory**. A system is a set of interconnected elements in which a change in one element affects all of the other elements. Key elements of any system include *inputs* (all of the variables that go into the system), *throughputs* (all of the things that make communication a process), and *outputs* (what the system produces). From a transactional communication perspective, a change in any aspect of the communication system (source, message, channel, receiver, noise, context, feedback) potentially influences all the other elements of the system. From a systems theory point of view, each element of communication is connected to all other elements of communication.

systems theory. Theory that describes the interconnected elements of a system in which a change in one element affects all the other elements.

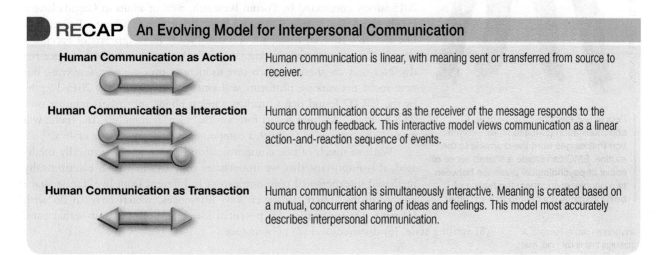

RECAP   **An Evolving Model for Interpersonal Communication**

Human Communication as Action	Human communication is linear, with meaning sent or transferred from source to receiver.
Human Communication as Interaction	Human communication occurs as the receiver of the message responds to the source through feedback. This interactive model views communication as a linear action-and-reaction sequence of events.
Human Communication as Transaction	Human communication is simultaneously interactive. Meaning is created based on a mutual, concurrent sharing of ideas and feelings. This model most accurately describes interpersonal communication.

Interpersonal Communication and Technology

Can you really communicate *interpersonally* with people on a smartphone or over the Internet without meeting them face to face? Yes, of course. You probably communicate this way every day, to both initiate and maintain relationships. When you post your thoughts on Facebook, Twitter, or Instagram, or use Snapchat or text message to communicate with your friends, you are using **electronically mediated communication (EMC)**.

electronically mediated communication (EMC). Communication that is not face to face, but rather is sent via a medium such as a cell phone or the Internet.

Increasingly, we rely on technology to make, keep, and drop friends, to self-disclose, to respond to and support others, and to coordinate other interactions. As author and social media expert Sherry Turkle has noted, "Those little devices in our pockets don't only change what we do, they change who we are."[14]

Comparing Electronically Mediated Communication with Face-to-Face Communication

Mediated communication is not new, of course. People have been communicating without being face to face for centuries; sending letters and other written messages is an age-old human way of relating to others. And even before written communication was widespread, humans used smoke signals and drum beats to communicate across long distances. What's new today is that there are so many different ways of *immediately* connecting with someone, such as using a smartphone, social networking applications (such as Facebook, LinkedIn, and Twitter), text messages, email, instant messaging, video messages (on YouTube, Skype, or Facetime), or a host of other electronically mediated ways of developing and maintaining interpersonal relationships. The different platforms for communicating change rapidly. Not that long ago, email was the hot new way of connecting; then there was instant messaging (IM). There is evidence that these two technologies are declining in use. In the second decade of the 21st century, texting and messaging from smartphones, as well as connecting via Instagram, Twitter, and Facebook, are among the most popular ways to communicate using EMC.

© WANG HSIU-HUA/Fotolia

People use electronically mediated communication (EMC) to share information that ranges from the dramatic to the routine. EMC can create a shared sense of social or psychological presence between two people, giving them the feeling of being instantly connected to each other.

We use EMC every day to share information. According to a January 2015 survey conducted by Forum Research, 59% of adults in Canada have a Facebook account, while 30% have a LinkedIn profile, 25% have a Twitter profile, and 16% have an Instagram account. Nearly three-quarters of Facebook users in Canada reported checking the site either once or more than once per day. Not only are these numbers sure to increase over the next few years, but new social networking platforms will emerge every year.[15] A 2015 Report by the CRTC found that Canadian wireless phone subscribers number over 28.8 million.[16] Another report forecasts that Canadian mobile data traffic will grow 700% from 2014 to 2019, a compound annual growth rate of 46%.[17]

With so much of our communication becoming electronically mediated, it is important that we understand the ways in which electronically mediated interpersonal communication is different from live, face-to-face conversations. There are seven key differences, which have to do with (1) time, (2) anonymity, (3) potential for deception, (4) non-verbal cues, (5) writing style, (6) distance, and (7) permanence.

asynchronous message. A message that is not read, heard, or seen exactly when it is sent; there is a time delay between the sending of the message and its receipt.

synchronous message. A message that is sent and received simultaneously.

social presence. The feeling communicators have of engaging in unmediated, face-to-face interactions even though messages are being sent electronically.

Time. When you interact with others using EMC, you can do so asynchronously. An **asynchronous message** is a message that is not read, heard, or seen at the same time it is sent; there is a time delay between when you send such a message and when someone else receives it. A text message sent to a friend's phone or a post on a friend's Facebook wall are examples of asynchronous messages.

Synchronous messages are those that are sent and received instantly and simultaneously. Face-to-face (FtF) conversations are synchronous—there is no time delay between when you send a message and when the other person receives it. A video conference is another example of a synchronous message.

The more synchronous an interaction, the more similar it is to FtF interactions. And the more a technology simulates a FtF conversation, the more it creates **social presence**, which is the feeling we have when we act and think as if we're involved in an unmediated, FtF conversation. When we send text or instance messages back and forth, we create a shared sense of social or psychological co-presence with our partners. Receiving a tweet from a friend gives us the feeling of being instantly connected to that person.

Another time difference between EMC and FtF messages is that it takes longer to tap out a typewritten message than to speak or to convey a non-verbal message. The amount of delay (which corresponds to silence in FtF interactions) can have an impact on the interpretation of a message's meaning. When texting, participants may expect to see a response to their message very quickly. This is one reason text messages are often very short and concise. A rapid succession of short messages imitates the back-and-forth of a FtF conversation and fosters a sense of synchronicity and social presence.

Anonymity. Because EMC allows people to be anonymous in their communications, they are more likely to be bolder, more honest, more outrageous, or more cruel than they would be in face-to-face communication. The phenomenon of Internet "trolls"—people who hide behind their anonymity to make deliberately offensive and hurtful comments about others— is a good example of this. The degree of anonymity you have online depends on the technology that you are using and the honesty of both you and your communication partners.

Potential for Deception. It's easy to lie when communicating electronically because with many forms of EMC you can't see or hear your audience. In a survey of 191 students at a college in the United States, 40% said that they had lied on the Internet: 15% about their age, 8% about their weight, 6% about appearance, 6% about marital status, and 3% about what sex they were.[18] In 2010, the documentary *Catfish* followed the filmmaker's discovery that the beautiful young woman with whom he had been carrying on an online relationship was in fact a middle-aged woman who had constructed several fake Facebook profiles and had been lying about her identity. The practice of online deception has become so widespread that Merriam-Webster expanded their dictionary definition of "catfish" to include "a person who sets up a false personal profile on a social networking site for fraudulent or deceptive purposes.[*]"

One of the things that draws people to social networking sites is the potential to create a new identity. Regardless of reality, on social media you can present yourself as the perfect parent, the ideal employee, or the most caring friend. You can even adopt an already-existing identity or totally fabricate one. Facebook has reported they they have around 170 million fake users … and those are just the ones that they know about![19] Online deception is almost as easy as typing. We say "almost," because you *can* assess the content of a written message for clues to deceit. In a study by Katherine Cornetto, American college-student respondents reported that the most common indicator of deception was someone's implausible statement or bragging.[20] In order to detect deception as friendships develop over the Internet, people come to depend on personal knowledge and impressions of their partners acquired over the course of their correspondence. Interestingly, Cornetto's study also found that those who reported lying most were the people most likely to suspect other users of lying.

Nonverbal Cues. Words and graphics become more important in EMC than in FtF communication, because in most forms of EMC you must rely solely on words to carry non-verbal messages. Of course, a YouTube video does include nonverbal messages, but even on YouTube some cues may be limited, such as the surrounding context and reactions from others. There are some basic things text users do to add emotion to their messages, including CAPITALIZING THE MESSAGE (equivalent to raising one's voice), making letters **bold,** and inserting emoticons—☺ to indicate happiness, ☹ to indicate sadness, and so on. The ability to tease or make sarcastic remarks is limited with EMC, because there is no tone of

---

[*]By permission. From Merriam-Webster's Collegiate® Dictionary, 11th Edition ©2016 by Merriam-Webster, Inc. (www.Merriam-Webster.com).

voice in the written message—so emoticons must provide information about the intended emotional tone of what is written. You can also write out an accompanying interpretation—LOL or JK (just kidding),—to compensate for the limited emotional cues.

There is also typically less emphasis on a person's physical appearance online than in FtF situations, unless you're using Facebook or Instagram. And in those forums, it's not only your own appearance that helps determine how others react to you; one study found that the physical attractiveness or unattractiveness of your "friends" rubs off on you. If you have friends who are perceived as attractive, you will be perceived as more popular and attractive.[21]

Writing Style. Texting or emailing someone allows you time to compose your message and craft it more carefully than you might in an FtF interaction. As a sender of written messages, you have more control over what you say and the impression you create; as the receiver of written messages, you no doubt realize that the other person has had the chance to shape his or her message carefully for its greatest impact on you.

However, not everyone is able to encode thoughts quickly and accurately into written words. One online scholar suggests that a person's typing ability and writing skills affect the quality of any relationship that is developed.[22] Not only do writing skills affect your ability to express yourself and manage relationships, they also affect how others perceive you. A text reading "whaddup? where u at? c u l8r" gives a very different impression from one reading "Hi Sarah. What are you doing this afternoon? Let me know if you want to meet later." Your written messages provide insights to others about your personality, skills, sense of humour, and even your values.

Distance. Although we certainly can and do send text messages to people who live and work in the same building we're in (or even the same room), there is typically greater physical distance between people who are communicating using EMC. When using the Internet or a cell phone, we can just as easily send a text or a video message to someone on the other side of the globe as we can to someone who is at the other side of the room.

Permanence. One important difference between EMC and FtF communication is the fact that a text, email, tweet, or Facebook posting provides a record of the communication, which the sender could come to regret in the future. There have been many recent instances of people losing their jobs and/or damaging their reputations through their social media activity. In 2010, two unionized workers at an automotive shop in British Columbia were fired after posting homophobic and violent Facebook status updates aimed at their manager.[23] This was the first known Canadian firing that was attributed to a Facebook posting, but there have been many more since. In 2013, two Toronto firefighters were fired after posting what were described as "misogynistic and offensive tweets," which were found to be in violation of city policy.[24] Also in 2013, in a case that made international headlines, a New York public relations executive posted an offensive tweet while on a flight to Africa, which resulted in the loss of her job and irreparable damage to her reputation.[25] Every year the number of cautionary tales increases. It is also wise to exercise caution even while engaging in what you think is "private" communication. While you might think you are exchanging "private and confidential" texts with a friend, your communication could be shared with hundreds of people (including strangers), and could end up following you around for years. The message is clear—think before you tweet … or text, or email, or update your Facebook status!

In addition to these seven differences between EMC and FtF messages, there are questions about who is more likely to use EMC messages. For example, researchers have asked whether people who spend a lot of time online generally have more or less personal contact with other people. A team of researchers led by Robert Kraut and Sara Kiesler made headlines when they published the results of their study, which concluded that the more people use the Internet, the less they will interact with others in person.[26] But other research contradicts this finding. Two follow-up studies found that people who use the Internet are more likely to have a greater number of friends, are more involved with community activities, and overall have greater levels of trust in other people. The most recent research seems to suggest that for some people—those who are already prone to being shy or introverted—there may be a link between Internet use and loneliness or feelings of social isolation. However, their isolation may not be because of their use of the Internet, but simply because they are less likely to make contact with others.[27] For those who are generally outgoing and who like to interact with others, the Internet is just another tool to reach out and make contact.

Increasingly, people use EMC forums such as Facebook not to substitute completely for FtF contact, but to enrich it. In fact, using EMC messages can result in relationships becoming more intimate in less time than they would through FtF interpersonal communication. Researchers have found that people develop hyperpersonal relationships using EMC. **Hyperpersonal relationships** are relationships formed primarily through EMC that become even *more personal* than equivalent FtF relationships, in part because of the absence of distracting external cues (such as physical qualities), an overdependence on just a few tidbits of personal information (which increases the importance of the information), and an idealization of the partner. Hyperpersonal relationships were first identified in a study in which pairs of students who were initially strangers interacted for up to an hour in a simulated instant-messaging situation, while another group of pairs met face to face for up to 15 minutes. Those in EMC interactions skipped the typical superficial getting-acquainted questions and used more direct questioning and disclosing with their partners.[28] Online pairs engaged in more intimate probes and responses and reached a similar level of understanding and ability to predict their partners' behaviours as those in FtF interactions.

A comprehensive study that investigated whether instant messages and text messages are more like speech or writing concluded that instant messages contain elements of both, but nonetheless differ from speech in grammar, style, syntax, and other language factors. Text messages are more like writing than like spoken messages. There are also gender differences: women's text and instant messages use more words, longer sentences, and more emoticons, and discuss and include more social and relational information than do men's messages.[29]

Understanding Electronically Mediated Communication

We've noted that EMC messages have both similarities to and differences from FtF messages. What theories and models of electronically mediated messages help us understand how relationships are developed and make predictions about how we will use EMC messages?

The communication models we've presented (communication as action, interaction, and transaction) on pages 8–9 are certainly applicable to EMC. There are times when EMC resembles the action model of communication. You post a message on a message board, blog, or Facebook wall and you get no immediate response from others. The communication is asynchronous—there's a time delay, so you're not really sure you've communicated with anyone. During some email or text-message exchanges, your communication is more like the communication-as-interaction model; you send a text message and you wait for the response. There's a time delay, but sooner or later you get a response. And then there are instances when you can see and hear the other person simultaneously, such as in a live conversation with someone via a webcam, which is a synchronous interaction. In this instance the EMC resembles the transactional communication model, in that communicating this way is almost like being there in person because of the immediacy of the communication.

Three theories have been developed to further explain and predict how EMC works.

Cues-Filtered-Out Theory. One early theory of communication via the Internet was called **cues-filtered-out theory**. This theory suggested that emotional expression is

hyperpersonal relationship. A relationship formed primarily through electronically mediated communication that becomes more personal than an equivalent face-to-face relationship because of the absence of distracting external cues, smaller amounts of personal information, and idealization of the communication partner.

cues-filtered-out theory. Theory that suggests that communication of emotions is restricted when people send messages to others via email or other electronic means because nonverbal cues such as facial expression and tone of voice are filtered out.

severely restricted when we communicate using only text messages; nonverbal cues such as facial expression, gestures, and tone of voice are filtered out. The assumption was that text messages were best used for brief, task-oriented communication such as sharing information or asking questions; text messages were assumed to be less effective in helping people establish meaningful relationships with one another.[30] The cues-filtered-out theory also suggests that, given the lack of these nonverbal cues and other social information, we'll be less likely to use EMC to manage relationships because of its limited ability to carry emotional and relational information. Although Facebook, Instagram, and Twitter present photos and ample personal information, communication through those forums is still not as rich as an FtF conversation.

Media Richness Theory. Another theory helps us make predictions about which form of media we will use to send certain kinds of messages. We use different types of media depending on the richness of a medium, that is, whether it allows us to express emotions and relational messages as well as send information. **Media richness theory** suggests that the richness of a communication channel is based on four criteria: (1) the amount of feedback that the communicator can receive, (2) the number of cues that the channel can convey and that can be interpreted by a receiver, (3) the variety of language that a communicator uses, and (4) the potential for expressing emotions and feelings.[31] Using these four criteria, researchers have developed a continuum of communication channels, from communication-rich to communication-lean. Figure 1.4 illustrates this continuum.

media richness theory. Theory that identifies the richness of a communication medium based on the amount of feedback it allows, the number of cues receivers can interpret, the variety of language it allows, and the potential for emotional expression.

FIGURE 1.4

A Continuum of Communication-Rich and Communication-Lean Channels

Adapted from L. K. Trevino, R. L. Draft, and R. H. Lengel, "Understanding Managers' Media Choices: A Symbolic Interactionist Perspective." In *Organizations and Communication Technology*, edited by J. Fulk and C. Steinfield (Newbury Park, CA: Sage, 1990), 71–94. © Steven A. Beebe

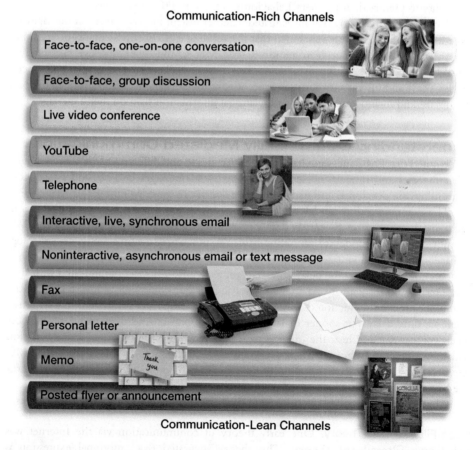

Communication-Rich Channels

Face-to-face, one-on-one conversation

Face-to-face, group discussion

Live video conference

YouTube

Telephone

Interactive, live, synchronous email

Noninteractive, asynchronous email or text message

Fax

Personal letter

Memo

Posted flyer or announcement

Communication-Lean Channels

BIZARRO © 2012 Dan Piraro. Dist. by King Features Syndicate.

Both the cues-filtered-out theory and media richness theory suggest that the restriction of nonverbal cues, which provide information about the nature of the relationship between communicators, hampers the quality of relationships that can be established using EMC. But a newer perspective suggests that although EMC may communicate fewer relational cues, we are eventually able to discern relational information.

Social Information-Processing Theory.

Social information-processing theory suggests that we *can* communicate relational and emotional messages via the Internet, *but it may take longer* to express messages that are typically communicated with facial expressions and tone of voice. A key difference between FtF and computer-mediated communication is the *rate* at which information reaches you. During an in-person conversation, you process a lot of information quickly; you process the words you hear as well as the many nonverbal cues you see (facial expression, gestures, and body posture) and hear (tone of voice and the use of pauses). During text-only interactions, there is less information to process (no audio cues or visual nonverbal cues), so it takes a bit longer for the relationship to develop—but it does develop as you learn more about your partner's likes, dislikes, and feelings.

Social information-processing theory also suggests that if you expect to communicate with your electronic communication partner again, you will likely pay more attention to the relationship cues—expressions of emotions that are communicated directly (as when someone writes "I'm feeling bored today") or indirectly (as when a friend responds to your long chatty email with only a sentence, which suggests he or she may not want to spend much time "talking" today).

When we use EMC, we often ask questions and interact with others to enhance the quality of our relationship with them. A study by W. Scott Sanders found that people who communicated via Facebook enhanced the nature of the relationship and reduced their uncertainty about others by asking questions based on information that was already present on the other person's Facebook page.[32] The pattern of differences between computer-mediated communication and face-to-face communication is still being explored as computer-mediated communication becomes an even more significant part of contemporary life.

In summary, we believe that EMC makes it possible for people to develop interpersonal relationships with others, whether they are miles away or in the next room. Lisa Tidwell and Joseph Walther use the "information superhighway" metaphor to suggest that EMC is not just a road for moving data from one place to another, but also a boulevard where people pass each other, occasionally meet, and decide to travel together.[33] You can't see very much of other drivers unless you do travel together for some time. There are highway bandits, to be sure, who are not what they appear to be—one must drive defensively—and there are conflicts and disagreements when travelling, just as there are in "off-road," or FtF, interactions.

social information-processing theory. Theory that suggests people can communicate relational and emotional messages via the Internet, although such messages take longer to express without nonverbal cues.

▶ RECAP   Theories of Electronically Mediated Communication

Theory	Description
Cues-Filtered-Out Theory	The communication of emotion and relationship cues is restricted in email or text messages because nonverbal cues, such as facial expression and tone of voice, are filtered out.
Media Richness Theory	The richness, or the amount of information a communication medium has, is based on the amount of feedback it permits, the number of cues in the channel, the variety of language used, and the potential for expressing emotions.
Social Information-Processing Theory	Emotional and relationship messages can be expressed via electronic means, although such messages take longer to be communicated without the immediacy of nonverbal cues.

Principles of Interpersonal Communication

Underlying our current understanding of interpersonal communication are five principles: interpersonal communication connects us to others, is irreversible, is complicated, is governed by rules, and involves both content and relationship dimensions.

Interpersonal Communication Connects Us to Others

Unless you live in a cave or have become a cloistered monk, you interact with others every day. Even if you work alone at home, you encounter other people in the course of living your life. The opportunities for interpersonal communication are everywhere. It is through inescapable interpersonal communication with others that we affect and are affected by other human beings.

Fundamental to an understanding of interpersonal communication is the assumption that the quality of interpersonal relationships stems from the quality of communication with others. This inescapable nature of interpersonal communication doesn't mean others will accurately decode your message; it does mean, however, that others are drawing inferences about you and your behaviour, inferences that may be right or may be wrong. Even as you silently stand in a crowded elevator, your lack of eye contact with others communicates your unwillingness to interact with fellow passengers. Your unspoken messages, even when you are asleep, provide cues that others interpret. Remember that people often judge you by your behaviour, not your intent. Your interpersonal communication is how you develop connections to others. Even in well-established interpersonal relationships, you may be evoking an unintended response to your behaviour.

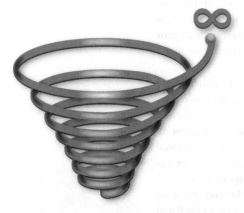

FIGURE 1.5

Interpersonal Communication Is Irreversible

This helical model shows that interpersonal communication never loops back on itself. It expands as the communication partners contribute their thoughts and experiences to the exchange.

Source: © F. E. X. Dance, *Human Communication Theory* (Holt, Rinehart & Winston, 1967), 294.

Interpersonal Communication Is Irreversible

"Disregard that last statement made by the witness," instructs the judge. Yet the clever lawyer knows that, once her client has stated that her husband gave her a black eye during an argument, the jury cannot really "disregard" the statement. This principle applies to all forms of oral communication. We may try to modify the meaning of a spoken message by saying something like "Oh, I really didn't mean it." But in most cases, the damage has been done. Once created, communication has a reality about it that is comparable to the physical property of matter; it can't be uncreated. As the helical model in Figure 1.5 suggests, once interpersonal communication begins, it never loops back on itself.

E-CONNECTIONS
Relating to Others

Communicating Through Text Message

You don't need a textbook to tell you that texting is an important way to keep in touch with others. A 2010 study from Nielsen found that the average teenager sends 3339 texts per month, with teen girls sending 4050 per month.[34] At the end of the first decade of the 21st century, text messages may be the most common way of interacting with others who are not physically present. One study found that 80% of people under 25 tended to text rather than phone a friend and leave a short message.[35]

Texting is a worldwide practice, in part because in most countries it's much cheaper to text than to call someone on the phone. Faye Siytangco, a young sales representative from the Philippines, said she wasn't surprised to see people bowing their heads at a funeral for a friend's father. But she was shocked when she realized they weren't bowing in prayer, but were texting their friends. According to contemporary Philippine custom, texting while something else important is going on is not a breach of etiquette; it's just what people do now.[36]

In June 2011, Kevin Newman, the 52-year-old Canadian journalist and news anchor, delivered the commencement address at the University of Western Ontario, then took his seat facing the audience and began typing into his iPhone. Appropriately enough, his address—which he read from his iPad—was on the increasing role of social media in shaping global events.[37]

Why are so many people, especially young people, communicating via text messages? If you frequently send text messages, you can answer the question yourself: it's fast, cheap, easy, and always available. There's no need to open a laptop or be near a computer. You don't have to worry about playing "telephone tag"—the recipient will read and respond to your message when he or she has time. And there's no need for small talk—text messaging lends itself to getting to the point.

As with all interpersonal communication, though, we need to be aware of the impression we are making on others. The Emily Post Institute published a series of rules for text messaging, including the following:[38]

Don't text-message anything confidential, private, or potentially embarrassing. You never know when someone might be looking over your significant other's shoulder—or worse yet, when your message might get sent to the wrong person...

If you text someone who doesn't have your phone number, start your message by stating who you are...

Just as you shouldn't answer your phone during a [face-to-face] conversation, you should not send a text message when you are engaged with someone else...

You shouldn't use text messaging when informing someone of sad news, business matters, or urgent meetings, unless it's to set up a phone call on the subject...

Finally, remember that as with email, you can't know for sure when the recipient is going to read his or her message—so don't panic if your text message doesn't get an immediate response.

Research evidence suggests that we will keep texting. It's convenient and it keeps us in touch with others. But don't forget the joys of a good face-to-face conversation or handwritten note. In 2011, Canadian actor Ryan Reynolds told *People* magazine that he recently sent a "good old-fashioned, handwritten" thank-you card to a director, adding that, "in this electronic-data age, not everything has to be pixels and light."[39]

© Golden Pixels LLC/Shutterstock

Instead, it continues to be shaped by the events, experiences, and thoughts of the communication partners. A Russian proverb nicely summarizes the point: "Once a word goes out of your mouth, you can never swallow it again." As discussed earlier in this chapter, this becomes even more of an issue when using EMC, as a record of the communication remains and may be reread, scrutinized, and discussed with others over and over again.

Interpersonal Communication Is Complicated

No form of communication is simple. If any were, we would know how to reduce the number of misunderstandings and conflicts in our world. Because of the number of variables involved in interpersonal exchanges, even simple requests are extremely complex.

"Gary, we need to not talk."

© Michael Maslin/Liza Donnelly

Communication theorists have noted that whenever you communicate with another person, there are really at least six "people" involved: (1) who you think you are; (2) who you think the other person is; (3) who you think the other person thinks you are; (4) who the other person thinks he or she is; (5) who the other person thinks you are; and (6) who the other person thinks you think he or she is.[40] Whew! And when you add more people to the interaction, it becomes even more involved.

Moreover, when humans communicate, they interpret information from others as symbols. A **symbol** is merely a representation of something else, and it can have various meanings and interpretations. Language is a system of symbols. In English, symbols do not resemble the words they represent. The word (symbol) for cow does not look at all like a cow; someone, somewhere, decided that "cow" should mean a beast that chews a cud and gives milk. The reliance on symbols to communicate poses a communication challenge; we are often misinterpreted. Sometimes we don't know the code. Only if you are conversant with Canadian English will you know that "riding" refers to an electoral district; "allophone" refers to a Quebecker whose first language is neither French nor English; and "poutine" is french fries with cheese curds and gravy.

Messages are not always interpreted as we intend them. Osmo Wiio, a Finnish communication scholar, points out the messiness of communicating with others when he suggests the following truths.

If communication can fail, it will.

The more communication there is, the more difficult it is for communication to succeed.[41]

Although we are not as pessimistic as Professor Wiio, we do suggest that the task of understanding each other is challenging.

Interpersonal Communication Is Governed by Rules

According to communication researcher Susan Shimanoff, a **rule** is a "followable prescription that indicates what behaviour is obligated, preferred, or prohibited in certain contexts."[42] The rules that help define appropriate and inappropriate communication in any given situation may be explicit or implicit. For your interpersonal communication class, explicit rules are probably spelled out in your syllabus, but your instructor has other rules that are more implicit. They are not written or verbalized because you learned them long ago: only one person speaks at a time, you raise your hand to be called on, you do not text message during class.

Interpersonal communication rules are developed by the people involved in the interaction and by the culture in which the individuals are communicating. Many times we learn communication rules from experience, by observing and interacting with others.

symbol. A representation of something else.

rule. A prescription for behaviour that indicates what is obligated, preferred, or prohibited in certain communication situations or contexts.

British researcher Michael Argyle and his colleagues asked people to identify general rules for relationship development and maintenance and then rate their importance. Here are the most important rules:[43]

Respect each other's privacy.

Do not reveal each other's secrets.

Look the other person in the eye during conversation.

Do not criticize the other person publicly.

Although we may modify rules to achieve the goals of our relationships, these general rules remain fairly constant. In interpersonal relationships, the rules of a relationship are mutually defined and agreed on. Most of us don't like to be told what to do or how to behave all the time. The expectations and rules are continually renegotiated as the relationship unfolds. Few of us learn relationship rules by copying them from a book. Most of us learn these rules from experience, through observing and interacting with family members and friends. Individuals who grow up in environments in which these rules are not observed may not know how to behave in close relationships.

For many of us, friendships are vital to our personal well-being. By improving our interpersonal communication skills, we can learn how to improve our friendships.

(© Ian Shaw/The Image Bank/Getty Images)

Interpersonal Communication Involves Both Content and Relationship Dimensions

The **content** of a communication message consists of the new information, ideas, or suggested actions that the speaker wishes to share. The **relationship dimension** of a communication message is usually more implied; it offers cues about the emotions, attitudes, and amount of power and control the speaker feels toward the other.

Your tone of voice, amount of eye contact, facial expression, and posture can reveal much about the true meaning of your message. If one of your roommates loudly and abruptly yells, "HEY, SLOB! WASH YOUR DISHES!" and another roommate sends the same verbal message but more gently and playfully, and with a smile—"Hey, slob. Wash your dishes"—both are communicating a message seeking the same outcome. However, the two messages have different relationship cues. The first, shouted message suggests that your roommate may be frustrated and angry with the state of the kitchen, whereas roommate number two's teasing request suggests he or she may be fondly amused by your failure to clean up after yourself.

Another way of distinguishing between the content and relationship dimensions of communication is to consider that the *content of a message* refers to what is said, and *relationship cues* refers to how it is communicated. This distinction explains why reading a transcript of what someone says can reveal a quite different meaning from actually hearing the person say the message.

Given these two dimensions of communication, one dimension can modify or contradict the other. Communication theorists have a word that describes how we can communicate about our communication: *metacommunication*. Stated in the simplest way, **metacommunication** is communication about communication; it can be nonverbal or verbal. Accurately decoding these unspoken or even verbalized metamessages helps you understand what people really mean.

content. New information, ideas, or suggested actions that a speaker wishes to share.

relationship dimension. The implied aspect of a communication message, which conveys information about emotions, attitudes, power, and control.

metacommunication. Verbal or nonverbal communication about communication.

You can express an idea nonverbally (by smiling to communicate that you are pleased), and you can also express your positive feeling verbally (by saying, "I'm happy to be here"). But sometimes your nonverbal communication can contradict your verbal message. You can say "Oh, that's just great" and use your voice to provide relational cues that express just the opposite of what the verbal content of the message means. The sarcasm communicated by the tone of your voice (a relationship cue) modifies the meaning of your verbal message (the content of your message).

In addition to nonverbal cues, which provide communication about communication, you can use words to explicitly talk about your message. For example, you can ask, "Is what I'm saying bothering you?" Your question is seeking information about the communication. We use metacommunication to check on how our message is being understood or to make sure we understand what someone else is saying. When you say "I'm not sure what you said is clear to me," you are using a metamessage to help you better understand the communication; it's a metamessage because you are talking about your talk. Here's another example of verbal metacommunication: "I'd like to talk with you about the way we argue." Again, you are using communication to talk about communication. Taking time to talk about the way you talk can help clarify misunderstandings. Being aware of the metamessage, in both its verbal and nonverbal forms, can help improve the accuracy of your interpretations of the meaning of message content as well as enhance the quality of your relationships with others.

Improving Your Own Interpersonal Communication Competence

Now that we have previewed the study of interpersonal communication, you may be saying to yourself, "Well, that's all well and good, but is it possible to improve my own interpersonal communication? Aren't some people just born with better interpersonal skills than others?" Just as some people have more musical talent or greater skill at passing a puck, evidence suggests that some people may indeed have an inborn, biological talent for communicating with others.

A growing body of research called the **communibiological approach** to communication suggests that some people inherit certain traits that affect the way they communicate with others. There may be a genetic basis for why people communicate as they do. For example, you or people you know may have been born to have more stage fright or anxiety when communicating with others. Additionally, some people may not be as comfortable interacting in interpersonal situations as others are.

So what are the implications of the communibiological approach to communication? Does this mean you can't improve your interpersonal communication? Absolutely not! Some researchers and teachers believe that the communibiological approach gives too much weight to biology and not enough to how we can learn to compensate for what nature did not give us.[44] The underlying premise of our study of interpersonal communication is that you can learn ways to enhance the quality of your interpersonal relationships.

Social learning theory suggests that we can learn how to adapt and adjust our behaviour toward others; how we behave is not solely dependent on our genetic makeup. By observing and interacting with others (hence the name *social learning*), we discover that we can adapt and adjust our behaviour. Although biology unquestionably plays a key role in how we behave, we can't blame biology for all aspects of our behaviour. We believe that people can learn how to enhance their communication competence.

To be competent in communication is to communicate in ways that are perceived to be both *effective* and *appropriate*. You communicate effectively when your message is understood by others and achieves its intended effect. For example, if you want your roommate to stop

communibiological approach. Theoretical perspective that suggests a person's communication behaviour can be predicted based on personal traits that result from his or her genetic background.

social learning theory. Theory of human behaviour that suggests we can learn how to adapt and adjust our behaviour toward others; how we behave is not solely dependent on our genetic or biological makeup.

using your hair dryer, and after you talk to your roommate he stops using your hair dryer, your message has been effective.

Competent communication should also be appropriate. By *appropriate*, we mean that the communicator should consider the time, place, and overall context of the message and should be sensitive to the feelings and attitudes of the listener. Who determines what is appropriate? *There is no single best way to communicate with others.* There are, however, avenues that can help you become both more effective and more appropriate when communicating with others. We suggest the following six-part strategy for becoming a more effective communicator.

Become Knowledgeable

By reading this chapter, you have already begun to improve your skills. Competent communicators are knowledgeable. They know how communication works. They understand the components, principles, and rules of the communication process. As you read on in this text, you will learn theories, principles, concepts, and rules that will permit you to explain and predict how humans communicate.

Understanding these things is a necessary prerequisite for enhancing your interpersonal effectiveness, but this kind of knowledge alone does not make you competent. You would not let someone fix your car's carburetor if he or she had only read a book on the subject. Knowledge must be coupled with skill, and we acquire skill through practice.

Become Skilled

Effective communicators know how to translate knowledge into action. You can memorize the characteristics of a good listener but still not listen well. To develop skill requires practice and helpful feedback from others who can confirm the appropriateness of your actions.

Learning a social skill is not that different from learning how to drive a car or operate a computer. To learn any skill, you must break it down into subskills that you can learn and practise. "Hear it, see it, do it, correct it" is the formula that seems to work best for learning any new behaviours. In this text we will examine the elements of complex skills such as listening, offer activities that will let you practise the skill, and provide opportunities for you to receive feedback and correct your application of the skill.

Become Motivated

Practising skills requires work. You need to be motivated to use your information and skill. You must want to improve, and you must have a genuine desire to connect with others if you wish to become a competent communicator. You may know people who understand how to drive a car and have the skill to drive yet are reluctant to get behind the wheel. Or perhaps you know someone who took a course in public speaking but is still too frightened to stand in front of a crowd. Similarly, you may pass a test about interpersonal communication principles with flying colours, but unless you are motivated to use your new-found skills, your interactions with others may not improve.

Become Adaptable

Effective communicators appropriately adapt their messages to others; they are flexible. In this text, we do not identify tidy lists of sure-fire strategies that you can use to win friends and influence people. The same set of skills is not effective in every situation, so competent communicators do not assume that "one size fits all." Rather, they assess each unique situation and adapt their behaviour to achieve the desired outcome. They examine the context, the situation, and the needs, goals, and messages of others to establish and maintain relationships.

Ethical communicators are sensitive to the needs of others.

(© Golden Pixels LLC/Shutterstock)

Become Ethical

Ethics are the beliefs, values, and moral principles by which we determine what is right or wrong. Ethics and ethical behaviour have long been a critical component of human behaviour. Effective interpersonal communicators are ethical. To be an ethical communicator means to be sensitive to the needs of others, to give people choices rather than forcing them to act a certain way. Unethical communicators believe that they know what other people need, even without asking them for their preferences. As we discuss in Chapter 6, being manipulative and forcing opinions on others usually results in a climate of defensiveness. Effective communicators seek to establish trust and to reduce interpersonal barriers. Ethical communicators keep confidences; they keep private information that others wish to be kept private. They also do not intentionally decrease others' feelings of self-worth. Another key element in being an ethical communicator is honesty. If you intentionally lie or distort the truth, then you are not communicating ethically or effectively.

Become Other-Oriented

It's not always about you. Lucy Van Pelt in the Peanuts cartoon seems startled to learn that the world does not revolve around her. Perhaps you know someone like Lucy. Sometimes we may need someone like Linus to remind us that we're not the centre of the universe. The signature concept for our study of interpersonal communication is the goal of becoming other-oriented in relationships. To be an other-oriented communicator is to consider the thoughts, needs, experiences, personality, emotions, motives, desires, culture, and goals of your communication partners, while still maintaining your own integrity. The choices we make in forming our messages, in deciding how best to express those messages, and in deciding when and where to deliver those messages will be made more effectively when we consider the other person's thoughts and feelings. To emphasize the importance of being an other-oriented communicator, throughout this text we will offer sidebar comments and questions to help you apply the concept of being other-oriented to your own interpersonal relationships.

Being other-oriented involves a conscious effort to consider the world from the point of view of those with whom you interact.[45] This effort occurs almost automatically when you are communicating with those you like or who are similar to you. Thinking about the thoughts and feelings of those you dislike or who are different from you is more difficult and requires more effort and commitment.

ethics. The beliefs, values, and moral principles by which people determine what is right or wrong.

Are people more self-focused today than in the past? Sociologist Jean Twenge suggests that people today are increasingly more narcissistic (self-focused) than they have been in previous generations—she dubs today's narcissistic generation "Generation Me." Her research found that "in the early 1950s, only 12% of teens aged 14 to 16 agreed with the statement 'I am an important person.' By the late 1980s, an incredible 80%—almost seven times as many—claimed they were important."[46] Using the Narcissistic Personality Inventory, an instrument designed to assess egocentrism and self-focus, Twenge and two of her colleagues found corroborating evidence for an increased self-focus among contemporary students.

We may find ourselves speaking without considering the thoughts and feelings of our listener when we have a need to purge ourselves emotionally or to confirm our sense of self-importance, but doing so usually undermines our relationships with others. A self-focused communicator often alienates others. Fortunately, research suggests that, almost by necessity, we adapt to our partner in order to carry on a conversation.[47] Adaptation includes such things as simply asking questions in response to our partner's disclosures, finding topics of mutual interest to discuss, selecting words and examples that are meaningful to our partner, and avoiding topics that we don't feel comfortable discussing with another person.

Adapting messages to others does not mean that we tell them only what they want to hear; that would be unethical. Nor does being considerate of others mean abandoning all concern for our own interests; that would be unwise. Other-oriented communicators maintain their own personal integrity while simultaneously being aware of the thoughts and feelings of others. Being other-oriented is more than just being "nice." It involves being principled enough to be considerate of others while making mindful choices about how and when to adapt our interpersonal messages.

How do you become other-oriented? Being other-oriented is really a collection of skills rather than a single skill. We devote considerable discussion throughout the text to developing this collection of essential communication skills.

Focusing on others begins with an accurate understanding of your self-concept and self-esteem; we discuss these foundation principles in the next chapter. As you will learn in Chapter 3, developing an accurate perception of both yourself and others is an important element of effectively relating to others.

BEING Other-ORIENTED

Being other-oriented means focusing on the interests, needs, and goals of another person. Think about a person who is important to you—it could be a family member, close friend, lover, or colleague. Consider the other-oriented nature of the relationship you have with this person. Are there specific things you say, gifts you have given, or activities you do with this person that demonstrate your focus on his or her interests, needs, and desires? What things does this person do that reflect his or her other-orientation toward you?

APPLYING AN OTHER-ORIENTATION
to Being an Effective Interpersonal Communicator

Effective interpersonal communicators are other-oriented communicators—they focus on the needs, interests, values, and behaviours of others while being true to their own principles and ethics. In this chapter we've previewed some of the knowledge needed, provided a rationale for being motivated to master interpersonal competencies, and offered a glimpse of the skills that enhance an other-orientation.

Knowledge. When you view communication as a transactive process rather than as a simplistic action or even an interactive process, you gain realistic insight into the challenge of communicating with others and the potential for misunderstandings. Knowing the messiness and dynamic nature of communication, as well as the various components of the process (source, message, channel, receiver, context, noise, and feedback), can help you better diagnose communication issues in your own relationships and improve your ability to accurately decode messages of others.

Motivation. As we've noted, learning about interpersonal communication has the potential to enhance both the quality of your relationships with others and your health. Developing your skill at and knowledge of interpersonal communication can enhance your confidence to improve your relationships with family members, friends, lovers, and colleagues.

Skill. To be other-oriented takes more than knowledge of the elements and nature of communication (although that's a good start), and more than a strong motivation to enhance your abilities. It takes skill. As you begin your study of interpersonal communication, you can be confident that in the chapters ahead you will learn how to listen to, respond to, use, and interpret verbal messages, express and interpret emotional meanings of messages, more accurately use and interpret nonverbal messages, manage conflict, and adapt to human differences. To be other-oriented is to have the knowledge, nurture the motivation, and develop the skill to relate to others in effective and ethical ways.

People gain insight into others' feelings by being sensitive to nonverbal messages as well as to the explicit verbal statements they make. We discuss verbal communication skills in Chapter 6 and nonverbal communication skills in Chapter 7. The skills and principles of managing conflict presented in Chapter 8 provide tools and ideas for understanding others when you disagree.

Becoming other-oriented also involves adapting to those who may be considerably different from you. Your communication partner may have a different cultural background,

be of the opposite sex, or be older or younger than you. In Chapter 4 we explore some of these differences, especially the cultural differences that can sometimes challenge effective and appropriate communication with others; we also suggest specific strategies to help you adapt to others who differ from yourself. Throughout the text, we include *Adapting to Differences: Understanding Others* boxes like the one that appears in this section to help you develop your sensitivity to important issues related to cultural diversity.

ADAPTING TO DIFFERENCES
Understanding Others

Cultural Differences Can Lead to Misinterpretation

In a culturally diverse society, we can make mistakes without meaning to offend or confuse the other person. Our goal is not to be insulting or misunderstood; it's just that values and practices differ from one culture to another, and sometimes the differences can lead to unintended errors.

Every culture has different rules for verbal and nonverbal communication. For example, in some cultures, it is considered rude to look another person directly in the eye when speaking, whereas in other cultures eye contact is seen as a sign of honesty and openness.

In many First Nations cultures, it is customary to respond to a question or

comment only after a lengthy period of observation and reflection in order to allow the listener to thoughtfully consider the speaker's words. The desire for adequate time to observe and reflect may explain why some First Nations students are not quick to respond verbally to questions asked in the classroom. This is often mistakenly interpreted by teachers as communicating shyness, passivity, or lack of knowledge rather than thoughtfulness and mutual respect.[48]

In addition, different cultures have different expectations for nonverbal communication. Depending on the culture, direct and sustained eye contact could

be understood as communicating respect, disrespect, aggression, flirtation, or focused attention and interest.

Chapters 9, 10, and 11 build on the principles of interpersonal relationships introduced in this chapter to help you understand how relationships evolve, are maintained, and sometimes end. The final chapter applies our discussion of other-oriented interpersonal communication to various contexts such as families, friends, and colleagues. Our goal is to help you better understand how you relate to others and to develop enhanced interpersonal skills.

What Is Interpersonal Communication, and Why Is It Important? (pages 2–7)

OBJECTIVES ❶ ❷ Compare and contrast definitions of communication, and explain why it is useful to study interpersonal communication.

Key Terms

communication 2
human communication 3
interpersonal
  communication 3
impersonal communication 3
relationship 4

mass communication 4
public communication 4
small-group communication 4
intrapersonal
  communication 5
depression 6

Critical Thinking Questions

1. Draw a relationship scale on a piece of paper, and label it "impersonal" at one end and "intimate" at the other. Place your family members, friends, and work colleagues on the scale. Why do some fall toward the "impersonal" end? What makes those relationships less personal than others? Discuss and compare your entries with those of classmates.

2. Ethics: Think about your primary goal for this course. Is it to develop communication strategies to help you achieve personal goals? Is it to develop sensitivity to the needs of others? What is behind your goal? Is your purpose ethical?

Activities

Briefly describe a recent interpersonal communication exchange that was *not* effective. Analyze the exchange. Write down some of the dialogue if you remember it. Did the other person understand you? Did your communication have the intended effect? Was your message ethical?

Web Resources

www.natcom.org This is the homepage of the National Communication Association, the largest professional association in the world. The site offers information, references, and resources about human communication.

The Communication Process

(pages 7–9)

OBJECTIVES ❸ ❹ Describe the key components of the communication process, and compare and contrast communication as action, interaction, and transaction.

Key Terms

source 7
encoding 7
messages 7
channel 7
receiver 7

decoding 7
noise 7
feedback 7
context 8
systems theory 9

Critical Thinking Questions

1. What makes interpersonal communication a complex process? Explain, drawing on some of your own everyday communication exchanges.

2. Think of some recent interpersonal communication exchanges you've had. Which communication model best captures the nature of each exchange? Analyze each exchange, identifying the components of communication discussed in this section of the chapter. Was feedback an important component? Were you and your partner experiencing the communication simultaneously? What was the context? What were sources of internal and external noise? Did you or your partner have problems encoding or decoding each other's messages?

Activities

Working with a group of your classmates or individually, develop your own model of interpersonal communication. Include all the components that are necessary to describe how communication between people works. Your model could be a drawing or an object that symbolizes the communication process. Share your model with the class, describing the decisions you made in developing it. Illustrate your model with a conversation between two people, pointing out how elements of the conversation relate to the model.

Web Resources

www.wcaweb.org The homepage of the World Communication Association includes a wealth of information, references, and resources about human communication.

Interpersonal Communication and Technology (pages 9–16)

OBJECTIVE ❺ Discuss electronically mediated communication's role in developing and maintaining interpersonal relationships.

Key Terms

electronically mediated
  communication (EMC) 9
asynchronous message 10
synchronous message 10
social presence 10

hyperpersonal relationship 13
cues-filtered-out theory 13
media richness theory 14
social information-processing
  theory 15

Critical Thinking Questions

1. Does electronically mediated communication make us more or less other-oriented than FtF communication? Explain. Think of the different types of EMC that you use in your daily life. How does each of these affect your social presence?

2. Ethics: There is a greater potential for deception with EMC than with face-to-face communication. What other ethical issues arise with EMC? What are some steps you can take to make sure you are communicating ethically via electronic media? And how do you evaluate the credibility and reliability of the electronically mediated communication you receive?

Activities

Keep a one-day log of your electronically mediated interactions (e.g., phone calls, Facebook messages, text messages). Describe each one, noting whether there was a greater emphasis on the content or the relational elements of the messages you exchanged during the interaction.

Principles of Interpersonal Communication, and Improving Your Own Interpersonal Communication Competence (pages 16–24)

OBJECTIVES ⑥ ⑦ Discuss five principles of interpersonal communication, and identify strategies that can improve your communication effectiveness.

Key Terms

symbol *18*
rule *18*
content *19*
relationship dimension *19*
metacommunication *19*

communibiological
 approach *20*
social learning theory *20*
ethics *22*

Critical Thinking Questions

1. What rules govern your relationship with your mother? Your father? Your communication professor? Your roommate? Your coach? Your spouse? Your siblings?

2. Ethics: Your parents want you to visit them for the holidays. You would rather spend the time with a friend. You don't want to hurt your parents' feelings, so you tell them that you are working on an important project and won't be able to come home for the holidays. Your message is understood. It achieves the intended effect: your parents don't seem to have hurt feelings, and you don't go home. Explain whether your message is ethical or unethical.

Activities

Review the discussion of principles of interpersonal communication that begins on page 16. Give an example from your own relationships that illustrates each principle.

Web Resources

www.khake.com/page66.html This website offers a host of resources and links to other sites that provide information about human communication.

© pikselstock/Fotolia

2

Interpersonal Communication and Self

66 People tell themselves stories and then pour their lives into the stories they tell. 99 —Anonymous

P hilosophers suggest that there are three basic questions to which we all seek answers: (1) Who am I? (2) Why am I here? and (3) Who are all these others? In this chapter, we will focus on these essential questions. Grappling with the question of who you are and seeking to define a purpose for your life are fundamental to understanding others and becoming other-oriented in your interpersonal communication and relationships.

Fundamentally, all your communication starts or ends with you. When you are the communicator, you intentionally or unintentionally code your thoughts and emotions to be interpreted by another. When you receive a message, you interpret the information through your own frame of reference. Your self-image and self-worth, as well as your needs, values, beliefs, and attitudes, serve as filters for your communication with others. As you develop and establish relationships, you may become more aware of these filters, and perhaps choose to alter them. A close relationship often provides the impetus for change.

To better understand the role that self-concept plays in interpersonal communication, we will explore the first two basic questions, "Who am I?" and "Why am I here?," by trying to discover the meaning of self. We will examine the multifaceted dimensions of our self-concept, learn how it develops, and compare self-concept with self-esteem. Then we will move to the third basic question, "Who are all these others?" What you choose to tell and not tell others about yourself reveals important clues about who you are, what you value, and how you relate to others. In addition, focusing on the needs, wants, and values of other people while maintaining your own integrity is the basis of being other-oriented.

Self-Concept: Who Do You Think You Are?

In Alice Munro's short story collection, *Who Do You Think You Are?*, a young girl is asked the title question by the people in her small town. As she grows up, her unclear self-concept has a negative impact on her relationships with others.

You can begin your journey of self-discovery by trying the exercise in the *Building Your Skills* box "Who Are You?" on page 29.

How did you answer the question "Who are you?" Perhaps your self-descriptions identify activities in which you participate. Or they may list groups and organizations to which you belong or some of the roles you assume, such as student, son or daughter, or parent. All of these things are, indeed, parts of your **self**, the sum total of who you are. Psychologist Karen Horney defines *self* as "that central inner force, common to all human beings and yet unique in each, which is the deep source of growth."[1]

Your answers are also part of your **self-concept**. Your self-concept is your subjective description of who you *think* you are—it is filtered through your own perceptions. For example, you may have great musical talent, but you may not believe in it enough to think of yourself as a musician. You can view self-concept as the labels you consistently use to describe yourself to others.

A healthy self-concept is flexible. It may change depending upon new experiences you have and new insights you gain. Although you may have used certain labels to describe yourself today, you may use different ones tomorrow or next week. However, core elements will remain stable. Who you are is also reflected in the attitudes, beliefs, and values that you hold. These are learned constructs that shape your behaviour and self-image. An **attitude** is a learned predisposition to respond to a person, object, or idea in a favourable or unfavourable way. Attitudes reflect what you like and what you don't like. If you like jazz music, butter pecan ice cream, and Labrador retrievers, you hold positive attitudes toward these things. You were not born with a fondness for butter pecan ice cream; you learned to like it, just as some people learn to enjoy the taste of snails, raw fish, or puréed turnips.

self. The sum total of who a person is; a person's central inner force.

self-concept. A person's subjective description of who the person thinks he or she is.

attitude. Learned predisposition to respond to a person, object, or idea in a favourable or unfavourable way.

Building Your Skills   Who Are You?

Consider this question: Who are you? More specifically, ask yourself this question 10 times. Write your responses in the spaces provided here or on a separate piece of paper. It may be challenging to identify 10 aspects of yourself; the Spanish writer Cervantes said, "To know thyself . . . is the most difficult lesson in the world." Your answers will help you begin to explore your self-concept and self-esteem in this chapter.

I am _____   I am _____

I am _____   I am _____

I am _____   I am _____

I am _____   I am _____

I am _____   I am _____

Beliefs are the ways in which you structure your understanding of reality—what is true and what is false. Most of your beliefs are based on previous experience. You believe that the sun will rise in the morning because it has risen every morning, and that you will get burned if you put your hand on a hot stove because it has happened to you or someone you know.

How are attitudes and beliefs related? They often function quite independently of one another. You may have a favourable attitude toward something and still believe negative things about it. You may believe, for example, that your university or college hockey team will not win the provincial championship this year, though you may be a big fan. Or you may believe that a God exists, yet not always like what you think that God does or doesn't do. Beliefs have to do with what is true or not true; attitudes reflect likes and dislikes.

Values are enduring concepts of good and bad, right and wrong. Your values are more resistant to change than either your attitudes or your beliefs. They are also more difficult for most people to identify. Values are so central to who you are that it is difficult to isolate them. For example, when you go to the supermarket, you may spend a few minutes deciding which cookies to buy, but you probably do not spend much time deciding whether you will steal the cookies or pay for them. Our values are instilled in us by our earliest interpersonal relationships; for almost all of us, our parents shape our values. The model in Figure 2.1 shows that values are central to our behaviour and concept of self, and that what we believe to be true or false stems from our values. Attitudes are at the outer edge of the circle because they are the most likely to change. You may like your co-worker today but not tomorrow, even though you *believe* the person will come to work every day and you still *value* the concept of friendship. Beliefs are between attitudes and values in the model because

beliefs. The ways in which you structure your understanding of reality—what is true and what is false.

values. Enduring concepts of good and bad, right and wrong.

▶ RECAP   Who You Are Is Reflected in Your Attitudes, Beliefs, and Values

	Definition	Dimensions	Example
Attitudes	Learned predispositions to respond favourably or unfavourably toward something.	Likes–Dislikes	You like mountain biking, horror movies, and cats.
Beliefs	The ways in which we structure reality.	True–False	You believe your parents love you.
Values	Enduring concepts of what is right and wrong.	Good–Bad	You value honesty and truth.

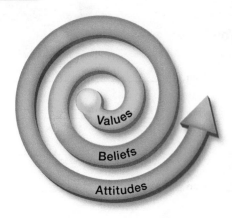

FIGURE 2.1

Values, Beliefs, and Attitudes in Relation to Self

they are more likely to change than our core values but don't change as much as our attitudes (likes and dislikes).

Mindfulness: Being Consciously Aware

Do you know what you're doing right now? "Of course," you may think, "I'm reading this text." But are you really aware of all of the fleeting thoughts bouncing around in your head, whether you're truly happy or sad, or even whether you may be twiddling a pencil, jiggling your leg, or in need of a snack? To be aware of who you are and what you may be thinking about is a more involved process than you may think. To be self-aware is to be mindful. **Mindfulness** is the ability to consciously think about what you are doing and experiencing rather than responding out of habit or intuition. If you've ever talked on the phone while driving (something illegal in many provinces), you may not have been mindful of, or consciously thinking about, where you were driving. Self-awareness is consciousness of who you are and what you are doing. Researchers have described three ways of being self-aware: subjective self-awareness, objective self-awareness, and symbolic self-awareness.[2]

Subjective Self-Awareness. **Subjective self-awareness** is the ability that people have to differentiate themselves from their environment. It is so basic an awareness that it may even seem not worth talking about. You know, for example, that you're not physically attached to the chair you may be sitting in. You are a separate being from everything that is around you.

Objective Self-Awareness. **Objective self-awareness** is the ability to be the object of one's own thoughts and attention. You have the ability to think about your own thoughts as you are thinking about them. Not only are you aware that you're separate from your environment (subjective self-awareness), but you can also ponder the distinct thoughts you are thinking. Of course, objective self-awareness, like subjective self-awareness, can be "turned on" and "turned off." Sometimes you are aware of what you are thinking or focusing on, while at other times you are completely unaware.

Symbolic Self-Awareness. **Symbolic self-awareness**, unique to humans, is our ability not only to think about ourselves, but to use language (symbols) to represent ourselves to others. For example, you have the ability to think about how to make a good impression on others. In an effort to make a positive impression on someone, you may say, "Good morning, Professor Gupta. I enjoyed your lecture yesterday," rather than just saying, "Hey." You make conscious attempts to use symbols to influence the way you are perceived by others.

mindfulness. The ability to consciously think about what you are doing and experiencing rather than responding out of habit or intuition.

subjective self-awareness. Ability to differentiate the self from the social and physical environment.

objective self-awareness. Ability to be the object of one's own thoughts and attention—to be aware of one's state of mind and that one is thinking.

symbolic self-awareness. Uniquely human ability to think about oneself and use language (symbols) to represent oneself to others.

One or Many Selves?

Shakespeare's famous line "To thine own self be true" suggests that you have a single self to which you can be true. Do you have just one self? Or is there a more real "you" buried somewhere within? "I'm just not myself this morning," sighs Denika as she drags herself out the front door to head for her office. If she is not herself, then who is she? Most researchers conclude that we have a core set of behaviours, attitudes, beliefs, and values that constitute our self—the sum total of who we are. However, our concept of self can and does change, depending on circumstances and influences.

In addition, our self-concepts are often different from the way others see us. We almost always behave differently in public than we do in private. Sociologist Erving Goffman suggests that, like actors and actresses, we have "on stage" behaviours when others are watching and "backstage" behaviours when they are not.[3]

Building Your Skills | Dimensions of Your Self

Take another look at your responses to the question, "Who are you?" Divide your list according to James's three components of the self. If nothing on your original list relates to one of these "selves," make a new entry here so that you have a response for each of them.

Material Self

References to the physical elements that reflect who you are.

Example:

I collect antiques.

_____
_____
_____
_____
_____

Social Self

References to interactions with others that reflect who you are.

Example:

I am a member of the Chess Club.

_____
_____
_____
_____
_____

Spiritual Self

References to your reflections about values, morals, and beliefs.

Example:

I believe in a higher spiritual being.

_____
_____
_____
_____
_____

Perhaps the most enduring and widely accepted framework for describing who you are was developed by the philosopher William James. He identified three components of the self: the material self, the social self, and the spiritual self.[4]

The Material Self. Perhaps you've heard the statement "You are what you eat." The material self goes a step further by suggesting, "You are what you have." The **material self** is a total of all the tangible things you own: your possessions, your home, your body. As you examine your list of responses to the question "Who are you?", note whether any of your statements refers to one of your physical attributes or something you own.

One element of the material self gets considerable attention in our culture: the body. Do you like the way you look? Most of us, if we're honest, would like to change something about our appearance. When there is a discrepancy between our desired material self and our self-concept, we may respond by attempting to eliminate the discrepancy. We may try to lose weight, develop our muscles, or change our hair colour. The multi-billion-dollar diet industry is just one of many that profit from our collective desire to change our appearance.

The Social Self. Look at your "Who are you?" list once more. How many of your responses relate to your **social self**, the part of you that interacts with others? William James believed that you have many social selves—that depending on the friend, family member, colleague, or acquaintance with whom you are interacting, you change the way you are. A person has, said James, as many social selves as there are people who recognize him or her.

For example, when you talk to your best friend, you are willing to reveal more thoughts and feelings than you would in a conversation with your communication professor, or perhaps even your parents. Each relationship that you have with another person is unique because you bring to it a unique social self.

The Spiritual Self. Your **spiritual self** consists of all your internal thoughts and introspections about your values and moral standards. It is not dependent on what you own or with whom you talk; it is the essence of who you think you are, and of your feelings about yourself, apart from external evaluations. It is an amalgam of your religious beliefs and your sense of who you are in relation to other forces in the universe. Your spiritual self is the part of you that answers the question "Why am I here?"

material self. Your concept of self as reflected in a total of all the tangible things you own.

social self. Your concept of self as developed through your personal, social interactions with others.

spiritual self. Your concept of self based on your thoughts and introspections about your values and moral standards.

▶ RECAP   William James's Dimensions of Self

	Definition	Examples
Material self	All of the physical elements that reflect who you are.	Possessions, car, home, body, clothes.
Social self	The self as reflected through your interactions with others; actually, a variety of selves that respond to changes in situations and roles.	Your informal self interacting with your best friend; your formal self interacting with your professors.
Spiritual self	Introspections about values, morals, and beliefs.	Religious belief or disbelief; regard for life in all its forms.

looking-glass self. Concept that suggests you learn who you are based on your interactions with others, who reflect your self back to you.

reflected appraisal. Another term for the looking-glass self. You learn who you are based on how others treat you.

How Your Self-Concept Develops

Some psychologists and sociologists have advanced theories that suggest we learn who we are through five basic means: (1) our interactions with other individuals, (2) our association with groups, (3) roles we assume, (4) our own labels, and (5) our personalities. Like James's framework, this one does not cover every base in our study of self, but its constructs can provide some clues about how our own self-concepts develop.

Interaction with Individuals. In 1902, Charles Horton Cooley first advanced the notion of the **looking-glass self**, which is the idea that we form our self-concepts by seeing ourselves in a kind of figurative looking glass; we learn who we are by interacting with others, much as we look into a mirror and see our reflection.[5] This is also referred to as **reflected appraisal**. In other words, we develop self-concepts that often match or correspond to the ways in which we believe others see us.

The process begins at birth. Our names, one of the primary ways we identify ourselves, are given to us by someone else. During the early years of our lives, our parents are the key individuals who shape who we are. If our parents encouraged us to play the piano, we probably played as children. As we become less dependent on our parents, our friends become highly influential in shaping our attitudes, beliefs, and values. Friends continue to provide feedback on how well we perform certain tasks. This, in turn, helps us shape our sense of identity as adults—we must acknowledge our talents in math, language, or art in our own minds before we can say that we are mathematicians, linguists, or artists.

Fortunately, not *all* feedback affects our sense of who we think we are. We are likely to incorporate the comments of others into our self-concept under three conditions: (1) How frequently the message is presented, (2) whether the message is perceived as credible, and (3) whether the message is consistent.

Frequent. We are more likely to believe another's statement if he or she repeats something we have heard several times. If one person casually tells you that you have a talent for singing, you are not likely to launch a search for an agent and a recording contract. However, if several individuals tell you on many different occasions that you have a talent for singing, you may decide to do something about it.

Credible. We are more likely to value another's statements if he or she has already earned our confidence. If you believe an individual is competent, trustworthy, and qualified to make a judgment about you, then you are more likely to believe the person's assessment.

"I don't want to be defined by who I am."

Consistent. We are likely to incorporate another's comments into our own concept of self if the comments are consistent with other comments and our own experience. If your boss tells you that you work too slowly, but for years people have been urging you to slow down, then your previous experience will probably encourage you to challenge your boss's evaluation.

Association with Groups. Reflect once more on your responses to the "Who are you?" question. How many responses associate you with a group? Religious groups, political groups, ethnic groups, social groups, study groups, and occupational and professional groups play important roles in determining our self-concept. Some of these groups we are born into; others we choose on our own. Either way, these group associations are significant parts of our identities. The *Canadian Connections* box features the compelling story of journalist Ian Stewart, who describes being shot while on the job. Still seeing himself as a writer and a journalist, he felt the need to document the tragic events and his slow recovery.

Canadian Connections   A Long Journey Home

These are a few excerpts from the story of Ian Stewart, a Canadian journalist who was shot on January 9, 1999, while covering a civil war in Africa. His award-winning story from November 24, 1999, is the account of his courageous struggle back toward health after being shot in the head.

I floated in a grey fog illuminated by the flickering of fluorescent lights. Someone was calling my name over and over, but the voice sounded far away. Blurry faces hovered over me. Shadows, then gone . . .

Wavering on that boundary between sleep and awareness, I couldn't lift my head from the pillow . . . Something was awfully wrong. Why couldn't I feel my leg?

Weeks drifted by. The mist that had enshrouded my brain began to lift. Destruction and death haunted my hospital dreams. Silhouettes of palm trees swayed against a cobalt sky streaked red and yellow by tracer bullets. Waking hours were no better. Lying on rubber sheets, I struggled to stop the walls as they spun by.

Adding to the torment, I have never been able to remember what happened when we were shot. With no recollection of the most cataclysmic moment of my life, each day is a battle against the incomprehensible.

Of course, I have been told how it happened. Our station wagon turned a corner and came upon five armed men in American-style jeans and flip-flops. Oddly, one was wearing a bowler hat. He raised his automatic rifle and fired a burst. Our escort returned fire, killing the shooter and another rebel. It was over in seconds. David had been cut by flying glass. I had been shot in the head. Myles had been killed instantly, the 24th AP journalist to die in the line of duty in the organization's 151 years . . .

Over the next several hours, David and AP Abidjan correspondent Tim Sullivan (now bureau chief) saved my life, pleading and cajoling my way onto a succession of airplanes that would hop across Africa and on to England and modern medical care. It was late Monday night by the time I was carried into London's Hospital for Neurology and Neurosurgery. With the dirty field dressing still around my head, I was wheeled past a shocked couple who had just rushed from Toronto . . .

I can't say when I began to realize the gravity of my wound. Because of the very nature of a brain injury, patients often find it hard to understand and almost impossible to accept. The consequences of my injury were almost entirely physical. My left arm and hand were paralysed, my left leg impaired . . .

But there were other complications. For days, I struggled just to understand where I was . . . My brain was a crystal goblet shattered into a million slivers of fading dreams and dashed hopes. I have been piecing it back together, one sliver at a time . . . Ten weeks after the shooting, I returned to my parents' home on Toronto's Lake Ontario waterfront.

For months I have struggled to adjust to life with a disability. I don't ever want to forget even the smallest detail of this experience. Two months after returning to Toronto, I have improved enough to walk with a cane. On June 3, a Thursday, I walk into a medical supply centre to return my wheelchair.

Once I was an athlete, a football player. Now I shuffle a few yards, stop to catch my breath, sit for a spell. As a wire service reporter, I used to whip out several stories a day. Now I spend months on this one, pecking at the keys with my one good hand. My therapist says that in time, my left arm will regain some function. How much is impossible to say . . .

Myles, David, and I were naive to hope our reporting could make people care about a little war in Africa. In fact, Freetown might never have made your daily newspaper had it not been for the death of one western journalist and wounding of another.

Will I continue to work as a journalist when I am well enough to work? Yes, and most likely I'll go back overseas.

Will I risk my life for a story again? No. Not even if the world cares next time.

In Canadian culture, behaviour among girls is in many ways quite distinct from that among boys.
© Tom McCarthy/PhotoEdit, Inc.

Associating with groups is especially important for people who are not part of the dominant culture. Members of the LGBTQ community, for example, may find the support provided by associating with other members of that community to be beneficial to their well-being. The groups you associate with provide not only information about your identity but also needed social support.

Roles We Assume. Look again at your answers to the "Who are you?" question. Perhaps you see words or phrases that signify a role you often assume. Father, aunt, sister, uncle, manager, salesperson, teacher, and student are labels that imply certain expectations for behaviour, and they are important in shaping self-concept. Couples who live together before they marry often report that marriage alters their relationship. Before, they may have shared domestic duties, such as doing dishes and laundry. However, when they assume the labels of "husband" and "wife," they may slip into traditional roles. Husbands don't do laundry. Wives don't mow the grass. These stereotypical role expectations that they learned long ago may require extensive discussion and negotiation. Couples who report the highest satisfaction with marriage agree on their expectations regarding roles ("We agree that I'll do laundry and you'll mow the grass").

One reason we assume traditional roles automatically is that our gender group asserts a powerful influence from birth on. As soon as parents know the sex of their child, many begin placing that child in the group by following cultural rules. They may paint the nursery pink for a girl, blue for a boy. Boys may get a catcher's mitt, a train set, or a hockey stick for their birthdays; girls may get dolls, frilly dresses, and tea sets. These cultural conventions and expectations play a major role in shaping our self-concept and our behaviour.

In 2011, a Toronto couple caused a controversy by deciding not to reveal the gender of their baby, Storm, to anyone, including friends and family. They didn't want their child's self-concept to be determined by gender roles. Storm's mother explained her decision as follows: "In fact, in not telling the gender of my precious baby, I am saying to the world, 'Please can you just let Storm discover for him/herself what s(he) wants to be?!'"[6]

Although it is changing, North American culture is still male-dominated. What we consider appropriate and inappropriate behaviour is often different for males and females. In group and team meetings, for example, task-oriented, male-dominated roles are valued more than feminine, relationship-building roles. We often applaud fathers who work 60 hours a week as "diligent and hard-working" but criticize mothers who do the same as "neglectful and selfish." This kind of example is becoming outdated as society slowly changes, but it can still be observed in many workplaces.

Although our culture defines certain roles as masculine or feminine, we do exercise individual choices about our gender roles. One researcher developed an inventory designed to assess whether you play traditional masculine, feminine, or androgynous roles.[7] Because an **androgynous role** is both masculine and feminine, this role encompasses a greater repertoire of actions and behaviours.

Self-Labels. Although our self-concept is deeply affected by others, we are not blank slates for them to write on. The labels we use to describe our own attitudes, beliefs, values, and actions also play a role in shaping our self-concept.

Where do we acquire our labels? We interpret what we experience; we are self-reflexive. **Self-reflexiveness** is the human ability to think about what we are doing while we are doing it. We talk to ourselves about ourselves. We are both participants and observers in all that we do. This dual role encourages us to use labels to describe who we are.

androgynous role. A gender role that includes both masculine and feminine qualities.

self-reflexiveness. Ability to think about what we are doing while we are doing it.

E-CONNECTION
Relating to Others

Your "Online Self" and Your "Offline Self"

Would people who know you only on Facebook or Twitter have the same impression of you if they met you in person? Would people with whom you communicate via email or a blog have the same image of you if they met you in person? Electronically mediated communication (EMC) makes it easier to control what information people learn about us. Because you have more control, does your online presentation of yourself differ from your live-and-in-person presentation of self? Do you try to enhance your "face" on Facebook in ways that are different from techniques you use when communicating in person? The ease and prevalence of EMC communication in the 21st century has spurred communication researchers to investigate these and other questions about how we present ourselves online.[8]

Communication researchers Lisa Tidwell and Joseph Walther wanted to know whether there are differences between face-to-face conversations and EMC conversations in the amount of information people share with others, their projection of confidence, and the overall effectiveness of communication. They found that when people communicate via email, they exchange information more directly with each other and perceive themselves and others to be more "conversationally effective" because they are more direct. Perhaps people perceive their communication as more effective because they can edit and revise what they say

online and have more control than when talking face to face. Email conversation partners also reported that they were more confident when communicating online than they were in their face-to-face encounters.[9]

In addition to perceiving ourselves as more effective and confident as well as sharing more personal information when communicating via email, we may be less truthful about ourselves when we are online compared with face-to-face communication. Two Internet researchers found strong evidence that people are much more likely to misrepresent themselves in cyberspace than in "realspace" relationships.[10] As we noted in Chapter 1, we're most likely to lie about our age, weight, and personal appearance when communicating online.[11]

Researchers have also found that people report their face-to-face relationships as being more serious in tone than their exclusively online relationships. And even though people made more expressions of commitment in their realspace relationships compared with their cyberspace relationships, research participants reported about the same levels of satisfaction with both types of relationships. They also reported similar potential for emotional growth in their romantic relationships, whether in realspace or cyberspace.

With our increased use of EMC, researchers have found that our sense of self is derived not only from face-to-face

interactions but also from the amount, kind, and quality of relationships we develop with people online. Canadian psychologist M. Kyle Matsuba examined how our self-concept (what he labelled "ego identity") is influenced by EMC.[12] He found that the clearer university students were about their own identity (self-concept), the less they developed online relationships. Or, stated the other way around, the less clear a person is about his or her own identity, the more likely he or she is to develop relationships online. (Note that this is a correlation rather than a cause-and-effect relationship.) Perhaps if we are not totally certain about who we are, we develop relationships with others online to help explore who we are. Matsuba also found a strong correlation between being a heavy user of the Internet and greater feelings of loneliness. (Again, he found a correlation rather than a cause-and-effect link between Internet use and loneliness; Internet use doesn't cause loneliness, but more people who feel lonely may use the Internet to connect with others.)

Because we can control our online persona more readily than our realspace presentation of self, we're more confident about what we say about ourselves online. The Internet, which offers the opportunity to develop many relationships with others quickly and efficiently, especially on social networking sites, can help us explore facets of ourselves and clarify our self-concept.

When you were younger, perhaps you dreamed of becoming an NHL hockey player or a movie star. Your coach or your teacher may have told you that you were a great player or a terrific actor, but as you matured, you probably began observing yourself more critically. You scored no goals; you did not get the starring role in local theatre productions. So you self-reflexively decided that you were not, deep down, a hockey player or an actor, even though others may have labelled you as "talented." However, sometimes, through this self-observation, we discover strengths that encourage us to assume new labels. One woman we know never thought of herself as "heroic" until she went through seventy-two hours of labour before giving birth!

Your Personality. The concept of personality is central to **psychology**, the study of how our thinking influences how we behave. According to psychologist Lester Lefton, your

psychology. Study of how thinking influences behaviour.

personality consists of a set of enduring internal predispositions and behavioural characteristics that, together, describe how you react to your environment.[13] Understanding the forces that shape your personality is central to increasing your awareness of your self-concept and how you relate to others.

Although there are numerous personality types in the world, psychologists today suggest that there are just five major personality traits, the combination of which determines your overall personality:[14]

Extraversion: The quality of being outgoing, talkative, and sociable

Agreeableness: The quality of being friendly, compassionate, trusting, and cooperative

Conscientiousness: The quality of being efficient, organized, self-disciplined, and dutiful,

Neuroticism: The quailty of being nervous, insecure, emotionally distressed, and anxious

Openness: The quality of being curious, imaginative, creative, and adventurous

Are you simply *born* with the personality you have or do you *learn* your behaviour by observing others? In other words, deos nature or nurture play the predominant role in shaping your personality? As we noted in Chapter 1, the **communibiological approach** to communication suggests that genetic makeup, or biology, is a major factor affecting how people communicate. Proponents of social learning theory, however, suggest that, although it's true that communication behaviour is influenced by genes, we should not forget that humans can learn to adjust and adapt.

One personality characteristic that communication researchers have spent considerable time studying is the level of comfort or discomfort with interactions with other people. Some people just don't like talking with others; in interpersonal communication situations, we may say those people are shy. **Shyness** is the behavioural tendency not to talk with others. One study found that about 40% of adults reported they were shy.[15] In public-speaking

personality. Enduring internal predispositions and behavioural characteristics that describe how people react to their environment.

extraversion. A personality trait describing someone as outgoing, talkative, having positive emotions, and sociable

agreeableness. A personality trait describing someone as friendly, compassionate, trusting, and cooperative.

conscientiousness. A personality trait describing someone as efficient, organized, self-disciplined, dutiful, and methodical.

neuroticism. A personality trait describing someone as nervous, insecure, emotionally distressed, and anxious.

openness. A personality trait describing someone as curious, imaginative, creative, and adventurous,

communibiological approach. Perspective that suggests that genetic and biological influences play a major role in influencing communication behaviour.

shyness. Behavioural tendency not to talk or interact with other people.

© Bruce Eric Kaplan/The New Yorker Collection/The Cartoon Bank

"My self-esteem was so low I just followed her around everywhere she would go."

situations, we say a person has stage fright; a better term to describe this feeling is **communication apprehension**. Communication apprehension, according to communication experts James McCroskey and Virginia Richmond, is "the fear or anxiety associated with either real or anticipated communication with another person or persons."[16] One study found that up to 80% of the population experiences some degree of nervousness or apprehension when they speak in public.[17] Another study found that about 20% of people are considerably anxious when they give a speech.[18] What makes some people apprehensive about communicating with others? Again, we get back to the nature–nurture issue. Heredity plays an important role in whether you are going to feel nervous or anxious when communicating with someone else. However, so does whether you were reinforced for talking with others as a child, as well as other experiences that are part of your culture and learning.

Your overall **willingness to communicate** with others is a general way of summarizing the likelihood that you will talk with others in a variety of situations. If you are unwilling to communicate, you will be less comfortable in a career such as sales or customer service that requires you to interact with people.

Understanding the factors that influence your self-concept—such as your interactions with individuals and groups, the roles you assume, your self-labels, and your personality, including your overall comfort level in communicating with others—can help you understand who you are and how you interact (or don't interact) with others. However, it's not only who you are that influences your communication; your overall sense of self-esteem or self-worth also affects how you express yourself and respond to others.

Self-Esteem: Your Self-Worth

Your **self-esteem** is closely related to your self-concept. Your self-concept is a description of who you are. The term **self-worth** is often used interchangeably with *self-esteem*. There is evidence that your overall feeling of self-worth is related to feeling and expressing positive messages toward others as well as being supportive of other people. You feel better about yourself if you behave in ways that researchers call being prosocial, which means your behaviours benefit others.

People derive their sense of self-worth from comparing themselves with others, a process called **social comparison**. Social comparison helps people measure how well they think they are doing compared with others. I'm good at playing soccer (because I beat others); I can't cook (because others cook better than I do); I'm not good at meeting people (most people I know seem to be more comfortable interacting with others); I'm not handy (but my brothers and sisters can fix a leaky faucet). Each of these statements implies a judgment about how well or badly you can perform certain tasks, with implied references to how well others perform the same tasks. A belief that you cannot fix a leaky faucet or cook like a chef may not in itself lower your self-esteem. But if there are several things you can't do well or many important tasks that you cannot seem to master, these shortcomings may begin to colour your overall sense of worth.

Improving Your Self-Esteem

We have already seen how low self-esteem can affect our own communication and interactions. In recent years, teachers, psychologists, ministers, rabbis, social workers, and even politicians have suggested that many of our societal problems stem from our collective feelings of low self-esteem. Our feelings of low self-worth may contribute to our choosing the

communication apprehension. Fear or anxiety associated with either real or anticipated communication with other people.

willingness to communicate. General characteristic that describes an individual's tendency to be shy or apprehensive about communicating with others.

self-esteem (self-worth). Your evaluation of your worth or value as reflected in your perception of such things as your skills, abilities, talents, and appearance.

social comparison. Process of comparing yourself to others who are similar to you to measure your worth and value.

Positive self-talk can help us focus on our own goals and improve our performance levels even when the goals seem insurmountable.
(© Canadian Cancer Society)

wrong partners; to becoming dependent on drugs, alcohol, or other substances; and to experiencing problems with eating and other vital activities. We owe it to society, as well as to ourselves, to maintain or develop a healthy sense of self-esteem.

Although no simple list of tricks can easily transform low self-esteem into feelings of being valued and appreciated, you can make improvements in the ways you think about yourself and interact with others. We'll explore seven proven techniques that have helped others.

Practise Positive Self-Talk

Every Canadian knows only too well the story of Terry Fox and his battle with the cancer that ended his young life. Through it all, he remained upbeat, and his positive attitude enabled him to run an equivalent to a marathon every day for 143 days. He has been described as Canada's true hero.

Intrapersonal communication is communication within one's own mind—self-talk. Realistic, positive self-talk can have a reassuring effect on your level of self-worth and on your interactions with others. Conversely, repeating negative messages about your lack of skill and ability can keep you from trying and achieving.

Of course, blind faith without hard work won't succeed. Self-talk is not a substitute for effort; it can, however, keep you on track and help you, ultimately, to achieve your goal.

Visualize a Positive Image of Yourself

Visualization takes the notion of self-talk one step further. Besides just telling yourself that you can achieve your goal, you can actually try to "see" yourself conversing effectively with others, performing well on a project, or emphasizing some other desirable behaviour. Recent research suggests that an apprehensive public speaker can manage his or her fears not only by developing skill in public speaking but also by visualizing positive results when speaking to an audience. If, for example, you tend to get nervous when meeting people at a party, imagine yourself in a room full of people, confidently introducing yourself to others with ease. Visualizing yourself performing well can yield positive results in changing long-standing feelings of inadequacy. Of course, your visualization should be realistic and coupled with a plan to achieve your goal.

Avoid Comparing Yourself with Others

Even before we are born, we are compared with others. Medical technology lets us see sonograms of fetuses still in the womb, so parents may begin comparing children with their siblings or other babies before birth. For the rest of our lives we are compared with others, and, rather than celebrating our uniqueness, comparisons usually point out who is bigger, brighter, and more beautiful. Most of us have had the experience of being chosen last to play on a sports team, being passed over for promotion, or standing unasked against the wall at a dance.

In North American culture, we may be tempted to judge our self-worth by our material possessions and personal appearance. If we know someone who has a newer car

intrapersonal communication. Communication within one's own mind, including self-talk.

visualization. A technique of imagining that you are performing a particular task in a certain way. Positive visualization can enhance your self-esteem.

(or simply a car, if we rely on public transportation), a smaller waistline, or a higher grade point average, we may feel diminished. Comparisons such as "She has more money than I have" or "He's in better shape than I am" are likely to deflate our self-worth.

Rather than focusing on others who are seemingly better off, focus on the unique attributes that make you who you are. Avoid judging your own value in comparison with that of others. A healthy, positive self-concept is fuelled not by judgments of others but by a genuine sense of worth that we recognize in ourselves.

Reframe Appropriately

Reframing is the process of redefining events and experiences from a different point of view. Just as reframing a work of art can give the painting a whole new look, reframing events that cause us to devalue our self-worth can change our perspective. If, for example, you get a report from your supervisor that says you should improve one area of your performance, instead of listening to the self-talk that says you're bad at your job, reframe the event within a larger context: tell yourself that one negative comment does not mean you are a worthless employee.

Of course, not all negative experiences should be lightly tossed off and left unexamined; you can learn and profit from your mistakes. However, it is important to remember that our worth as human beings is not contingent on a single letter grade, a single response from a prospective employer, or a single play in a hockey game.

Develop Honest Relationships

Having at least one other person who can help you objectively and honestly reflect on your virtues and vices can be extremely beneficial in fostering a healthy, positive self-image. As we noted earlier, other people play a major role in shaping our self-concept and self-esteem. The more credible the source of information, the more likely we are to believe it. Later in the chapter, we discuss how honest relationships are developed through the process of self-disclosure. Honest, positive support can provide encouragement for a lifetime.

Let Go of the Past

Your self-concept is not a fixed construct. Nor was it implanted at birth to remain constant for the rest of your life. Things change. You change. Others change. Individuals with low self-esteem may be fixating on events and experiences that happened years ago and refusing to let go of them. Looking back at what we can't change only reinforces a sense of helplessness. Constantly replaying negative experiences in our mind serves only to make

---

BEING Other-ORIENTED

We all need support and encouragement from others from time to time. When have other people helped you manage a difficult situation or period of your life? What are the qualities in others that you look for when you need social support? What are talents and skills that you possess that will help you provide useful social support to others?

reframing. The process of redefining events and experiences from a different point of view.

social support. Expression of empathy and concern for others that is communicated while listening to them and offering positive and encouraging words.

talk therapy. Technique in which a person describes his or her problems and concerns to a skilled listener in order to better understand the emotions and issues that are creating the problems.

By becoming a detective, you can find clues in the behaviour of others to determine if the assumptions you've made about them are accurate. Reflect on times when you have accurately identified the emotions of another person and compare those instances to other times when you weren't as accurate. What kinds of clues help you accurately predict others' moods and feelings?

our sense of worth more difficult to change. Becoming aware of the changes that have occurred, and can occur, in your life can assist you in developing a more realistic assessment of your value.

Seek Support

You provide **social support** when you express care and concern as well as listen and empathize with others. Perhaps you just call it "talking with a friend." Having someone be socially supportive is especially important to us when we experience stress and anxiety or are faced with a vexing personal problem.

Social support from a friend or family member can be helpful, but some of your self-image problems may be so ingrained that you need professional help. A trained counsellor, clergy member, or therapist can help you sort through them. The technique of having a trained person listen as you verbalize your fears, hopes, and concerns is called **talk therapy**. You talk, and a skilled listener helps you sort out your feelings and problems. There is power in being able to put your thoughts, especially your negative thoughts and emotions, into words. By saying things out loud to an open, honest, empathetic listener, we gain insight and can sometimes figure out why we experience the hurts and difficulties that we do. If you are not sure to whom to turn for a referral, you can start with your school counselling services. Or, if you are near a medical-school teaching hospital, you can contact the counselling or psychotherapy office there for a referral.

Because you have spent your whole lifetime developing your self-esteem, it is not easy to make big changes. However, as we have seen, talking through our problems can make a difference. As communication researchers Frank E. Dance and Carl Larson see it, "Speech communication empowers each of us to share in the development of our own self-concept and the fulfillment of that self-concept."[19]

▶ RECAP   Strategies for Improving Your Self-Esteem

Engage in positive self-talk	If you receive a low grade on an essay, tell yourself that you have a lot of interesting ideas and that you will do better next time.
Visualize	If you feel nervous before a meeting, visualize everyone in the room congratulating you on your great ideas.
Avoid comparisons	Rather than compare yourself to others, focus on your positive qualities and what you can do to enhance your own talents and abilities.
Reframe appropriately	If you experience one failure, keep the larger picture in mind rather than focusing on that isolated incident.
Develop honest relationships	Cultivate friends in whom you can confide and who will give you honest feedback for improving your skills and abilities.
Let go of the past	Try not to dwell on negative experiences in your past; instead, focus on ways to enhance your abilities in the future.
Seek support	Talk with professional counsellors who can help you identify your gifts and talents.

Self and Interpersonal Relationships

Your self-concept and self-esteem filter every interaction with others. They determine how you approach, respond to, and interpret messages. Specifically, your self-concept and self-esteem affect your ability to be sensitive to others, your self-fulfilling prophecies, your interpretation of messages, your own social needs, and your typical communication style.

Self and Others

Your image of yourself and your sense of self-worth directly affect how you interact with others. Who you think you are affects how you communicate with other people.

We defined human communication as the way we make sense of the world and share that sense with others by creating meaning through verbal and nonverbal messages. **Symbolic interaction theory** is indeed based on the assumption that we make sense of the world based on our interactions with others. We interpret what a word or symbol means based, in part, on how other people react to our use of that word or symbol. We learn, for example, that certain four-letter words have power because we see people react when they hear the words. Even our own understanding of who we think we are is influenced by who others tell us we are. For example, you don't think you're a good dancer, but after several of your friends tell you that you have dazzling dance moves, you start believing that you *do* have dancing talent. Central to understanding ourselves is understanding the importance of other people in shaping our self-understanding. Symbolic interaction theory has had a major influence on communication theory because of the pervasive way our communication with others influences our very sense of who we are.

George Herbert Mead is credited with the development of symbolic interaction theory, although Mead did not write extensively about his theory.[20] One of Mead's students, Herbert Blumer, actually coined the term *symbolic interaction* to describe the process through which our interactions with others influence our thoughts about others, our life experiences, and ourselves. Mead believed that we cannot have a concept of our own self-identity without interactions with other people.

Because the influence of others on your life is so far-reaching, it's sometimes hard to be consciously aware of how other people shape your thoughts. One of the ways to be more mindful of the influence of others is to become increasingly other-oriented—sensitive to the thoughts and feelings of others—which is essential for developing quality relationships with others. Becoming other-oriented involves recognizing that your concept of self (who *you* think you are) is different from how others perceive you—even though it's influenced by others, as suggested by symbolic interaction theory. Mead suggests that we come to think of ourselves both as "I," based on our own perception of ourselves, and as "me," based on the collective responses we receive from others and interpret. Being aware of how your concept of self ("I") differs from the perceptions others have of you ("me") is an important first step in developing an other-orientation.

Although it may seem complicated, it's really quite simple: You affect others and others affect you. Your ability to predict how others will respond to you is based on your skill in understanding how your sense of the world is similar to and different from theirs. To enhance your skill in understanding this process, you need to know yourself well. But understanding yourself is only half the process; you also need to be other-oriented. One of the best ways to improve your ability to be other-oriented is to notice how others respond when you act on the predictions and assumptions you have made about them. If you assume that your friend, who is out of work and struggling to make ends meet, will like it if you pick up the cheque for lunch, and she offers an appreciative "Thank you so much," you have received confirmation that your generosity was appreciated and that your hunch about how your friend would react to your gesture was accurate.

Self and Your Future

What people believe about themselves often comes true because they expect it to come true. Their expectations become a **self-fulfilling prophecy**. If you think you will fail the math quiz because you have labelled yourself inept at math, then you must overcome not only your math deficiency but your low expectations of yourself. Research suggests that you can create your own obstacles to achieving your goals by being too critical of yourself—or

BEING Other-ORIENTED

You develop your perception of yourself as an "I" based on your self-talk or the messages you tell yourself. Your perception of "me" is based on what you believe others say about you. Are you aware of your own perceptions of yourself ("I") compared with how others see you ("me")? Compare and contrast the information you use to develop your concept of yourself and your self-esteem with the information others use to form their perceptions of you.

symbolic interaction theory. Theory that people make sense of the world based on their interpretation of words or symbols used by others.

self-fulfilling prophecy. The idea that when people expect their beliefs about themselves to come true, they often do.

you can increase your chances for success by having a more positive mindset. Your attitudes, beliefs, and general expectations about your performance have a powerful and profound effect on your behaviour.

Self and Interpretation of Messages

Do you remember Eeyore, the donkey from A.A. Milne's classic children's stories about Winnie-the-Pooh and his friends? Eeyore lived in the gloomiest part of the Hundred Acre Wood and had a self-image to match. Perhaps you know, or have known, an Eeyore—someone whose low self-esteem colours how he or she interprets messages and interacts with others. According to research, such people are more likely to[22]

- Be more sensitive to criticism and negative feedback from others.

- Be more critical of others.

- Believe they are not popular or respected by others.

- Expect to be rejected by others.

- Dislike being observed when performing.

- Feel threatened by people who they feel are superior.

- Expect to lose when competing with others.

- Be overly responsive to praise and compliments.

- Evaluate their overall behaviour as inferior to that of others.

The Pooh stories offer an antidote to Eeyore's gloom in the character of the optimistic Tigger, who assumes that everyone shares his exuberance for life. If, like Tigger, your sense of self-worth is high, research suggests that you will

- Have higher expectations for solving problems.

- Think more highly of others.

- Be more likely to accept praise and accolades from others without feeling embarrassed.

- Be more comfortable having others observe you when you perform.

- Be more likely to admit you have both strengths and weaknesses.

- Be more comfortable when you interact with others who view themselves as highly competent.

- Expect other people to accept you for who you are.

- Be more likely to seek opportunities to improve skills that need improving.

- Evaluate your overall behaviour more positively than would people with lower self-esteem.[23]

Self and Interpersonal Needs

According to social psychologist Will Schutz, our concept of who we are, coupled with our need to interact with others, profoundly influences how we communicate. Schutz identifies three primary social needs that affect our degree of communication: the need for inclusion, the need for control, and the need for affection.[24]

The **need for inclusion** suggests that each of us has a need to be included in the activities of others. We all need human contact and fellowship. We need to be invited to join others, and perhaps we need to invite others to join us. The level and intensity of this

BEING Other-ORIENTED

Some things about ourselves we learn from others: elements of our personality (both positive and negative characteristics), talents we possess, and other pieces of information that others share. What aspects of your personality or talents did you learn about from others, and might not have known about if someone had not shared them with you? How have others helped you learn about yourself?

need for inclusion. Interpersonal need to be included and to include others in social activities.

need differs from person to person, but even loners desire some social contact. Our need to include others and be included in activities may stem, in part, from our concept of ourselves as either a "party person" or a loner.

The second need, the **need for control**, suggests that we also need some degree of influence over the relationships we establish with others. We may also have a need to be controlled because we desire some level of stability and comfort in our interactions with others. If we view ourselves as people who are comfortable being in charge, we are more likely to give orders than take them.

And finally, we each have a **need for affection**. We need to give and receive love, support, warmth, and intimacy, although the amounts we need vary enormously from person to person. If we have a high need for affection, we will more likely place ourselves in situations where that need can be met. The greater our inclusion, control, and affection needs are, the more likely it is that we will actively seek others as friends and initiate communication with them.

Self and Communication Style

Our self-concept and self-esteem affect not only the way we feel about ourselves, the way we interpret messages, and our personal performance, but also the way we deliver messages and treat other people. Each of us has a **communication style** (or **social style**) that is identifiable by the habitual ways in which we behave toward others. The style we adopt helps others interpret our messages. As they get to know us, other people begin to expect us to behave in a certain way, based upon previous associations with us.

How do we develop our communication style? Many communication researchers, sociologists, and psychologists believe that we have certain underlying traits or personality characteristics that influence how we interact with others. Some scholars believe these traits stem from genetics: we are born with certain personality characteristics; we are who we are because that's the way we are made. Others emphasize the **social learning approach**: we communicate as we do because of our interactions with others, such as our parents and friends. The truth is that we cannot yet explain exactly how we come to communicate as we do.

Even though we don't know the precise role of nature or nurture in determining how we communicate, most inventories of personality or communication style focus on two primary dimensions that underlie how we interact with others—assertiveness and responsiveness. **Assertiveness** is the tendency to make requests, ask for information, and generally pursue our own rights and best interests. An assertive style is sometimes called a "masculine" style. By *masculine*, we don't mean that only males can be assertive, but in many cultures, being assertive is synonymous with being masculine. You are assertive when you seek information if you are confused or when you direct others to help you get what you need.

Responsiveness is the tendency to be sensitive to the needs of others. Being other-oriented and sympathetic to the pain of others and placing the feelings of others above your own feelings are examples of being responsive. Researchers sometimes label responsiveness a "feminine" quality. Again, this does not mean that only women are or should be responsive but only that many cultures stereotype being responsive as a traditional behaviour of females.

What is your communication style? To assess your style of communication on the assertiveness and responsiveness dimensions, take the "Sociocommunicative Orientation" test by James McCroskey and Virginia Richmond in the *Building Your Skills* box. You may discover that you test higher in one dimension than in the other. It's also possible to be high on both or low on both. Assertiveness and responsiveness are two different dimensions; you need not have just one or the other.

What many of you will want to know is "What is the best communication style? Should I be assertive or responsive?" The truth is, there is no one best style for all situations. Sometimes the appropriate thing to do is to assert yourself—to ask or even demand that

need for control. Interpersonal need for some degree of domination in our relationships as well as the need to be controlled.

need for affection. Interpersonal need to give and receive love, personal support, warmth, and intimacy.

communication style (social style). Your consistent way of relating to others based upon your personality, self-concept and self-esteem.

social learning approach. Theoretical perspective that suggests the origins of our communication styles lie in what we learn, directly and indirectly, from other people.

assertiveness. Tendency to make requests, ask for information, and generally pursue your own rights and best interests.

responsiveness. Tendency to be sensitive to the needs of others, including being sympathetic to the pain of others and placing the feelings of others above your own feelings.

Building Your Skills   Sociocommunicative Orientation

Directions: The following questionnaire lists 20 personality characteristics. Please indicate the degree to which you believe each of these characteristics applies to you, as you normally communicate with others, by marking whether you (5) strongly agree that it applies, (4) agree that it applies, (3) are undecided, (2) disagree that it applies, or (1) strongly disagree that it applies.

There are no right or wrong answers. Work quickly; record your first impression.

_____ 1. Helpful
_____ 2. Defends own beliefs
_____ 3. Independent
_____ 4. Responsive to others
_____ 5. Forceful
_____ 6. Has strong personality
_____ 7. Sympathetic
_____ 8. Compassionate
_____ 9. Assertive
_____ 10. Sensitive to the needs of others
_____ 11. Dominant
_____ 12. Sincere
_____ 13. Gentle
_____ 14. Willing to take a stand
_____ 15. Warm
_____ 16. Tender
_____ 17. Friendly
_____ 18. Acts as a leader
_____ 19. Aggressive
_____ 20. Competitive

Scoring: Items 2, 3, 5, 6, 9, 11, 14, 18, 19, and 20 measure assertiveness. Add the scores on these items to get your assertiveness score. Items 1, 4, 7, 8, 10, 12, 13, 15, 16, and 17 measure responsiveness. Add the scores on these items to get your responsiveness score. Scores range from 50 to 10. The higher your score, the higher your orientation as assertive and responsive.

Source: James C. McCroskey and Virginia P. Richmond, *Fundamentals of Human Communication: An Interpersonal Perspective* (Prospect Heights, IL: Waveland Press, 1996), 91. Printed with permission from Virginia P. Richmond.

you receive what you need and have a right to receive. In other situations, it may be more appropriate to be less confrontational. Maintaining the quality of the relationship by simply listening and being thoughtfully responsive to others may be best. The appropriateness of your communication style involves issues we will discuss in future chapters, such as how you adapt to culture and gender differences, your needs, the needs and rights of others, and the goal of your communication.

▶ RECAP How Self-Concept and Self-Esteem Affect Interpersonal Communication and Relationships

Term	Definition	Examples
Message interpretation and interaction	Feelings of high or low self-esteem affect how you understand and react to messages.	If you have high self-esteem, you are more likely to accept praise without embarrassment.
Self-fulfilling prophecy	What you believe about yourself will come true because you expect it to come true.	You expect to have a terrible time at a party, and you behave in such a way that you don't enjoy the party.
Communication style	Your self-concept and self-esteem contribute to habitual ways of responding to others.	Your image of yourself influences your expressive or assertive behaviour toward others.

Self and Disclosure to Others

self-disclosure. Purposefully providing information to others that they would not learn if you did not tell them.

When we interact with others, we reveal information about ourselves; in other words, we self-disclose. **Self-disclosure** occurs when we purposefully provide information to others about ourselves that they would not learn if we did not tell them. Self-disclosure ranges from revealing basic information about yourself, such as where you were born, to admitting your deepest fears and most private fantasies. Disclosing personal information not only provides a basis for another person to understand you better, it also conveys your level of trust and acceptance of the other person.

We are much more likely to self-disclose to someone whom we trust and feel close to, and we are less likely to self-disclose if we think we'll lose someone's respect and admiration.[25] Because others self-disclose, you are able to learn information about them and deepen your interpersonal relationships with them.[26] Another factor that has been found to influence the amount of self-disclosure is your overall mood. If you are feeling good about yourself and are in a positive mood, you are more likely to self-disclose. That's why someone who has consumed more alcohol than is advisable and is feeling mellow and "happy" (as well as having lowered inhibitions) may share more details about his or her life than you wish to hear. Someone who is sober and feeling less positive may be less likely to share intimate, personal information.[27]

We introduce the concept of self-disclosure in this chapter because it's an important element in helping us understand ourselves. If you have a Facebook page, you may want to monitor your level of self-disclosure when posting photos and comments about your daily routine. Social media researcher Bradley Bond found that women are more likely to self-disclose more information on a wider range of topics on Facebook than are men.[28] Women are also "marginally more likely to report being sexually expressive on their profiles."[29] Because self-disclosure is the primary way we establish and maintain interpersonal relationships, we'll discuss self-disclosure in considerable detail in Chapter 9.

To disclose information to others, you must first have **self-awareness**, an understanding of who you are. In addition to just thinking about who you are, asking others for information about yourself and then listening to what they tell you can enhance your

self-awareness. A person's conscious understanding of who he or she is.

ADAPTING TO DIFFERENCES
Understanding Others   How Universal Is "The Golden Rule"?

It's clear that there are cultural differences among the world's people, including differences in language, food preferences, housing preferences, and a host of other elements; these differences have existed as long as there have been people. Anthropologists and communication scholars who study intercultural communication, a topic we'll discuss in more detail in Chapter 4, teach the value of adapting to cultural differences in order to understand others better. But is it possible that despite their clear differences, there is a universally held principle that influences the behaviour of all people? The question is not a new one. Scholars, theologians, and many others have debated for millennia whether there are any universal values that inform all human societies.

The importance of being other-oriented rather than self-absorbed is not a new idea. Most world religions emphasize some version of the same spiritual principle, known in Christianity as the Golden Rule: Do unto others as you would have others do unto you. There is convincing evidence that this rule has been the foundation of most ethical codes throughout the world. The following principles underlying various religious traditions emphasize the universal importance accorded to being other-oriented.[30]

Hinduism This is the sum of duty: Do nothing to others that would cause pain if done to you.

Buddhism One should seek for others the happiness one desires for one self.

Taoism Regard your neighbour's gain as your own gain, and your neighbour's loss as your loss.

Confucianism Is there one principle that ought to be acted on throughout one's whole life? Surely it is the principle of loving-kindness: do not unto others what you would not have them do unto you.

Zoroastrianism The nature alone is good that refrains from doing unto another whatsoever is not good for itself.

Judaism What is hateful to you, do not do to others. That is the entire law: all the rest is but commentary.

Islam No one of you is a believer until he desires for his brother that which he desires for himself.

Christianity Do unto others as you would have others do unto you.

Do you find this list of variations on the Golden Rule from different world religions convincing evidence that being other-oriented is a universal value? Are there additional underlying values or principles, such as how the poor or the elderly should be treated, that should inform our interactions with others?

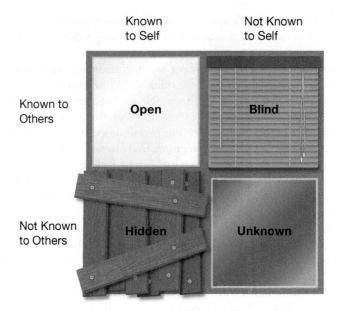

FIGURE 2.2

The Johari Window

self-awareness. A variety of personality tests, such as the Myers-Briggs personality inventory, may provide you with additional insight into your interests, style, and ways of relating to others. Most colleges and universities have a career services office where you can take vocational aptitude tests to help you identify careers that fit who you are.

The **Johari Window model** nicely summarizes how your awareness of who you are is influenced by your own level of disclosure, as well as by how much others share information about you with you. (The name "Johari Window" sounds somewhat mystical and exotic, but "Johari" is simply a combination of the first names of the creators of the model, Joseph Luft and Harry Ingham.)[31] As Figure 2.2 shows, the model looks like a set of panes in a window, with the window representing your self. This self includes everything about you, even things you don't yet see or realize. One axis is divided into what you have come to know about yourself and what you don't yet know about who you are. The other axis represents what someone else may know and not know about you. The intersection of these categories creates a four-panel, or four-quadrant, window.

Open: Known to Self and Known to Others. Quadrant 1 is an *open* area. The open area contains information that others know about you and that you are also aware of—such as your age, your occupation, and other things you might mention about yourself. At first glance, all four quadrants in the window appear to be the same size, but that may not be the case (in fact, it probably isn't). In the case of quadrant 1, the more you reveal about yourself, the larger this quadrant will be. Put another way, the more you open up to others, the larger the open area will be.

Blind: Not Known to Self but Known to Others. Quadrant 2 is a *blind* area. This part of the window contains information that other people know about you but that you do not know. Perhaps when you were in grade school, someone put a sign on your back that said "Kick me." Everyone was aware of the sign but you. The blind area of the Johari Window represents much the same situation. For example, you may see yourself as generous, but others may see you as a tightwad. As you learn how others see you, the blind area of the

Johari Window model. Model of self-disclosure that reflects the movement of information about yourself from blind and unknown quadrants to hidden and open ones.

Johari Window gets smaller. Generally, the more accurately you know yourself and perceive how others see you, the better your chances of establishing open and honest relationships with others.

Hidden: Known to Self but Not Known to Others. Quadrant 3 is a *hidden* area. This area contains information that you know about yourself but that others do not. You can probably think of many facts, thoughts, feelings, and fantasies that you would not want anyone else to know. They may be feelings you have about another person or something you've done privately in the past that you'd be embarrassed to share with others. The point here is not to suggest you should share all information in the hidden area with others. It is useful to know, however, that part of who you are is known by some people but remains hidden from others.

Unknown: Not Known to Self or Others. Quadrant 4 is an *unknown* area. This area contains information that is unknown to both you and others. These are things you do not know about yourself yet. Perhaps you do not know how you will react under certain stressful situations. Maybe you are not sure what stand you will take on a certain issue next year or even next week. Other people may also not be aware of how you would respond or behave under certain conditions. Your personal potential, your untapped physical and mental resources, are unknown. You can assume that this area exists because eventually some (though not necessarily all) of these things become known to you, to others, or to both you and others. Because you can never know yourself completely, the unknown quadrant will always exist; you can only guess at its current size because the information it contains is unavailable to you.

We can draw Johari Windows to represent each of our relationships (see Figure 2.3). Window A shows a new or restricted relationship for someone who knows himself or herself very well. The open and blind quadrants are small, but the unknown quadrant is also small. Window B shows a very intimate relationship, in which both individuals are open and disclosing.

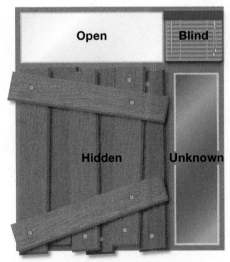

(A) A new relationship for someone who is very self-aware

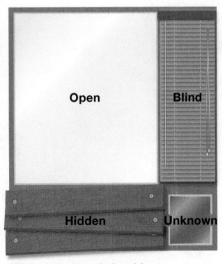

(B) An intimate relationship

FIGURE 2.3

Variations on Johari Windows

APPLYING AN OTHER-ORIENTATION
to Self and Interpersonal Communication

In this chapter we've discussed the significance of your self-perception and self-esteem and how these self-perceptions affect your relationships with others. Although we've emphasized the importance of being other-oriented, we conclude the chapter by echoing Polonius's advice to his son: Be true to yourself.

To be other-oriented doesn't mean only behaving in people-pleasing ways in order to ingratiate yourself to others. Rather, as an other-oriented communicator, you are aware of the thoughts and feelings of others but remain true to your own ethics and beliefs. For example, if you object to watching violent movies and a group of your friends invites you to see a "slasher" film, you don't have to attend with them. Nor do you have to make a self-righteous speech about your feelings about violent movies; you can simply excuse yourself after calmly saying you don't like that kind of movie. You don't have to do what others do simply to be popular. As your mother may have said when you were growing up, "If all your friends jumped off a cliff, would you jump too?" In essence, your mother was echoing Polonius's counsel to be true to yourself rather than blindly following the herd to be popular.

The word *credo* means belief. What's your personal credo or set of beliefs? Being aware of your personal beliefs—whether those beliefs are about things philosophical or spiritual, about human nature, or about the political and social issues of the day—can serve as an anchoring point for your interactions with others. Without knowing where your "home" is—your personal credo—you won't know how far away from "home" you travel as you make your way in the world and relate to others.

Self-Concept: Who Do You Think You Are? (pages 28–37)

OBJECTIVE ➊ Define, compare, and contrast the meanings of "self-concept" and "self-esteem."

Key Terms

self *28*
self-concept *28*
attitude *28*
beliefs *29*
values *29*
mindfulness *30*
subjective self-awareness *30*
objective self-awareness *30*
symbolic self-awareness *30*
material self *31*
social self *31*
spiritual self *31*
looking-glass self *32*
reflected appraisal *32*
androgynous role *34*

self-reflexiveness *34*
psychology *35*
personality *36*
extraversion *36*
aggreeableness *36*
conscientiousness *36*
neuroticism *36*
openness *36*
communibiological approach *36*
shyness *36*
communication apprehension *37*
willingness to communicate *37*

Critical Thinking Questions

1. Make a list of all the groups, clubs, and organizations to which you belong. Rank them from most important to you to least important. What does your ranking tell you about these groups in reference to your self-concept? For example, which groups have you joined more from a desire to belong or for the prestige of the group than because of an interest in or passion for the group's cause?

2. Ethics: Considering again Shakespeare's line "To thine own self be true," can you think of instances when you have not been true to yourself, in your actions, the role(s) you assumed, and/or your interactions with others? Did you know at the time that you were behaving in a way that was not compatible with your values? Do you think others were aware of this? Explain.

Activities

Rank the following list of values from 1 to 12 to reflect their importance to you. In a group with other students, compare your answers. Discuss how your ranking of these values influences your interactions with others.

____Honesty   ____Justice
____Salvation   ____Wealth
____Comfort   ____Beauty
____Good health   ____Equality

____Human rights   ____Freedom
____Peace   ____Mercy

Web Resources

www.queendom.com Assess your personality and other communication-related variables.

Self-Esteem: Your Self-Worth, and Improving Your Self-Esteem (pages 37–40)

OBJECTIVES ➋ ➌ Identify factors that shape the development of your self-concept, and list and describe strategies for improving your self-esteem.

Key Terms

self-esteem (self-worth) *37*
social comparison *37*
intrapersonal communication *38*

visualization *38*
reframing *39*
social support *40*
talk therapy *40*

Critical Thinking Questions

1. Describe a recent event or communication exchange that made you feel better or worse about yourself. What happened that made you feel good? Or what made you feel bad—inadequate, embarrassed, or unhappy? In general, how do your communication exchanges influence your self-esteem? Explain. How might visualization or other strategies help?

2. Do you find that you make social comparisons with others that affect your self-esteem? If so, what qualities of others most influence your own view of yourself: appearance, material possessions, skills/talent, something else? Explain.

3. How does electronically mediated communication (EMC) influence the comparisons you described in Question 2, and, in turn, your self-esteem? Do Facebook profiles play a role? Do the mass media play a role in creating those comparisons?

4. Ethics: Many self-help books claim to provide sure-fire techniques for enhancing self-esteem and thus enriching your social life. Do you think these claims are ethical? Why or why not?

Activities

Briefly describe an upcoming situation that makes you anxious, such as working on a group project, calling a prospective employer about a job, or competing in a sporting event. What strategies are you employing to deal with your nervousness? Describe how visualization might help. Share with your classmates a positive scenario, describing the successful outcome.

Web Resources

www.social-anxiety.com Go to this site to learn more about shyness and social phobias; the site also offers case studies.

Self and Interpersonal Relationships
(pages 40–48)

OBJECTIVE 4 Describe how your self-concept and communication style affect your relationships with others.

Key Terms

symbolic interaction
  theory *41*
self-fulfilling prophecy *41*
need for inclusion *42*
need for control *43*
need for affection *43*
communication style
  (social style) *43*

social learning
  approach *43*
assertiveness *43*
responsiveness *43*
self-disclosure *44*
self-awareness *45*
Johari Window
  model *46*

Critical Thinking Questions

1. Provide an example of a recent communication exchange with a friend, classmate, family member, or work colleague that revealed that some aspect of your perception of yourself differed from how the other person perceived you. Why do you think the perceptions differed? Did knowing the other person's perception change your behaviour and/or your own perceptions, or not? Explain.

2. Describe a situation in which your expectations of the outcome became a self-fulfilling prophecy. Was the outcome positive or negative? Did your self-esteem have an impact? Explain.

3. Have you ever shared personal information and found that what you revealed wasn't well received or wasn't received as you intended? How did you handle the situation?

4. Ethics: Is it always best to be honest when self-disclosing? What types of self-disclosure might be inappropriate? Are

there times when it would be appropriate to withhold information? Is that ethical? Explain.

5. Ethics: Carmelita would like to become better friends with Hector. She decides to disclose some personal information to Hector, hoping that this self-disclosure will increase feelings of intimacy between them. Is it ethical to self-disclose to others as a strategy to enhance intimacy in a relationship?

Activities

1. Create a Johari Window that includes in square 3 ("hidden," or known to self but not to others) five or six adjectives that best describe your personality as you see it. Then ask a close friend to fill in square 2 ("blind," or known to others but not known to self) with five or six adjectives to describe your personality. Separately, ask a classmate you've just met to fill in square 2 as well. Compare and contrast. Are the adjectives used by your close friend and the acquaintance you've just met similar or different? Is there any overlap? Now fill in square 1 ("open," or known to self and others) with any adjectives that both you and either of the other participants chose. What does this tell you about what you disclose about yourself to others?

2. Go through your library of music downloads and CDs and identify a selection that best symbolizes you, based on either the lyrics or the music. Bring your selection to class to play for your classmates. Tell why this music symbolizes you. Discuss with classmates how your choice of music provides a glimpse of your attitudes and values, as well as a vehicle for self-expression.

Web Resources

www.usgs.gov/humancapital/documents/JohariWindow.pdf This Johari Window Workbook contains more information about the Johari Window, as well as an informative exercise that will help you develop and expand your "open area" when working with others.
www.typefocus.com Take this online personality assessment by TypeFocus, a leading developer of online personality type resources.
www.hc-sc.gc.ca/fn-an/nutrition/weights-poids/index-eng.php This site from Health Canada discusses positive self- and body image.
www.shyness.com This site, sponsored by the Shyness Institute, has a host of resources on shyness, including symptoms, causes, consequences, and treatment.

© Russell Sadur/Dorling Kindersley Limited

3

Interpersonal Communication and Perception

66 What we see depends mainly on what we look for. 99 —John Lubbock

51

Look at the photo below. What do you think is happening? Do you see the boy as lost, running away from home, or in some kind of trouble? What might he be feeling? Why does he have the police officer's hat on? What do you think the officer is saying to the little boy? Is she reprimanding him or comforting him? Your interpretation of what is happening in the photograph reflects interpersonal perception, which we discuss in this chapter.

In Chapter 1 we defined human communication as the process of making sense of the world and sharing that sense with others by creating meaning through the use of verbal and nonverbal messages. In this chapter, we discuss the first half of that definition: the process of making sense of our world. How we make sense out of what we experience is the starting point for what we share with others. As human beings, we interpret and attribute meaning to what we observe or experience, particularly if what we are observing is other people. We tend to make inferences about their motives, personalities, and other traits based on their physical qualities and behaviours. Those who are skilled at making observations and interpretations have a head start in developing effective interpersonal relationships. Those who are other-oriented, who are aware of and sensitive to the communication behaviours of others, will likely be better at accurately perceiving others.

Before we turn to the role that perception plays in interpersonal communication, let's first take a closer look at the interpersonal perception process itself.

perception. Experiencing the world and making sense out of what is experienced.

interpersonal perception. The process of selecting, organizing, and interpreting one's observations of other people.

What do you think is happening in this photograph? Your interpretation reflects interpersonal perception.

(© Disability Images/Alamy Stock Photo)

Understanding Interpersonal Perception

What is perception? **Perception** is the process of experiencing your world and then making sense out of what you experience. Although you experience your world through your five senses, your perceptions of people go beyond simple interpretations of sensory information. **Interpersonal perception** is the process by which you decide what people are like and give meaning to their actions. It includes making judgments about personality and drawing inferences from what you observe.

When you meet someone new, you select certain information to attend to (you note whether the person is male or female, has an accent, smiles, uses a friendly tone of voice), as well as particular personal information (the person is from Lunenburg, Nova Scotia). You then organize the information under some category that is recognizable to you, such as "a friendly Maritimer." Then you interpret the organized perceptions: this person is trustworthy, honest, hardworking, and likable.

Stage One: Selecting

Sit for a minute after you read this passage and try to tune into all the sensory input you are receiving: consider the feel of your socks against your feet, the pressure of the floor on your heels, the pressure of the piece of furniture against your body as you sit, the buzzing sounds from various sources around you—this "white noise" might come from a refrigerator, a personal computer, fluorescent lights, water in pipes, voices, passing traffic, or your own heartbeat or churning stomach. What do you smell? What do you see?

Without moving your eyes, turn your awareness to the images you see in the corner of your vision. What colours do you see? What shapes? What taste is in your mouth? How do the pages of this book feel against your fingertips? Now stop reading and consider all these sensations. Try to focus on all of them at the same time. You can't.

Principles of Selection. Why do we select certain sounds, images, and sensations, and not others? Four principles of selection frame the process of how we select what we see, hear, and experience: selective perception, selective attention, selective exposure, and selective recall.

Selective perception occurs when we see, hear, or make sense of the world around us based on factors such as our personality, beliefs, attitudes, hopes, fears, culture, likes, and dislikes. We literally see and don't see things because of our tendency to perceive selectively. Your eyes and brain do not work like a camera, which records everything in the picture. When you take a photo, you capture what was in the viewfinder. Your brain doesn't necessarily process everything you see through your viewfinder. Similarly, your ear is not a microphone that picks up every sound.

Selective attention is the process of focusing on specific stimuli; we selectively lock on to some things in our environment and ignore others. As in the selective perception process, we have a tendency to attend to those things around us that relate to our needs and wants. When you're hungry, for example, and you're looking for a place to grab a quick bite of lunch, you'll probably be more attentive to fast-food advertising and less focused on ads for cars. We also attend to information that is moving, interesting, new, or noisy. Web page designers, for example, give a lot of thought to ways of catching our attention with advertisements that pop up, blink, or flash.

Selective exposure is our tendency to put ourselves in situations that reinforce our attitudes, beliefs, values, or behaviours. The fact that we're selective about what we expose ourselves to means that we are more likely to be in places that make us feel comfortable and support the way we see the world than to be in places that make us uncomfortable. Whom do you usually find at a Catholic church on Sunday mornings? Catholics. Who attends a Liberal Party convention? Liberals. If you perceive yourself to be a good student who does everything possible to get high grades, you will do your best to attend class. We expose ourselves to situations that reinforce how we make sense out of the world.

Selective recall occurs when we remember things we want to remember and forget or repress things that are unpleasant, uncomfortable, or unimportant to us. Because our brains don't operate like cameras or microphones, not all that we see or hear is recorded in our memories so that we can easily retrieve it. Some experiences may simply be too painful to remember. Or we just don't remember some information because it's not relevant or needed (like the address of a website you clicked on yesterday).

BEING Other-ORIENTED

We are constantly selecting cues from our environment and then using those cues to help us perceive and form impressions of others. Are you aware of the behaviours that you typically notice about other people? What do you focus on when selecting information about other people and forming impressions of them?

---

selective perception. Process of seeing, hearing, or making sense of the world around us based on such factors as our personality, beliefs, attitudes, hopes, fears, and culture, as well as what we like and don't like.

selective attention. Process of focusing on specific stimuli, locking on to some things in the environment and ignoring others.

selective exposure. Tendency to put ourselves in situations that reinforce our attitudes, beliefs, values, or behaviours.

selective recall. Process that occurs when we remember things we want to remember and forget or repress things that are unpleasant, uncomfortable, or unimportant to us.

Thin Slicing: Making a Judgment Based on a Small Sample of Behaviour. Have you ever gone to a grocery store and enjoyed the free samples that are sometimes offered to encourage you to buy various products? The grocer hopes that if you like the small sample, you'll want to purchase more. Perhaps after tasting a thin slice of cheese, you'll buy a pound of it. The concept of **thin slicing** in the perception process works the same way. You sample a little bit of someone's behaviour and then generalize as to what the person may be like, based on the information you have observed. Journalist Malcolm Gladwell wrote a popular book called *Blink: The Power of Thinking Without Thinking*, in which he pointed to several examples of how people thin slice to make judgments of others.[1] For example, Gladwell reviewed research that found that a patient was less likely to sue a physician for malpractice if the doctor had effective "people skills." Doctors who took the time to listen, respond positively, empathize, and, in short, be other-oriented, were less likely to be sued than doctors who were not other-oriented. As patients, we thin slice when we make a judgment about the overall credibility of a doctor based on just one aspect of the doctor's behaviour—his or her bedside manner.

thin slicing. Observing a small sample of someone's behaviour and then making a generalization about what the person is like based on the sample.

superimposing. Placing a familiar structure on information you select.

Stage Two: Organizing

Look at the four items in Figure 3.1. What does each of them mean to you? If you are like most people, you will perceive item A as a rabbit, item B as a telephone number, C as the word *interpersonal*, and D as a circle. Strictly speaking, none of those perceptions is correct. We'll discuss why after we explore the second stage of perception: organization.

We organize our world by creating categories, linking together the categories we've created, and then seeking closure by filling in any missing gaps in what we perceive. Let's examine each of these in greater detail.

We Create Categories. After we perceive certain stimuli, we organize them into convenient, understandable, and efficient categories that let us make sense of what we have observed. Organizing, or chunking, what we perceive makes it easier to process complex information because it lets us impose the familiar on the unfamiliar and because we can more easily store and recall simple patterns.

One of the ways we create categories is by superimposing a familiar structure on information we select. To **superimpose** is to use a framework we're already familiar with to interpret information that may, at first, look formless. We look for the familiar in the unfamiliar. For example, when you looked at item A in Figure 3.1, you saw the pattern of dots as a rabbit because *rabbit* is a concept you know and to which you attach various meanings. The set of dots would not have meaning for you in and of itself, nor would it be meaningful to you to attend to each particular dot or to the dots' relationships to one another. It would be possible to create a mathematical model of the dots indicating their placement on an x–y grid, but such a model would be extremely complex and difficult to observe and remember. It's much easier to organize the dots by superimposing something that is stored in your memory: a rabbit. For similar reasons, people have organized patterns of stars in the sky into the various constellations and have given them names that reflect their shapes, like the bear, the crab, and the big and little dippers.

People also search for and apply patterns to their perceptions of other people. You might have a friend who jogs and works out at a gym. You put these together to create a pattern and label the friend as "athletic." That label represents a pattern of qualities you use in relating to your friend, a pattern that we discuss later in the chapter.

A.

B. **5 5 5   4 4 3 3**

C. **N T R P R S N L**

D.

FIGURE 3.1
What Do You See?

We Link Categories. Once we have created categories, we link them together as a way of further making sense of how we have chunked what we experience. We link the categories though a process called punctuation. **Punctuation** is the process of making sense out of stimuli by grouping, dividing, organizing, separating, and further categorizing information.

Just as punctuation marks on this page tell you when a sentence ends, punctuation in the perception process makes it possible for you to see patterns in information. To many people, item B in Figure 3.1 looks like a telephone number because it has three numbers followed by four numbers. However, the digits could just as easily represent two totally independent numbers: five hundred fifty-five followed by the number four thousand, four hundred thirty-three. How we interpret the numbers depends on how we punctuate or separate them. When we record information, we use commas, periods, dashes, and colons to signal meanings and interpretations. In our minds, we sometimes impose punctuation marks where we believe they should be. For example, perhaps you mentally put a dash between 555 and 4433, even though no dash appears there.

When it comes to punctuating relational events and behaviours, people develop their own separate sets of standards. You will sometimes experience difficulties and disagreements because of differences in how you and your communication partner choose to punctuate a conversational exchange or a shared sequence of events. For example, a husband and wife are having a disagreement because she wants him to help with the housework, and he reacts by withdrawing. The husband punctuates their interactions in such a way that he sees his withdrawing as a reaction to what he perceives as "nagging." The wife, in contrast, sees herself as pursuing the matter because her husband keeps withdrawing. The husband and wife punctuate their perceptions differently because they each perceive different starting points for their interaction. Resolving such conflicts involves having the parties describe how they have punctuated the event and agree on a common punctuation.

We Seek Closure. Another way we organize information is by seeking closure. **Closure** is the process of filling in missing information or gaps in what we perceive. Looking again at Figure 3.1, you can understand people's inclination to label the figure in item D a circle, even though circles are continuous lines without gaps. We apply the same principles in our interactions with people. When we have an incomplete picture of another human being, we impose a pattern or structure, classify the person on the basis of the information we do have, and fill in any missing information. For example, when meeting someone for the first time who looks and acts like someone you already know, you may make assumptions about your new acquaintance based on the characteristics of the person you already know. You close the gaps in the missing information about your new acquaintance based on the characteristics of the person well known to you. Many of us are uncomfortable with uncertainty; creating closure is a way of helping us make better sense out of what is new and unfamiliar.

Stage Three: Interpreting

Once you have selected and organized stimuli, the next step is to interpret the stimuli. You see your best friend across a crowded room at a party. Your friend waves to you, and you say to yourself, "He wants to talk with me." Or you nervously wait as your literature teacher hands back the results of the last exam. When the professor calls your name, she frowns ever so slightly; your heart sinks. You think, "I must have bombed the test." Or, while you were out, your administrative assistant left you a note saying that your sister has called. You're worried. You reflect, "My sister never uses her daytime cell phone minutes to call during the day. There must be something wrong." In each of these situations, you're trying to make sense out of the information you hear or see. You're attempting to interpret the meaning of the verbal and non-verbal cues you experience.

punctuation. Making sense out of stimuli by grouping, dividing, organizing, separating, and categorizing information.

closure. The filling in of missing information.

▶ RECAP   The Interpersonal Perception Process

Term	Explanation	Examples
Selection	The first stage in the perceptual process, in which we select certain sensations to focus our awareness on.	Sitting in your apartment, where you hear lots of traffic sounds and car horns, you focus on a particular rhythmic car honking that seems to be right outside your door.
Organization	The second stage in the perceptual process, in which we assemble stimuli into convenient and efficient patterns or categories.	You link the honking horn to your anticipation of a friend arriving to pick you up for a movie that starts in five minutes.
Interpretation	The final stage in perception, in which we assign meaning to what we have observed.	You decide the honking horn must be your friend's signal to you to come out to the car quickly because she is running late.

impressions. Collection of perceptions about others that you maintain and use to interpret their behaviours.

impression formation theory. Theory that explains how you develop perceptions about people and how you maintain and use those perceptions to interpret their behaviours.

passive perception. Perception that occurs without conscious effort, simply in response to one's surroundings.

active perception. Perception that occurs because you seek out specific information through intentional observation and questioning.

Forming Impressions and Interpreting the Behaviour of Others

Impressions are collections of perceptions about others that we maintain and use to interpret their behaviours. Impressions tend to be very general: "She seems nice," "He was very friendly," or "What a nerd!" According to **impression formation theory,** we form these impressions based on our perceptions of physical qualities (what people look like), behaviour (what people do), what people tell us, and what others tell us about them. When we first meet someone, we form a first impression without having much information, and we often hold on to this impression (even if it's an inaccurate one) throughout the relationship. So it's important to understand how we form impressions of others. Researchers have found that we often give special emphasis to the first things we see or the last things we observe about another person. We also generalize from specific positive or negative perceptions we hold.

Our perceptions of others affect how we communicate with them, and their perceptions of us affect the way they interact with us. It's through our perceptions that we develop general as well as specific impressions of other people. (And they do the same—they rely on their perceptions to develop impressions of us.) How much we notice about another person relates to our level of interest and need. We perceive others either passively or actively.

Passive perception occurs simply because we are alive and our senses are operating. We see, hear, smell, taste, and feel things around us without any conscious attempt to do so. No one teaches you to be passively perceptive; you simply respond to your surroundings. Similarly, you don't have to think about perceiving others; you just do it because you're alive.

Active perception doesn't just happen. It is the process of actively finding out specific information by intentionally observing and sometimes questioning others. We're engaged in activeperception when we make a conscious effort to figure out what we are observing. Do you like to "people watch"? If you have some time on your hands while waiting for a friend, you may start just looking at people and making guesses about what these strangers do for a living, whether they are friendly, grumpy, peaceful, or petulant, where they are from, or whether they are

We form impressions of others both passively and actively, and our own implicit assumptions and expectations colour those impressions.

(© Jupiterimages/BananaStock/Thinkstock/Getty Images)

married. When people watching, you are involved in active perception. You consciously make assumptions about the personalities and circumstances of those you observe.

As we make these assumptions and form impressions of others, most of us rely on an **implicit personality theory,** our personal set of assumptions and expectations or a pattern of associated qualities that we attribute to people, which allows us to understand them—whether we met them 10 minutes ago or 10 years ago. An implicit personality theory provides a way of organizing the vast array of information we have about people's personalities.

Although an implicit personality theory describes how we organize and interpret our perceptions of people's personalities in general, we develop specific categories for people, called constructs. A **construct,** according to psychologist George Kelly, is a bipolar quality (that is, a quality with two opposite categories) or a continuum that we use to classify people.[2] We may pronounce someone good or bad, athletic or nonathletic, warm or cold, funny or humourless, selfish or generous, beautiful or ugly, kind or cruel, and so on. So we don't necessarily classify people in absolute terms—they are categorized in degrees.

As we meet and observe people, we draw on our own implicit personality theory to help us reduce our uncertainty about others. **Uncertainty reduction theory** suggests that one of the primary reasons we communicate at all is to reduce our uncertainty about what we see and experience. By making guesses and assumptions about people, we reduce our uncertainty. If we can reduce our uncertainty about other people, then we can predict their reactions and behaviours, adapt our behaviours and strategies, and therefore maximize the likelihood of fulfilling our own social needs. Being able to reduce uncertainty and increase predictability gives us greater control when communicating with others. Although this might sound calculating, it really isn't. If you enjoy outdoor activities such as camping and hiking, one of your goals in establishing social relationships is probably to find others who share your interest. So actively observing, questioning, and consciously processing information to determine a potential friend's interests can help you assess whether the relationship will meet your goals. And in the spirit of being other-oriented, you will also be able to assess whether you can meet the goals and interests of the other person. In Chapter 5 we discuss ways to improve your ability to gain information through more effective listening.

Now let's take a closer look at several typical ways most of us form impressions of others: our tendency to emphasize what we see first or what we observe last when interacting with others, and our tendency to generalize from our perceptions of them as positive or negative.

We Form Impressions of Others Online: The Social Media Effect.

Increasingly, others evaluate you based upon what you have posted on your Facebook page. The photos you post, as well as the information you decide to include on your Facebook profile, provide both explicit and implicit cues about your interests, personality, and communication style. But there's evidence that what others say about you on Facebook posts, tweets, or other social media is more likely to have an effect on how others perceive you than is what *you* post. Specifically, Sonia Utz found that what other people said about individuals on their Facebook pages had more impact on whether they were perceived positively or negatively than how the individuals described themselves.[3] Although some researchers have found that Facebook lurkers can gain accurate perceptions of your personality based only on your Facebook information, what others say about you has more credibility.[4] Other people may also be making inferences about your popularity, personality, and sincerity simply by noting the number of friends you have on your Facebook wall. One research team found that if you have too few or too many Facebook friends, other people may find it unusual and thereby lower their impression of your attractiveness or credibility.[5] Specifically, people with 102 friends were perceived as less socially attractive than people who had 302 friends. Yet if you have 502 or 1000 friends, you are perceived as less socially attractive. Thus there is a curvilinear relationship (think of an upside down "U" as charting the relationships) between

implicit personality theory. Your unique set of beliefs and hypotheses about what people are like.

construct. Bipolar quality used to classify people.

uncertainty reduction theory. Theory that claims people seek information in order to reduce uncertainty, thus achieving control and predictability.

the number of friends you have and how positively you are perceived by others. Too few or too many friends is likely to lower your social attractiveness as perceived by others.

We Emphasize What Comes First: The Primacy Effect.

There is evidence that when we form impressions of others, we pay more attention to our first impressions. The process of attending to the first pieces of information that we observe about another person is called the **primacy effect**. The primacy effect was documented in a famous study on impression formation theory conducted by Solomon Asch.[6] Individuals were asked to evaluate two people based on two lists of adjectives. The list for the first person had the following adjectives: *intelligent, industrious, impulsive, critical, stubborn,* and *envious.* The list for the other person had the same adjectives, but in reverse order. Although the content was identical, respondents gave the first person a more positive evaluation than the second. One explanation for this is that the first words in each list created a first impression that respondents used to interpret the remaining adjectives. In a similar manner, the first impressions we form about someone often affect our interpretation of subsequent perceptions of that person.

We Emphasize What Comes Last: The Recency Effect.

Not only do we give more weight to our first impressions, but we also give considerable attention to our most recent experiences and impressions. The tendency to put a lot of stock in the last thing we observe is called the **recency effect**. For example, if you have thought for years that your friend is honest but today you discover that she lied to you about something important, that lie will have a greater impact on your impression of her than the honest behaviour she has displayed for years. Similarly, if, during a job interview, you skilfully answered all of the interviewer's questions yet your last answer to a question was not the answer the interviewer was looking for, you may not get the job. If you're going to make mistakes in an interview, it's best not to do it at the beginning of the interview (primacy effect) or at the end of the conversation (recency effect).

We Generalize Positive Qualities: The Halo Effect.

One feature common to most of our implicit personality theories is the tendency to put people into two categories: those we like and those we don't like. When we observe people we like, there is often a **halo effect**: we attribute a variety of positive qualities to them without personally confirming the existence of these qualities. If you like me, you will add a "halo" to your impression of me, determining that I am nice to other people, warm and caring, fun to be with, and have a great sense of humour.

We Generalize Negative Qualities: The Horn Effect.

Just as we can use the halo effect to generalize about someone's positive qualities, the opposite can also happen. We sometimes make many negative assumptions about a person because of one unflattering perception. This is called the **horn effect**, named for the horns associated with images of a devil. If you don't like the way someone looks, you might also decide that person is selfish or stingy and attribute a variety of negative qualities to that individual, using your implicit personality theory. As evidence of the horn effect, research suggests that during periods of conflict in our relationships, we are more likely to attribute negative behaviours to our feuding partner than we are to ourselves. A little bit of negative information can affect how we perceive other attributes of a person.

Interpreting the Behaviour of Others

"I know why Jessica is always late for our meetings. She just doesn't like me," says Alisha. "She also just wants people to think she's too busy to be bothered with our little group." Alisha not only seems to have formed a negative impression of Jessica, but she also has a

primacy effect. Tendency to attend to the first pieces of information observed about another person in order to form an impression.

recency effect. Tendency to attend to the most recent information observed about another person in order to form or modify an impression.

halo effect. Attributing a variety of positive qualities to those we like.

horn effect. Attributing a variety of negative qualities to those we dislike.

Canadian Connections   Michaëlle Jean

What is your impression of Michaëlle Jean, the former governor general of Canada?

(© Robert Wagenhoffer/STRRTW/The Canadian Press)

While she was Canada's governor general, Michaëlle Jean had her share of supporters and detractors. Opinions and perceptions were bound to vary, just as they do about many well-known political or business figures. So who is this person and what did people think of her?

Jean was born in Port-au-Prince, Haiti. In 1968, as a result of violence in the country, her family fled Haiti and settled in Quebec. Her father had been arrested, jailed, and tortured under the dictatorship of Duvalier.

She was 11 years old. As a child in Montreal, she encountered her first racist experiences. For example, she had children touching her black skin to see if she was "real."

Jean went on to complete a degree in Spanish and Italian and a master's degree in comparative literature. During her studies she became involved with helping women and children who were victims of domestic violence. In the late 1980s her focus turned to journalism, and by 1988 she was a well-known reporter on Radio-Canada's *Actuel*. She continued this career in news reporting, hosting CBC Newsworld's *The Passionate Eye* and *Rough Cuts*. With her husband, Jean-Daniel Lafond, she made several documentaries.[1]

In her new role as governor general, which she held from 2005 to 2010, she was met with a variety of views and feelings. One author described her as the "most controversial choice" for governor general, a description based largely upon her husband's controversial films and how she was chosen for the post.[2] Another author described her as "Canada's empathetic governor general" and compared her to Oprah Winfrey.[3] One article quoted Paul

Benoit, of the Monarchist League of Canada, describing her as "quite young, very dynamic, has rapport with a lot of the younger audience." That article also described her as an "inspired choice."[4]

While she is the same person, how people view her history, her relationships, and her behaviour will be based on perception. As you read about Michaëlle Jean and her speeches and decisions as governor general, what do you think and feel about her?

1. CBC News, "In Depth: Governor General Michaelle Jean," *CBC News Online*, October 11, 2005, www.cbc.ca/news /background/governorgeneral/michaelle _jean.html, retrieved January 9, 2009.

2. Paul Wells, "GG Jean's Appointment Raises Complex Questions," *Maclean's*, August 29, 2005, available at www .thecanadianencyclopedia.com/index .cfm?PgNm=TCESearch&Params =M1, retrieved January 9, 2009.

3. Aaron Wherry, "Canada's Empathetic Governor General," *Maclean's*, January 14, 2008, available at www .thecanadianencyclopedia.com/index .cfm?PgNm=TCE&Params=M1A RTM0013189, retrieved January 9, 2009.

4. CBC News, "Jean Called an 'Inspired Choice' for Governor," www.cbc.ca /canada/story/2005/08/03/gg050803 .html.

hunch as to why Jessica is late for meetings. Alisha is attributing meaning to Jessica's behaviour. Even though Jessica could have just forgotten about the meeting or gotten caught in traffic, Alisha thinks Jessica's lateness is caused by feelings of superiority and contempt. Alisha's assumptions about Jessica can be explained by several theories about the way we interpret the behaviour of others. Based on a small sample of someone's behaviour, we develop our own explanations of why people do what they do. Attribution theory, standpoint theory, and intercultural communication theory can offer perspectives on how to make sense of what we perceive.

Attribution Theory: We Attribute Motives to Others' Behaviour. Attribution theory explains how we ascribe specific motives and causes to the behaviours of others. It helps us interpret what people do and why they are doing it. Suppose a student sitting next to you in

attribution theory. Theory that explains how we generate explanations for people's behaviours.

class gets up in the middle of the lecture and walks out. Why did the student leave? Did the student become angry at something the instructor said? No, the lecturer was simply describing types of cloud formations. Was the student sick? You remember noticing that the student looked a little flushed and occasionally winced. Maybe the student had an upset stomach. Or maybe the student is a bit of a rebel and often does things like leave in the middle of a class.

Social psychologist Fritz Heider says that we are "naive psychologists"[7] because we all seek to explain the motives people have for their actions. We are naive because we do not create these explanations in a systematic or scientific manner but rather by applying common sense to our observations. Developing the most credible explanation for the behaviour of others is the goal of the **attribution** process.

Causal attribution theory identifies three potential causes for any person's action: circumstance, a stimulus, or the person herself or himself. Attributing to circumstance means that you believe a person acts in a certain way because the situation leaves no choice. This way of thinking places responsibility for the action outside the person. You would be attributing to circumstance if you believed the student quickly left the classroom because of an upset stomach. Concluding that the student left because the instructor said something inappropriate would be attributing the student's action to the stimulus (the instructor). However, if you knew the instructor hadn't said anything out of line and that the student was perfectly healthy, you might place the responsibility for the action on the student. Attributing to the person means that you believe there is some quality about the person that caused the observed behaviour.

To explore how attributions to a person affect us, interpersonal communication researchers Anita Vangelisti and Stacy Young wanted to know whether intentionally hurtful words inflict more pain than unintentionally hurtful comments.[8] As you might suspect, if we think someone intends to hurt us, spiteful words have more sting and bite than if we believe someone does not intend to hurt our feelings. Our attributions are factors in our impressions.

attribution. The reasons we develop to explain the behaviours of others.

causal attribution theory. One theory of attribution, based on determining whether a person's actions are caused by circumstance, a stimulus, or the person.

standpoint theory. The theory that a person's social position, power, or cultural background influences how the person perceives the behaviour of others; where you stand makes a difference in what you see.

Standpoint Theory: We Use Our Own Point of Reference About Power. **Standpoint theory** is yet another framework that seeks to explain how we interpret the behaviour of others. The theory is relatively simple: we each see the world differently because we're each viewing it from a different position. Some people have positions of power and others do not; the resources we have to help us make our way through life provide a lens through which we view the world and the people in it.

Standpoint theory explains why people with differing cultural backgrounds have different perceptions of others' behaviour. In the early 19th century, German philosopher Georg Hegel noted this simple but powerful explanation of why people see and experience the world differently.[9] Hegel was especially interested in how one's standpoint was determined

ADAPTING TO DIFFERENCES
Understanding Others

The Power of Perspective

As noted in our discussion of standpoint theory, where you stand makes a difference in what you see and how you interpret human behaviour. Since the recent nationwide debate about the rights of gays and lesbians to marry, discussion about perceptions of the power and influence of different cultural groups has become more common. Religious leaders, political leaders, and most Canadians in general are becoming much more sensitive to how deeply these beliefs about what is right, wrong, moral, immoral, just, and unjust are held across different groups.

Men and women, blacks and whites, Jews and Christians, Muslims and Hindus, Hispanics and Asians, Aboriginals and non-Aboriginals, English Canadians and French Canadians, gay people and straight people—all experience life from their own cultural standpoint, which means they all have perceptions about their influence on others. To become more other-oriented is to become aware of your own perceived place in society and to be more sensitive to how that position of power or lack of power affects how you perceive others with a different standpoint.

To explore applications of standpoint theory in your life, consider the following questions:

1. How would you describe your standpoint in terms of power and influence in your school, at work, or in your family? Have you ever experienced rejection, alienation, or discrimination based on how others perceived you?

2. How would other people in your life (parents, siblings, children, co-workers, employers, or friends) describe your power and influence on them?

3. How does your standpoint influence your relationship with others? Identify a specific relationship with a teacher, co-worker, or family member in which different standpoints influence the quality of the relationship in either positive or negative ways.

4. What can you do to become more aware of how your standpoint influences your interactions with others? How can your increased awareness enhance the quality of your interpersonal communication with others?

▶ RECAP   How We Organize and Interpret Interpersonal Perceptions to Perceive Others

Theory	Definition	Examples
Impression formation theory	We form the general perspectives we have of others based on general physical qualities, behaviours, and disclosed information.	"He has a nice smile, so he must be a friendly and honest person."
Implicit personality theory	We form our own personal general theory about the way people think and behave.	"If she is intelligent, then she must be caring, too."
Attribution theory	We develop explanations for the behaviours of others.	"I guess she didn't return my call because she doesn't like me."
		"He's just letting off steam because he had a bad week of exams."
Causal attribution theory	We ascribe a person's actions to circumstance, a stimulus, or the person himself or herself.	"He didn't go to class because his alarm didn't go off."
		"He didn't go to class because it was a makeup session."
		"He didn't go to class because he is bored by it."
Standpoint theory	We interpret the behaviour of others through the lens of our own social position, power, or cultural background.	"He won't join the fraternity because he doesn't understand how important that network can be to his professional career."
Intercultural communication theory	Our cultural experiences and backgrounds influence how we view the world.	"I don't understand why our Japanese guests greet us by bowing. We don't do that in Canada."

Our own cultural framework has a profound effect on how we interpret everything we experience, including our interactions with others. Do people in your own culture typically behave like those in this photo? If not, what is your reaction to what you see here?

(© Paul Thuysbaert/Grapheast/Alamy Stock Photo)

in part by one's power and influence. For example, people who have greater power and more influence in a particular culture may not be aware of their power and influence and how it affects their perceptions of others. People with less power (which in many cultures includes women and people of colour) may be acutely aware of the power they don't have.

As evidence of standpoint theory, one team of researchers found that people who perceived that they were the victims of someone's lying to them or cheating them had a more negative view overall of the communication with their communication partner than with someone who they perceived did not lie or cheat.[10] This makes sense, doesn't it? If our point of view is that a certain person can't be trusted in one situation, we are less likely to trust the person in other situations.

Intercultural Communication Theory: We Draw on Our Own Cultural Background. When Alisha thought Jessica was rude and thoughtless because she always arrived at their meetings late, Alisha was attributing meaning to Jessica's behaviour based on Alisha's cultural assumptions about when meetings usually begin. According to Alisha, if a meeting is supposed to start at 10:00 a.m., it's important to be prompt and be ready to begin on time. But Jessica comes from a culture with a different approach to time; in Jessica's culture, meetings *never* begin on time. In fact, it's polite, according to Jessica, to be fashionably late so that the meeting leader can greet people and make any last-minute preparations for the meeting. To show up on time would be disrespectful. Both Jessica and Alisha are making sense out of their actions based on their own cultural framework. Jessica and Alisha aren't the only ones who interpret behaviour through their cultural lens—we all do.

Culture is a learned system of knowledge, behaviours, attitudes, beliefs, values, and norms that is shared by a group of people. Our culture is reflected not only in our behaviour but in every aspect of the way we live our lives. The categories of things and ideas that identify the most profound aspects of cultural influence are known as *cultural elements*. According to one research team, cultural elements include the following:[11]

- Material culture: housing, clothing, automobiles, and other tangible things
- Social institutions: schools, governments, religious organizations
- Belief systems: ideas about individuals and the universe
- Aesthetics: music, theatre, art, dance
- Language: verbal and nonverbal communication systems

As you can see from the list, cultural elements are not only things we can see and hear, but also ideas and values. And because these elements are so prevalent, they have an effect on how we interpret all that we experience.

Our culture is like the air we breathe, in that we're often not aware that it's there—we simply go about our daily routines, usually not conscious that we are breathing. Because our culture is ever-present and is constantly influencing our thoughts and behaviour, it has a profound impact on how we experience the world. If you come from a culture in which horsemeat is a delicacy, you'll likely savour each bite of your *cheval tartare* (raw horsemeat), because you've learned to enjoy it. Yet if eating horsemeat is not part of your cultural heritage, you will have a different perception if you're served this dish, which is

culture. Learned system of knowledge, behaviours, attitudes, beliefs, values, and norms shared by a group of people.

common in France. So it is with how we interpret the behaviour of other people who have different cultural expectations than we do. In some countries, men kiss each other on the cheek when greeting one another, or they may walk arm in arm down the sidewalk when conversing. These are considered normal and natural aspects of human interaction. Yet in North America, these behaviours may be perceived differently because of different cultural expectations.

Identifying Barriers to Accurate Interpersonal Perceptions

Think about the most recent interaction you have had with a stranger. Do you remember the person's age, gender, race, or body size? Did the person have any distinguishing features, such as a beard, tattoos, or a loud voice? The qualities you recall will most likely serve as the basis for attributions you make about that person's behaviour. However, these attributions, based on your first impressions, might be highly inaccurate. We each see the world from our own unique perspective. This perspective is clouded by a number of distortions and barriers that contribute to inaccurate interpersonal perception.

We Stereotype

Preconceived notions about what they expect to find may keep people from seeing what is before their eyes and ears. We see what we want to see, and we hear what we want to hear. We **stereotype** others, which means that we attribute a set of qualities to a person because of his or her membership in a particular category. The word *stereotype* was originally a printing term, referring to a metal plate that was cast from type set by a printer. The plate would print the same page of type over and over again. When we stereotype people, we place them into inflexible, all-compassing categories. We "print" the same judgments on anyone placed into a given category. We may even choose to ignore contradictory information that we receive directly from the other person. Instead of adjusting our conception of that person, we adjust our perception. The halo and horn effects discussed earlier are reflections of this tendency. For example, if an instructor gets an excellent paper from a student who she has concluded is not particularly bright or motivated, she may tend to find errors and shortcomings that are not really there, or she may even accuse the student of plagiarism.

We Ignore Information

Sometimes we overlook important information because we give too much weight to information that is obvious and superficial. Why do we ignore important information that may be staring us in the face? The answer lies in what we learned about attribution theory. We tend to explain the motives for a person's actions on the basis of the most obvious information rather than on any in-depth information we might have. When meeting someone new, we perceive his or her physical qualities first: colour of skin, body size and shape, age, gender, and other obvious physical characteristics. We overattribute to these qualities because they are so vivid and available. We have all been victims of these kinds of attributions, some of us more than others. Often, we are unaware that others are making biased attributions because they do not express them openly. However, sometimes we can tell by the way others react to us and treat us.

stereotype. A set of qualities that you attribute to a person because of the person's membership in some category.

We Overgeneralize

We treat small amounts of information as if they were highly representative. This tendency also leads us to draw inaccurate, prejudicial conclusions. Your authors, for example, may talk to two students from your school, and then we may generalize by applying the impression we have of those two students to the entire student population. In a similar way, we tend to assume that the small sampling we have of another person's behaviour is a valid representation of who that person is. As we saw in Figure 3.1, we create a rabbit even when we have only a few dots on which to base our perception.

To overgeneralize is similar to the concept of thin slicing discussed earlier in the chapter. Although we use a small sample of information to reach a conclusion, a problem occurs when the conclusion we reach from a brief observation is inaccurate. Overgeneralization occurs when the thin-sliced information we use to reach a conclusion is wrong. When making snap judgments from only bits of information, realize the potential for making an inaccurate conclusion.

We Oversimplify

We prefer simple explanations to complex ones. When Terry picks you up late to go to a movie, she says, "Sorry, I lost track of the time." The next day, Christine also picks you up late to go to a movie. She says, "Sorry. You wouldn't believe how busy I've been. I ran out of hot water when I was showering and my hair dryer must be busted. It kept shutting off. Then I stopped to get something to eat and it took forever to get my order. Then it turned out they had it all messed up and had to redo it." Who's explanation can you accept more easily—Terry's or Christine's?

Usually, we prefer simple explanations; they tend to be more believable and easier to use in making sense of another's actions. In reality, our behaviours are affected by a multitude of factors, as Christine's explanation indicates. Unfortunately, it takes a lot of effort to understand what makes another person do what he or she does—more effort than we are typically willing to give.

We Impose Consistency

We overestimate the consistency and constancy of others' behaviours. When we organize our perceptions, we also tend to ignore fluctuation in people's behaviours and see them as consistent. We believe that if someone acted a certain way one day, he or she will continue to act that way in the future. Perhaps you have embarrassed yourself in front of a new acquaintance by acting in a foolish and silly manner. At another encounter with this new acquaintance, you realize that the person is continuing to see your behaviour as foolish, even though you don't intend it to be seen that way. The other person is imposing consistency on your inconsistent behaviour.

In fact, everyone's behaviour varies from day to day. Some days we are in a bad mood, and our behaviour on those days does not represent what we are generally like. As intimacy develops in relationships, we interact with our partners in a variety of activities that provide a more complete picture of our true nature.

Stereotypes can help us make sense out of the wide range of stimuli we encounter every day. However, we also need to make sure we don't overuse stereotypes and fail to see people as individuals.

(© Jacopo Pandolfi/Photonica World/Getty Images)

We Focus on the Negative

We give more weight to negative information than to positive information. Job interviewers often ask interviewees to describe their strengths and weaknesses. If you describe five great strengths and one

The SIDE Model We use what cues are available online to stereotype others, just as we do in face-to-face interactions. In fact, we may be *more* likely to stereotype others online than in person; when we are online, we have to make more inferences about the other person because there are fewer cues and it takes longer for relationship cues to emerge. This theory is called the **social identity model of deindividuation effects (SIDE).**[1] We are more likely to reduce someone to a stereotype—or, to use a technical term, to *deindividuate* them—online because we have fewer cues to help us develop a clear impression.

One study found that Asian–American women were stereotypically perceived as shyer and more introverted, compared to African-American women, when communicating via email but not when communicating by telephone.[2] The fewer cues available, the more likely stereotypical perceptions of the other person were to emerge. Since email offers fewer cues than the telephone (the telephone is a richer medium), stereotyping is more likely in the media-lean email context. Another study found that people make stereotypical judgments about another person's gender when communicating via email when they aren't certain whether the person they are interacting with is a male or female.[3] We use whatever cues we have, such as language style and even topics discussed, to help us form a stereotypical impression of the other person.

Another interesting study suggests that people may form stereotyped impressions about you based on the perceived physical attractiveness of photos of the friends you have posted on your Facebook page.[4] If your friends appear to be attractive, research suggests *you* will be perceived as more attractive and will make a more positive impression on others than if your friends are perceived as less attractive.[5] In short, you look good if you have friends who look good. This finding suggests that people form stereotypes not only on the basis of the qualities of other people, but also from context cues about those with whom others associate.[6]

Research Implications: So What? We are more likely to overgeneralize and to oversimplify because we have limited information available. The problem is that with less relational information or fewer cues in general, we may be even more inaccurate in making stereotypical judgments of others online. So what should we do? Consider these suggestions:

1. First, be mindful of the potential for developing inaccurate stereotypes online. Being aware of the problem is the first step in avoiding the problem.

2. Second, as you become aware that you may be making an inaccurate stereotype based on limited online information, be cautious of the conclusions you draw about others' personality and character.

3. Third, as you prepare your online profile on Facebook or other e-formats, look at your information with the other-oriented perspective of how others may perceive you online.

weakness, it is likely that the interviewer will attend more to the one weakness you mention than to the strengths. We seem to recognize this bias and compensate for it when we first meet someone by sharing only positive information about ourselves.

In another of the Solomon Asch experiments on impression formation, participants heard one of the following two lists of terms describing a person: (1) intelligent, skilful, industrious, warm, determined, practical, cautious; or (2) intelligent, skilful, industrious, cold, determined, practical, cautious.[12] The only difference in these two lists is the use of "warm" in the first list and "cold" in the second. Despite the presence of six other terms, those with the "cold" list had a much more negative impression of the person than those with the "warm" list. One piece of negative information can have a disproportionate effect on our impressions and negate the effect of several positive pieces of information.

social identity model of deindividuation effects (SIDE). Theory that people are more likely to stereotype others with whom they interact online, because such interactions provide fewer relationship cues and the cues take longer to emerge than they would in face-to-face interactions.

We Blame Others, Assuming They Have Control

People are more likely to believe that others are to blame when things go wrong than to believe that the problem was beyond their control. Your parents were looking forward to celebrating their 25th wedding anniversary. They planned a quiet family celebration at a restaurant. You set your smartphone to remind you one week before the anniversary dinner to buy them a present to give to them at the dinner. You hadn't anticipated, however, that you'd lose your phone. When your home phone rang and your mom asked "Where are you?," it all came jarringly back: today was their anniversary, and you'd forgotten it. Not only did you forget to buy them a present, but you forgot to attend the dinner. Your parents were hurt. Your mother's quivering "How could you forget?" still sears your conscience. Your parents' hurt feelings evolved into anger. They think you just didn't care enough about them to remember such an important day. Rather than thinking that there might be an explanation for why you forgot their important day, they blame you for your thoughtlessness. Although they certainly have a right to be upset, their assuming that you don't care about them is an example of what researchers call a fundamental attribution error.

A **fundamental attribution error** occurs when a person believes that the cause of a problem is something personally controllable rather than something uncontrollable. For example, fundamental attribution error would predict that you're more likely to assume that the person who cuts you off in traffic is a jerk rather than that he's trying to get out of the way of the truck that's tailgating him. If you assume another person made a conscious choice to hurt you instead of considering that there may be other reasons for the person's behaviour that are beyond the person's control, you've made a fundamental attribution error.

We Avoid Responsibility

People are more likely to save face by believing that they are not the cause of a problem. In other words, people assume that other people or events are more than likely the source of problems or events that may put them in an unfavourable light. In one classic episode of *The Simpsons*, Bart Simpson creates a popular catch phrase by saying "I didn't do it" when he clearly was the cause of a calamity. Whether he is lighting Lisa's hair on fire, calling Moe's tavern asking for Al Coholic, or putting baby Maggie on the roof, Bart defends himself from judgment simply by saying, "I didn't do it." We chuckle at Bart's antics and would never stoop to such juvenile pranks. Yet there is evidence that when we do cause a problem or make a mistake, we are more likely to blame someone else rather than ourselves. Bart's "I didn't do it" approach to life represents self-serving bias.

When we avoid taking responsibility for our own errors and mistakes, we are guilty of what researchers call the self-serving bias. **Self-serving bias** is the tendency to perceive our own behaviour as more positive than others' behaviour. Sociologist Erving Goffman was one of the first to note this tendency when he wrote his classic book, *The Presentation of Self in Everyday Life*.[13] We are likely, for example, to attribute our own personal success to hard work and effort rather than to external, uncontrollable causes. You get an A on your anthropology paper because, you think, "I'm smart." When you get an F on your history paper, it's because your neighbour's loud party kept you up all night and you couldn't study. Self-serving bias is the tendency to take credit for the good things that happen to you and to say "I didn't do it" or "it's not my fault" when bad things happen to you. The self-serving bias is one of the obstacles to becoming other-oriented. Blaming others and blaming external causes rather than owning up to our own foibles can keep us from taking an honest look at ourselves. Of course, there are many times when, in fact, you "didn't do it." The challenge lies in sorting out when you are at fault and when you are not. Self-serving bias makes it difficult to make that decision objectively. However, simply being aware of your self-serving bias may help you become more objective and accurate in identifying the causes of calamities in your life.

fundamental attribution error. Attributing another person's behaviour to internal, controllable causes rather than to external, uncontrollable causes.

self-serving bias. The tendency to perceive our own behaviour as more positive than others' behaviour.

▶ RECAP Barriers to Accurate Perceptions

Ignoring information	We give too much weight to information that is obvious and superficial.
Overgeneralizing	We treat small amounts of information as if they were highly representative.
Oversimplifying	We prefer simple explanations to complex ones.
Stereotyping	We allow our pre-existing rigid expectations about others to influence our perceptions.
Imposing consistency	We overestimate the consistency and constancy of others' behaviour.
Focusing on the negative	We give more weight to negative information than to positive information.
Blaming others by assuming they have control	We are more likely to believe that others are to blame when things go wrong than to assume that the cause of the problem was beyond their control.
Avoiding responsibility	We save face by believing that other people, not ourselves, are the cause of problems; when things go right, it's because of our own skills and abilities rather than help from others.

Improving Interpersonal Perception Skills

With so many barriers to perceiving and interpreting other people's behaviour accurately, what can you do to improve your perceptual skills? Increasing your awareness of the factors that lead to inaccuracy will help initially, and you will find further suggestions in this section. Ultimately, your improvement will depend on your willingness to do three things: (1) to grow as you expand your experiences, (2) to communicate about your perceptions with others, and (3) to seek out and consider others' perceptions of you. Realize that you have had a lifetime to develop these barriers and that it will take time, commitment, and effort to overcome their effects.

Just by reading this chapter, you've gained a greater understanding of how the perception process affects your relationship with others. Use your knowledge of the perceptual process to sharpen your own perceptions and conclusions. Here are additional strategies to help you become a more accurate perceiver.

Link Details with the Big Picture

The famous fictional detective Sherlock Holmes was particularly skilled at taking a small piece of information or evidence and using it to reach a broader conclusion. Skilled perceivers keep the big picture in mind as they look for clues about a person. In this chapter, we have encouraged you to become more sensitive to details when observing others. However, be cautious of taking one scrap of evidence and spinning out inaccurate conclusions about a person. Just because someone may dress differently from you or have a pronounced accent, don't rush to judgment about the person's competence based on such few snatches of information. Look and listen for other cues about your new acquaintance that can help you develop a more accurate understanding of who that person is. Try not to use the early information to cast a quick or rigid judgment that may be inaccurate. Look at all the details you've gathered.

This driver may be making the fundamental attribution error—assuming that the other person's behaviour was under his control, when in fact it may not have been.

(© Vladimir Mucibabic/Fotolia)

BEING **Other**-ORIENTED

Being willing not only to accept criticism from others but also to seek it can enhance a relationship, if both people are sensitive when sharing and listening. Can you think of criticism that a close friend or family member has shared with you that strengthened the quality of your relationship with that person? Have you heard criticism that caused a relationship to deteriorate? What kind of shared information makes a relationship stronger? What kinds of criticism may be damaging to a relationship?

Become Aware of Others' Perceptions of You

The best athletes don't avoid hearing criticisms and observations from their coaches. Instead, they seek out as much feedback as they can about what they are doing right and wrong. Olympic training often involves the use of videotaped replays and computer analysis so that athletes can see themselves as others see them and use that perspective to improve their performance. It is difficult to be objective about our own behaviour, so feedback from others can help us with our self-perceptions. The strongest relationships are those in which the partners are willing to share and to be receptive to each other's perceptions.

Check Your Perceptions

Throughout this chapter we've encouraged you to be more mindful of your communication with others. It may seem as though we're expecting you to be a mind reader—to just look at someone and know precisely what he or she is thinking. Mind reading may be a good circus act, but it's not a well-documented way of enhancing your perception of others. What does seem to work is to check your perceptions of others.

You can check out the accuracy of your perceptions and attributions in two ways: indirectly and directly. **Indirect perception checking** involves seeking additional information through passive perception, either to confirm or to refute your interpretations. If you suspect someone is angry at you but is not admitting it, for example, you could look for more cues in his or her tone of voice, eye contact, and body movements to confirm your suspicion. You could also listen more intently to the person's words and language.

Direct perception checking involves asking straight out whether your interpretation of what you perceive is correct. Asking someone to confirm a perception shows that you are committed to understanding his or her behaviour. If your friend's voice sounds weary and her posture is sagging, you may assume that she is depressed or upset. If you say, "I get the feeling from your tone of voice and the way you're acting that you're kind of down and depressed; what's wrong?," your friend can then either provide another interpretation—"I'm just tired; I had a busy week"—or expand on your interpretation: "Yeah, things haven't been going very well. . . ." Your observation might also trigger a revelation: "Really? I didn't realize I was acting that way. I guess I am a little down."

indirect perception checking. Seeking additional information through passive perception to confirm or refute your interpretations.

direct perception checking. Asking for confirmation from the observed person of an interpretation or a perception about him or her.

Become Other-Oriented

Effective interpersonal perception depends on the ability to understand where others are coming from, to get inside their heads, to see things from their perspectives.

Becoming other-oriented involves a two-step process: social decentring (consciously thinking about another's thoughts and feelings) and empathizing (responding emotionally to another's feelings). What does your boss think and feel when you arrive late for work? What would your spouse think and feel if you brought a dog home as a surprise gift? Throughout

this book we offer suggestions for becoming other-oriented, for reminding yourself that the world does not revolve around you. Being other-oriented enables you to increase your understanding of others and improve your ability to predict and adapt to what others do and say.

To improve your ability to socially decentre and to empathize, strive for two key goals: (1) to gather as much information as possible about the circumstances that are affecting the other person; and (2) to gather as much information as possible about the other person.

Be Sensitive to Cultural Differences

Although Chapter 4 deals with diversity and cultural differences in greater detail, it is appropriate to touch on the subject here. Cultures can influence perception in many ways. For example, in some Asian cultures, eye contact is seen as disrespectful, especially to those in authority. Yet in North America, if no eye contact is given, many people feel the person is lying or hiding something. By simply realizing that cultures differ in what they consider acceptable or unacceptable behaviour, you will be less likely to make perceptual errors. The potential for interpersonal communication problems will diminish if you keep these simple ideas with you when interpreting a person's behaviour if he or she is from a culture different from your own.

BEING Other-ORIENTED

Being other-oriented may sound like a simple set of techniques that can solve all relationship problems. But it's not that simple. And we don't claim that if you *are* other-oriented, all your relational challenges will melt away. Can you think of situations in which you believed you were being other-oriented yet the relationship continued to experience turbulence and challenges? What are the limitations of being other-oriented?

APPLYING AN OTHER-ORIENTATION
to Interpersonal Perception

We continue to stress the importance of considering the thoughts and feelings of others as a way to enhance the quality of our interpersonal relationships. When forming impressions of others and striving to perceive them accurately, it's especially important to consider what the other person may be thinking and feeling. To help you become more other-oriented, we offer several questions you could ask yourself. You don't need to ponder each question every time you meet someone new—that would be unrealistic. But in situations in which it's especially important to form an accurate impression of someone (whether you're interviewing the person for a job or thinking about asking the person out on a date), consider these questions:

- What factors or circumstances are affecting the other person right now?

- How can I determine whether there are factors I don't know about or don't fully understand about the other person? Should I ask specific questions?

- What do I know about this person that explains his or her behaviours?

- What might be going on in the other person's mind right now?

- What might the other person be feeling right now?

- What other possible explanations could there be for the person's actions?

- What would I be thinking if I were in the same situation as this person?

- How would I be feeling if I were in the same situation as this person?

- What would most other people think if they were in that situation?

- How would most other people feel if they were in that situation?

Understanding Interpersonal Perception (pages 52–56)

OBJECTIVE ❶ Define perception and explain the three stages of interpersonal perception.

Key Terms

perception 52
interpersonal perception 52
selective perception 53
selective attention 53
selective exposure 53

selective recall 53
thin slicing 54
superimposing 54
punctuation 55
closure 55

Critical Thinking Questions

1. Describe your current environment. What is going on around you at the moment? Is there noise in the room? Noise outside the room? What do you see? What can you smell? Are you being distracted by technology—TV, radio, iPod, cell phone, etc.? Are there other people around? What are you attending to most closely? What sensory input are you selecting? Are you perceiving other things that you are able to ignore or tune out? Explain.

2. Do you ever "people watch"? If so, do you find that you thin slice, or make judgments about the people you are observing? What cues do you tend to focus on?

Activities

Find a magazine ad or illustration, a photograph, or a painting that shows a group of people, and bring it to class. In groups of four or five, pass around the pictures. For each picture, write down a few words to describe your perceptions of what you see. What are the people doing? What is their relationship to one another? What is each person like? How is each person feeling? Why are they doing what they are doing? After you've finished, share what you wrote with the others in your group. Try to determine why people's descriptions of what they saw differed. What factors influenced your perceptions?

Web Resources

http://members.tripod.com/nwacc_communication/id4.htm Visit this site and explore the meaning of self-concept and perception while gaining knowledge about yourself through an interactive exercise.

Forming Impressions and Interpreting the Behaviour of Others (pages 56–63)

OBJECTIVE ❷ List and describe the strategies we use to form impressions and interpret the behaviour of others.

Key Terms

impressions 56
impression formation
   theory 56
passive perception 56
active perception 56
implicit personality theory 57
construct 57
uncertainty reduction
   theory 57

primacy effect 58
recency effect 58
halo effect 58
horn effect 58
attribution theory 59
attribution 60
causal attribution theory 60
standpoint theory 60
culture 62

Critical Thinking Questions

1. Describe a recent situation in which your first impression of someone turned out to be inaccurate. What led you to form this initial impression? What were your initial perceptions? What then led you to change those perceptions?

2. Think of a recent interaction with a friend, family member, or work colleague in which you interpreted the person's behaviour incorrectly. Did you attribute specific motives to the person's behaviour? What led you to ascribe these motives? What was the outcome of the exchange?

Activities

Pair up with someone in class whom you do not know and with whom you have not interacted before. Without saying anything to each other, write down 10 words that you think apply to the other person. Now chat together for five minutes. On a separate section of your paper, write down any additional words that you believe apply to the person; you can also go back and cross out any of the words in the first list that you now think don't apply. Share both lists of words with each other. Discuss the reasons each of you chose each word.

Identifying Barriers to Accurate Interpersonal Perceptions (pages 63–67)

OBJECTIVE ❸ Identify the factors that distort the accuracy of our interpersonal perceptions.

Key Terms

stereotype 63
social identity model of
   deindividuation effects
   (SIDE) 65

fundamental attribution
   error 66
self-serving bias 66

Critical Thinking Questions

1. What do you think contributes to the tendency to perceive others inaccurately? How might the effects of those factors be minimized or eliminated?

2. Think about some of your recent interpersonal conflicts. How would you describe your perception of the problem in each conflict? How do you think the others would describe their perceptions of the problem? What role did perception play in contributing to or resolving the conflict?

3. Choose several "friends" from Facebook or another social networking site—people you don't know well but who have nonetheless "friended" you. What impressions do you have of these people? Do you tend to place them into a category based on their profile information, wall posts, or photos? What factors lead you to categorize them in this way? Are your perceptions positive or negative? What attribution errors might you be making?

4. Ethics: Do you have a right in an intimate relationship to expect your partner to share his or her perceptions of you, whether those perceptions are positive or negative? Explain your reasoning.

Activities

1. Make a list to share with classmates of between 5 and 10 stereotypes of different groups or categories of people. Compare and contrast your list and your classmates' lists. What factors contribute to the forming of these stereotypes?

2. Ask a classmate to make a list of adjectives that he or she would use to describe you. Then discuss with the classmate how many of these characteristics are based on stereotypes. How many are based on other perceptual barriers such as lack of information?

Web Resources

https://implicit.harvard.edu/implicit/demo At this site you can test your implicit attitudes to explore any prejudices and stereotypes you might have.

Improving Interpersonal Perception Skills (pages 67–69)

OBJECTIVE ④ Identify and apply suggestions for improving interpersonal perceptions.

Key Terms

indirect perception   **direct perception checking** *68*
checking *68*

Critical Thinking Questions

1. Describe a recent communication exchange in which you needed to be other-oriented. How did you "step back" to understand what the other person was thinking and feeling? Did you express empathy? Explain how you did so.

2. Ethics: If you are aware of how you are distorting your own perceptions and attributions, should you try to change? Are people morally obligated to perceive others accurately? Explain your reasoning.

Activities

Think of a person in your life whose recent behaviour and/or communication has puzzled or angered you. Put yourself in the person's place and analyze why he or she is behaving in this way. List the questions you need to ask yourself to help understand your perceptions and determine whether these perceptions are accurate. What perception-checking steps do you need to take? What, specifically, do you need to do to adjust your perceptions and have more effective communication with this person?

Web Resources

http://sds.hss.cmu.edu/risk Make better decisions by understanding the domain in which they take place. The Center for Risk Perception and Communication will help you measure perceptions and evaluate communication.

4

Interpersonal Communication and Diversity: Adapting to Others

66 He who is different from me does not impoverish me—he enriches me. 99 —Antoine de Saint Exupéry

© Jasmin Merdan/Fotolia

Diversity of culture, language, religion, and a host of other factors is increasingly commonplace in contemporary society. This diversity creates the potential for misunderstanding and even conflict stemming from the different ways we make sense of the world and share that sense with others. Although as human beings we share many things in common, our interpersonal interactions with others make it obvious that many people look different from us and communicate in ways that are different from ours.

In the first three chapters, we acknowledged the influence of diversity on interpersonal relationships. In this chapter, we examine in more detail the impact that people's differences have on their lives and suggest some communication strategies for bridging those differences in our interpersonal relationships. Our premise for this discussion of diversity is that in order to live comfortably in the 21st century, people must learn to appreciate and understand our differences instead of ignoring them, suffering because of them, or wishing that they would disappear. As suggested by the statistics in the Canadian Connections box, Canada is becoming increasingly diverse. With this diversity comes a growing awareness that learning about differences, especially cultural differences, can affect every aspect of people's lives in positive ways.

A central goal of your study of interpersonal communication is to learn how to better relate to others. Some of the factors that contribute to diversity and may interfere with developing relationships include differences in age, learning style, gender, religion, race and ethnicity, sexual orientation, social class, and culture. We will emphasize the role of cultural differences and how these differences affect our interpersonal communication, while also noting a variety of ways that we may seem strange to one another.

Understanding Diversity: Describing Our Differences

How are we different? Let us count the ways. No, let's not—that would take up too much space! There is an infinite number of ways in which we are different from one another. Unless you have an identical twin, you look different from everybody else, although you may have some things in common with a larger group of people (such as skin colour, hair style, or clothing choice). Communication researchers have, however, studied several major differences that affect the way we interact with one another. To frame our discussion of diversity and communication, we'll note differences in gender, sexual orientation, race and ethnicity, age, and social class. Each of these differences—some learned and some based on biology, on economic status, or simply on how long someone has lived—has an effect on how we perceive others and interact with them. Following our discussion of some classic ways in which we are diverse, we'll turn our attention to cultural differences and then note the barriers that cultural differences can create. We'll conclude the chapter by identifying strategies to enhance the quality of interpersonal communication with others, despite our differences.

Differences in age and ability are just two types of diversity that might cause barriers to effective communication.
(© goodluz/Shutterstock)

Canadian Connections

Canada's Increasing Diversity

Canada continues to be a cultural mosaic of many races and cultures, a fact which was highlighted in the 2011 National Household Survey (NHS). Here are a few of its interesting findings:

- The 2011 NHS enumerated 6.8 million foreign-born individuals in Canada representing 20.6% of the total population. This is the highest percentage among the G8 countries.

- After Canadian, the other most frequently reported origins in 2006, either alone or with other origins, were English, French, Scottish, Irish, and German.

- Over 200 ethnic origins were reported by the total Canadian population. Of

these, 13 different ethnic origins surpassed the 1 million mark.

- In the 2006 census, 16.2% of Canadians identified themselves as members of visible minorities. In 2011, this number rose to 19.1%. Visible minorities are defined by the Employment Equity Act as "persons, other than Aboriginal peoples, who are non-Caucasian in race or non-white in colour."

- Combined, the three largest visible minority groups—South Asians, Chinese, and Blacks—accounted for 61.3% of the visible minority population.

- Most of the 1.2 million people who immigrated to Canada between 2006 and 2011 settled in a metropolitan area.

Just over 62.5 of these recent immigrants live in the three largest metropolitan areas—Toronto, Montreal, and Vancouver. In contrast, just over 35.2% of Canada's total population lived in these three cities.

- The 2011 NHS enumerated 6.8 million foreign-born individuals in Canada representing 20.6% of the total population.

- Among foreign-born individuals, 61.2% were able to carry on a conversation in English or French and at least one non-official language.

Source: Statistics Canada, "2011 National Household Survey: Immigration, place of birth, citizenship, ethnic origin, visible minorities, language and religion," *The Daily*, May 8, 2013; http://www.statcan.gc.ca/daily-quotidien/130508/dq130508b-eng.htm. © Steven A. Beebe

Sex and Gender

Perhaps the most obvious form of human diversity is the existence of female and male human beings. A person's **sex** is determined by biology; only men can impregnate; only women can menstruate, gestate, and lactate. In contrast to sex differences, *gender differences* reflect learned behaviour that is culturally associated with being a man or a woman. Gender role definitions are flexible: a man can adopt behaviour associated with a female role in a given culture, and vice versa. **Gender** refers to psychological and emotional characteristics that cause people to assume masculine, feminine, or androgynous (having a combination of both feminine and masculine traits) roles. Your gender is learned and socially reinforced by others, as well as by your life experiences and genetics. Some researchers prefer to study gender as a co-culture (a subset of the larger cultural group). We view gender as one of many basic elements of culture.

In the predominant culture of North America, someone's gender is an important thing to know. Yet how different are men and women? John Gray, author of the popular book *Men Are from Mars, Women Are from Venus*, would have us believe that the sexes are so different from each other that we approach life as if we lived on two different planets.[1] However, communication researchers have challenged many of Gray's stereotypical conclusions.[2] Although researchers have noted some differences in the way men and women interact, to label *all* men and *all* women as acting in prototypical ways may cause us to assume differences that aren't really there.

Deborah Tannen, author of several books on communication between the sexes, views men and women as belonging to different cultural groups.[3] She suggests that female–male communication is cross-cultural communication, with all the challenges of communicating with people who are different from us.

Research conclusions can result in uncertainty about sex and gender differences. Are there really fundamental differences in the way men and women communicate? Researchers have documented some differences, but the differences may have more to do with why we communicate than how. There is evidence that men tend to talk to accomplish something or to complete a task. Women are often more likely to use conversation to establish and

sex. Biologically based differences that determine whether one is male or female.

gender. Socially learned and reinforced characteristics that include one's biological sex and psychological characteristics (femininity, masculinity, androgyny).

maintain relationships. Tannen summarizes the difference as follows: *men often communicate to report; women often communicate to establish rapport.* Research suggests that many men tend to approach communication from a content orientation, meaning that they view the purpose of communication as primarily information exchange. You talk when you have something to say. Women, research suggests, tend to use communication for the purpose of relating or connecting to others. So the point of difference isn't in the way the sexes actually communicate but in their motivations or reasons for communicating.

Sexual Orientation

During the past decades, gays and lesbians have become more assertive in expressing their rights within society. Many legal battles are being fought by gays and lesbians to obtain the equal rights afforded their heterosexual peers. Their victories include the extension of Canadian Pension Plan survivor benefits to same-sex partners and the nationwide legalization of same-sex marriage. Although being gay lesbian is a source of pride for many, it remains a source of stigma for others. The incidence of suicide among gay and lesbian teenagers is significantly higher than among heterosexual teens.[4] Although gays and lesbians are gaining legal rights and protections, they are still subject to discriminatory laws and social intolerance. Yet the gay and lesbian communities are important co-cultures within the larger Canadian culture.

An effective and appropriate interpersonal communicator is aware of and sensitive to issues and attitudes about sexual orientation in contemporary society. Homophobia—the irrational fear of, aversion to, or discrimination against homosexuality and gays or lesbians—continues to exist among many people. Just as you have been taught to avoid biased expressions that degrade someone's race or ethnicity, it is equally important to avoid using language that demeans a person's sexual orientation.

Although we may not intend anything negative, sometimes we unintentionally offend someone through more subtle use and misuse of language. For example, gays and lesbians usually prefer to be referred to as "gay" or "lesbian" rather than "homosexual." In addition, the term "sexual orientation" is preferred over "sexual preference" when describing a person's sexual orientation. Our language should reflect and acknowledge the range of human relationships that exist. Our key point is this: be sensitively other-oriented as you interact with those whose sexual orientation is different from your own.

Race and Ethnicity

Racial and ethnic differences among people are often discussed and sometimes debated. According to *Random House Webster's Unabridged Dictionary*, **race** is based on the genetically transmitted physical characteristics of a group of people who are also classified together because of a common history, nationality, or geographical location.[5] A person's racial classification is typically based on visible physiological attributes—phenotypes—which include skin colour, body type, hair colour and texture, and facial attributes. Skin colour and other physical characteristics affect our responses and influence the way people of different races interact.

Although it may seem neat and tidy to classify individuals genetically as belonging to one race or another, it's not quite that simple. There really aren't vast genetic differences between people who have been assigned to racial categories. That's why many scholars suggest that we think of race as a category that not only emphasizes biological or genetic characteristics, but also includes cultural, economic, social, geographic, and historical elements. The term *race*, therefore, is a fuzzy, somewhat controversial way of classifying people.

Ethnicity is a related term, yet scholars hold that it differs from race. **Ethnicity** is a *social classification* based on a variety of factors, such as nationality, religion, language, and ancestral heritage (race), that are shared by a group of people who also share a common geographic origin.

race. Genetically transmitted physical characteristics of a group of people.

ethnicity. Social classification based on nationality, religion, language, and ancestral heritage, shared by a group of people who also share a common geographical origin.

Simply stated, an ethnic group comprises those who have self-labelled themselves as such based on a variety of factors that may or may not include race. In making distinctions between race and ethnicity, one researcher defines ethnicity as "a common origin or culture based on shared activities and identity related to some mixture of race, religion, language and/or ancestry."[6] In this formulation, while ethnicity may include race, race is a separate category that is based on genetic or biological factors. But other research has found that those genetic or biological distinctions are not clear-cut. A key distinction between race and ethnicity is that one's ethnicity is a *socially constructed* category that emphasizes culture and a host of other factors other than one's racial or genetic background. Not all Asians (race), for example, have the same cultural background (ethnicity). Nationality and geographical location are especially important in defining an ethnic group. Those of Irish ancestry are usually referred to as an ethnic group rather than as a race. The same could be said of Britons, Norwegians, and Spaniards.

Ethnicity, like race, fosters common bonds that affect communication patterns. On the positive side, ethnic groups bring vitality and variety to Canadian society. On the negative side, members of these groups may experience persecution or rejection by members of other groups in society.

One of the most significant problems that stem from attempts to classify people by racial or ethnic type is the tendency to discriminate and to unfairly, inaccurately, or inappropriately ascribe stereotypes to racial or ethnic groups. **Discrimination** is the unfair or inappropriate treatment of other people based on their group membership. One of the goals of learning about diversity and becoming aware of both differences and similarities among groups is to eliminate discrimination and stereotypes that cause people to rigidly and inappropriately prejudge others.

Age

Different generations tend to view life differently because they have experienced different cultural and historical events. If your grandparents experienced the Great Depression of the 1930s, they may have different attitudes about savings accounts than you or even your parents do. The generation gap is real and has implications for the relationships we develop with others.

Generational differences have an effect not just on communication with your parents or other family members, but on a variety of relationships, including those with teachers, bosses, classmates, and co-workers. There is considerable evidence that people hold stereotypical views of others based on others' perceived age. In addition, a person's age has an influence on his or her communications with others. For example, one study found that older adults have greater difficulty in accurately interpreting the nonverbal messages of others than younger people do.[7] Neil Howe and William Strauss, researchers who have investigated the role of age and generation on society, define a generation as "a society-wide peer group, born over a period roughly the same length as the passage from youth to adulthood, who collectively possess a common persona."[8] "Baby boomers" is the label for one such generation, people born between 1943 and 1960. Perhaps your parents or grandparents are Boomers. "Generation X" is the term used for people born between 1961 and 1981. If you were born between 1982 and 2002, you and your generation have been labelled "Millennials."[9] According to Howe and Strauss, as a group, "Millennials are unlike any other youth generation in living memory. They are more numerous, more affluent, better educated, and more ethnically diverse."* Table 4.1 summarizes labels for and common characteristics and values of several generational groups.

discrimination. Unfair or inappropriate treatment of people based on their group membership.

---

*Howe and Strauss (see citation in Table 4.1), p. 4.

TABLE 4.1   Summary of Generational Characteristics

Generation Name	Birth Years	Typical Characteristics
Matures	1925–1942	• Work hard • Have a sense of duty • Are willing to sacrifice • Have a sense of what is right • Work quickly
Baby Boomers	1943–1960	• Value personal fulfillment and optimism • Crusade for causes • Buy now, pay later • Support equal rights for all • Work efficiently
Generation X	1961–1981	• Live with uncertainty • Consider balance important • Live for today • Save • Consider every job as a contract
Millennials	1982–2002	• Are close to their parents • Feel "special" • Are goal-oriented • Are team-oriented • Focus on achievement

Source: Information summarized from N. Howe and W. Strauss, *Millennials Rising: The Next Great Generation* (New York: Vintage, 2000).

Your generation has important implications for communication, especially as you relate to others in both family and work situations. Each generation has developed its own set of values, which are anchored in social, economic, and cultural factors stemming from the times in which the generation has lived. Our values—our core conceptualizations of what is fundamentally good or bad, right or wrong—colour our way of thinking about and responding to what we experience. Generational and age differences may create barriers and increase the potential for conflict and misunderstanding. For example, one team of researchers that investigated the role of generations in the workforce found that, paradoxically, Generation X workers are both more individualistic (self-reliant) and more team-oriented than Boomers are.[10] Boomers are more likely to have a sense of loyalty to their employers, expect long-term employment, value a pension plan, and experience job burnout from overwork. Generation Xers, in contrast, seek a more balanced approach between work and personal life, expect to have more than one job or career, value good working conditions over other job factors, and have a greater need to feel appreciated. Of course, these are broad generalizations and do not apply to all people in these categories.

Social Class

As the Canadian Charter of Rights and Freedoms says, "every individual is equal," but there is dramatic evidence that class differences do exist and affect communication patterns. Social psychologist Michael Argyle reports that the cues we use to identify class distinctions are (1) way of life, (2) family, (3) job, (4) money, and (5) education.[11] As teacher and researcher Brenda Allen puts it, "Social class encompasses a socially constructed category of identity that involves more than just economic factors; it includes an entire socialization process."[12] Such a socialization process influences the nature and quality of the interpersonal relationships we have with others. Although sociologists are the primary academic group

Canada is a multicultural country.
(© Megapress/Alamy Stock Photo)

of scholars who study social class, psychologists, business professionals, marketing specialists, and communication scholars also are interested in how a person's social class has an effect on his or her thoughts and behaviour. Class differences influence whom we talk with, whether we are likely to invite our neighbours over for coffee, and whom we choose as our friends and lovers. Social class also is used by advertisers to target sales pitches to specific types of people.

Principles that describe how social classes emerge from society include the following:

1. Virtually every organization or group develops a hierarchy that makes status distinctions.

2. We are more likely to interact with people from our own social class. There seems to be some truth to the maxim "Birds of a feather flock together." Most of us must make a conscious effort if we want to expand beyond our class boundaries.

3. People who interact with one another over time tend to communicate in similar ways; they develop similar speech patterns and use similar expressions.

4. Members of a social class develop ways of communicating class differences to others by the way they dress, the cars they drive, the homes they live in, the schools they attend, and other visible symbols of social class.

5. It is possible to change one's social class through education, employment, and income.

Differences in social class and the attendant differences in education and lifestyle affect whom we talk with and even what we talk about. These differences influence our overall cultural standpoint, from which we perceive the world.

Understanding Culture: Dimensions of Our Mental Software

We have noted ways that differences in gender, sexual orientation, race and ethnicity, age, and social class contribute to an overall cultural perspective that influences how we relate to others. As we discussed in Chapter 3, **culture** is a learned system of knowledge, behaviours, attitudes, beliefs, values, and norms that is shared by a group of people. In the broadest sense, culture includes how people think, what they do, and how they use things to sustain their lives. Researcher Geert Hofstede describes culture as the "mental software" that touches every aspect of how we make sense out of the world and share that sense with others.[13] Just like software in a computer, our culture influences how we process information. To interact with other people is to be touched by the influence of culture and cultural differences.

culture. Learned system of knowledge, behaviour, attitudes, beliefs, values, and norms that is shared by a group of people.

world view. Individual or cultural perceptions about key beliefs and issues, which influence interactions with others

Your culture and your life experiences determine your **world view**—the general cultural perspective on such key issues as death, God, and the meaning of life that shapes how you perceive and respond to what happens to you. Your cultural world view shapes your thoughts, language, and actions; it permeates all aspects of how you interact with society. You cannot avoid having a world view. Your personal world view is so pervasive that you may not even be aware of it. Just as a fish may not be aware of the water in its fish bowl, you may not be aware of how your world view influences every aspect of your life—how you see and what you think. Your world view is one of the primary ways you make sense out of the world—it's how you interpret what happens to you. A person from a small town in Atlantic Canada, for example, is more likely to say "hello" to a stranger on the street than someone from a large city such as Toronto or Vancouver. Your cultural "software" influences with whom you initiate conversation. Cultural differences also predict how and where you send and receive text messages. One study found that people from India prefer private and semi-private places (such as their home) rather than public places (such as a restaurant or bar) to send and receive text messages.[14] Sometimes when we speak of culture, we may be referring to a co-culture. A **co-culture** is a distinct culture within a larger culture. The differences of gender, sexual orientation, race and ethnicity, age, and social class that we discussed earlier are subcultures within the predominant culture. In the 2011 National Household Survey, for example, more than 200 different ethnic origins were reported; as well, significant religious co-cultures included Amish, Mennonite, Mormon, Islamic, and Jewish religious groups. Often, because they are in the minority, members of a co-culture not only *feel* marginalized, they *are* marginalized in employment, education, housing, and other aspects of society. To enhance their power and self-identity, members of co-cultures may develop their own rules and norms. For example, teens develop their own slang, wear certain kinds of clothing, value certain kinds of music, and engage in other behaviours that make it easier for them to be identified apart from the larger culture.

Cultural Elements

Categories of things and ideas that identify the most profound aspects of cultural influence are known as *cultural elements*. According to one research team, cultural elements include the following:

- *Material culture:* housing, clothing, automobiles
- *Social institutions:* schools, governments, religious organizations
- *Individuals and the universe:* system of beliefs
- *Aesthetics:* music, theatre, art, dance
- *Language:* verbal and nonverbal communication systems[15]

How We Learn Our Culture

As we grow, we learn to value these cultural elements. You were not born with a certain taste in food, music, clothes, and automobiles. Through **enculturation**, the process of communicating a group's culture from generation to generation, you learned what you liked by choosing from among the elements that were available within your culture. Your friends, colleagues, the media, and, most importantly, your family communicate information about these elements and advocate choices for you to make. How you celebrate holidays, your taste in clothing styles, and your religious beliefs are learned through the enculturation process.

Cultures are not static; they change as new information and new influences penetrate their stores of knowledge. We no longer believe that bathing is unhealthy, or that we can safely use makeup made with lead. These changes resulted from scientific discoveries, but other changes take place through **acculturation**; we acquire other approaches, beliefs, and values by coming into contact with other cultures. Today, acupuncture, yoga, tai chi, and karate studios are commonplace in most cities across Canada. Hummus (from the eastern Mediterranean) and basmati rice (from South Asia) are available in every supermarket, and restaurants offer a variety of fare, from Mexican to Italian to Thai. In less obvious ways, "new" perspectives from other cultures have also influenced our thoughts, actions, and relationships.

co-culture. A distinct culture within a larger culture, such as the gay and lesbian co-culture.

enculturation. The process of communicating a group's culture from generation to generation.

acculturation. The process of acquiring new approaches, beliefs, and values through exposure to other cultures.

Pomp and Circumstance. Which elements of culture are conveyed through Canada's changing of the guard ceremony on Parliament Hill? How do these cultural elements combine to shape the identity of Canadians?

(© Sean Kilpatrick/The Canadian Press)

cultural values. What a given group of people values or appreciates.

cultural context. Aspects of the environment and/or nonverbal cues that convey information not explicitly communicated through language.

This girl's clothing and pets reflect the aesthetics and lifestyle of her Inuit culture.

(© Mike Beedell Photography)

Cultural Values

Identifying what a given group of people values or appreciates can provide insight into the behaviour of an individual raised within that group. Although **cultural values** vary greatly across the world, researchers have identified six dimensions of culture that that exist in all the cultures that they have studied. Think of these dimensions as general ways of describing how culture is expressed in the behaviour of groups of people. The six dimensions are (1) individualism (an emphasis on the individual) versus collectivism (an emphasis on the group); (2) an emphasis on the surrounding context, including nonverbal behaviours, versus little emphasis on context; (3) masculine values that emphasize accomplishment versus feminine values that emphasize nurturing; (4) degree of tolerance for uncertainty; (5) approaches to power; and (6) short- or long-term approaches to time.

Individualism: One and Many. One of the most prominent dimensions of a culture is that of individualism versus collectivism. Individualistic cultures such as those in North America value individual achievement and personal accomplishment. Conversely, collectivistic cultures, including many Asian cultures, value group and team achievement and strive to attain goals for all members of the family, group, or community. In collectivistic cultures, individuals expect more support from others; they also experience more loyalty to and from the community. Because collectivistic cultures place more value on "we" than "I," teamwork approaches usually succeed better in their workplaces.

Context: High and Low. Individuals from different cultures use cues from the **cultural context** to varying degrees to enhance messages and meaning. This insight led anthropologist Edward T. Hall to categorize cultures as either high- or low-context.[16]

In **high-context cultures**, nonverbal cues are extremely important in interpreting messages. **Low-context cultures** rely more explicitly on language and use fewer contextual cues to send and interpret information. Individuals from high-context cultures may perceive people from low-context cultures as less attractive, knowledgeable, and trustworthy, because they violate unspoken rules of dress, conduct, and communication. Individuals from low-context cultures often are not skilled in interpreting unspoken, contextual messages. For example, Darrin grew up in Calgary, Alberta, a low-context culture, and is spending a semester as an exchange student in Tokyo, Japan, a high-context culture. He may want to tone down his gestures, facial expressions, and other overly expressive nonverbal cues when talking with his classmates. The challenge is to be aware of culture differences and preferences without going to extremes in adapting to another person. As in all other-oriented conversations, before premeditating how you will adapt your communication style, you may want to observe and listen. You want to be appropriately sensitive without overadapting based on stereotypes or expectations.

Gender: Masculine and Feminine. Some cultures emphasize traditional male values, whereas others place greater value on female perspectives. These values are not really about biological sex differences but about overarching approaches to interacting with others. People from backgrounds with **masculine cultural values** tend to value more traditional roles for both men and women. Masculine cultures also value achievement, assertiveness, heroism, and material wealth. Research reveals that men tend to approach communication from a content orientation, meaning that they view communication as functioning primarily for information exchange. Men talk when they have something to say. This is also consistent with the tendency of men to base their relationships, especially their male friendships, on sharing activities rather than talking.

Men and women from backgrounds with **feminine cultural values** tend to value such things as caring for the less fortunate, being sensitive toward others, and enhancing the overall quality of life. Women tend to approach communication for the purpose of relating or connecting to others, of extending themselves to other people in order to know them and be known by them. What women talk about is less important than the fact that they're talking, because talking implies relationship.

Of course, rarely is a culture on the extreme end of the continuum; many are somewhere in between. For centuries, most countries in Europe, Asia, and the Americas have had masculine cultures. Men and their conquests dominate history books; men have been more prominent in leadership and decision making than women. But today many of these cultures are moving slowly toward the middle—legal and social rules are encouraging more gender balance and greater equality between masculine and feminine roles.

Power: Centralized and Decentralized. Some cultures value an equal or decentralized distribution of power, whereas others accept a concentration of hierarchical power in a centralized government and other organizations. In the latter, hierarchical bureaucracies are common, and people expect some individuals to have more power than others. Russia, France, and China all rank high on the concentrated power scale. Those that often strive for greater equality and distribution of power and control include many (but not all) citizens from Australia, Denmark, New Zealand, and Israel. People from these latter countries tend to minimize differences in power between people.

Time: Short Term and Long Term. A culture's orientation to time falls on a continuum between long term and short term. People from a culture with a long-term orientation to time place an emphasis on the future and tend to value perseverance and thrift, because these are virtues that pay off over a long period of time. A long-term time orientation also implies a greater willingness to subordinate oneself for a larger purpose, such as the good of society

high-context culture. Culture in which people derive much information from nonverbal and environmental cues.

low-context culture. Culture in which people derive much information from the words of a message and less information from nonverbal and environmental cues.

masculine cultural values. Achievement, assertiveness, heroism, and material wealth.

feminine cultural values. Relationships, caring for the less fortunate, and overall quality of life.

or the group. In contrast, a culture that tends to have a short-term time orientation values spending rather than saving (because of a focus on the immediate rather than the future), tradition (because of the value placed on the present and the past), and making sure that an individual is respected and that his or her dignity is upheld. It also expects that results will soon follow the actions and effort expended on a task. Short-term cultures place a high value on social and status obligations.

Cultures or societies with a long-term time orientation include many Asian cultures such as China, Hong Kong, Taiwan, and Japan. Short-term time orientation cultures include Pakistan, the Czech Republic, Nigeria, Spain, and the Philippines. Both Canada and the United States are closer to the short-term time orientation than the long-term time orientation, which suggests an emphasis on valuing quick results from projects and greater pressure toward spending rather than saving, as well as a respect for traditions.

▶ RECAP Understanding Culture: Dimensions of Our Mental Software

Cultural Dimension	Countries That Score Higher on This Cultural Dimension	Countries That Score Lower on This Cultural Dimension
Individualism: Societies that place greater emphasis on individualism generally value individual accomplishment more than do societies that value collective or collaborative achievement.	United States, Australia, Great Britain, Canada, Netherlands, New Zealand, Italy, Belgium, Denmark, Sweden, France	Guatemala, Ecuador, Panama, Venezuela, Colombia, Indonesia, Pakistan, Costa Rica, Peru, Taiwan, South Korea
Context: High-context societies prefer to draw information from the surrounding context, including nonverbal messages. Low-context societies tend to prefer information to be presented explicitly, usually in words.	Japan, China, Saudi Arabia, Italy, Greece	Switzerland, Germany, Sweden, Denmark, Finland, United States, Australia
Gender: Societies with greater emphasis on masculinity value achievement, assertiveness, heroism, material wealth, and more clearly differentiated sex roles. People from more feminine cultures tend to value caring, sensitivity, and attention to quality of life.	Japan, Australia, Venezuela, Italy, Switzerland, Mexico, Ireland, Jamaica, Great Britain	Sweden, Norway, Netherlands, Denmark, Costa Rica, Finland, Chile, Portugal, Thailand
Uncertainty: People in societies with less tolerance for uncertainty generally like to know what will happen next. People in other societies are more comfortable with uncertainty.	Greece, Portugal, Guatemala, Uruguay, Belgium, Japan, Peru, France, Argentina, Chile	Singapore, Jamaica, Denmark, Sweden, Hong Kong, Ireland, Great Britain, Malaysia, India, Philippines, United States, Canada
Power: Societies with a more centralized power distribution generally value greater power differences between people; people in such societies are generally more accepting of fewer people having authority and power than are people from societies in which power is more decentralized.	Malaysia, Guatemala, Panama, Philippines, Mexico, Venezuela, Arab countries, Ecuador, Indonesia, India	Austria, Israel, Denmark, New Zealand, Ireland, Sweden, Norway, Finland, Switzerland, Great Britain
Time: People in societies with a long-term orientation to time tend to value perseverance and thrift. People in societies with a short-term orientation to time value both the past and the present, tradition, saving "face," and spending rather than saving.	China, Hong Kong, Taiwan, Japan, Vietnam, South Korea, Brazil, India, Thailand, Hungary, Singapore, Denmark, Netherlands	Pakistan, the Czech Republic, Nigeria, Spain, Philippines, Canada, Zimbabwe, Great Britain, United States, Portugal, New Zealand

Barriers to Effective Intercultural Communication

Intercultural communication occurs when individuals or groups from different cultures communicate. The process of listening and responding to people from different cultural backgrounds can be challenging: the greater the difference in culture between two people, the greater the potential for misunderstanding and mistrust.

Misunderstanding and miscommunication occur between people from different cultures because of different coding rules and cultural norms, which play a major role in shaping patterns of interaction. The greater the difference between the cultures, the more likely it is that they will use different verbal and nonverbal codes. When you encounter a culture that has little in common with your own, you may experience **culture shock**, or a sense of confusion, anxiety, stress, and loss. If you are visiting or actually living in the new culture, your uncertainty and stress may take time to subside as you learn the values and codes that characterize the culture. However, if you are simply trying to communicate with someone from a background very different from your own—even on your home turf—you may find the suggestions in this section helpful in closing the communication gap.

The first step to bridging differences between cultures is to find out what hampers effective communication. What keeps us from connecting with people from other cultures? Sometimes it is different meanings created by different languages or by different interpretations of nonverbal messages. Sometimes it is our inability to stop focusing on ourselves and begin focusing on the other. We'll examine some of these barriers first, then discuss strategies and skills for overcoming them.

Colourful celebrations like this powwow can reinforce healthy ethnic pride. But if ethnic pride is taken to extremes, the resulting ethnocentrism may act as a barrier between groups.

(© Luc Novovitch/Alamy Stock Photo)

intercultural communication. Communication between or among people who have different cultural traditions.

culture shock. Feelings of stress and anxiety a person experiences when encountering a culture different from his or her own.

You don't have to travel the globe to communicate with people who live on the other side of the world. It's increasingly likely that you will interact electronically with others who have cultural or ethnic perspectives different from yours. Research suggests that you or one or more of your work colleagues will work in an international location: according to a *Business Week* survey, most workers thought that by 2017 they would have a colleague with whom they would work closely but who lived in another country.[17] Social networking sites like Facebook, Instagram, or Snapchat, as well as other Internet-based or phone-based connections, make it easy to interact with international friends and colleagues. As more companies are outsourcing customer service to international venues, it's also increasingly likely that you may be speaking to someone in another country when making a call about a problem with your computer or your TV or some other customer-service need. It's challenging enough bridging cultural differences when you're interacting face

to face. It can be even more challenging communicating electronically with others who have different cultural perspectives from yours.

Here are some tips and strategies for enriching electronic intercultural connections with others.

- If you are communicating with someone who is from a high-context culture (such as someone from Japan or another Asian country) in which nonverbal messages are especially important and you are using a leaner communication medium such as texting, consider providing more explicit references to your feelings and emotions by using emoticons or more explicitly stating your feelings and emotional reactions to messages.

- Consider asking more questions than you normally would if you were interacting face to face to clarify meanings and the interpretation of messages.

- Use "small talk" and comments about the weather, what your typical day is like, and other low-level disclosures to build a relationship. Then look for reciprocal responses from your communication partner that indicate a relationship is naturally evolving.

- Summarize and paraphrase messages that you receive more often than you might normally, in order to increase the accuracy of message content.

- Remember the difference between your time zone and the other person's time zone.

- If you find a relationship is awkward or you notice an increase in conflict, use the richest medium you can—use the phone instead of texting or sending email, or use a webcam instead of the phone. If you're merely sharing routine, noncontroversial information, a lean medium (such as texting) should be fine.

Most people are ethnocentric to some degree. But extreme ethnocentrism can be a major interpersonal communication barrier. What symptoms may indicate when an ethnocentric mindset may be interfering with the quality of communication with another person? What are examples of comments that might signal that someone believes his or her cultural approaches are superior to another person's culture?

ethnocentrism. Belief that your cultural traditions and assumptions are superior to those of others.

Ethnocentrism

> All good people agree,
> And all good people say,
> All nice people like Us, are We,
> And everyone else is They.

In a few short lines, 19th-century British writer Rudyard Kipling captured the essence of what sociologists and anthropologists call ethnocentric thinking. Members of all societies tend to find comfort in the familiar and often denigrate or distrust others. Of course, with exposure to other cultures and experience communicating with those who are different from them, they may learn to put themselves in others' shoes and be more accepting of differences.

> … if you cross over the sea,
> Instead of over the way,
> You may end by (think of it!) looking on We
> As only a sort of They.

In a real sense, a main lesson of the sociology of intergroup relations is to begin to "cross over the sea," to learn to understand why other people think and act as they do and to be able to empathize with their perspectives.

Ethnocentrism stems from a conviction that your own cultural traditions and assumptions are superior to those of others. In short, it is the opposite of other-orientation, which embraces and appreciates the elements that give another culture meaning. This kind of cultural snobbery is one of the fastest ways to create a barrier that inhibits, rather than enhances, communication.

Different Communication Codes

You are on your first trip to Calgary. You step off the bus and look around for Stampede Park, and you realize that you have gotten off at the wrong stop. You see a corner grocery store with "Stampede Park" painted on a red sign. So you walk in and ask the man behind the counter, "How do I get to the Calgary Stampede, please?" The man smiles, shrugging his shoulders, but he points to a transit map pasted onto the wall behind the counter.

Today, even when you travel within Canada, you are likely to encounter people who do not speak your language. Obviously, this kind of intercultural difference poses a formidable communication challenge, and even when you do speak the same tongue as another, he or she may come from a place where the words and gestures have different meanings. Your ability to communicate will depend on whether you can understand each other's verbal and nonverbal codes.

In the example above, although the man behind the counter did not understand your exact words, he noted the cut of your clothing, your backpack, and your anxiety. From this, he deduced that you were asking for directions, and you could understand what his gesture toward the transit map meant. Unfortunately, not every communication between the users of two different languages is this successful.

Even when language is translated, there can be missed or mangled meanings. Note the following examples of mistranslated advertisements:

- A General Motors auto ad with "Body by Fisher" became "Corpse by Fisher" in Flemish.

- A Colgate-Palmolive toothpaste named "Cue" was advertised in France before anyone realized that Cue also happened to be the name of a widely circulated pornographic book about oral sex.

- Pepsi-Cola's "Come Alive with Pepsi" campaign, when it was translated for the Taiwanese market, conveyed the unsettling news that "Pepsi brings your ancestors back from the grave."

- Parker Pen could not advertise its famous "Jotter" ballpoint pen in some languages because the translation sounded like "jockstrap" pen.

- One American airline operating in Brazil advertised that it had plush "rendezvous lounges" on its jets, unaware that in Portuguese (the language of Brazil), "rendezvous" implies a special room for making love.[18]

Stereotyping and Prejudice

All French people dress fashionably.

All Asians are good at math.

All Canadians are polite and apologetic.

These statements are stereotypes. They are all inaccurate. To **stereotype** someone is to push him or her into an inflexible, all-encompassing category. In Chapter 3, we saw how our tendency to simplify sensory stimuli can lead us to adopt stereotypes as we interpret the behaviour of others. When we stereotype, we "print" the same judgment over and over again, failing to consider the uniqueness of individuals, groups, or events. This becomes a barrier to effective intercultural communication.

stereotype. To place a person or group of persons into an inflexible, all-encompassing category.

Can stereotypes play a useful role in interpersonal communication? The answer is a resounding "no" if our labels are inaccurate or if they assume superiority on our part. However, sometimes it may be appropriate to draw on generalizations. If, for example, you are walking lost and alone in an unfamiliar neighbourhood late at night and you realize that you have heard the same set of footsteps behind you for several blocks, it would be a good idea to increase your speed and try to find a place where there are other people. You would be wise to prejudge that the person following you might have some malicious intent. In most situations, however, **prejudice**—prejudging someone before you know all the facts—inhibits effective communication. If you decide that you like or dislike (usually dislike) someone simply because he or she is a member of a certain group or class of people, you will not give yourself a chance to communicate with the person in a meaningful way. Prejudice usually involves negative attitudes toward members of a specific social group or culture.

Certain prejudices are widespread. Although there are more females than males in the world, in many societies females are prejudged to be less valuable than males. One study found that even when a male and a female hold the same type of job, the male's job is considered more prestigious than the female's.[19] Discrimination is often a result of prejudice. When people discriminate, they treat members of groups differently from their own in negative ways. In the past, people of different gender, race, ethnicity, or sexual orientation were often victims of discrimination socially and politically. Today, discrimination of these kinds in hiring and promotion is illegal in Canada, but our social attitudes have not kept pace with the law. Stereotyping and prejudice are still formidable barriers to effective interpersonal communication. While many people do not actively engage in discrimination, many still hold negative attitudes and stereotypes of people different from themselves.

Assuming Similarity

Just as it is inaccurate to assume that all people who belong to another social group or class are worlds apart from you, it is usually erroneous to assume that others act and think as you do. Even if they appear to be like you, all people are not alike. While this statement is not profound, it has profound implications. We often make the mistake of assuming that others value the same things we do, maintaining a self-focused perspective instead of an other-oriented one. As you saw in Chapter 3, focusing on superficial factors, such as appearance, clothing, and even a person's occupation, can lead to false impressions. Instead, we must take the time to explore a person's background and cultural values before we can determine what we really have in common.

prejudice. Prejudging someone before you know all of the facts or background of that person.

Assuming Differences

Although it may seem to contradict what we just noted about assuming similarities, another barrier to intercultural communication is to automatically assume that another person is different from you. It can be just as detrimental to communication to assume someone is different from you as it is to assume that others are similar to you. The fact is, human beings do share common experiences, while at the same time there are differences.

The point of noting that humans have similarities as well as differences is not to diminish the role of culture as a key element that influences communication, but to recognize that despite cultural differences, we are all members of the human family. The words "communication" and "common" resemble each other. We communicate effectively and appropriately when we can connect to others based on what we hold in common. Identifying common cultural issues and similarities can help us establish common ground with others.

How are we all alike? Cultural anthropologist Donald Brown has compiled a list of hundreds of "surface" universals of behaviour and language use that have been identified. According to Brown, people in all cultures

- Have beliefs about death
- Have a childhood fear of strangers
- Divide labour on the basis of sex
- Experience envy, pain, jealousy, shame, and pride
- Use facial expressions to express emotions
- Have rules for etiquette
- Experience empathy
- Value some degree of collaboration or cooperation
- Experience conflict and seek to manage or mediate conflict[20]

Of course, all cultures do not have the same beliefs about death or divide labour according to sex in the same ways, but all cultures address these issues. Linguist and scholar Steven Pinker is an advocate of common human values. Drawing on the work of anthropologists Richard Shweder and Alan Fiske, Pinker suggests that the following value themes are universally present in some form or degree in societies across the globe:

- It is bad to harm others and good to help them.
- People have a sense of fairness; we should reciprocate favours, reward benefactors, and punish cheaters and those who do harm.
- People value loyalty to a group and sharing in a community or group.
- It is proper to defer to legitimate authority and to respect those with status and power.
- People should seek purity, cleanliness, and sanctity while shunning defilement and contamination.[21]

In summary, "… avoidance of harm, fairness, community (or group loyalty), authority, and purity … are the primary colors of our moral senses."[22]

What are the practical implications of trying to identify common human values or characteristics? Here's one implication: if you are speaking about an issue on which you and another person fundamentally differ, identifying a larger common value—such as the value of peace, prosperity, or the importance of family—can help you find a foothold so that the other person will at least listen to your ideas. It's useful, we believe, not just to categorize our differences but also to explore how human beings are similar to one another.

Discovering how we are alike can provide a starting point for human understanding. Yes, we are all different, but we share things in common as well. Communication effectiveness is diminished when we assume we're all different from one another in every aspect, just as communication is affected negatively if we assume we're all alike. We're more complicated than that.

RECAP   Barriers to Effective Intercultural Communication

Ethnocentricism	Assuming that one's own culture and cultural traditions are superior to those of others
Different communication codes	Allowing differences in language and the interpretation of nonverbal cues to lead to misunderstanding
Stereotyping and prejudice	Rigidly categorizing and prejudging others based on limited information
Assuming similarity	Assuming that other people respond to situations as we do; failing to acknowledge and consider differences in culture and background
Assuming differences	Assuming that other people are always different from and have nothing in common with us; failing to explore common values and experiences that can serve as bridges to better understanding

Improving Intercultural Communication Competence

It is not enough just to point to the barriers to effective intercultural communication and say, "Don't do that." Although identifying the causes of misunderstanding is a good first step to becoming interculturally competent, most people need help with specific strategies to help them overcome these barriers. In this text, and in this chapter, we want to focus attention on the interpersonal communication strategies that can lead to intercultural communication competence.

Intercultural communication competence is the ability to adapt your behaviour toward another in ways that are appropriate to the other person's culture. To be interculturally competent is to be more than merely aware of what is appropriate or simply sensitive to cultural differences. To be interculturally competent is to behave toward others in ways that are appropriate—but prior to behaving appropriately, an individual needs to have knowledge about another culture and the motivation to adapt or modify his or her behaviour.

Although we've identified stages in the process of becoming interculturally competent, the question remains: How do you achieve intercultural communication competence? The remaining portion of this chapter presents specific strategies to help you bridge differences between you and people who have a different cultural perspective from yours.

Developing Bridging Strategies

Three strategies to help you bridge differences between yourself and people from different cultural backgrounds are developing appropriate knowledge, developing motivation, and developing skill.

- *Develop Appropriate Knowledge.* One of the barriers to effective intercultural communication is having different communication codes. Improving your knowledge of how others communicate can reduce the impact of this barrier. We offer strategies to help you learn more about other cultures by actively pursuing information about others.

intercultural communication competence. Ability to adapt one's behaviour toward another in ways that are appropriate to the other person's culture.

- *Develop Motivation.* **Motivation** is an internal state of readiness to respond to something. A competent communicator wants to learn and improve. Developing strategies to appreciate others who are different from you may help you appreciate different cultural approaches to communication and relationships. We suggest you endeavour to be tolerant of uncertainty and to avoid knee-jerk negative evaluations of others.

- *Develop Skill.* Developing **skill** in adapting to others focuses on specific behaviours that can help overcome barriers and cultural differences. As we discussed in Chapter 1, becoming other-oriented is critical to the process of relating to others.

Developing Knowledge: Strategies to Understand Others Who Are Different from Us

Knowledge is power. To increase your knowledge of others who are different from you, we suggest that you actively seek information about others, ask questions and listen to the answers, and establish common ground. Let's discuss these strategies in more detail.

Seek Information. Seeking information about a culture or even about a specific communication situation can be a useful strategy to enhance the quality of intercultural communication. Why? Because seeking information helps manage uncertainty and anxiety that we may feel when we interact with people who are different from us. Sometimes we feel uncomfortable in intercultural communication situations because we just don't know how to behave. We aren't sure what our role should be; we can't quite predict what will happen when we communicate with others because we're in a new or strange situation. Actively seeking information about a culture or about people from a culture other than your own can help you manage some of the anxiety and uncertainty you may experience when you communicate in new cultural contexts. Seeking new information can also help counter inaccurate information and prejudice.

motivation. Internal state of readiness to respond to something.

skill. Behaviour that improves the effectiveness or quality of communication with others.

You can also prepare yourself by studying the culture. If you are going to another country, courses in the history, anthropology, art, or geography of that place can give you a head start on communicating with understanding. One of this book's authors was invited to a wedding for a Native Canadian friend, and part of the ceremony was "smudging." Prior to attending, the author learned about what it was and how it is done (if you don't know, here is a learning opportunity). Learn not only from books, magazines, and the Internet but also from individuals whenever possible.

Given the inextricable link between language and culture, the more you learn about another language, the more you will understand the traditions and customs of the culture. Politicians have long known the value of using the first languages of their minority constituents. Speaking even a few words can signify your interest in learning about the language and culture of others.

Ask Questions and Listen Effectively. When you encounter a person from another background, asking questions and then pausing to listen is a simple technique for gathering information and also for confirming the accuracy of your expectations and assumptions. Some cultures, such as the Japanese, have rigid expectations regarding gift giving. It is better to ask what these expectations are than to assume that your good old down-home manners will see you through.

When you ask questions, be prepared to share information about yourself, too. Otherwise, your partner may feel as if you are interrogating him or her as a way to gain power and dominance rather than from a sincere desire to learn about cultural rules and norms.

Studying interpersonal communication helps us learn to bridge differences in age, gender, race, or ability that might act as barriers to effective communication.

(© Bob Mahoney/The Image Works)

Communication helps to reduce the uncertainty that is present in any relationship. When you meet people for the first time, you are highly uncertain about who they are and what they like and dislike. When you communicate with someone from another culture, the uncertainty level is particularly high. As you begin to interact, you exchange information that helps you develop greater understanding. If you continue to ask questions, eventually you will feel less uncertain about how the person is likely to behave.

Just asking questions and sharing information about yourself is not sufficient to bridge differences in culture and background. It is equally important to listen to what others share. In Chapter 5 we provide specific strategies for improving your listening skills.

Develop a "Third Culture." Several researchers suggest that one of the best ways to enhance understanding when communicating with someone from a different cultural background is to develop a **third culture**. This is created when the communication partners join aspects of separate cultures to create a third, "new" culture that is more comprehensive and inclusive than either of the two separate cultures.

According to one intercultural communication researcher, F. L. Casmir, a third-culture approach to enhancing the quality of intercultural communication occurs when the people involved in the conversation construct "a mutually beneficial interactive environment in which individuals from two different cultures can function in a way beneficial to all involved."[23]

How do you go about developing a third culture? In a word: talk. Developing a third culture does not just happen all at once; it evolves from dialogue. The communicators construct a third culture together. After they realize that cultural differences may divide them, they may develop a third culture by making a conscious effort to develop common assumptions and common perspectives for the relationship. Dialogue, negotiation, conversation, interaction, and a willingness to let go of old ways and experiment with new frameworks are the keys to developing a third culture as a basis for a new relationship.

Consider the example of Fiona, a businesswoman from Halifax, and Xiaoxian, a businesswoman from Shanghai. In the context of their business relationship, it would be difficult for them to develop a comprehensive understanding of each other's cultural traditions. If, however, they openly acknowledged the most significant of these differences and sought to create a third culture by identifying explicit rules and norms for their interaction, they might be able to develop a more comfortable relationship with each other.

As described by Benjamin Broome, the third culture "is characterized by unique values and norms that may not have existed prior to the dyadic [two-person] relationship."[24] Broome labels the essence of this new relationship **relational empathy**, which permits varying degrees of understanding rather than requiring complete comprehension of another's culture or emotions.

The cultural context includes all the elements of the culture (learned behaviours and rules, or "mental software") that affect the interaction. Do you come from a culture that takes a tea break each afternoon at 4:00? Does your culture value hard work and achievement or relaxation and enjoyment? Creating a third culture acknowledges the different cultural contexts and interactions participants have experienced and seeks to develop a new context for future interaction.

third culture. Establishing common ground by joining separate cultures to create a third, "new," more comprehensive and inclusive culture.

relational empathy. The essence of the third culture, permitting varying degrees of understanding rather than complete comprehension of another's culture or emotions.

▶ RECAP   Develop Knowledge to Enhance Understanding

Seek information about the culture	Learn about a culture's world view.
Ask questions and listen	Reduce uncertainty by asking for clarification and listening to the answer.
Develop a third culture	Create common ground.

Developing Motivation: Strategies to Accept Others

Competent communicators want to learn and improve. They are motivated to enhance their ability to relate to others and to accept others as they are. A key to accepting others is to develop a positive attitude of tolerance and acceptance of those who are different from us. We propose three strategies to help improve your acceptance and appreciation of others who are different from you: tolerate ambiguity, develop mindfulness, and avoid negative judgments about others.

Tolerate Ambiguity. Communicating with someone from another culture produces uncertainty. It may take time and several exchanges to clarify a message. Be patient and try to expand your capacity to tolerate ambiguity if you are speaking to someone with a markedly different world view.

When Ken and Rita visited Montreal, they asked their hotel concierge to direct them to a church of their faith, and they wound up at one with a predominantly Haitian congregation. They were not prepared for the exuberant chanting and verbal interchanges with the minister during the sermon. They weren't certain whether they should join in or simply sit quietly and observe. Ken whispered to Rita, "I'm not sure what to do. Let's just watch and

---

ADAPTING TO DIFFERENCES
Understanding Others

Tao: A Universal Moral Code

It's clear that there are cultural differences among the world's people, and that these differences have existed since there have *been* people. Anthropologists and communication scholars who study intercultural communication teach us the value of adapting to cultural differences in order to understand others better. However, are there any universal values that are or have been embraced by all humans? The question is not a new one; scholars, theologians, and many others have debated for millennia whether there are any universal underpinnings for all human societies. C. S. Lewis, a British scholar, author, and educator who taught at both Oxford and Cambridge, argued that there are universal ethical and moral principles that undergird all societies of civilized people, regardless of their religious beliefs, cultural background, or government structure.[1] For Lewis, the existence of Natural Laws, or what he called a Tao—a universal moral code—informs human ethical decisions. In his book *The Abolition of Man*, he presented eight universal principles, or laws. He did not claim that all societies have followed these laws—many of them have been clearly violated and continue to

be violated today—but he did suggest that they provide a bedrock of values against which all societies may be measured. Here are his eight laws:

1. The Law of General Beneficence: Do not murder, be dishonest, or take from others what does not belong to you.

2. The Law of Special Beneficence: Value your family members.

3. Duties to Parents, Elders, and Ancestors: Especially hold your parents, those who are a generation older than you, and your ancestors with special honour and esteem.

4. Duties to Children and Posterity: We have a special obligation to respect the rights of the young and to value those who will come after us.

5. The Law of Justice: Honour the basic human rights of others; each person is of worth.

6. The Law of Good Faith and Veracity: Keep your promises and do not lie.

7. The Law of Mercy: Be compassionate to those less fortunate than you.

8. The Law of Magnanimity: Avoid unnecessary violence against other people.

To support his argument that these are universal values, Lewis offered quotations from several well-known sources, including religious, historical, and political writings, both contemporary and centuries old. Lewis implied that these eight laws may be viewed as a universal Bill of Rights, and that they constitute an underlying set of principles that either implicitly or explicitly guide all civilized society. Do you agree? Is it useful to search for underlying principles of humanness? Despite cultural differences, are there underlying values or principles that should inform our interactions with others? Is there truly a universal human theory of communication? Or might it do more harm than good to suggest that universal principles underlie what it means to behave and communicate appropriately and effectively?

1. *The Abolition of Man* by C.S. Lewis, copyright (c) C.S. Lewis Pte. Ltd. 1943, 1946, 1978. Extract reprinted by permission.

Source: Based on The Abolition of Man by C.S. Lewis. © Steven A. Beebe

see what's expected of us." In the end, they chose to sit and clap along with the chanting rather than become actively involved in the worship. Rita felt uncomfortable and conspicuous, though, and had to fight off the urge to bolt; but after the service several members of the congregation came up to greet Ken and Rita, invited them to lunch, and expressed great happiness in their visit. "You know," said Rita later in the day, "I'm so grateful that we sat through our discomfort. We might never have met those terrific people. Now I understand why their worship is so noisy—they're just brimming over with joy."

Develop Mindfulness. "Our life is what our thoughts make it," said Marcus Aurelius in *Meditations*. To be **mindful** of cultural differences is to be consciously aware of them, to acknowledge that there is a connection between thoughts and deeds when you interact with a person from a background different from your own. William Gudykunst asserts that being mindful is one of the best ways to approach any new cultural encounter.[25] Remember that there are and will be cultural differences, and try to keep them in your consciousness. Also, try to consider the other individual's frame of reference or world view and to use his or her cultural priorities and assumptions when you are communicating. Adapt your behaviour to minimize cultural noise and distortion.

You can become more mindful through self-talk, something we discussed in Chapter 2. Self-talk consists of rational messages to yourself to help you manage your emotions or discomfort with a certain situation. Imagine that you're working on a group project with several of your classmates. One classmate, Suji, was born in Iran. When interacting with you, he consistently gets about 30 cm away, whereas you're more comfortable with 90 to 120 cm between you. When Suji encroaches on your space, you could "be mindful" of the difference by mentally noting, "Suji sure likes to get close to people when he talks to them. This might represent a practice in his culture." This self-talk message makes you consciously aware that there may be a difference in your interaction styles. If you still feel uncomfortable, instead of blurting out "Hey, man, why so close?," you could express your own preferences with an "I" message: "Suji, I'd prefer a bit more space between us when we talk."

> **BEING Other-ORIENTED**
>
> Being motivated to establish positive relationships with others who are different from us is a key aspect of communicating in interculturally competent ways. What are "self-talk" messages that you could tell yourself (such as "I may feel uncomfortable right now, but I'll keep listening to this person") to motivate you to increase your intercultural competence?

RECAP Develop Motivation to Accept Others

Tolerate ambiguity	Take your time and expect some uncertainty.
Develop mindfulness	Be conscious of cultural differences rather than ignoring the differences.
Avoid negative judgments	Resist thinking that your culture has all the answers.

Developing Skills: Strategies to Adapt to Others Who Are Different from Us

To be skilled is to be capable of putting what you know and want to achieve into action. The underlying skill in being interculturally competent is the ability to be flexible, to be other-oriented, and to adapt to others.

Develop Flexibility. When you interact with someone from another background, your responding skills are crucial. You can learn only so much from books; you must be willing to learn as you communicate. Every individual is unique, so cultural generalizations that you learn from research may not always apply. It is not accurate to assume, for example, that all French people are preoccupied with food and fashion. Many members of minority groups in Canada find it draining to correct these generalizations in their encounters with others. Pay close attention to the other person's nonverbal cues when you begin conversing;

mindful. Consciously aware of cultural differences.

then adjust your communication style and language, if necessary, to put the person at ease. Avoid asking questions or making statements based on generalizations.

Become Other-Oriented. Throughout this text, we have emphasized the importance of becoming other-oriented—focusing on others rather than on yourself—as an important way to enhance your interpersonal competence. We have also discussed the problems ethnocentrism can create when you attempt to communicate with others, especially with those whose culture is different from your own.

It's important to be flexible in your responses to other cultures and people with different backgrounds. Travelling in other countries can hone your intercultural communication skills.

(© Wesley Roberts/Alamy Stock Photo)

Although our focus in this discussion will be on how to increase other-orientation in intercultural interactions, the principles apply to all interpersonal interactions. The major difference between intercultural interactions and those that occur within your own culture is primarily the obviousness of the differences between you and the other person. To become other-oriented is to do two things: first, to take into account another person's thoughts and perspective, and second, to consider what the other person may be experiencing emotionally. These are skills we've emphasized before. The first skill is called social decentering. The second skill is empathy.

Social decentring is a *cognitive process* in which you take into account the other person's thoughts, values, background, and overall perspective. The greater the difference between you and another person, the more difficult it is to accomplish social decentering. As you meet someone from a different culture, ask yourself, "What might this person be thinking right now?" Of course, since you're not a mind reader, you won't be able to know definitively what someone is thinking. But you can think about what most people that you know might be thinking, or draw on your own experiences. Be sure to keep the other person's world view and cultural values in mind as you make inferences about his or her cognitive perspective. After considering his or her cognitive point of view, consider what the person may be experiencing emotionally.

Empathy is an *emotional reaction* that is similar to the one being experienced by another person.[26] Empathy is about *emotions*, whereas social decentering is about cognitive processes. You develop empathy as you draw on your own experiences (what you felt in a similar situation), your knowledge of other people in general, and what you know about the specific person you are interacting with. It's impossible to ever experience the emotions of another person with complete confidence and accuracy. But to be empathic is to do your best to put yourself in someone else's place emotionally and consider what that person is feeling. Being in touch emotionally is hard work, and some people are just naturally more empathic toward others.

Research has consistently found that your ability to be emotionally responsive can enhance your skill in communicating with others who are different from you. Specifically, if you can monitor and then appropriately adapt your emotional response to others, you are more likely to be perceived as socially skilled, a perception that will enhance interpersonal relationships with others. Yet if you tend to shut down and consistently suppress your emotional reactions to the extent that you are perceived to be difficult to figure out, other people may perceive you as less socially skilled.

Appropriately Adapt Your Communication to Others. The logical extension of being flexible and becoming other-oriented is to adapt your communication to enhance the

social decentring. A cognitive process in which we take into account another person's thoughts, feelings, values, background, and perspectives.

empathy. Process of developing an emotional reaction that is similar to the reaction being experienced by another person. Feeling what another person is feeling.

quality and effectiveness of your interpersonal communication. **Adaptation** means adjusting your behaviour to others to accommodate differences and expectations. Appropriate adaptation occurs in the context of the relationship you have with the other person and what is happening in the communication environment.

Communication accommodation theory holds that all people adapt their behaviour to others to some extent. Those who appropriately and sensitively adapt to others are more likely to experience more positive communication. Adapting to others doesn't mean you only tell others what they want to hear and do what others want you to do. Such placating behaviour is not wise, effective, or ethical. Nor are we suggesting that you adapt your behaviour only so that you can get your way; the goal is effective communication, not manipulation. We *are* suggesting, however, that you be aware of what your communication partner is doing and saying, especially if there are cultural differences, so that your message is understood and you don't unwittingly offend others. Although it may seem common sense, being sensitive to others and adapting behaviours to others are not as common as you might think.

Sometimes people adapt their behaviour based on what they think someone will like. At other times, they adapt their communication after realizing they have done something wrong. When you modify your behaviour in anticipation of an event, you **adapt predictively**. For example, you might decide to buy a friend flowers to soften the news about breaking a date because you know how much your friend likes flowers. When you modify your behaviour after an event, you **adapt reactively**. For example, you might buy your friend flowers to apologize for a fight.

You often adapt your messages to enhance message clarity. There are at least four reasons that explain why you may adapt your communication with another person:

- *Information.* You adapt your message in response to specific information that you already know about your partner, such as what he or she may like or dislike, or information that your partner has shared with you.

- *Perceived Behaviour.* You adapt your communication in response to what you think the other person is thinking, what you see the person doing, and your observations of the person's emotional expressions and moods.

- *History.* You adapt your messages to others based on previous conversations, past shared experiences, and personal information that others have shared with you.

- *Communication Context.* You adapt your message depending on where you are; you may whisper a brief comment to someone during a movie, yet shout a comment to someone when attending a loud rock concert.

In intercultural interactions, people frequently adapt communication in response to the feedback or reactions they are receiving during a conversation. An other-oriented communicator is constantly looking and listening to the other person in order to appropriately adapt his or her communication behaviour. Table 4.2 describes how we adapt our verbal messages to others and provides some examples.

People in conversations also adapt to nonverbal cues. They will often raise or lower their voice in response to the volume of a partner, or lean toward a partner who leans toward them. We will discuss such nonverbal cues in Chapter 6.

Adaptation across intercultural contexts is usually more difficult than adaptation within your own culture. Imagine shaking hands with a stranger and having the stranger hold on to your hand as you continue to talk. In Canada, hand holding between strangers violates nonverbal norms, but in some cultures, maintaining physical contact while talking is expected. Pulling your hand away from this person would be rude. What may be mannerly in one culture is not always acceptable in another. Adapting to these cultural differences means developing that "third culture" we talked about earlier in the chapter.

BEING Other-ORIENTED

At the heart of being other-oriented is adapting your behaviour toward others in mindful and ethical ways. Review the adaptation strategies presented in Table 4.2. Identify other examples of various ways of adapting to others. Which strategies are easiest for you to use, and which are the most challenging for you?

---

adaptation. Adjusting behaviour in accord with what someone else does. We can adapt based on the individual, the relationship, and the situation.

communication accommodation theory. Theory that suggests all people adapt their behaviour to others' to some extent.

adapt predictively. Modify or change behaviour in anticipation of an event.

adapt reactively. Modify or change behaviour after an event.

TABLE 4.2   How Do We Adapt to Others?

Type of Adaptation	Examples
Topical Adaptation (including self-disclosures): Choosing topics of conversation because of interests or things you have in common with your partner, including sharing information about yourself	• Talking about a class you both attend • Mentioning an article you read about a TV show your partner really likes • Telling someone about your depression because you believe he or she cares
Explanatory or Elaborated Adaptation: Providing additional information or detail because you recognize that your communication partner has certain gaps in his or her information	• Telling a story about Ike, whom your partner doesn't know, and explaining that Ike is your uncle • Describing Facebook to your grandparent, who doesn't know what the Internet is • Telling someone, "I know my behaviour might seem a little erratic, but I'm under a lot of pressure at work right now and my parents are on my case"
Adaptation Through Withholding or Avoiding Information: Not providing explanations of something your partner already knows; not providing information to avoid an anticipated undesired reaction from your partner; or not providing information because of a fear of how your partner might potentially use the information (such as sharing the information with other people)	• Not elaborating on the parts of an auto engine when describing a car problem because you know your partner is knowledgeable about cars • Not telling someone you saw his or her lover with another because he or she would be hurt • Not mentioning your interest in a mutual friend because you know the listener would blab about it to the mutual friend
Adaptation Through Examples, Comparisons, and Analogies: Choosing messages you believe your partner will find relevant	• Describing a person who is not known by your partner by comparing the person to someone your partner knows • Explaining roller-blading by comparing it to ice skating because your partner is an avid ice skater
Adaptation Through Language Choice: Choosing or avoiding specific words because of the anticipated effect on your partner; consciously selecting words that you believe are understandable to your partner; or using words that have a unique meaning to you and your partner	• Using formal address in response to status differences: "Thank you, Professor Smith" • Using slang when the relationship is perceived as informal • Using nicknames, inside jokes, or teasing comments with close friends

Source: © Mark V. Redmond, 1994. Adapted with permission.

Taking an other-oriented approach to communication means considering the thoughts, feelings, background, perspectives, attitudes, and values of your partners and adjusting your interaction with them accordingly. Other-orientation leads to more effective interpersonal communication, regardless of whether you are dealing with someone in your family or a person from another country.

RECAP   Develop Skill to Adapt to Others

Develop flexibility	Learn to "go with the flow."
Become other-oriented	Put yourself in the other person's mental and emotional mindset; adapt to others; listen and respond appropriately.
Adapt your communication to others	Adjust your behaviour to others to accommodate differences and expectations.

APPLYING AN OTHER-ORIENTATION
to Diversity: The Platinum Rule

When interacting with someone who is dramatically different from you, if you want to be truly other-oriented, you may need to go beyond what is known to most Westerners as "The Golden Rule": "Do unto others as you would have others do unto you." Or, as succinctly stated by the Buddha, "Consider others as yourself." But when interacting with someone who is quite different from you, treating him or her as you'd like to be treated may not achieve relational benefits. If you like hip-hop music but your friend prefers Mozart, taking her to a Mos Def concert may make you feel good about following the Golden Rule (that's how *you'd* like to be treated)—but the concert might be painful for her if she'd rather be listening to Mozart's Horn Quintet in E flat, K. 407. Whether it's taste in music or food, greeting rituals, or a host of other culturally determined

behaviours, the ultimate other-oriented behaviour would be what communication researcher Milton Bennett calls the Platinum Rule: Do to others as they themselves would like to be treated.[27] Rather than treating people as *you* would like to be treated, interact with others the way you think *they* would like to be treated. According to Bennett, at its essence, empathy is "the imaginative, intellectual and emotional participation in another person's experience."[28] The goal, according to Bennett, is to attempt to think and feel what another person thinks and feels and to go beyond that by taking positive action toward others in response to your empathic feelings.

But is the Platinum Rule always helpful, or even possible? As you ponder the virtues and challenges of becoming other-oriented and adapting your communication behaviour to

enhance your intercultural communication competence, consider the following questions:

- Is the Platinum Rule always desirable? Are there situations when it would be inappropriate to follow the Platinum Rule? Explain your answer.

- What are some obstacles to applying the Platinum Rule, especially with people who are culturally different from you?

- How can the Platinum Rule be useful when you are having a disagreement with another person?

- Think about a time when you applied the Platinum Rule. What was the effect on the person with whom you were communicating?

Understanding Diversity: Describing Our Differences (pages 73–78)

OBJECTIVE ❶ Describe five human differences that influence communication.

Key Terms

sex *74*
gender *74*
race *75*

ethnicity *75*
discrimination *76*

Critical Thinking Questions

1. What type of diversity do you find on campus? In the workplace? In your community? Do you find that you communicate differently with people from different groups and cultures? Explain.

2. How have gender differences played a role in your own communication or interactions with others? Explain.

Activities

How well do you think you could predict someone's reactions to finding out that a parent or another close relative had just died? Rank each of the following from 1 (the person whose reaction you could predict most confidently) to 6 (the person whose reaction you'd be least confident about predicting).

a. _____ A close friend of your own sex, age, race, and cultural background

b. _____ A 60-year-old male Chinese farmer

c. _____ A university student 20 years older than you but of your own race, sex, and cultural background

d. _____ A 10-year-old Métis girl from Saskatoon

e. _____ A university student of a different race but your own age, cultural background, and sex

f. _____ A university student of the opposite sex but your own age, race, and cultural background

Which characteristics of each person do you believe provide the best information on which to base your judgments? Why? What would you need to know about each person to feel comfortable in making a prediction? How could you get that information?

Web Resources

www.yforum.com Visitors to the National Forum on People's Differences can ask questions about religion, culture, gender, ethnicity, sexual preference, or other topics that might be too personal or embarrassing to ask someone in person.

Understanding Culture: Dimensions of Our Mental Software (pages 78–82)

OBJECTIVE ❷ Define culture and identity and describe the six dimensions of culture.

Key Terms

culture *78*
world view *78*
co-culture *79*
enculturation *79*
acculturation *79*
cultural values *80*

cultural context *80*
high-context cultures *81*
low-context cultures *81*
masculine cultural values *81*
feminine cultural values *81*

Critical Thinking Questions

1. Name the co-cultures to which you belong. Would you describe your co-cultures as low- or high-context, masculine or feminine? Explain. What beliefs and norms characterize these co-cultures? What does your culture or co-culture value?

2. Is it ethical or appropriate for someone from one culture to attempt to change the cultural values of someone from a different culture? For example, Culture A practises polygamy, which means that one husband can be married to several wives. Culture B practises monogamy, which means that one husband can be married to only one wife. Should a person from Culture B attempt to make someone from Culture A change his or her ways? Why or why not?

Activities

Bring to class a fable, folktale, or children's story from a culture other than your own. As a group, analyze the cultural values implied by the story or characters in the story.

Barriers to Effective Intercultural Communication, and Improving Intercultural Communication Competence (pages 83–96)

OBJECTIVES ❸ ❹ List and describe barriers that inhibit effective intercultural communication, and identify and apply strategies to improve intercultural competence

Key Terms

intercultural
    communication *83*

culture shock *83*

ethnocentrism *84*

stereotype *85*

prejudice *86*

intercultural communication
    competence *88*

motivation *89*

skill *89*

third culture *90*

relational empathy *90*

mindful *92*

social decentring *93*

empathy *93*

adaptation *94*

communication
    accommodation theory *94*

adapt predictively *94*

adapt reactively *94*

Critical Thinking Questions

1. What is the problem in assuming that other people are like us? How does this create a barrier to effective intercultural communication?

2. Christine, a Canadian, has just been accepted as a foreign exchange student in Germany. What potential cultural barriers might she face? How should she manage these potential barriers?

3. What are appropriate ways to deal with someone who consistently utters racial slurs and demonstrates prejudice toward racial or ethnic groups? Using MySearchLab, find an article that suggests some ways to deal with this type of behaviour. Share your article and findings with your class or small group.

Activities

In small groups, identify examples from your own experiences of each barrier to effective intercultural communication discussed in the text. Use one of the examples as the basis for a skit to perform for the rest of the class. See whether the class can identify which intercultural barrier your group is depicting. Also, suggest how the skills and principles discussed in the chapter might have improved the communication in the situation you role-play.

Web Resources

http://chocd.umsl.edu The Connecting Human Origin and Cultural Diversity Program provides suggestions for the development of social justice and cultural awareness curricula.

© David Gilder/Shutterstock

5

Listening and Responding Skills

66We have two ears and one mouth so we may listen more and talk the less. **99** —Epictetus

Think about your best friend. What are some of the qualities you most admire in this person? Many people would respond that one of the most valued qualities in a friend is his or her just being there—supporting, comforting, and listening. As theologian Henri Nouwen so eloquently put it,

> Listening is much more than allowing another to talk while waiting for a chance to respond. Listening is paying full attention to others and welcoming them into our very beings.[1]

To say it more simply, friends listen. They listen even if we sometimes say foolish things. The skill of listening to others is one of the most important skills of interpersonal communication. Skilled communicators do more than impassively listen—they appropriately respond to what we say, confirming that they understand and care for us by providing both verbal and nonverbal feedback.

Listening and responding skills are important for several reasons. Some researchers suggest that because listening is the first communication skill we learn (because we respond to sounds even while in our mother's womb), it's also the most important skill. Listening plays a key role in helping us learn to speak.

Another reason listening is important: you spend more time listening than participating in any other communication activity. In fact, you spend more time listening to others than doing almost anything else. Typical North American college students spend more than 80% of an average day communicating with other people, and as the pie chart in Figure 5.1 shows, of the total time they spend communicating, 55% is spent listening to others.[2] Throughout your years in elementary school, high school, and post-secondary education, you have probably taken many courses designed to help you improve your written communication skills. Now, how much formal training have you had in listening? In this chapter, we focus on this often neglected, yet absolutely essential, skill for developing quality interpersonal relationships. Listening is the process by which people learn the most about others. In addition, we explore ways to respond appropriately to others.

listening. Selecting, attending to, constructing meaning from, remembering, and responding to verbal and nonverbal messages

hearing. The physiological process of decoding sounds.

selecting. The process of sorting through various sounds competing for your attention.

Listening Defined

"Did you hear what I said?" demands a father who has been lecturing his son on the importance of hanging up his clothes. In fact, the boy has heard him, but he may not have been listening. **Listening** is a complex process of selecting, attending to, constructing meaning from, remembering, and responding to verbal and nonverbal messages. When we listen, we hear words and try to make sense out of what we hear. The essence of being a good listener is being able to accurately interpret the messages expressed by others. **Hearing** is the physiological process of decoding sounds: sound vibrations reach your eardrum and cause the middle ear bones—the hammer, anvil, and stirrup—to move. Eventually, these sound vibrations are translated into electrical impulses that reach the brain. In order to listen to something, you must first (1) select that sound from competing sounds. Then you must (2) attend to it, (3) understand it, and (4) remember it. When you (5) respond to the sound, you confirm that listening—not merely hearing—has occurred.

Selecting

Selecting a sound is the process of choosing one sound from all the various sounds competing for your attention. As you listen to someone in an interpersonal context, you focus on the words and nonverbal messages of your

FIGURE 5.1

What You Do with Your Communication Time

partner. Even now, as you are reading this text, there are undoubtedly countless noises within earshot. Stop reading for a moment and sort through the various sounds around you. Do you hear music? Is there noise from outside? How about the murmur of voices, the tick of a clock, the hum of a computer, the whoosh of an air conditioner or furnace? To listen, you must select which of these sounds will receive your attention.

Attending

After selecting a sound, you then focus on or **attend** to it. You may attend to the sound for a moment and then move on or return to other thoughts or other sounds. As we discussed in Chapter 3, your attention is sometimes selective. Either consciously or unconsciously, you are more likely to attend to those messages that meet your needs and are consistent with your attitudes or interests. Information that is surprising or intense, or that somehow relates to you, may capture your attention. And conflict, humour, new ideas, and real or concrete things command your attention more easily than abstract theories that do not relate to your interests or needs.

Healthy family relations result when parents and children are able to develop people-oriented listening styles.

(© Dorothy Littell Greco/The Image Works)

Understanding

While hearing is a physiological phenomenon, **understanding** is the process of assigning meaning to the sounds you select and to which you attend. There are several theories about how you assign meaning to words you hear, but there is no universally accepted notion of how this process works. We know that people understand best if they can relate what they are hearing to something they already know. For this reason, the use of analogy and comparison is effective when explaining complex material or abstract ideas.

A second basic principle about how people understand others is that the greater the similarity between individuals, the greater the likelihood for more accurate understanding. Individuals from different cultures who have substantially different religions, family lifestyles, values, and attitudes often find it a challenge to understand each other, particularly in the early phases of a relationship.

attending. The process of focusing on a particular sound or message.

understanding. Assigning meaning to messages.

A third principle is that you understand best what you also experience. Perhaps you have heard the Montessori school philosophy: I hear, I forget; I see, I remember; I experience, I understand. Hearing alone does not create understanding. People hear over one billion words each year, but understand only a fraction of that number. Understanding happens when we derive meaning from the words we hear.

Remembering

Remembering is the process of recalling information. Some researchers theorize that you store every detail you have ever heard or witnessed; your mind operates like a computer's hard drive, but you cannot retrieve all the data. Have you ever found that you had no memory of what your professor covered in a particular lecture, even though you know you were in class that day?

Our brains have both short-term and long-term memory storage systems. Short-term memory is where you store almost all the information you hear. You look up a phone number, mumble it to yourself, and then something distracts you. A minute later, you have to look up the number again because it did not get stored in your long-term memory. Our short-term storage area is very limited. Just as airports have only a few short-term parking spaces but many spaces for long-term parking, our brains can accommodate only a few things of fleeting significance but many more pieces of important information. We forget hundreds of bits of insignificant information that pass through our brains each day.

The information we store in long-term memory includes events, conversations, and other data that are significant for us. We tend to remember dramatic and vital information, as well as seemingly inconsequential details connected with such information. Many Canadians have vivid memories of the day Justin Trudeau became Prime Minister, or the day NDP leader Jack Layton died, or the day Sidney Crosby scored the winning goal in the Canada–U.S. hockey game at the Vancouver Olympics.

Responding

Interpersonal communication is interactive; it involves both talking and **responding**. You respond to people to let them know you understand their messages. Responses can be nonverbal; direct eye contact and head nods let your partner know you're paying attention. Or you can respond verbally, by asking questions to confirm the content of the message ("Are you saying you don't want us to spend as much time together?") or by making statements that reflect the feelings of the speaker ("So you're frustrated that you have to wait for someone to drive you where you want to go"). We will discuss responding skills in more detail later in the chapter.

remembering. Recalling information that has been communicated.

responding. Confirming your understanding of a message.

▶ RECAP   What Is Listening?

Selecting	Sorting through various sounds that compete for your attention
Attending	Focusing on a particular sound or message
Understanding	Assigning meaning to messages
Remembering	Recalling information that has been communicated
Responding	Confirming your understanding of a message

Overcoming Contemporary Listening Challenges

Listening may be an even more important skill today than in the past. Why? There are two reasons: recorded messages and noise. Today's technology makes it increasingly likely that you will be listening to recorded messages. This is called *asynchronous listening*—listening to a message communicated at another time, when no one is available to receive it. Retrieving messages through voicemail is an example of asynchronous listening. Listening to recorded messages can be tricky because you can't stop the person to ask for clarification or to have information repeated. Without immediate feedback, there is greater potential for you to misunderstand a message. Yes, you can replay a message one or more times to make sure you understand it, but no matter how often you replay it, you'll never be able to ask for more details or for an example to help you understand the message. Yet another problem with asynchronous listening is that you are only *listening* to these recorded messages; you aren't *seeing* the person delivering the message. Without the nonverbal cues that you pick up when you can see the sender of a message, the true meaning of the message may be more elusive.

Another contemporary listening challenge is noise. The prevalence of smartphones and Bluetooth technology means that you may have more sounds competing for your attention, and this can sap your listening effectiveness. Perhaps even now, as you're reading this book, you hear music—either something you've selected as background for your reading or music from an out-of-sight but not out-of-earshot source. In addition, ring tones, pings indicating the arrival of a text or email message, electronic beeps from machines announcing that your clothes and dishes are washed, and other e-reminders punctuate our days and can be potential distractions as we listen to others. Fortunately, there are strategies that can help enhance your listening, whether the issue is noise or asynchronous listening.

Overcoming Asynchronous Listening Barriers. One of the things you can do to help manage the recorded messages you receive is to customize the recorded message that invites a caller to leave you a message. For example, your recorded message could remind callers to speak slowly or to repeat key information, such as phone numbers or email addresses. In addition, when you listen to your messages, do so when you're not distracted by other tasks. Trying to remember key information when driving, watching TV, or doing household chores makes listening even more difficult. Listen to your messages in a quiet place with pen and paper ready to capture key details that you'll need later. Of course, you can replay a message to make sure you get key information or to confirm that you've heard the message accurately.

Although recorded messages can be an efficient way of sharing simple information or confirming appointments, without feedback and the opportunity to seek clarification, a voice message is not conducive to managing relational conflict, especially when the topic under discussion is an emotional one. It is best to use the richest possible communication medium when dealing with difficult or sensitive topics.

Overcoming Noise Barriers. Often the solution to noise distractions is simple: get away from the noise. Turn off the music, shut off your cell phone, or move away from the distracting noise. In order to do that, you first need to be aware that noise is indeed noise. Because music and other audio distractions are everywhere, you may not be aware of their power to distract you. If someone else is the source of the noise, when appropriate, consider politely asking the person to keep it down, or to go elsewhere. Sometimes just being aware that the noise is causing a listening distraction allows you to take steps to create a calmer environment that is more conducive to effective listening.

Listening Styles

Although we've described the typical elements in the listening process, not everyone has the same style or approach to listening. Your **listening style** is your preferred way of making sense out of the messages you hear. Some people, for example, prefer to focus on facts and analyze the information they hear. Others seem more interested in focusing on the feelings and emotions expressed. What's your listening style? Knowing your style can help you adapt and adjust when listening to others. Listening researchers Debra Worthington, Graham Bodie, and Christopher Gearhart, building on the extensive work of other listening researchers, have found that people tend to listen using one or more of four listening styles: relational, analytic, critical, or task-oriented.[3]

listening style. Preferred way of making sense out of the spoken messages we listen to.

Relational Listening Style

Relational listeners tend to prefer listening to people's expressions of their emotions and feelings. A person with a relational listening style searches for common interests and seeks to empathize with the feelings of others—she or he connects emotionally with the sentiments and passions others express.[4] Relational listeners are less apprehensive when communicating with others in small groups and interpersonal situations.[5]

Research shows that relational listeners have a greater tendency to be sympathetic to the person they are listening to.[6] A sympathetic listener is more likely to voice concern for the other person's welfare when that person is sharing personal information or news about a stressful situation. A sympathetic listener says things like "Oh, Pat, I'm so sorry to hear about your loss. You must feel so lonely and sad." There is evidence that relational listeners may be more empathic; they seem to have greater skill in understanding the thoughts and feelings of others.[7] One study found that jurors who are relational listeners are less likely to find the plaintiff at fault in a civil court trial, perhaps because of their tendency to empathize with others.[8]

Analytical Listening Style

Analytical listeners focus on facts and tend to withhold judgment before reaching a specific conclusion. They would make good judges because they generally consider all sides of an issue before making a decision or reaching a conclusion. Analytical listeners tend to listen to an entire message before assessing the validity of the information they hear. To help analyze information, they take the perspective of the person to whom they are listening; this helps them suspend judgment. They also like information to be well organized so that they can clearly and easily analyze it. While listening to a rambling personal story, the analytical listener focuses on the facts and details rather than on the emotions being expressed. Analytical listeners prefer listening to rich message content and then find ways of organizing or making sense out of the information.

Critical Listening Style

Critical listeners are good at evaluating information they hear. They are able to hone in on inconsistencies in what someone says. They are comfortable listening to detailed, complex information and focusing on the facts, yet they are especially adept in noting contradictions in the facts presented. Critical listeners are also likely to catch errors in the overall logic and reasoning that is being used to reach a conclusion.

Critical listeners tend to be a bit more skeptical than relational listeners about the information they hear. Researchers call this skepticism **second-guessing**—questioning the assumptions underlying a message.[9] It's called second-guessing because instead of assuming that what they hear is accurate or relevant, listeners make a second guess about the accuracy of the information they are listening to. Accuracy of information is especially important to critical listeners, because if they are going to use the information in some way, it should be valid.

Task-Oriented Listening Style

Task-oriented listeners are interested in focusing more on achieving a specific outcome or accomplishing a task than on focusing on the communication relationship when they are listening to others. They emphasize completing a specific transaction, such as solving a problem, taking action, or making a purchase. The task-oriented listener focuses on verbs—what needs to be done. Consequently, they don't like to listen to rambling, descriptive messages that don't seem to have a point. They appreciate efficient communicators who are sensitive to how much time is involved in delivering a message. They also like messages to be well organized so that they can focus on the outcomes. Task-oriented listeners want to do

relational listeners. Those who prefer to focus on the emotions and feelings communicated verbally and nonverbally by others.

analytical listeners. Those who withhold judgment, listen to all sides of an issue, and wait until they hear the facts before reaching a conclusion.

critical listeners. Those who prefer to listen for the facts and evidence to support key ideas and an underlying logic; they also listen for errors, inconsistencies, and discrepancies.

second-guessing. Questioning the ideas and assumptions underlying a message; assessing whether the message is true or false.

task-oriented listeners. Those who are focused on achieving a specific outcome or accomplishing a task; they emphasize completing a specific transaction.

something with the information they hear; they want it to serve a purpose or function; and they become impatient with information that doesn't seem to have a "bottom line."

Understanding Your Listening Style

How does knowing about listening styles benefit you? For one, knowing your own listening style can help you adapt and adjust to the listening situation. If, for example, you are a relational listener and you're listening to a message that has little information about people but many technical details, be aware that you will have to work harder to stay tuned in to the message.

Also, it can be useful to be aware of the listening styles of others so you can communicate messages they are more likely to listen to. If you know your spouse is an analytical listener, then communicate a message that is rich in information; that's what your spouse prefers. Tell the analytical listener, "Here are three things I have to tell you." Then say them. The information preview tells your analytical listener that you are about to convey three pieces of information. Of course, it may be difficult to determine someone's listening style, especially if you don't know him or her very well. But it is both easier and worth the time to consider the listening styles of people you *do* know well (your family members, your coworkers, your boss). Knowing your own and others' listening styles can help you adapt your communication to enhance the accuracy of your own listening and the appropriateness of the way in which you communicate to others.

Listening Barriers

Even though we spend so much of our communication time listening, most of us don't listen as well as we should. Twenty-four hours after we hear a speech, a class lecture, or a sermon, we forget more than half of what was said. Within another 24 hours, we forget half of what we remembered, so we really remember only a quarter of the lecture.

Our interpersonal listening skills may be even worse. When you listen to a speech or lecture, you have a clearly defined listening role; one person talks, and you are expected to listen. However, in interpersonal situations, you may have to alternate quickly between speaking and listening. This takes considerable skill and concentration. Often you are thinking of what you want to say next rather than listening.

Most interpersonal listening problems can be traced to a single source: ourselves. While listening to others, we also "talk" to ourselves. Our internal thoughts are like a play-by-play sportscast. We mentally comment on the words and sights that we select and to which we attend. If we keep those comments focused on the message, they may be useful, but we often attend to our own internal dialogues instead of to others' messages. Then our listening effectiveness plummets.

Inattentive listening is a bit like channel surfing when we watch TV—switching from channel to channel, avoiding things that don't interest us, and focusing for brief periods on attention-grabbing program "bites." When we listen to others, we may fleetingly tune in to the conversation for a moment, decide that the content is uninteresting, and then focus on a personal thought. These thoughts are barriers to communication, and they come in a variety of forms. Let's explore several listening barriers that keep us from catching others' meaning.

Information overload can prevent us from being able to communicate effectively with people around us.
(© auremar/Fotolia)

Self-Absorption

Self-absorbed listeners are focused on their needs rather than those of their communication partner; to them, the message is about themselves alone, not the other person. During conversations with a self-absorbed communicator, it is difficult sustaining communication about anything except the self-absorbed partner's ideas, experiences, and stories. This problem is also called **conversational narcissism**. To be narcissistic is to be in love with oneself, as was the mythical Greek character Narcissus, who fell in love with his own reflection in a pool of water.

The self-absorbed listener is actively involved in doing several things other than listening and is much more likely to interrupt others in mid-sentence, often in search of ways to focus the attention on him- or herself. The self-absorbed listener is also not focusing on his or her partner's message but is instead thinking about what he or she is going to say next. This focus on an internal message can keep a listener from selecting and attending to the other person's message.

How do you control this listening problem in yourself? First, diagnose it. Note consciously when you find yourself drifting off, thinking about your agenda, or looking at your phone rather than concentrating on the speaker. Second, work on strengthening your powers of concentration when you find that your internal messages are distracting you from listening well.

Unchecked Emotions

Words are powerful symbols that affect our attitudes, our behaviour, and even our blood pressure. Words arouse us emotionally, which can also affect us physically. **Emotional noise** occurs when our emotions interfere with communication effectiveness. If you grew up in a home in which swearing was forbidden, then four-letter words may be distracting to you. Words that insult your religious, ethnic, or sexual identity can also provoke an intense emotional reaction.

Sometimes it is not specific words but rather concepts or ideas that cause an emotional eruption. Some talk-radio hosts try to boost their ratings by purposely using language that elicits passionate responses. Although listening to such conflict can be interesting and entertaining, when your own emotions become aroused, you may lose your ability to listen effectively. Strong emotions can interfere with focusing on the message of another.

The emotional state of the speaker may also affect your ability to understand and evaluate what you hear. If you are listening to someone who is emotionally distraught, you will be more likely to focus on his or her emotions than on the content of the message. When you are communicating with someone who is emotionally excited, you should remain calm and focused, and try simply to communicate your interest in the other person.

Your listening challenge is to avoid emotional sidetracks and to keep your attention focused on the message. When your internal dialogue is kicked into high gear by objectionable words or concepts, or by an emotional speaker, make an effort to quiet it down and steer back to the subject at hand.

Criticizing the Speaker

The trapdoor spider is an ambush predator; it lurks unseen in its burrow, waiting to jump out and devour unsuspecting prey as it passes by. Perhaps you know someone who is an **ambush listener**. This is a person who is quick to pounce on the speaker to argue, criticize, or find fault with what the other person has said. Although the ambush listener may look as if she or he is listening, in reality this type of listener is just waiting for an opportunity to attack or criticize the speaker.

Being critical of a speaker may distract us from focusing on their message. Superficial factors such as clothing, body size and shape, age, and ethnicity all affect our interpretation

---

BEING Other-ORIENTED

When someone "pushes your hot buttons" and you find yourself becoming emotionally upset, what can you do to calm yourself and remain centred? First, simply be aware that you are becoming emotionally upset. Then take action (such as focusing on your breathing) to lower the tension you are feeling. What are other strategies to help you remain calm when someone "pushes your buttons"?

---

conversational narcissism. Focusing on personal agendas and being self-absorbed rather than focusing on the needs and ideas communicated by others.

emotional noise. Emotional arousal that interferes with communication effectiveness.

ambush listener. A person who is overly critical and judgmental when listening to others.

ADAPTING TO DIFFERENCES
Understanding Others | Who Listens Better, Men or Women?

Research provides no definitive answer to this question. There is evidence, however, that men and women listen differently and have different expectations about the role of listening and talking. According to language expert Deborah Tannen, one of the most common complaints wives have about their husbands is "He doesn't listen to me anymore." Complaints about lack of communication are usually at the top of women's lists of reasons for divorce but are mentioned much less often by men. Why are women often more dissatisfied with the listening and talking process than men? Tannen's explanation: women and men expect different things from conversations.[10]

Different Attention Styles. Research suggests that men and women may have different attention styles.[11] When men listen, they may be looking for a new structure or organizational pattern, or to separate bits of information they hear. They continually shape, form, observe, inquire, and direct energy toward a chosen goal. Women are described as more subjective, empathic, and emotionally involved as they listen. They are more likely to search for relationships among parts of a pattern and to rely on more intuitive perceptions of feelings. They are also more easily distracted by competing details. These differences in attention styles and the way men and women process information can potentially affect listening, even though we have no direct evidence linking attention style to listening skill.

Different Listening Goals. There may also be gender-related differences in listening goals. There is evidence that when men listen, they are more likely to listen to solve a problem; men tend to be more instrumental and task-oriented, while women may listen to enhance understanding.[12]

What does this research imply about both attention styles and listening goals? It may mean that men and women focus on different parts of messages and have different listening objectives. In any case, gender-based differences in attention style and information processing can affect relationship development and may account for some of the relational problems experienced by husbands and wives, lovers, siblings, and male and female friends.

Different Listening Focus. There may also be gender differences in the way people focus on a listening task. Research suggests that men are more likely to have difficulty attending to multiple messages; when they are focused on one message, they may have more difficulty than women in carrying on a conversation with another person. Men have a tendency to lock on to a single message, whereas women seem more adept at shifting between two or more simultaneous messages.[13]

Different Listening Perceptions. Although it may seem that men and women have somewhat different approaches to listening, it is still not clear whether men and women are really that different when it comes to relating to

one another. Communication researchers Stephanie Sargent and James Weaver suggest that pop psychology conclusions, which erroneously promote dramatic differences between the way men and women listen, may simply be perpetuating stereotypes of the way men and women *think* they are supposed to listen.[14] Although there is research that suggests men and women may differ somewhat in the way they respond to information, the difference may not be based in a person's biological sex; it is more likely a reflection of gender differences (socially constructed cultural or co-cultural learned approaches).

So when it comes to enhancing communication and listening to one another, it is best to start not from the position that men and women are from different planets, but rather from the position that they share common needs.

BIZARRO © 2008 Dan Piraro. Dist. by King Features Syndicate.

of a message. It is important to monitor your internal dialogue to make sure you are focusing on the message rather than criticizing the messenger. Good listeners say to themselves, "While it may be distracting, I am simply not going to let the appearance of this speaker keep my attention from the message."

Differing Speech Rate and Thought Rate

Your ability to think faster than people speak is another listening pitfall. The average person speaks at a rate of 125 words a minute. Some folks talk a bit faster, others more slowly. In contrast, your brain can process up to 600 or 800 words a minute. The difference between

Are Cell Phones in the Classroom a Valuable Learning Tool or an Unnecessary Distraction?

There is no doubt that cell phones make it easier to communicate with our families and friends. However, anyone who has had a conversation with someone who is simultaneously texting someone else, reading emails, or watching a video on their smartphone knows cell phones can distract users from face-to-face communication. And most of us have had the frustrating experience of trying to focus on a movie in a darkened theatre only to have our attention drawn toward the lit-up phone screens of moviegoers who seem compelled to text, tweet, or email throughout the movie.

So, with their potential for distraction, should cell phones be allowed in Canadian classrooms?

In September 2010, Ontario's then premier, Dalton McGuinty, caused a controversy when he stated his opinion that Ontario schools should be open to using cell phones in the classroom. "Telephones and BlackBerrys and the like are conduits for information today, and one of the things we want to do is to be well-informed," he said. Andrea Horwath, then leader of the NDP, argued that allowing cell phones in schools would hinder students' learning, saying, "I have a son and he's distracted enough already."[15]

While the rest of Canada has always left the decision of whether to allow handheld devices in the classroom up to individual principals and teachers, until September 2011, the Toronto District School Board, Canada's largest, had a policy banning cell phones from classrooms. Although the board-wide ban was lifted, many schools still implement policies banning phones.

Some educators and educational researchers see the potential of cell phones and smartphones as learning tools, allowing students to take notes, look up information, and interact with teachers and classmates. However, many teachers are skeptical about the usefulness of the devices for learning, instead seeing them as a harmful distraction. And, surprisingly, many students agree. A recent survey conducted by the Ontario Student Trustees' Association found that 72% of Ontario high school students surveyed don't want cell phones to be used as classroom learning tools. Zane Schwartz, a grade 12 student and student trustee with the Toronto District School Board, says that students use phones "to text or communicate with friends. It's a great communication tool, not necessarily an educational tool." Natalie Rizzo, also in grade 12 and a student trustee for the Toronto Catholic District School Board, says that while phones would provide opportunities for classroom research, "at the end of the day, nothing is better than face-to-face learning and I guess it would be a distraction or something students don't think is necessary."[16]

your mental ability to handle words and the speed at which they arrive at your cortical centres can cause you to daydream and tune the speaker in and out, giving you the illusion that you are concentrating more attentively than you actually are.

You can turn your listening speed into an advantage if you use the extra time instead to summarize what a speaker is saying. By periodically creating mental summaries during a conversation, you can dramatically increase your listening ability and make the speech-rate/thought-rate difference work to your advantage.

Information Overload

We live in an information-rich age. We are all constantly bombarded with sights and sounds, and experts suggest that the volume of information competing for our attention is likely to become even greater in the future. Incoming messages and information on computers, cell phones, and other technological devices can interrupt conversations and distract us from listening to each other.

Be on the alert for these information interruptions when you are talking with others. Don't assume that because you are ready to talk, the other person is ready to listen. If your message is particularly sensitive or important, you may want to ask your listening partner, "Is this a good time to talk?" Even if he or she says yes, look for eye contact and a responsive facial expression to make sure the positive response is genuine.

External Noise

As you will recall, the communication models we saw in Chapter 1 all include the element of noise—distractions that take your focus away from the message. Many households seem to be addicted to noise. Often there is a TV on (sometimes more than one), a computer game beeping, and music emanating from another room. These and other sounds compete for your attention when you are listening to others.

Besides literal noise, there are other potential sources of distraction. A tweet about the latest details in a political scandal may "shout" for your attention just when your son wants to talk with you about his day at school. A desire to listen to the podcast you just downloaded may drown out your partner's attempts to discuss your finances. The Internet, music, TV, books, and video games can all lure you away from more important listening tasks.

Distractions make it difficult to sustain attention to a message; however, you can make a choice: you can attempt to listen through the labyrinth of competing distractions, or you can modify the environment to reduce them. Putting down your phone or iPad and establishing eye contact with the speaker can help to minimize the noise barrier.

Listener Apprehension

Not only do some people become nervous and apprehensive about speaking to others, but some are also anxious about listening to others. **Listener apprehension** is the fear of misunderstanding or misinterpreting, or of not being able to adjust psychologically to messages spoken by others. Because some people are nervous or worried about missing the message, they *do* misunderstand the message; their fear and apprehension keep them from absorbing it. If you are one of those people who are nervous when listening, you may experience difficulty understanding all you hear.

If you're an apprehensive listener, you will have to work harder when you listen to others. When listening to a public speech, it may be acceptable to record it or to start taking notes; it's usually not appropriate to make a recording or take notes during interpersonal conversations. If you're on the phone, you can take notes when you listen to help you remember the message content, but recording phone conversations without the other speaker's consent is unethical and illegal. Whether you're face to face with the speaker or on the phone, what you can do is try to mentally summarize the message as you're listening to it. Concentrating on the message in this way can help take your mind off your anxiety and help you focus on the message.

listener apprehension.
The fear of misunderstanding, misinterpreting, or being unable to adjust to the spoken messages of others.

▶ RECAP   Overcoming Barriers to Listening

Listening Barriers	To Overcome the Barrier:
Self-absorption	Consciously become aware of your internal focus and shift attention.
Unchecked emotions	Use self-talk to manage emotions.
Criticizing the speaker	Focus on the message, not the messenger.
Differing speech and thought rate	Use the difference between speech rate and thought rate to mentally summarize the message.
Information overload	Realize when you are—or when your partner is—tired or distracted and not ready to listen.
External noise	Take charge of the listening environment by eliminating distractions.
Listener apprehension	Concentrate on the message as you mentally summarize what you hear.

Improving Your Listening Skills

Many of the listening problems we have identified stem from focusing on ourselves rather than on the messages of others. Dale Carnegie, in his classic book *How to Win Friends and Influence People*, offered this tip to enhance interpersonal relationships: "Focus first on being interested, not interesting."[17] In essence, he was affirming the importance of being other-oriented when listening to others.

You can begin improving your listening skills by following three steps you probably first encountered in elementary school—(1) stop, (2) look, and (3) listen—and then two more: (4) ask questions and (5) reflect content by paraphrasing. Simple as they may seem, these steps can provide the necessary structure to help you refocus your mental energies and improve your listening power. Let's consider each step separately.

Stop

What should you *not* do in order to be a better listener? You should stop attending to "self-talk." Your internal, self-generated messages may distract you from giving your undivided attention to what others are saying.

We tend to place more importance on speaking than on being silent and waiting for someone to speak.[18] Yet we need silence in order to truly listen to, understand, and connect with the other person. Silence is indeed golden in that it provides the space for the other person to connect and be accepted.

Most interpersonal listening problems can be traced to a single source—ourselves. While listening to others, we also "talk" to ourselves. Our internal thoughts are like a play-by-play sportscast. We mentally comment on the words and sights that we select and to which we attend. If we keep those mental comments focused on the message, they may be useful. But we often attend to our own internal monologues instead of to others' messages, causing our listening effectiveness plummets. Two listening researchers conducted a study to identify the specific behaviours of good listeners. What they discovered supports our advice that the first thing you have to do be a better listener is to stop focusing on your own mental messages. Specifically, you should take the following actions during what the researchers called the "pre-interaction phase" of listening.

- Put your own thoughts and biases aside.
- Be there mentally as well as physically.
- Make a conscious, mindful effort to listen.
- Take adequate time to listen; don't rush the speaker; be patient.
- Be open-minded.[19]

It boils down to this: when you listen, you are either on-task or off-task. When you are on-task, you are concentrating on the message; when you're off-task, your mind may be a thousand miles away. What's important is to be mindful of what you are doing. You can increase your motivation to listen by reminding yourself of why the information you are listening to important.

Two researchers studied how to enhance the performance of "professional listeners" who work in call centres—places where customers call to order products, make product suggestions, or even offer complaints.[20] They found that customers preferred listeners who were focused and communicated that they were devoting their full attention to the caller. Specially trained listeners who avoided distractions, honed in on the essence of a caller's message, and stopped to focus on what the callers were telling them increased customers' confidence and satisfaction in the speaker–listener relationship. The researchers also concluded that the ability to stop and focus on the comments of others can be taught. People who learn how to stop mental distractions can improve their listening comprehension.

Look

Nonverbal messages are powerful. As the primary ways in which we communicate feelings, emotions, and attitudes, they play a major role in the total communication process, particularly in the development of relationships. Facial expressions and vocal cues, as well as eye contact, posture, and use of gestures and movement, can dramatically colour the meaning of a message. When the nonverbal message contradicts the verbal message, we almost always believe the nonverbal message.

Accurately interpreting nonverbal messages can help you "listen between the lines" by noting what someone is not saying verbally but expressing nonverbally. By attending to your partner's unspoken message, you are looking for the **meta-message**—the message about the message. Meta communication, as you learned in Chapter 1, is communication about communication. The nonverbal meta-message provides a source of information about the emotional and relational impact of what a speaker may be expressing with the verbal message. For example, a friend may not explicitly say that he or she is angry, upset, or irritated, but his or her nonverbal cues let you know that your friend is not happy. You take in more information when you listen with your eyes as well as your ears.

Another reason to look at someone is to establish eye contact, which signals that you are focusing your interest and attention on him or her. If your eyes are glancing over your partner's head, looking for someone else, or if you are constantly peeking at your watch, your partner will rightfully get the message that you're not really listening. We often signal our desire to change roles from listener to speaker by increasing our eye contact or shifting our posture to appear more alert. It is important to maintain eye contact and monitor your partner's nonverbal signals when you are speaking as well as listening.

It is also important, however, not to be distracted by nonverbal cues that may prevent us from interpreting the message correctly. Do pay attention to the speaker's facial expressions, gestures, and posture, but don't let these nonverbal behaviours distract you from what the speaker is saying.

Listen

After making a concerted effort to stop distracting internal dialogue and to look for nonverbal cues, you will then be in a better position to understand the verbal messages of others. Listening involves more than merely focusing on facts; it involves searching for the essence of the speaker's thoughts.

Research suggests that effective listeners are active rather than passive when listening. For example, during the normal course of actively listening to another person, effective listeners

- just listen—they do not interrupt

- respond appropriately and provide both verbal feedback ("Yes, I see," "I'm not sure I understand") and nonverbal feedback (eye contact, nodding, frowning)

- make appropriate contributions to the conversation

Effective listeners are not only goal-oriented (listening for the point of the message) but are also people-oriented (listening to appropriately affirm the person). To maximize your listening effectiveness, we offer the following specific strategies and tips:

1. *Determine your listening goal.* You listen to other people for several reasons—to learn, to enjoy yourself, to evaluate, or to provide empathic support. With so many potential listening goals and options, it is useful to decide consciously what your listening objective is.

   If you are listening to someone give you directions to the park, then your mental summaries should focus on the details of when to turn left and how many streets past the stoplight you go before you turn right. These details are crucial to achieving your objective. If, in contrast, your neighbour is telling you about her father's triple bypass operation, then your goal is to empathize. Your job is to listen patiently and to provide

meta-message. A message about a message; the message a person is expressing via non verbal means (such as by facial expression, eye contact, or posture) about the message articulated with words.

emotional support; it is probably not important that you be able to recall when her father checked into the hospital or other details. Clarifying your listening objective in your own mind can help you use appropriate skills to maximize your listening effectiveness.

2. *Transform listening barriers into listening goals.* If you can transform the listening barriers you read about earlier into listening goals, you will be well on your way to improving your listening skills. Possible goals include not focusing on your personal agenda, using self-talk to manage emotional noise, and not criticizing the speaker. Remind yourself before each conversation to do mental summaries that capitalize on the differences between your information processing rate and the speaker's verbal delivery rate. In addition, make it your business to choose a communication environment that is free of distraction from other incoming information or noise.

3. *Mentally summarize the details of the message.* This suggestion may seem to contradict the suggestion to avoid focusing only on facts, but if your goal is to be able to recall information, it is important to have a grasp of the details your partner provides. As we noted earlier, you can process words much more quickly than a person speaks. So, periodically, summarize the names, dates, and locations in the message. Organize the speaker's factual information into appropriate categories or try to place events in chronological order. Without a full understanding of the details, you will likely miss the speaker's major point.

4. *Mentally weave these summaries into a focused major point or series of major ideas.* Facts usually make the most sense when we can use them to help support an idea or major point. So, as you summarize, try to link the facts you have organized in your mind with key ideas and principles. Use the facts to enhance your critical thinking as you analyze, synthesize, evaluate, and finally summarize the key points or ideas your listening partner is making.

5. *Practise listening to challenging material.* To improve or maintain any skill, you need to practise it. Listening experts suggest that listening skills deteriorate if people do not practise what they know. Listening to difficult, challenging material can sharpen listening skills, so good listeners practise by listening to documentaries, debates, and other challenging material rather than sitcoms and material that entertains but does not engage them mentally.

▶ RECAP   How to Improve Your Listening Skills

Listening Skill	Definition	Action
Stop	Tune out distracting, competing messages.	Become conscious of being distracted; use self-talk to remain focused.
Look	Become aware of the speaker's nonverbal cues; monitor your own nonverbal cues to communicate your interest in the speaker.	Establish eye contact; avoid fidgeting or performing other tasks when someone is speaking to you. Listen with your eyes.
Listen	Create meaning from your partner's verbal and nonverbal messages.	Mentally summarize details; link these details with main ideas.

Improving Empathic Listening Skills

Listening involves more than merely comprehending the words of others; it's also about understanding and experiencing the feelings and emotions expressed. Cultivating **empathy**—feeling what someone else is feeling—is at the core of being other-oriented. When you have had a bad day—perhaps you failed an exam, or had a fight with your

empathy. Understanding and experiencing the feelings of another.

partner—you may seek out a friend or family member to talk about it. You're not necessarily looking for solutions to your problems; you just want someone to focus attention on you, to listen, and to care about what you are saying. You are seeking someone who will empathize.

How do you enhance your empathic listening skills? First, try to imagine what the other person may be thinking; this process is called *social decentring*. Second, try to feel what the other person may be feeling; this process is called *empathizing*.

Imagine What Your Partner Is Thinking. As noted in Chapter 4, **social decentring** is a *cognitive process* in which you take into account another person's thoughts, values, background, and perspectives as you interact with him or her. This process involves viewing the world from the other person's point of view. The greater the difference between you and your communication partner, the more difficult it is to accomplish social decentring.

There are three ways to socially decentre: (1) Develop an understanding of another person based on how you have responded when something similar has happened to you, (2) base your understanding on knowledge you have about the specific person, or (3) make generalizations about someone based on your understanding of how you think most people would behave.[21]

Imagine What Your Partner Is Feeling. As we've noted, empathy is an *emotional reaction* that is similar to the one being experienced by another person. In contrast to social decentring, which is a cognitive reaction to what the other person is experiencing, empathizing is feeling what the other person feels. Empathy is not a single skill but rather a collection of skills, including compassionate listening and active listening, that help you predict how others will respond.

Compassionate Listening Diana Rehling suggests that **compassionate listening**— being open, nonjudgmental, and nondefensive—is a needed approach to listening to combat feelings of isolation, separation, and loneliness.[22] Listening with passion or acceptance takes empathic listening one step further because the listener is not only trying to experience the emotional response of others, but also accepting it, honoring it, and compassionately trying to confirm the worth of the other person. There is clear evidence that being empathic is linked to being a better listener.[23] Your ability to empathize with others is influenced by your personality and how you were raised, as well as by your listening habits and your skill level. For example, boys whose fathers are affectionate and nurturing grow up with a greater capacity for empathy. There is also evidence that boys whose fathers are less affectionate toward them may have a tendency to compensate for the lack of close nurturing from their dads by expressing more affection toward their sons.[24] So your capacity for empathy is both learned—based on your experiences, especially with your parents—and part of your nature.

social decentring. A cognitive process in which we take into account another person's thoughts, feelings, values, background, and perspectives.

compassionate listening. Open, nonjudgmental, nondefensive listening.

RECAP   How to Be an Empathic Listener

What to Do	How to Do It
Social decentring: A cognitive process of thinking about the other person's thoughts, values, background, and perspectives	• Think how you would react in the given situation.
Empathizing: An emotional reaction similar to the emotion being experienced by another person	• Think how the other person would react, based on what you know about his or her previous experiences and behavior.
	• Stop focusing on your own thoughts and needs and imagine what the other person is feeling.
	• Look for nonverbal cues that express emotion.
	• Listen for the meaning of words and the meaning behind the words.
	• Respond actively, not passively.
	• Experience the emotion of the other person.

Building Your Skills

Enhancing Listening by Identifying the Major Idea and Details of a Message

How skilled are you at noting both the major ideas and details of a message? To become a skilled listener, you must know how to identify both. How do you do that?

- First, identify the major idea as you listen. Ask yourself, "What is the key idea? What does this person want or expect from me?" Or, "Is there one main idea or are several ideas jumbled together?" Consider: Is your goal to *remember* the information, *take some action, empathize* with the speaker, or *just listen* to reflect and be a sounding board.?

- Second, identify the overall emotional tone of the message. Is the speaker calm, angry, happy, peaceful, upset? Assessing the emotion of the speaker can help you identify the speaker's purpose.

- Third, try to identify the overall organizational pattern. Is the speaker telling a story in chronological order? Is the message organized around general topics? Or is the speaker elaborating on reasons that something is true or false? Perhaps there is no logical organization in which case you'll have to find a way to organize the ideas in your own mind.

- Fourth, identify the specific details or essential pieces of information that help tell the story or make the speaker's point. You can better chunk the message into manageable details if you know what the overarching story or key idea is.

- Finally, link the details you hear with what seems to be the speaker's purpose. Linking details with the major idea will both help you remember the details and confirm your understanding of the main point of the message.

Here's a chance to practice your skill in identifying and remembering bits of information, as well as the main meaning of a message. Read each of the following statements. After you have read each statement, cover it with your hand or a piece of paper.

First, list as many of the details as you can recall from the message. Second, summarize your understanding of the major idea or key point of the message. As a variation on this activity, rather than reading the statement, have someone read the statement to you, and then identify the details and major idea.

Statement 1: "I'm very confused. I reserved our conference room for 1 p.m. today for an important meeting. We all know that conference space is tight. I reserved the room last week with the administrative assistant. Now I learn that you are planning to use the conference room at noon for a two-hour meeting. It's now 11 a.m. We need to solve this problem soon. I have no other option for holding my meeting. And if I don't hold my meeting today, the boss is going to be upset."

Statement 2: "Hello, Marcia? I'm calling on my cell phone. Where are you? I thought you were supposed to meet me at the circle drive 45 minutes ago. You know I can't be late for my seminar this evening. What do you mean, you're waiting at the circle drive? I don't see you. No, I'm at Switzler Hall circle drive. You're where? No, that's not the circle drive I meant. I thought you'd know where I meant. Don't you ever listen? If you hurry, I can just make it to the seminar."

Statement 3: "Oh, Mary, I just don't know what to do. My daughter announced that when she turns 18 next week she's going to shave her head, get a large tattoo, and put a ring in her nose and eyebrow. She said it's something she's always wanted to do and now she can do it without my permission. She's always been such a sweet, compliant girl, but she seems to have turned wacky. I've tried talking with her. And her father isn't much help. He thinks it may look 'cool.' I just don't want her to look like a freak when she has her senior picture taken next month."

Improving Critical Listening Skills

After putting it off for several months, you've decided to buy a new cell phone. As you begin to talk to your friends, you find a bewildering number of factors to consider: Do you want a prepaid plan? A plan that includes text messaging? Do you want to be able to check email and surf the web? Receive TV signals? How many weekend minutes, evening minutes, or daily minutes of calling time do you need? You decide to head to a store to see if a salesperson can help you sort through the maze of options. The salesperson is friendly enough, but you become even more overwhelmed with the number of options to consider. As you try to make this decision, your listening goal is not to empathize with those who extol the virtues of cell phones. Nor do you need to take a multiple-choice test on the information they share. To sort through the information, you need to listen critically.

critical listening. Listening in which the goal is to evaluate and assess the quality, appropriateness, value, or importance of information.

Critical listening involves listening to evaluate the quality, appropriateness, value, or importance of the information you hear. *The goal of a critical listener is to use information to* *make a choice.* Whether you're selecting a new phone, deciding whom to vote for, choosing a potential date, or evaluating a new business plan, you will be faced with many opportunities to use your critical listening skills in interpersonal situations.

Assess Information Quality. A critical listener seeks to identify both good information and information that is flawed or less helpful. We call this process *information triage. Triage* is a French term that usually describes the process used by emergency medical personnel to determine which of several patients is the most severely ill or injured and needs immediate medical attention. **Information triage** is a process of evaluating and sorting out information. An effective critical listener performs information triage; he or she is able to distinguish useful and accurate information and conclusions from information that is less useful and conclusions that are inaccurate or invalid.

How do you develop the ability to perform information triage? Initially, listening critically involves the same strategies as listening to comprehend, which we discussed earlier. Before you evaluate information, it's vital that you first *understand* the information. Second, examine the logic or reasoning used in the message. And finally, be mindful of whether you are basing your evaluations on facts (something observed or verifiable) or inference (a conclusion based on partial information).

Avoid Jumping to Conclusions. Imagine that you are a detective investigating a death. You are given the following information: (1) Leo and Moshia are found lying together on the floor; (2) Leo and Moshia are both dead; (3) Leo and Moshia are surrounded by water and broken glass; (4) on the sofa near Leo and Moshia is a cat with its back arched, apparently ready to defend itself.

Given these sketchy details, do you, the detective assigned to the case, have any theories about the cause of Leo and Moshia's demise? Perhaps they slipped on the water, crashed into a table, broke a vase, and died (that would explain the water and broken glass). Or maybe their attacker recently left the scene, and the cat is still distressed by the commotion. Clearly, you could make several inferences (conclusions based on partial information) as to the probable cause of death. Oh yes, there is one detail we forgot to mention: Leo and Moshia are fish. Does that help?

People often spin grand explanations and hypotheses based on incomplete information. Making inferences, people may believe that the "facts" clearly point to a specific conclusion. Determining the difference between a fact and an inference can help you more accurately use language to reach valid conclusions about what you see and experience.

What makes a fact a fact? Most people, when asked this question, respond by saying, "A fact is something that has been proven true." If that is the case, *how* has something been proven true? In a court of law, a **fact** is something that has been observed or witnessed. Anything else is speculation or inference.

> "Did you see my client in your house, taking your jewellery?" asks the defendant's clever attorney.
>
> "No," says the plaintiff.
>
> "Then you do not know for a fact that my client is a thief."
>
> "I guess not," the plaintiff admits.

Problems occur when we respond to something as if it were a fact (something observed) when in reality it is an **inference** (a conclusion based on speculation):

> "It's a fact that you will be poor all your life."
>
> "It's a fact that you will fail this course."

information triage. Process of evaluating information to sort good information from less useful or less valid information.

fact. Something that has been directly observed to be true and thus has been proven to be true.

inference. Conclusion based on speculation.

Both of these statements, although they may very well be true, misuse the term *fact*. If you cannot recognize when you are making an inference instead of stating a fact, you may give your judgments more credibility than they deserve. Being sensitive to the differences between facts and inferences can improve both critical listening and responding skills.

Improving Your Responding Skills

We've offered several strategies for responding to others when your goal is to comprehend information, empathize with others, or evaluate messages. Regardless of your communication goal, we'll now present several additional strategies to enhance your skill in responding to others. To respond effectively to others, consider the timing of the response, usefulness of the information, amount of detail, and descriptiveness of the response.

Provide Well-Timed Responses

Feedback is usually most effective when you offer it at the earliest opportunity, particularly if your objective is to teach someone a skill. For example, if you are teaching someone how to make your famous egg rolls, you provide a step-by-step commentary as you watch your pupil. If he or she makes a mistake, you don't wait until the egg rolls are finished to say that he or she left out the cabbage. Your pupil needs immediate feedback to finish the rest of the sequence successfully.

Sometimes, however, if a person is already sensitive and upset about something, delaying feedback can be wise. Use your critical thinking skills to analyze when feedback will do the most good. Rather than automatically offering immediate correction, use the just-in-time (JIT) approach and provide feedback just before the person might make another mistake. If, for example, your daughter typically rushes through math tests and fails to check her work, remind her right before her next test to double-check her answers, not immediately after the test she just failed. To provide feedback about a relationship, select a mutually agreeable place and time when both of you are rested and relaxed; avoid hurling feedback at someone "for his or her own good" immediately after he or she offends you.

Provide Useful Information

When you provide information to someone, be certain that it is useful and relevant. How can you make sure your partner can use the information you share? Try to understand your partner's mindset. Ask yourself, "If I were this person, how would I respond to this information? Is it information I can act on? Or might it make matters worse?" Under the guise of effective feedback, we may be tempted to reveal to others our complete range of feelings and emotions. However, research suggests that selective feedback is best. In one study, married couples who practised selective self-disclosure were more satisfied than couples who told everything they knew or were feeling.[25] Immersing your partner in information that is irrelevant or that may be damaging to the relationship may be cathartic, but it will not enhance the quality of your relationship or improve understanding.

Avoid Unnecessary Details

When you are selecting meaningful information, try to cut down on the volume. Don't overwhelm your listener with details that obscure the key point of your feedback. Give only the highlights that will benefit the listener. Be brief.

Be Descriptive Rather Than Evaluative

"You're an awful driver!" shouts Patrick at his girlfriend, Carmen. Although Patrick may feel that he has provided Carmen with simple feedback about her skills, Carmen will probably not respond well, or even listen closely, to his feedback. If Patrick tries to be more descriptive and less evaluative, then she might be inclined to listen. Less offensive comments might include "Carmen, you're going 70 in a 50-kilometre zone," or "Carmen, I get really nervous when you zigzag so fast through traffic." These statements describe Carmen's behaviour rather than rendering judgments about her that are likely to trigger a defensive, passive listening reaction.

RECAP   **Suggestions for Improving Responding Skills**

Responding Strategy	Example
Provide well-timed responses	Sometimes immediate feedback is best; at other times provide a just-in-time (JIT) response when it will do the most good.
Provide meaningful information	Select information that your partner can act on rather than making vague comments or suggestions that are beyond his or her capabilities.
Avoid unnecessary details	Avoid information overload; don't bombard your listener with too much information; keep your comments focused on major points.
Be descriptive	Don't evaluate your listening partner; focus on behaviour rather than personality.

Enhancing Your Empathic Responding Skills

When your listening and responding goal is to empathize with another person, simply imagining the emotional response of another person may not lead you to an appropriate response. Paraphrasing not only the content of what someone says but also the emotion behind the words may be helpful. And your partner may be seeking more than understanding; he or she may be seeking social support. When your listening partner wants and needs to know that you care about him or her, there are ways of responding that can enhance empathy and provide meaningful emotional support.

Paraphrase Emotions. The bottom line in empathic responding is to make certain that you accurately understand how the other person is feeling. You can paraphrase, beginning with such phrases as

"So you are feeling . . ."

"You must feel . . ."

"So now you feel . . ."

In the following example of empathic responding, the listener asks questions, summarizes content, and summarizes feelings.

David: I think I'm in over my head. My boss gave me a job to do, and I just don't know how to do it. I'm afraid I've taken on too much.

Mike: (Thinks how he would feel if he were given an important task at work but did not know how to complete the task, then asks for more information.) What job did she ask you to do?

David: I'm supposed to do an inventory of all the items in the warehouse on the new computer system and have it finished by the end of the week. I don't have the slightest idea of how to start. I've never even used that system.

Mike: (Summarizes feelings.) So you feel panicked because you may not have enough time to learn the system *and* do the inventory.

BEING **Other**-ORIENTED

To be able to paraphrase
the essential ideas of
others, you will need to be
focused not only on what
someone is saying, but
also on how someone is
expressing his or her ideas.
Listen for the emotional
message underlying the
words to identify what the
other person is expressing.
What are clues that help
you identify other people's
emotional state when you
listen "between the lines"?

David: Well, I'm not only panicked; I'm afraid I may be fired.

Mike: (Summarizes feelings.) So your fear that you might lose your job is getting in the way of just focusing on the task and seeing what you can get done. It's making you feel like you made a mistake in taking this job.

David: Yes—that's exactly how I feel.

Note that toward the end of the dialogue, Mike has to make a couple of tries to summarize David's feelings accurately. Also note that Mike does a good job of listening and responding without giving advice. Just by being an active listener, you can help your partner clarify a problem. For tips on listening actively, refer to the "Listen" subsection on pp. 111.

We have discussed responding empathically and listening actively using a tidy step-by-step textbook approach. In practice, you may have to back up and clarify content, ask more questions, and rethink how you would feel before you attempt to summarize how someone else feels. Conversely, you may be able to summarize feelings *without* asking questions or summarizing content if the message is clear and it relates to a situation with which you are very familiar. Overusing paraphrasing can slow down a conversation and make the other person uncomfortable or irritated. But if you use it judiciously, paraphrasing can help both you and your partner stay focused on the issues and ideas at hand.

Reflecting content or feeling through paraphrasing can be especially useful in the following situations:

- Before you take an important action

- Before you argue or criticize

- When your partner has strong feelings or wants to talk over a problem

- When your partner's meaning is unclear

- When you encounter new ideas

Sometimes, however, you truly don't understand how another person really feels. At times like this, be cautious about telling others, "I know just how you feel." It may be more important simply to let others know that you care about them than to grill them about their feelings.

If you do decide to use paraphrasing skills, keep the following guidelines in mind:

- Use your own words.

- Don't go beyond the information communicated by the speaker.

- Be concise.

- Be specific.

- Be accurate.

Do *not* use paraphrasing skills if you aren't able to be open and accepting, if you do not trust the other person to find his or her own solution, if you are using these skills as a way of hiding yourself from another, or if you feel pressured, hassled, or tired. And as we have already discussed, overuse of paraphrasing can be distracting and unnatural.

Don't be discouraged if your initial attempts to use these skills seem awkward and uncomfortable. Any new skill takes time to learn and use well. The instructions and samples you have read should serve as guides rather than as hard-and-fast prescriptions to follow during each conversation.

Express Helpful Social Support. There are times when it is clear that a communication partner is experiencing stress, pain, or a significant life problem. Just by listening and empathizing you can help ease the pain and help the person manage the burden. Specifically, you provide **social support** when you offer positive, sincere, supportive messages, both verbal and nonverbal, when helping others deal with stress, anxiety, or uncertainty. Providing social support isn't the same as expressing pity for another person; it's providing a response that lets the other person know that he or she is both understood and valued. Nor does offering social support mean giving advice to solve the problem or take away the fear. Giving social support means providing messages that help the person seek his or her own solution.

An ability to listen empathically is important when you discern that someone needs social support. What do researchers suggest are the best ways to provide supportive, empathic, comforting messages to others? Although there are no magic words or phrases that will always ease someone's stress and anxiety, here's a summary of social support messages that seem to be appreciated by others:

- Clearly express that you want to provide support. ("I would really like to help you.")

- Appropriately communicate that you have positive feelings for the other person. ("You mean a lot to me." "I really care about you.")

- Express your concern about the situation that the other person is in right now. ("I'm worried about you right now because I know you're feeling _____ [stressed, overwhelmed, sad, etc.].")

- Indicate that you are available to help. ("I can be here for you when you need me.")

- Let the other person know how much you support her or him. ("I'm here for you, and I'll always be here for you.")

- Acknowledge that the other person is in a difficult situation. ("This must be very difficult for you.")

- Paraphrase what the other person has told you about the issue or problem that is causing stress. ("So you became upset when she told you she didn't want to see you again.")

- Ask open-ended questions to see if the other person wants to talk. ("How are you doing now?")

- Let the other person know that you are listening and being supportive by providing conversational continuers such as "Yes, then what happened?" or "Oh, I see," or "Uh-huh."

- After expressing your compassion, empathy, and concern, just listen.

Some types of responses are less helpful when providing social support. Here are a few things *not* to do, based on the conclusions of communication researchers:

- Don't tell the other person that you know exactly how he or she feels.

- Don't criticize or negatively evaluate the other person; he or she needs support and validation, not judgmental comments.

- Don't tell the other person to stop feeling what he or she is feeling.

- Don't immediately offer advice. First, just listen.

social support. Positive, sincere, supportive messages, both verbal and nonverbal, offered to help others deal with stress, anxiety, or uncertainty.

Developing empathy requires more than simply understanding someone's situation. A person who is truly empathic "feels with" the other person—he or she experiences the emotions the other person is feeling.

(© Charles O. Cecil/Alamy Stock Photo)

- Don't tell the other person that "it's going to get better from here" or that "the worst is over."

- Don't tell the other person that there is really nothing to worry about or that "it's no big deal."

- Don't tell the other person that the problem can be solved easily. ("Oh, you can always find another girlfriend.")

- Don't blame the other person for the problem. ("Well, if you didn't always drive so fast, you wouldn't have had the accident.")

- Don't tell the other person that it is wrong to express feelings and emotions. ("Oh, you're just making yourself sick. Stop crying.")

Improving Your Confirmation Skills

Couple A:

> *Wife to husband:*   "I just don't feel appreciated anymore."
>
> *Husband to wife:*   "Margaret, I'm so very sorry. I love you. You're the most important person in the world to me."

Couple B:

> *Wife to husband:*   "I just don't feel appreciated anymore."
>
> *Husband to wife:*   "Well, what about my feelings? Don't my feelings count? You'll have to do what you have to do. Can we eat early? I'm going over to Dave's to watch the Flames game."

confirming response. Statement that causes another person to value himself or herself more.

disconfirming response. Statement that causes another person to value himself or herself less.

It doesn't take an expert in interpersonal communication to know that Couple B's relationship is not warm and confirming. Researchers have studied the specific kinds of responses people offer to others.[26] Some responses are confirming; other responses are disconfirming. A **confirming response** is an other-oriented statement that causes others to value themselves more; Wife A is likely to value herself more after her husband's confirming response. A **disconfirming response** is a statement that causes others to value themselves less. Wife B knows firsthand what it's like to have her feelings ignored and disconfirmed. Are you aware of whether your responses to others confirm them or disconfirm them? To help you be more aware of the kinds of responses you make to others, we'll provide some examples of both confirming and disconfirming responses.

Confirming Responses

The underlying principle of confirming responses is that we are judged more by our words and actions than by our intent. Since it is those who receive your messages who determine whether they have the effect you intended, formulating confirming responses requires careful listening and attention to the other person.

Does it really matter whether we confirm others? Marriage researcher John Gottman used video cameras and microphones to observe couples interacting in an apartment over an extended period of time. He found that a significant predictor

Effective critical listening skills are crucial in a business environment.

(© Rachel Epstein/PhotoEdit, Inc.)

ZITS © 1999 Zits Partnership. Dist. by King Features Syndicate.

of divorce was neglecting to confirm or affirm one's marriage partner during typical, everyday conversation—even though couples who were less likely to divorce spent only a few seconds more confirming their partner than couples who eventually did divorce. His research conclusion has powerful implications: long-lasting relationships are characterized by supportive, confirming messages.[27] The everyday kinds of confirmation and support we offer need not be excessive—sincere, moderate, heart-felt support is evaluated as the most positive and desirable kind. Here are several kinds of confirming responses:

Direct Acknowledgment. When you respond directly to something another person says to you, you are acknowledging not only the statement, but also that the person is worth responding to.

Joan:　　It's a great day to eat lunch outside.

Mariko:　Yes, it's a beautiful day. I'm glad you suggested it, Joan.

Agreement About Judgments. When you confirm someone's evaluation of something, you are also affirming that person's sense of taste and judgment.

Nancy:　I loved the drum solo in that last song.

Victor:　Yes, I think it was the best part of the performance.

Supportive Response. When you express reassurance and understanding, you are confirming a person's right to his or her feelings.

Jesse:　I'm disappointed that I only scored 60 on my interpersonal communication test.

Sarah:　I'm sorry to see you so frustrated, Jesse. I know that test was important to you.

Clarifying Response. When you seek greater understanding of another person's message, you are confirming that he or she is worth your time and trouble. Clarifying responses also encourage the other person to talk in order to explore his or her feelings.

Jeff:　I'm not feeling very good about my family situation these days.

Tyrone:　Is it tough with you and Margo working different shifts?

Expression of Positive Feeling. We feel confirmed or valued when someone else agrees with our expression of joy or excitement.

Lorraine:　I'm so excited! I was just promoted to assistant manager.

Dorette:　Congratulations! I'm so proud of you! You deserve it.

Compliment. When you tell people you like what they have done or said, what they are wearing, or how they look, you are confirming their sense of worth.

Jean-Christophe: Did you get the invitation to my party?

Manny: Yes! It looked so professional. I didn't know you were so talented.

In each of these examples, note how the responder provides comments that confirm the worth or value of the other person. But keep in mind that confirming responses should be sincere. Offering false praise is manipulative, and your communication partner will probably sniff out your phoniness.

Disconfirming Responses

Some statements and responses can undermine another person's self-worth. We offer these categories so that you can both avoid using them and recognize them when someone uses them to chip away at your self-image and self-esteem.

Impervious Response. When a person fails to acknowledge your statement or attempt to communicate, even though you know he or she heard you, you may feel a sense of awkwardness or embarrassment.

Rosa: I loved your speech, Tre.

Tre: (No response, verbal or nonverbal.)

Interrupting Response. When you interrupt someone, you are implying that what you have to say is more important than what the other person has to say. In effect, your behaviour communicates that *you* are more important than the other person is. You may simply be enthusiastic or excited when the words tumble out of your mouth; nonetheless, be especially mindful of not interrupting others. An interrupting response is a powerful disconfirming behaviour, whether you are aware of its power or not.

Anna: I just heard on the news that—

Sharon: Oh yes. The stock market just went down 100 points.

Irrelevant Response. An irrelevant response is one that has nothing at all to do with what you were saying. Chances are your partner is not listening to you at all.

Matt: First we're flying down to Rio, and then to Quito. I can hardly wait to—

Peter: They're predicting a hard freeze tonight.

Impersonal Response. A response that intellectualizes and uses the third person distances the other person from you and has the effect of trivializing what you say.

Diana: Hey, Bill. I'd like to talk with you for a minute about getting your permission to take my vacation in July.

Bill: One tends to become interested in recreational pursuits about this time of year, doesn't one?

Incoherent Response. When a speaker mumbles, rambles, or makes some unintelligible effort to respond, you may end up wondering if what you said was of any value or use to the listener.

Paolo: George, here's my suggestion for how to divide up the work on our presentation. If you summarize the main points of the first two chapters, I'll look at the third and fourth, and then we can both provide our analysis.

George: Huh? Well . . . so . . . well . . . hmmm . . . I'm not sure.

Incongruous Response. When a verbal message is inconsistent with nonverbal behaviour, people usually believe the nonverbal message, but they usually feel confused as well. An incongruous response is like a malfunctioning traffic light with red and green lights flashing simultaneously—you're just not sure whether the speaker wants you to go or stay.

Sue: Honey, do you want me to go grocery shopping with you?

Steve: (Shouting) OF COURSE I DO! WHY ARE YOU ASKING?

Although it may be impossible to eliminate all disconfirming responses from your repertoire, becoming aware of the power of your words and monitoring your conversation for offensive phrases may help you avoid unexpected and perhaps devastating consequences.

APPLYING AN OTHER-ORIENTATION
to Listening and Responding Skills

It's impossible to be other-oriented without listening to and observing others. Listening to comprehend information, to empathize, or to critically evaluate what others are saying is the quintessential other-oriented skill. The following poem by an anonymous author, simply called "Listen," nicely summarizes the reason why listening is such an important interpersonal skill.

Listen

When I ask you to listen to me
and you start giving advice,
you have not done what I
asked.
When I ask you to listen to me
and you begin to tell me why
I shouldn't feel that way, you
are trampling on my
feelings.

When I ask you to listen to me
and you feel you have to do
something to solve my problems,
you have failed me, strange as
that may seem.
Listen! All I asked was that you
listen. Not talk or do—just
hear me.
Advice is cheap: 50 cents will get
you both Dear Abby and Billy
Graham in the same newspaper.
And I can do for myself; I'm not
helpless. Maybe discouraged and
faltering, but not helpless.
When you do something for me that
I can and need to do for myself,
you contribute to my fear and
weakness.
But when you accept as a simple
fact that I do feel what I feel,
no matter how irrational, then I
quit trying to convince you and

can get about the business of
understanding what's behind this
irrational feeling.
And when that's clear, the answers
are obvious and I don't need
advice.
Irrational feelings make sense when
we understand what's behind
them.
Perhaps that's why prayer works,
sometimes, for some people—
because God is mute, and
doesn't give advice or try to fix
things.
God just listens and lets you work it
out for yourself.
So, please listen and just hear me,
and, if you want to talk, wait a
minute for your turn, and I'll listen
to you.

Anonymous

Listening Defined (pages 100–103)

OBJECTIVE ❶ Define listening and describe five elements of the listening process

Key Terms

listening *100*　　　　　　understanding *101*
hearing *100*　　　　　　　remembering *102*
selecting *100*　　　　　　responding *102*
attending *101*

Critical Thinking Questions

1. Describe two recent communication exchanges in which you were an effective or ineffective listener. What factors contributed to your listening skill (or lack of skill)?

2. Ethics: If you weren't really listening when someone was speaking to you, should you admit you weren't listening and ask the person to repeat what he or she said? Or should you say you couldn't hear or got distracted? Is it best to be honest in such a situation?

Activities

Over the next week, in your numerous communication exchanges with friends, family members, professors, and work colleagues, make an effort to listen carefully and effectively. Then, following each exchange, make a list of at least five items that you remember (things you discussed). Is there a difference in what you remember in each case? What factors contribute to your ability to listen, attend to, and remember details of each communication?

Web Resources

http://psychologytoday.tests.psychtests.com/take_test.php?idRegTest =3206 This site offers a self-test of your knowledge of listening and responding to others.

Listening Styles (pages 103–105)

OBJECTIVE ❷ Identify characteristics of four listening styles.

Key Terms

listening style *103*　　　　critical listeners *104*
relational listeners *104*　　second-guessing *104*
analytical listeners *104*　　task-oriented listeners *104*

Critical Thinking Questions

1. What is your primary listening style? How do you know?

2. Describe several situations in which you might modify or adapt your primary listening style. Do you find that you consciously adapt your communication to others' listening styles? When and why? What factors contribute to the need to adapt your listening style?

Activities

Consider others with whom you frequently communicate. How would you characterize their listening styles? Make a list of people you know who are primarily relational, critical, or analytical listeners. Do some of these people use different styles at different times? What cues help you to identify their styles? With which type of listeners do you find it easiest to communicate? Explain.

Web Resources

www.nasuad.org/documentation/I_R/ActiveListening.pdf This list provides tips and suggestions for being a better listener and for providing helpful feedback to others.
Try a "Listening Self-Assessment" to learn about your current listening skills and the areas in which you may need to improve.

Listening Barriers (pages 105–109)

OBJECTIVE ❸ Identify several important barriers to effective listening.

Key Terms

conversational narcissism *106*　　ambush listener *106*
emotional noise *106*　　　　　　listener apprehension *109*

Critical Thinking Questions

1. What daily challenges do you encounter in listening, and, in particular, attending to messages? Pause to consider some of the "noise" around you right now, including electronic and internal (emotional) or external distractions. What effect does this noise have on your ability to listen to others?

2. In this age of communication technologies, what strategies can you use to reduce information overload and listen more effectively to others' messages?

3. Jason and Chris are roommates. They both work hard each day and come home exhausted. What suggestions would you offer to help them listen to each other effectively, even when they are tired?

Improving Your Listening, Responding, and Confirmation Skills (pages 109–123)

OBJECTIVES ❹ ❺ Identify ways to improve your other-orientation and listening skills, and identify responding skills and understand strategies for improving them.

Key Terms

meta-message *111*

empathy *112*

social decentring *113*

compassionate listening *113*

critical listening *114*

information triage *115*

fact *115*

inference *115*

social support *119*

confirming response *120*

disconfirming response *120*

Critical Thinking Questions

1. Miranda and Salvador often disagree about who should handle some of the child-rearing tasks in their home. What are some effective listening skills and strategies they can use in discussing these tasks and making sure they understand each other?

2. Ethics: Your roommate (or partner or spouse) wants to tell you about his day. You are tired and really don't want to hear all the details. Should you fake attention so that you won't hurt his feelings, or simply tell him you are tired and would rather not hear the details right now?

Activities

How empathetic are you? The Empathy Quotient (EQ) is a psychological self-assessment questionnaire that measures an individual's levels of empathy. It was developed by Simon Baron-Cohen and Sally Wheelwright at the Autism Research Centre (ARC) at the University of Cambridge. To take the test and find out your score, visit http://psychology-tools.com/empathy-quotient.

Web Resources

http://discoveryhealth.queendom.com/eiq_abridged_access.html   This online test, provided by Discovery Health, will help you assess your emotional intelligence.

www.listen.org The homepage of the International Listening Association includes tips and resources to enhance listening skills.

6

Verbal Communication Skills

© CREATISTA/Shutterstock

66 Words can destroy. What we call each other ultimately becomes what we think of each other, and it matters. 99 —Jeanne J. Kirkpatrick

Words are powerful. Those who use them skilfully can exert great influence with just a few of them. Consider these notable achievements:

Shakespeare expressed the essence of the human condition in Hamlet's famous "To be or not to be" soliloquy—just 363 words long.

Several religions accept a comprehensive moral code expressed in even fewer words: the Ten Commandments.

In politics, the right words (delivered in the right way) can launch a career: former U.S. president Barack Obama first drew the public's attention with his address at the Democratic National Convention in 2004, while he was a state senator. Similarly, Canada's Prime Minister Justin Trudeau entered the political spotlight after delivering the eulogy at his father's funeral in 2000.

Words have great power in our private lives as well. In this chapter we will examine ways to use words more effectively in interpersonal relationships. We'll investigate how to harness the power that words have to affect emotions, thoughts, and actions, and we'll describe links between language and culture. We will also identify communication barriers that may keep you from using words effectively and note strategies and skills for managing those barriers. Finally, we will examine the role of speech in establishing supportive relationships with others.

According to one study, a person's ability to use words—more specifically, to participate in conversation with others—is one of the best predictors of communication competence.[1] Another study found that people who simply didn't talk much were perceived as being less interpersonally skilled than people who spent what was considered to be an appropriate amount of time engaged in conversation with others.[2] This chapter is designed to help you better understand the power of words and to use them with greater skill and confidence.

Throughout our discussion of the power of verbal messages, we invite you to keep one important idea in mind: *you are not in control of the meaning others derive from your messages.* Meaning is created by others. That is, words don't have meaning; people create meaning.

How Words Work

As you read the printed words on this page, how are you able to make sense out of these black marks? When you hear words spoken by others, how are you able to interpret those sounds? Although there are several theories that attempt to explain how we learn language and assign meaning to both printed and spoken words, there is no single, universally held view that neatly clarifies the mystery.

Words Are Symbols

As we noted in Chapter 1, words are **symbols** that represent something else. A printed word triggers an image, sound, concept, or experience. Take the word "cat" for instance. The word may conjure up in your mind's eye a hissing creature with bared claws and fangs. Or perhaps you envision a cherished pet curled up by a fireplace.

The classic model in Figure 6.1 was developed by Charles Ogden and Ivor Richards to explain the relationships between *referents, thoughts, and symbols.*[3] **Referents** are the things the symbols (words) represent. **Thought** is the mental process of creating a category, idea, or image triggered by the referent or the symbol. So, these three elements—words, referents, and thoughts—are inextricably linked. Although some scholars find this model too simplistic to explain how we link all words to a meaning, it does illustrate the process for most concepts, people, and tangible things.

symbols. A word, sound, or visual device that represents a thought, concept, or object.

referents. The things that a symbol represents.

thought. The mental process of creating a category, idea, or image triggered by a referent or symbol.

FIGURE 6.1
Triangle of Meaning

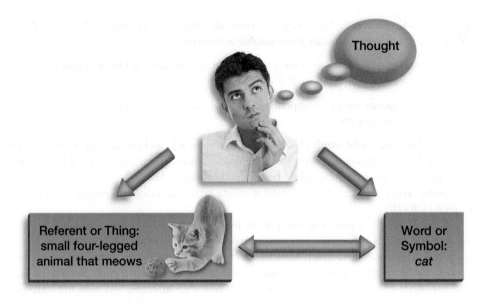

The association between a word and the thing it symbolizes is not always clear. The meaning of a word is attributed by a person based on his or her experiences; meaning does not reside within the word itself. When your friend says, "Have you seen Billy Elliot?" (meaning the Broadway show) and you say, "I don't know who he is" because you were thinking about a person you thought you should know, you are attributing a different meaning to the words *Billy Elliot* than did your friend. You both are using the same words, but thinking about different things. As illustrated in Figure 6.2, in the almost overlapping circles, sometimes the meaning for a word is shared between you and another person. Yet at other times, what you mean by a word is completely misunderstood; the circles are barely touching to suggest low or almost no shared meaning.

Words Are Denotative and Connotative

Language creates meaning on two levels: the denotative and the connotative.

The **denotative meaning** of a word creates content. The denotation of a word is its restrictive or literal meaning. For example, here is one dictionary definition for the word "school":

> An institution for the instruction of children; an institution for instruction in a skill or business; a college or a university.[4]

This definition is the literal or denotative definition of the word; it describes what "school" means in North American culture.

denotative meaning. The restrictive or literal meaning of a word.

connotative meaning. The personal and subjective meaning of a word.

The **connotative meaning** of a word conveys feelings. Words have personal and subjective meanings for us. The word "school" to you might mean a wonderful, exciting place where you meet your friends, have a good time, and learn new information and skills. To others, "school" could be a restrictive, burdensome obligation that stands in the way of making money and getting on with life. The connotative meaning of a word is more individualized. The denotative or objective meaning of the word "school" can be found in any dictionary; your connotative,

High shared meaning   Low shared meaning

FIGURE 6.2

subjective response to the word exists only in your mind. The words "house" and "home" have approximately the same *denotative* meaning: a residence or dwelling place. However, if you look up your local real estate listings online, you will find that the word "home" is used much more frequently. This is because the *connotative* meaning of "home" is different from that of "house": people associate "home" with feelings of security, love, family, and comfort.

Words Are Concrete and Abstract

Words can be placed along a continuum from abstract to concrete. We call a word "concrete" if we can experience the thing it refers to with one of our senses; if we can see it, touch it, smell it, taste it, or hear it, then it's concrete. If we cannot do these things, then the word is abstract. We can visualize the progression from abstract to concrete as a ladder. In Figure 6.3 (see below), the term at the bottom, red Mercedes 500, is quite specific and concrete. You're more likely to have a clear mental picture of a red Mercedes than a clear image of the word "transportation," on the top rung, which could mean anything from walking to flying in a 747. In general, the more concrete the language, the easier it is for others to understand.

Most of us can agree on the denotative meaning for the word "school," but the connotative meaning will be different for everybody.

(© Blend Images—Andersen Ross/Brand X Pictures/Getty Images)

Words Are Arbitrary

In English, as in all languages, words arbitrarily represent something else. There's not an obvious reason why many words represent what they refer to. The word "dog," for example, does not sound like a dog or look like a dog. Yet there is a clear connection in your mind between your pet terrier and the word "dog." The words we use have agreed-upon general meanings, but there is not typically a logical connection between a word and what it represents. Yes, some words, such as "buzz," "hum," "snort," and "giggle," do re-create the sounds they represent. Words that, when pronounced, sound like the event or thing they are signifying are called onomatopoetic words. You probably learned about **onomatopoeia** in an English class. Many words can trace their origin to other languages. However, most of the time words have an arbitrary meaning. Therefore, unless we develop a common meaning for a word, misunderstanding and miscommunication may occur.

onomatopoeia. A word that imitates a sound associated with what is named; also, the use of such a word.

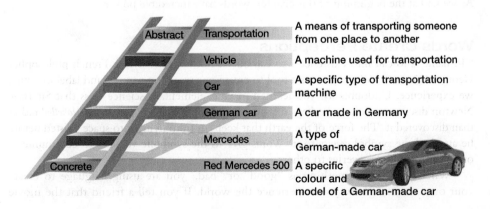

Abstract	Transportation	A means of transporting someone from one place to another
	Vehicle	A machine used for transportation
	Car	A specific type of transportation machine
	German car	A car made in Germany
	Mercedes	A type of German-made car
Concrete	Red Mercedes 500	A specific colour and model of a German-made car

FIGURE 6.3

A Ladder of Abstraction

Words Are Culture-Bound

Culture consists of the rules, norms, values, and mores of a group of people, which have been learned and shaped from one generation to the next. The meaning of a symbol such as a word can change from culture to culture. Some years ago, General Motors sold a car called a Nova. In English, "nova" means bright star—an appropriate name for a car. In Spanish, however, it sounds like the words *no va*, which translate as "It does not go." As you can imagine, this name was not a great sales tool for the Spanish-speaking market.

One way to measure how words reflect culture is to consider the new words that become new entries in dictionaries. Here are some new additions to the 11th edition of Webster's *New World College Dictionary*, published in 2012:

Webisode: an episode that can be viewed at a website

Vlog: A web log (blog) that contains video material

Bromance: A close nonsexual relationship between men

Frenemy: One who is both a friend and an enemy

Sexting: the sending of sexually explicit messages or images by cellphone

Man Cave: a room that is used as a man's personal space

The study of words and meaning is called *semantics*. One important type of semantic theory, known as **symbolic interaction**, holds that as a society we are bound together because of our common use of symbols. Originally developed by sociologists as a way of making sense out of how societies and groups are linked together,[5] the theory of symbolic interaction also illuminates how we use our common understanding of symbols to form interpersonal relationships. Common symbols foster links in understanding and, therefore, lead to satisfying relationships. Of course, even within a given culture, we misunderstand each other's messages. However, the more similar the cultures of the communication partners, the greater the chance for a meeting of meanings.

The Power of Words

> Sticks and stones may break my bones, but words can never hurt me.

This old schoolyard chant may provide a ready retort for the desperate victim of name-calling, but it is hardly convincing. With more insight, the poet Robert Browning wrote, "Words break no bones; hearts though sometimes"; and in his book *Science and Sanity*, mathematician and engineer Alfred Korzybski argued that the words we use (and misuse) have tremendous effects on our thoughts and actions.[6] Browning and Korzybski were right. As we said at the beginning of this chapter, words have incredible power.

Words Create Perceptions

"To name is to call into existence—to call out of nothingness," wrote French philosopher Georges Gusdorff.[7] Words give us a tool to create our world by naming and labelling what we experience. Undoubtedly, you learned in your elementary science class that Sir Isaac Newton discovered gravity. Perhaps it would be more accurate to say that he *labelled* rather than discovered it. The force of the earth that keeps us from flying into space existed before he attached the symbol *gravity* to it. Words give us the symbolic vehicles to communicate our creations and discoveries to others.

When you label something as "good" or "bad," you are using language to create your own vision of how you experience the world. If you tell a friend that the movie

symbolic interaction. A theory that suggests societies are bound together through the common use of symbols.

you saw last night was vulgar and obscene, you are not only providing your friend with a critique of the movie, but you are also communicating your sense of what is appropriate and inappropriate.

You create your self-worth largely with self-talk and with the labels you apply to yourself. Although emotions may sometimes seem to wash over you like ocean waves, there is evidence that you have the ability to control your emotions based on your ability to control what you think about, as well as the choice of words you use to describe your feelings. In Chapter 2 we talked about the appraisal theory of emotions, which holds that we exert considerable control over our emotions based on how we frame what is happening to us. If you get fired from a job, you might say that you feel angry and helpless, or you might declare that you feel liberated and excited. The first response might lead to depression, and the second to happiness. Your words and corresponding outlook even have the power to affect your health. The concept of reframing, discussed in Chapter 2 as a way to improve self-concept, is based on the power of words to "call into existence" whatever we describe with them.

Words Influence Thoughts

Words can distort how we view and evaluate others. When we label someone as kind, devious, fashionable, or disorganized, it distorts our perception of the other person. Read the *Canadian Connections* feature for research findings on the use of labels to signify a cultural group and how these labels may affect our perceptions of a group.

There is, in fact, scientific evidence that words influence our thoughts. As Figure 6.4 illustrates, the process of hearing, seeing, or saying words influences different parts of the brain. How we use words literally changes our brain activity.

Because words have the power to influence our thoughts, the meaning of a word resides within us rather than in the word itself. Words symbolize meaning, but the precise meaning of a word originates in the mind of the sender and the receiver. The meaning of a word is not static; it evolves as a conversation unfolds. Your meanings for words and phrases change as you gain additional experiences and have new thoughts about the words you use.

FIGURE 6.4

Words Influence Brain Activity

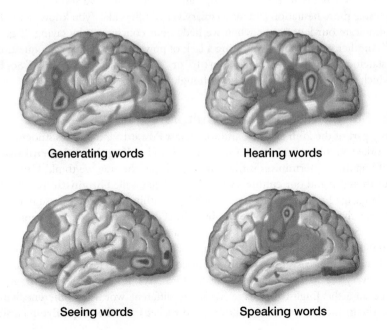

Generating words   Hearing words

Seeing words   Speaking words

Canadian Connections

Labels Are Words That Affect Our Evaluation of Others

The words we use to label people of other cultures and groups affect how we evaluate them. A study examined labels and their effects on people's attitudes toward Canada's Native peoples. In the past, Native Canadians were often simply labelled "Indians" with no thought about the impact of this labelling. More recently, a variety of labels have been used to refer to Canada's indigenous peoples. The labels "Aboriginal Peoples," "Native Peoples," "Native Indians," "First Nations People," and "Native Canadians" were used in the study to assess attitudes, stereotypes, and emotions toward several target groups, including Native Canadians themselves. The results indicate that how

groups are labelled affects our perceptions in both positive and negative ways.[1] In other words, these labels affect whether a group or a person with a particular label will be evaluated more positively or negatively. And once we have evaluated another group, our behaviour may be based on that label and evaluation. In the study, the labels "Native Canadians" and "First Nations People" elicited the least favourable evaluations compared with the other three labels.

Although this study was done in the late 1990s, it still serves as a reminder of how the words we use to label groups or people are powerful influences. Although attitudes cannot always predict behaviour,

there is little doubt that attitudes often do influence behaviour in positive and negative ways. To learn more about the attitude–behaviour relationship, you may want to examine some texts in social psychology.

Note:

1. Darrell W. Donakowski and Victoria M. Esses, "Native Canadians, First Nations, or Aboriginals: The Effect of Labels on Attitudes Toward Native Peoples," *Canadian Journal of Behavioural Science*, 28(2) (1996): 86–91. © Steven A. Beebe.

Words Influence Actions

A paraphrase of a well-known verse from the book of Proverbs in the Bible tells us, "As a person thinks, so is he or she." Words not only have the power to create and influence your thoughts, they also influence your actions—because your thoughts, which are influenced by words, affect how you behave. Advertisers have long known that slogans and catch phrases sell products. Political candidates also know that the words they use influence whether they will get your vote.

Research suggests that the very way we use language can communicate the amount of power we have in a conversation with others.[8] We use language in ways that are both powerful and powerless. When we use powerless speech, we are less persuasive and have less influence on the actions of others. Powerless speech is characterized by more frequent use of pauses, which may be filled with "umm," "ahhh," and "ehh." We also express our lack of power by using more hesitation and unnecessary verbal fillers like "you know" and "I mean." We communicate our low power when we hedge our conclusions by saying "I guess" and "sort of." Another way of communicating a lack of power is by tacking on a question at the end of a statement, such as "I'm right, aren't I?" or "This is what I think, OK?" So, the very way in which you speak can influence the thoughts and actions of others.

linguistic determinism. A theory that describes how use of language determines or influences thoughts and perceptions.

linguistic relativity. The theory that each language includes some unique features that are not found in other languages.

Sapir-Whorf hypothesis. Based on the principles of linguistic determinism and linguistic relativity, the hypothesis that language shapes our thoughts and culture, and our culture and thoughts affect the language we use to describe our world.

Words Shape and Reflect Culture

In the early part of the 20th century, anthropologist Edward Sapir and his student Benjamin Whorf worked simultaneously to refine a theory called **linguistic determinism**.[9] The essence of linguistic determinism is that language shapes the way we think. Our words also reflect our thoughts and our culture. A related principle, called **linguistic relativity**, states that each language has unique elements embedded within it. Together these two principles form the underlying elements in the **Sapir-Whorf hypothesis**, which proposes that language shapes our culture and culture shapes our language.

To support the theory, Benjamin Whorf studied the languages of several cultures, particularly that of Hopi Native Americans. He discovered that in Hopi, one word (*masa'ytaka*) is used for every creature that flies, except for birds. While this seems odd to an English-speaker, because the English language has many different words for different flying creatures (and things such as airplanes, balloons, and rockets), for the Hopi, flying creatures (or objects) constitute a single category. Whorf saw this as proof of his hypothesis that the words we use reflect our culture and our culture influences our words.

Similarly, today's highly developed technological culture has given rise to many new words that reflect the importance we place on technology; terms such as "PC," "hard drive," and "gigabyte" weren't part of your grandparents' language. Also, the fact that a certain type of behaviour is now labelled attention-deficit/hyperactivity disorder (ADHD) is an example of how words can create a reality in a culture. Your grandfather might argue that there weren't any ADHD kids in his day—some kids were just "rowdy."[10]

Words not only reflect your culture; there is evidence that they mould it. When Wendell Johnson, a speech therapist, noticed that very few Native Americans in a certain tribe stuttered, he also found that their language had no word for stuttering.[11] He concluded that few people had this affliction because it never entered their minds as a possibility. Perhaps you've heard that Inuit have 50 different words for snow. Even though they really don't have quite that many, the Inuit do have more words for snow than, for example, most residents of Florida do. In Canada, we

Surfers have created their own special language as part of the culture they share.

(© Zac Macaulay/The Image Bank/Getty Images)

are quite familiar with bilingual food containers such as cereal boxes. French–English bilingualism is so pervasive in Canadian culture that most of us don't give this kind of labelling a second thought. We just automatically turn to the side that we can read most easily.

These examples also show that the words we use and listen to affect our **world view**—how we interpret what we experience. The words you use to describe your view of the world reflect and further shape your perspective, and you, in turn, help to shape your culture's collective world view through your use of language.

Words Affect the Quality of Our Relationships

What you say and how you say it have a strong impact on how you relate to others. As we noted in Chapter 1, relating to another person is like dancing with the person. When you dance with a partner, your moves and counter-moves respond to the rhythm of the music and the moves your partner makes. In our interpersonal relationships with others, we "dance" as we relate to our communication partners with both language and nonverbal cues (something we'll discuss in more detail in the next chapter). A good conversation has a rhythm created by both communicators as they listen and respond to each other. Even our "small talk"—our everyday, sometimes brief responses and exchanges with others ("Nice weather we're having")—is important in establishing how we feel about others. The words we use, especially in our daily conversations, are directly related to the quality of the relationships we have with others.

Interpersonal communication researcher Steve Duck suggests that we literally talk a relationship into being.[12] Through talk, we establish relationships with other people. What do we talk about? One research team simply looked at what satisfied couples talked about with each other during the course of a week. The team found that the most frequent topic was the couples themselves—what they did during the day and how they were feeling—followed by general observations, and then responses to each other such as "Yes, I see" and "Uh huh"—what researchers call *backchannel talk*. The researchers also found that we're

world view. A culturally acquired perspective for interpreting experiences.

more likely to have conflict with our partners during the weekend as well as to use humour, to talk about household tasks, and to make general plans about the future.[13] Couples were least satisfied with their partners on Saturdays and Wednesdays; Monday was the day they were most satisfied. So, what we talk about and the way we talk to others form the basis of how we relate to others.

Communication Barriers: Managing Misunderstandings

Have you ever had a conversation in which the other person misinterpreted your meaning and became offended as a result? As most of us have experienced firsthand, words have the power to create monumental misunderstandings as well as deep connections. Although it is true that meanings are in people, not in words, sometimes assumptions or inaccurate use of words hinder understanding. How do you manage the inevitable misunderstandings that occur even between the best of friends? Read on.

Be Aware of Missed Meaning

A student pilot was on his first solo flight. When he called the tower for flight instructions, the control tower said, "Would you please give us your altitude and position?" The pilot said, "I'm 180 cm tall, and I'm sitting up front."

Bypassing occurs when the same words mean different things to different people. Meaning is fragile, and the English language is imprecise in many areas. One researcher estimated that the 500 words we use most often in our daily conversations with others have over 14 000 different dictionary definitions, and this number does not take into account personal connotations. It is no wonder that bypassing is a common communication problem.

How do you avoid bypassing and missing someone's meaning? Using the listening and responding skills we talked about in the previous chapter is key to enhancing communication accuracy. Ask questions if you're uncertain of the meaning. Listen and paraphrase your understanding of the message.

bypassing. Miscommunicating because of different understandings of the same words.

malapropism. The confusion of one word or phrase for another.

Be Clear and Precise in the Words You Choose

In Shakespeare's *A Midsummer Night's Dream*, the character of Bottom says "We will meet; and there we may rehearse most obscenely and courageously." He means "obscurely" or "secretively," but he says "obscenely," which means something else entirely.

This example illustrates a **malapropism**—a confusion of one word or phrase for another that sounds similar to it. The word comes from the name of a character in Richard Sheridan's 18th-century play *The Rivals*. Mrs. Malaprop had a tendency to utter such mixed-up phrases as "He is the very pineapple of politeness" (instead of "pinnacle") and "My affluence over my niece is very small" (instead of "influence"). You have probably heard people confuse such word pairs as "construction" and "instruction," and "subscription" and "prescription." Although this confusion

"Actually, I prefer the term Arctic-American."

may at times be humorous, it can also result in failure to communicate clearly. So, too, can using words out of context, using inappropriate grammar, or putting words in the wrong order. Confusion is the inevitable result, as illustrated by this note written to a landlord:

> The toilet is blocked and we cannot bathe the children until it is cleared.

This is a funny example, but in fact, unclear language can launch a war or sink a ship. It is vital to remember that *meanings are in people, not in words*. We give symbols meaning; we do not receive inherent meaning *from* symbols. For most communication, the object is to be as specific and concrete as possible. Vague language creates confusion and frustration.

Besides avoiding malapropisms and being careful not to use the wrong words, how else can you speak with clarity? Consider these strategies:

- Think about what you mean before you speak. Speaking without thinking, or rushing to make a point without having a point can lead to misunderstandings. For many years people who worked at the large computer company IBM had a one-word sign on their desks: *Think*. This is good advice when clarity is the goal.

- Observe the reaction your listener provides as you are speaking. Watching for feedback that you're not making sense (a grimace, a frown, or a quizzical look) can help you assess whether you are being clear.

- Use appropriate examples; they need not be elaborate or highly detailed, but a well-told example can add clarity to your conversations.

- Ask the other person whether he or she has questions and whether or not he or she understands you.

- Consider the perspective and background of the person or persons to whom you are speaking. If you are other-oriented, you will assess how someone else will respond to your message and try to select those symbols that he or she is most likely to interpret as you intend.

Be Specific and Avoid Overgeneralizations

For most communication, the object is to be as specific and concrete as possible. Vague language creates confusion and frustration. But is it possible to be too specific? It is if you use a restricted code that has a meaning your listener does not know. A **restricted code** is a set of words that have a particular meaning to a subgroup or culture. If you send many text messages, you probably use a restricted code when you use what are called *textisms*—brief abbreviations for common words, such as "c u" for "see you" or the ubiquitous "LOL" for "laughing out loud." To you, such restricted code is clear, but to someone who doesn't receive many text messages, these abbreviations can result in head-scratching confusion.

We sometimes develop abbreviations or specialized terms that make sense and save time when we speak to others in our group. Musicians, for example, use special terms that relate to reading and performing music. Most computer users know that a "screamer" is someone who sends email messages typed in all capital letters. Ham radio operators use codes to communicate over the airwaves. Yet, in each instance, this shorthand language would make little sense to an outsider. In fact, groups that rely on restricted codes may have greater cohesiveness because of this shared "secret" language, or **jargon**. Whatever your line of work or social group, it's a good idea to guard against lapsing into phrases that can only be interpreted by a few.

When people have known each other for a long time, they may also use restricted codes for their exchanges. Often married couples communicate using short-hand speech that no outsider could ever interpret. To enhance the clarity of your messages with others, especially people who don't know you well, be as specific as you can to reduce uncertainty.

restricted code. The use of words with a particular meaning known only to a subgroup or culture.

jargon. A shared language of terms used within a subgroup.

An additional challenge to clarity is the tendency to use language to make unqualified, often untrue generalizations called **allness statements**. Allness statements deny individual differences or variations. Statements such as "All women are poor drivers" and "All Canadians love hockey" are generalizations that imply the person making the pronouncement has examined all the information and has reached a definitive conclusion. Although our world would be much simpler if we *could* make such statements without straining reality, reality rarely, if ever, provides evidence to support sweeping generalizations. For example, although research conclusions document differences between the way men and women communicate, it is inaccurate to say that all women are more emotional and that all men are task-oriented. Empathic, other-oriented speakers avoid making judgments of others based only upon conventional wisdom or traditionally held attitudes and beliefs. If you respond to others (of a different gender, sexual orientation, or ethnicity) based on stereotypical concepts, you will diminish your understanding and the quality of the relationship.

One way to avoid untrue generalizations is to remind yourself that your use and interpretation of a word is unique. Saying the words "to me" either to yourself or out loud before you offer an opinion or make a pronouncement can help communicate to others (and remind yourself) that your view is uniquely yours. Rather than announcing "Curfews for teenagers are ridiculous," you could say, "To me, curfews for teenagers are ridiculous," or "I think that curfews for teenagers are ridiculous."

Indexing your comments and remarks is another way to avoid generalizing. To index is to acknowledge that each individual is unique. Rather than announcing that all doctors are abrupt, you could say, "My child's pediatrician spends a lot of time with me, but my internist never answers my questions." This helps you remember that doctors are not all the same.

Be Aware of Changes in Meaning

You change. Your world changes. An ancient Greek philosopher said it best: "You can never step in the same river twice."[14] Yet we sometimes use words with an implicit assumption that our world doesn't change. Word meanings can change over time. A **static evaluation** is a statement that fails to recognize change. Labels in particular have a tendency to freeze-frame our awareness. Someone who was a nerd in high school might today be a successful, polished businessperson; the old label does not fit.

In addition, some people suffer from "hardening of the categories": their world view is so rigid that they can never change or expand their perspective. After all, the world is a moving target, and just when we think we have things neatly figured out and categorized, something shifts. Our labels, then, may not reflect the buzzing, booming, zipping process of change. It is important to acknowledge that perception is a process and to avoid trying to nail things down permanently into all-inclusive categories.

General semanticists use the metaphorical expression "The map is not the territory" to illustrate the concept of static evaluation. Like a word, a map symbolizes or represents reality. Yet our road system is constantly changing. New roads are built, old ones are closed. If you were to use a 1949 map to guide you from St. Andrews, New Brunswick, to Winnipeg, Manitoba, the current highway system would not even be on it, and you would probably lose your way. Similarly, if we use old labels and do not adjust our thinking to accommodate change, we will be semantically lost.

To avoid static evaluation yourself, try dating your observations and indicate to others the time period from which you are drawing your conclusions. For example, if your cousin comes to town for a visit, say, "When I last saw you, you loved to listen to Céline Dion" rather than greeting her at the airport with the newest Céline Dion CD. This allows for the possibility that your cousin's tastes may have changed since you saw her last.

BEING Other-ORIENTED

People change. Yet our labels for and descriptions of others tend to freeze our perceptions because of the power of words to affect our thoughts and perceptions. When interacting with others, how can you avoid the tendency to "step in the same river twice" and treat people as if they didn't change?

allness statements. Unqualified often untrue generalizations.

indexing. A way of avoiding allness statements by separating one situation, person, or example from others.

static evaluation. Pronouncing judgment on something without taking changes into consideration.

Most importantly, try to observe and acknowledge changes in others. If you are practising what you know about becoming other-oriented, you are unlikely to erect this barrier.

Be Aware of Polarizing, "Either-Or" Extremes

Describing and evaluating what we observe in terms of extremes, such as good or bad, old or new, beautiful or ugly, brilliant or stupid, is known as **polarization**. General semanticists remind us that the world in which we live comes not in black and white but in a variety of colours, hues, and shades. If you describe things in extremes, leaving out the middle ground, then your language does not accurately reflect reality, and because of the power of words to create, you may believe your own pronouncements.

"You either love me or you don't love me," says Kamal.

"You're *always* trying to control me," replies Lise.

Both people are overstating their case, using language to polarize their perceptions of the experience.

Family counsellors who listen to family feuds find that the tendency to see things from an either–or point of view is a classic symptom of a troubled relationship. Placing the entire blame on your partner for a problem in your relationship is an example of polarizing. Few relational difficulties are exclusively one-sided.

Be Unbiased and Sensitive to Others' Differences

Using words that reflect your biases toward other cultures or ethnic groups, the other gender, people with a different sexual orientation, or people who are different from you in some other way can create a barrier for your listeners. Because words, including the words used to describe people, have power to create and affect thoughts and behaviour, they can affect the quality of relationships with others. Although TV and radio shows and magazine articles may debate the merits of political correctness, there is no doubt that sexist or racially stereotypical language can offend others.

Hate speech is any word or phrase that is intended to offend and show disrespect for another person because of his or her race, ethnicity, cultural background, gender, age, sexual orientation, disability, social class, occupation, personal appearance, mental capacity, or any other personal aspect that could be perceived as demeaning. Some people use words to *intentionally* express their prejudice, bias, ignorance, or just plain meanness toward other people, hoping to hurt someone. Like the sticks and stones that are hurled at others to intentionally inflict harm, hate speech is uttered with the explicit purpose of hurting someone. In Canada, the *Charter of Rights and Freedoms* provides for freedom of speech. Yet do people have the legal right to direct hurtful, venomous comments toward others, knowing that such comments will create mental anguish? Your college or university may have a speech code that prohibits hate speech, yet critics of such codes argue that it's impossible to prove the motivation or intent of someone who uses such language.

An other-oriented communicator avoids language that would intentionally hurt someone. We'll address three issues in language use that can reflect poorly on the speaker and affect interpersonal relationship with others: sexist language, ethnic or racially biased language, and demeaning language.

polarization. Describing and evaluating what we observe in extremes, such as good or bad, old or new, beautiful or ugly.

hate speech. Words or phrases intended to offend or show disrespect for someone's race, ethnicity, cultural background, gender, or some other aspect of their personality.

The term *policeman* fails to accurately describe the person shown here. A more inclusive term would be *police officer*.

(© aijohn784/Fotolia)

Avoid Sexist Language. Sexist language is the use of words that reflect stereotypical attitudes or that describe roles in exclusively male or female terms.

Words such as "alder*man*," "mail*man*," and "*man*kind" ignore the fact that women are part of the workforce and the human race. Contrast these with "city councillor," "letter carrier," and "humankind," which are gender neutral and allow for the inclusion of both men and women. Or, rather than eliminating the word "man" from your vocabulary, try to use appropriate labels when you know the gender of the subject. A male police officer is a "policeman"; a female police officer is a "policewoman." Rather than "salesperson," you could say "salesman" or "saleswoman," depending on the gender of the seller.

Many of our social conventions also diminish or ignore the importance of women:

Sexist	Unbiased
I'd like you to meet Dr. and Mrs. John Chao.	I'd like you to meet Dr. Susan Ho and Dr. John Chao. They are husband and wife.
	or I'd like you to meet John Chao and Susan Ho. They're both doctors at the Hôtel Dieu.
Let me introduce Mr. Tom Bertolone and his wife Beverly.	Let me introduce Beverly and Tom Bertolone.

We have, however, made more substantial progress in reflecting changes and changed attitudes toward women in the professional arena. Compare the terms we now use to describe workers with those used in the 1950s:

Terms Used Today	Terms Used in 1950s
Flight attendant	Stewardess
Firefighter	Fireman
Police officer	Policeman
Physician	Female doctor
Office workers	Girls at work
Ms.	Miss/Mrs.
People/humans	Mankind

Consciously remembering to use non-sexist language will result in several benefits. First, non-sexist language reflects non-sexist attitudes. Your attitudes are reflected in your

speech, and your speech affects your attitudes. Monitoring your speech for sexist remarks can help you monitor your attitudes about sexist assumptions. Second, using non-sexist language will help you become more other-oriented. Monitoring your language for sexist remarks will reflect your sensitivity to others. Third, non-sexist language will make your speech more contemporary and unambiguous. By substituting the word "humankind" for "mankind," for example, you can communicate that you are including all people, not just men, in your observation or statement. Finally, your non-sexist language will empower others. By eliminating sexist bias from your speech, you will help confirm the value of all the individuals with whom you interact.

In addition to the debate over language that refers to gender, there is considerable and controversial discussion about the language used to describe sexual orientations. The principle of being other-oriented includes sensitivity in your choice of words when you speak of someone's sexual orientation. Labelling someone a "fag," "queer," or "dyke" is not only likely to be offensive and hurtful to the person being labelled; it will also reflect poorly on the sensitivity of the person doing the labelling. We're not suggesting that certain words be expunged from dictionaries or never uttered; we are suggesting that when describing others, people should be sensitive to how others wish to be addressed and discussed.

Avoid Ethnically or Racially Biased Language. Besides monitoring your language for sexual stereotypes, avoid racial and ethnic stereotypes. Monitor your speech so you are not, even unconsciously, using phrases that depict a racial or ethnic group in a negative or stereotypical fashion. How do you feel about being called a Canuck? A student writer for an American university paper who used the term "Canucks" to refer to the many Canadians moving into the entertainment field in the United States was fired for it. He was later rehired after a large number of Canadians said that they did not find the term offensive.[15] Expressions such as "Indian giver" or "I jewed him down" (to negotiate a good price) demonstrate an insensitivity to members of other cultural groups. The underlying principle in avoiding biased language is to be other-oriented and to imagine how the listener might react to your words. As illustrated in the *Canadian Connections* feature on page 132, how we label others can affect our perceptions. A sensitive, other-oriented communicator keeps abreast of changes in preferred labels and adopts the designations currently preferred by members of the ethnic groups themselves.

Avoid Demeaning Language. Language barriers are created not only when someone uses sexist or racially biased language but also when someone disparages a person's age, mental or physical ability, or social standing. Calling someone a "geezer," "retard," or "trailer trash" may seem harmless or humorous to some, but others may perceive these labels as insensitive or insulting.

Age-based discrimination is a growing problem in the workplace. In some occupations, as a worker moves into his or her 50s, it may be difficult to change jobs or find work. Despite laws designed to guard against age discrimination, it clearly exists. As we have noted, the language that people use has power to affect attitudes and behaviour. This is why using negative terms to describe the elderly can be a subtle—or sometimes not-so-subtle—way of expressing disrespect toward an older generation.

Also monitor the way you talk about someone's social class. Although some societies and cultures make considerable distinctions among classes, it is nonetheless offensive today to use words that are intended to demean someone's social class. Terms such as "welfare recipients," "manual labourers," and "blue-collar workers" are often used derogatorily. Avoid labelling someone in a way that shows disrespect toward the person's social standing, education, or socioeconomic status.

BEING **Other**-ORIENTED

There will be many times when you find you need to offer an opinion or express your reaction to something someone has said or done. What are effective ways of using the principles and skills presented in this chapter to be both honest and supportive of others?

RECAP   Managing Communication Barriers

Barrier	Definition	Example
Bypassing	Confusion caused by the fact that the same word may evoke different meanings for different people	"W.C." might mean "wayside chapel" to a Swiss person and "water closet" to a British person.
When speaking, provide specific examples; when listening, ask questions to clarify the meaning.		
Lack of clarity	Inappropriate or imprecise use of words	Sign in Acapulco hotel: "The manager has personally passed all the water served here."
When speaking, use more precise language. Provide short, specific examples or indicate the probability of something happening: "There's a 40% chance I won't go shopping today." When listening, paraphrase the message to ensure that you understand it accurately.		
Allness	Tendency to lump things or people into all-encompassing categories	"All Albertans drive pickup trucks and wear cowboy hats."
When speaking, say "To me" before you offer a generalization to indicate that the idea or perception is your own. Index a generalized statement by using phrases that separate one situation, person, or example from another. When listening, ask the speaker whether he or she intends to mean that *every* situation or person fits the generalization presented.		
Static evaluation	Statement labelling people, objects, or events without considering change	You still call your 28-year-old nephew a juvenile delinquent because he spray-painted your fence when he was 11.
When speaking, put a date on your observation: "In 1989 I thought he was a difficult child to manage." When listening, ask the speaker whether the observation remains true today or if the same generalization applies now.		
Polarization	Use of either/or terms—good or bad, right or wrong	"You're either with me or against me."
When speaking, avoid either/or terms and blaming something on a specific cause. When listening, ask the speaker whether a statement really reflects an all-or-nothing, either/or proposition.		
Biased language	Language that reflects gender, racial, ethnic, age, ability, or class biases	"His mom is a mailman."
When speaking, be mindful of how insensitive language can hurt someone. Avoid using labels or derogatory terms. When listening, try to keep your emotions in check when others use inappropriate words or insensitive, derogatory phrases. You can't control what others do or say, only what you do and say and how you react. Consider appropriately but assertively communicating that a word, label, or phrase offends you.		

Words of Support

"I'm going to win this argument."

"You're wrong and I'm right. It's as simple as that."

"We're going to do it my way or else!"

None of these statements is likely to result in a positive communication climate. All three are likely to result in debate rather than true dialogue. The words you hear and use are central to your establishing a quality or positive relationship with others. Author and researcher Daniel Yankelovich points out that the goal of conversations with others should be to establish a genuine dialogue rather than verbally arm-wrestle a partner in order to win the argument.[16] A true dialogue involves establishing a climate of equality, listening with empathy, and trying to bring assumptions into the open. Expressing equality, empathy,

ADAPTING TO DIFFERENCES
Understanding Others

Do Men and Women Speak the Same Language?

In Chapter 4 we noted that gender makes a difference in how we interact with others. John Gray's popular self-help book *Men Are from Mars, Women Are from Venus*[17] has been heralded by some as "the book that saved our relationship," yet some communication scholars have concluded that Gray has overstated his case in claiming that there are vast differences in the ways men and women speak to each other.[18] The thing to keep in mind is that the differences are not so extensive that they cannot be bridged. Men and women do indeed speak the same language, but they may have different assumptions about the function of talk in the development of relationships.

Julia Wood is a communication researcher who has criticized John Gray for oversimplifying the differences in how men and women talk to one another. She acknowledges that women tend to use talk to establish and maintain relationships more so than men. In reviewing the literature on women's speech, Wood found the following:[19]

- Women tend to seek to establish equality between themselves and others by using such phrases as "I know just how you feel" or "Yes, the same thing has happened to me."

- Women are more likely to show emotional support for others using statements such as "How wonderful" or "Oh, that sounds very frustrating."

- Women often spend time conducting conversational "maintenance work,"—for example, trying to keep the conversation from lagging by asking open-ended questions that prompt a more detailed response.

- Women are more likely to be inclusive—to make sure everyone present is invited to talk.

- Women also have been found to be more tentative in the way they use language. They may use more qualifiers when they talk, saying things like "*I thought* it was kind of boring" (rather than just saying "It was boring"). Tentativeness is also expressed by ending a phrase with a question—called a tag question—such as "That was a good class, wasn't it?"

- Women tend to spend more time when composing email messages to ensure that the message fits with social norms.[20]

- Women are more likely than men to pick up on relational cues in email messages.

One study found that when composing email messages, women were perceived to express more interpersonal sensitivity and emotional warmth than were men.[21] Women also tend to be adaptive to their message sender when composing an email; compared to men, they wrote more personalized and polite email messages to friends their own age and more formal email messages to their professors.[22] So language differences between men and women have been found to exist both in person and online.

In contrast, men tend to use their verbal messages for "proving oneself and negotiating prestige."[23] Rather than talking about a relationship, men are more likely to engage in mutual activities to communicate friendship, such as going to a movie together or participating in sports or other activities of mutual interest. Wood's literature review suggests the following:[24]

- Men are less likely to present information that indicates their vulnerabilities. Men talk to establish their power, status, and worth.

- Men also talk to accomplish tasks rather than to express feelings—they are more instrumental in the way they use language. Men talk to seek information, share information, and solve problems.

- Men tend to use speech to sustain and even dominate a conversation; there is evidence that they interrupt others more than women do.

- Men are, according to research, more assertive and less tentative when talking with others.

- Men speak in more general, abstract ways and often are less concrete and specific when describing situations and events.

- Men tend to provide fewer responsive cues such as "I'm listening," "yes," "uh-hum," and "I'm with you."

Yet, despite differences, researchers have also found much similarity, which is why many communication researchers and educators suggest that it's not helpful to compare and contrast the way men and women speak as if they were from separate planets. For example, one research study suggests that it's not true that women talk more than men; both men and women use about the same number of words during a typical day of conversation.[25] Communication researcher Anthony Mulac has concluded that although there are some differences between the speech of men and women, the differences are not significant enough to explain why conflicts may occur. Mulac found that when reading written transcripts of conversations, it was difficult for readers to identify whether the speakers were men or women.[26]

Deborah Tannen suggests that differences between men and women can be described as cultural differences.[27] The strategies for bridging cultural differences that we discussed in Chapter 4 can be useful in enhancing the quality of communication between men and women: be mindful of different communication assumptions, tolerate some uncertainty and ambiguity in communication, ask questions, seek more information before reacting (or overreacting) to messages, be other-oriented, and adapt communication messages.

and openness and avoiding biases are more likely to occur if you approach conversations as dialogue rather than debate. In true dialogue, people look for common ground rather than using a war of words to defend a position.

For more than three decades, Jack Gibb's observational research has been used as a framework for both describing and prescribing verbal behaviours that contribute to feelings of either supportiveness or defensiveness.[28] Gibb spent several years listening to and observing groups of individuals in meetings and conversations, noting that some exchanges seemed to create a supportive climate, whereas others created a defensive one. Words and actions, he concluded, are tools we use to let someone know whether we support them or not. Now let's consider how you can use words to create a supportive climate rather than an antagonistic or defensive one.

Describe Your Own Feelings Instead of Evaluating the Behaviour of Others

Most of us don't like to be judged or evaluated. Criticizing and name-calling, obviously, can create relational problems, but so can our attempts to diagnose others' problems or win their affection with insincere praise. In fact, any form of evaluation creates a climate of defensiveness. As Winston Churchill declared, "I am always ready to learn, although I do not always like being taught." Correcting others, even when we are doing it "for their own good," can cause them to become defensive.

One way to avoid evaluating others is to eliminate the accusatory "you" from your language. Statements such as "You always come in late for supper" or "You need to pick up the dirty clothes in your room" attack a person's sense of self-worth and usually result in a defensive reaction.

extended "I" language. Brief preface to a feedback statement, intended to communicate that you don't want your listener to take your message in an overly critical way.

Instead, use the word "I" to describe your own feelings and thoughts about a situation or event: "I find it hard to keep your supper warm when you're late," or "I don't enjoy the extra work of picking up your dirty clothes." When you describe your own feelings instead of berating the receiver of the message, you are in essence taking ownership of the problem. This approach leads to greater openness and trust because your listener does not feel rejected or that you are trying to control him or her. Also, when you express your emotions, make sure you choose the right words to communicate your feelings.

Sometimes simply using an "I" message may be too subtle to take the sting out of the negative message you want to express. You may need to add a longer justification when you provide negative, emotional information to another. We call this using **extended "I" language**, which is a brief preface to a feedback statement, intended to communicate that you don't want the person to think you don't value or care about him or her even though you have a negative message to share. Saying something like "I don't want you to misinterpret what I'm about to say, because I really do care about you" or "I don't think it's entirely your fault, but I'm feeling frustrated when I experience …" may have a better chance of enhancing communication than simply beginning a sentence with the word "I" instead of "You." Remember, there are no magic words for enhancing communication. However, strategies of being other-oriented do seem to enhance the quality of communication. See the *Building Your Skills* box "Practise Using 'I' Language," which will help you practise expressing your feelings accurately and effectively.

Using descriptive "I" language rather than evaluative "you" language can help you manage tension and disagreement. How might the young man in this photo begin a conversation about his feelings in this situation?

(© AlikeYou/Shutterstock)

Building Your Skills | Practise Using "I" Language

An essential skill in being supportive rather than defensive is describing what you want with "I" language rather than "you" language. Rephrase the following "you" statements into "I" statements.

"You" Language

1. You are messy when you cook.
2. Your driving is terrible.
3. You never listen to me.
4. You just lie on the couch and never offer to help me.
5. You always decide what movie we see.

"I" Language

_____

_____

_____

_____

_____

Solve Problems Instead of Trying to Control Others

Most of us don't like it when others attempt to control us. Someone who presumes to tell us what's good for us, instead of helping us puzzle through issues and problems, is likely to engender defensiveness. Open-ended questions such as "What seems to be the problem?" and "How can we deal with the issue?" create a more supportive climate than critical comments such as "Here's where you're wrong" or commands such as "Don't do that!"

Be Genuine Rather Than Manipulative

To be genuine means that you honestly seek to be yourself rather than someone you are not. It also means taking an honest interest in others and considering the uniqueness of each individual and situation, avoiding generalizations or strategies that focus only on your own needs and desires. A manipulative person has hidden agendas; a genuine person uses words to discuss issues and problems openly and honestly.

If your goal is to look out only for your own interests, your language will reflect your self-focus. At the heart of being genuine is being other-oriented—being sincerely interested in those with whom you communicate. Although it's unrealistic to assume you will become best friends with everyone you meet, you *can* work to develop an unselfish interest in others. It may be hard to do, but the effort will be rewarded with a more positive communication climate.

Empathize Instead of Remaining Detached from Others

Empathy is one of the hallmarks of supportive relationships. As we learned earlier, empathy is the ability to understand the feelings of others and to predict the emotional responses they will have to different situations.

Being empathic is the essence of being other-oriented. The opposite of empathy is neutrality. To be neutral is to be indifferent toward another. Even when you express anger or irritation toward another, you are investing some energy in the relationship.

An essential skill in being supportive rather than defensive is describing what you want with "I" language rather than "you" language. Could the use of "I" language help this couple?

(© Jason Stitt/Shutterstock)

Developing empathy is a quintessential skill of being other-oriented. Yet, if you empathize and then feel smug or self-righteous about being empathic, your efforts to relate to another person may appear manipulative. How can you empathize with another person without focusing on yourself or appearing self-serving?

Research suggests that one of the most important things we can do to be empathic and supportive is simply what we have been suggesting throughout this book: be other-oriented. Interpersonal communication researcher Amy Bippus determined that what most people want from others during times of stress are messages of empathy and sensitivity to their feelings, followed by problem solving, relating, refraining from general negativity, and offering a different perspective. The positive interpersonal outcomes that resulted from providing other-oriented messages were a more upbeat mood, feelings of empowerment, and more focused, calmer thoughts.[29]

Be Flexible Rather Than Rigid Toward Others

Most people don't like someone who always seems certain that he or she is right. A "you're wrong, I'm right" attitude creates a defensive climate. This does not mean that you should have no opinions and go through life blithely agreeing to everything. Nor does it mean that there is never one answer that is right and others that are wrong. However, instead of making rigid pronouncements, you can use phrases such as "I may be wrong, but it seems to me …" or "Here's one way to look at this problem." This manner of speaking gives your opinions a softer edge that allows room for others to express their own point of view.

Present Yourself as Equal Rather Than Superior

You can antagonize others by letting them know that you view yourself as better or brighter than they are. You may be gifted and intelligent, but it's not necessary to announce it, and although some people have the responsibility and authority to manage others, "pulling rank" does not usually produce a cooperative climate. With phrases such as "Let's work on this together" or "We each have a valid perspective," you can avoid erecting walls of resentment and suspicion.

Also, avoid using abstract language to impress others. Keep your messages short and clear, and use informal language. When you communicate with someone from another culture, you may need to use an **elaborated code** to get your message across. This means that your messages will have to be more explicit, but they should not be condescending. For example, if you were trying to explain to a French exchange student what a black fly

elaborated code. Using many words and various ways of describing an idea or concept to communicate its meaning.

RECAP | Using Supportive Communication and Avoiding Defensive Communication

Supportive Communication Is . . .	Defensive Communication Is . . .
Descriptive: Use "I" language that describes your own feelings and ideas.	**Evaluative:** Avoid using "you" language that attacks the worth of another person.
Problem-Oriented: Aim communication at solving problems and generating multiple options.	**Controlling:** Don't attempt to get others to do only what you want them to do in order to control the outcome.
Spontaneously Genuine: Develop a here-and-now orientation. Be honest and authentic rather than fake and phony.	**Strategically Manipulative:** Avoid planning your conversation in advance to get what you want. Don't develop a script to manipulate and accomplish your goal.
Empathic: Be emotionally involved in the conversation; attempt to understand what your partner is thinking and feeling.	**Neutrally Detached:** Avoid being emotionally indifferent or creating the impression that you don't care how another person is feeling.
Provisionally Flexible: Be open to receiving new information; demonstrate flexibility in the positions you take.	**Certain and Rigid:** Don't take a dogmatic, entrenched, or rigid position on issues; be willing to listen to others.
Equal: Adopt a communication style based on mutual respect and assume each person has a right to express ideas and share information.	**Superior:** Avoid assuming an attitude or mindset that you and your ideas are better than others.

is, first you would have to translate "fly" into French, and then you would have to provide scientific, descriptive, and narrative evidence to help the student understand how these tiny, biting insects terrorize people in the northern part of Ontario.

Underlying the goal of creating a supportive rather than a defensive communication climate is the importance of providing emotional support when communicating with others. A basic principle of all healthy interpersonal relationships is the importance of positive, supportive messages that communicate liking or affection. Providing verbal messages of comfort and support, not surprisingly, enhances the quality of a relationship; as a relationship develops over time and the communication partners gain more credibility and influence, messages of comfort play an even more important role in maintaining the quality of the interpersonal relationship. We use not only words of comfort but, as you will learn in Chapter 7, nonverbal expressions of comfort as well.

How to Apologize

In this chapter we've talked about the power of words and how communication can sometimes create problems and damage a relationship. There are times, if we're honest with ourselves, that we aren't as other-oriented as we should be, and we may say and do things that we shouldn't. We're human; we make mistakes. Words, however, not only inflict pain but also have power to repair relational damage.

One of the ways to mend a relational rift when we have made a mistake is to offer an **apology**—to explicitly admit that we made an error and to ask the person we offended to forgive us. An apology helps us save face and can repair relational stress. One research team found that people who received an apology felt less anger, were less likely to be aggressive, and had a better overall impression of the offender.[30] An apology can calm a turbulent relationship.

Communication researchers Janet Meyer and Kyra Rothenberg found that the seriousness of the offence and the quality of the relationship we have with another person determine whether we are likely to apologize and the kind of apology we should offer.[31] Committing a serious blunder or error is more likely to result in an apology than committing a mild offence—especially if we believe we've hurt someone. We're also more likely to apologize to someone if we feel guilty or embarrassed by something we've said or done. And the more interpersonally intimate we are with someone, the more likely we are to apologize.

What kinds of apologies are most effective? One of the most effective ways to apologize is simply to honestly and sincerely admit that you were wrong. It's not enough just to say, "I'm sorry I hurt you." A true apology acknowledges that the offending individual was wrong. Thus, it's better to say it explicitly: "I was wrong." Assuming responsibility for the error and offering to do something to repair the damage are specific kinds of behaviours that enhance the effectiveness of an apology. Also, it may not be best to apologize immediately after you make a mistake; an apology given too quickly may be perceived as insincere—the offended person may think that you're just trying to quickly dismiss the error. If you wait a short time before apologizing, your apology will be perceived as more sincere and heartfelt. Being perceived as sincerely remorseful is one of the keys to an effective apology.

The words we use can hurt others. We can also use words to repair the damage we have done by offering an apology expressing that we were wrong (not simply sorry), we are sincerely remorseful, we want to do something to repair the damage, and

apology. Explicit admission of an error, along with a request for forgiveness.

An apology can help you save face when you have made a relationship blunder and can relieve tension between you and another person.

(© Jupiterimages/Thinkstock/Getty Images)

we understand how much we may have hurt our communication partner. A well-worded apology can help restore lustre to a relationship that may have become tarnished. Words have power—to hurt and to heal.

How to Be Assertive

At times you run across people who are verbally aggressive, obnoxious, or worse—they may try to coerce or intimidate you into doing things you'd rather not do. Being other-oriented doesn't mean you should ignore such boorish behaviour. Nor do you have to respond in the same way you have been treated. Rather than return mean-spirited aggressiveness with an equally inappropriate stream of aggressive words or rude behaviour, consider using your verbal skills to be appropriately assertive. To be **assertive** is to make requests, ask for information, stand up for your rights, and generally pursue your own best interests without denying your communication partner's rights.

Each individual has rights. You have the right to refuse a request someone makes of you, the right to express your feelings as long as you don't trample on the feelings of others, and the right to have your personal needs met if this doesn't infringe on the rights of others. Assertive people let their communication partners know when a message or behaviour is infringing on their rights.

As we mentioned earlier, the freedom to express your opinion is protected by law, as is the freedom from aggressive behaviour (including sexual harassment). In the workplace, for example, you have the right to be assertive and to not tolerate any kind of harassment. Your college or university also has policies that protect your rights and procedures to report harassment or aggression. The *Canadian Human Rights Act* also holds that others are responsible for taking action, too: for example, teachers and principals are responsible if harassment occurs in their classroom or school or anywhere school-related activities are taking place, and employers are responsible if harassment occurs in their workplace or wherever their employees do work-related activities.

Some people confuse the terms "assertive" and "aggressive." Being **aggressive** means pursuing your interests by denying the rights of others. Assertiveness is other-oriented; aggressiveness is exclusively self-oriented. Aggressive people blame, judge, and evaluate to get what they want. Aggressive communicators use defensive communication tactics, including such intimidating nonverbal cues as steely stares, a bombastic voice, and flailing gestures. Assertive people can ask for what they want without judging or evaluating their partners.

When presenting the dos and don'ts of appropriate verbal communication in this chapter, we've often emphasized strategies for initiating communication with others. Sometimes what's most challenging is to respond appropriately when another person (who has not taken a course in interpersonal communication) comes at you with an inappropriately aggressive, argumentative, or defensive message, especially if the inappropriate message that's hurled at you takes you by surprise. You do not have to be passive when you are on the receiving end of such messages. We suggest instead that an effective communicator is appropriately assertive.

assertive. Able to pursue one's own best interests without denying the rights of one's communication partner.

aggressive. Pursuing one's own interests by denying the rights of others.

▶ RECAP   Assertiveness vs. Aggressiveness

Assertiveness	Aggressiveness
Expresses your interests without denying the rights of others	Expresses your interests and denies the rights of others
Is other-oriented	Is self-oriented
Describes what you want	Evaluates the other person
Discloses your needs using "I" messages	Discloses your needs using "you" messages

Behaving Assertively: Five Steps

Many people have a tendency to withdraw in the face of controversy, even when their rights are being violated or denied. However, you can develop skill in asserting yourself by practising five key suggestions.

Describe. *Describe how you view the situation.* To assert your position, you first need to describe how you view the situation. You need to be assertive because the other person has not been other-oriented. For example, Doug is growing increasingly frustrated with Maria's tardiness for weekly staff meetings. He approaches the problem by first describing his observation: "I've noticed that you're usually 15 minutes late to our weekly staff meetings." A key to communicating your assertive message is to monitor your nonverbal message, especially your voice. Avoid sarcasm or excessive vocal intensity. Calmly yet confidently describe the problem.

Disclose. *Disclose your feelings.* After describing the situation from your perspective, let the other person know how you feel.[32] Disclosing your feelings will help build empathy and avoid lengthy harangues about the other person's unjust treatment. "I feel you don't take our weekly meetings seriously," continues Doug as he asserts his desire for Maria to be on time to the meetings. Note that Doug does not talk about how others are feeling ("Every member of our group is tired of your coming in late"); he only describes how *he* feels.

Identify Effects. Next, you can *identify the effects of the other person's behaviour* on you or others. "When you're late, it disrupts our meeting," says Doug.

Be Silent. *Wait.* After taking the first three steps, simply wait for a response. Some people find this step hard. Again, make sure to monitor your nonverbal cues. Make sure your facial expression does not contradict your verbal message. Delivering an assertive message with a broad grin might create a double bind for your listener, who may not be sure what the primary message is—the verbal one or the nonverbal one.

Paraphrase. *Paraphrase content and feelings.* After the other person responds, paraphrase both the content and the feelings of the message. Suppose Maria says, "Oh, I'm sorry. I didn't realize I was creating a problem. I have another meeting that usually goes overtime. It's difficult for me to arrive at the start of our meeting on time." Doug could respond, "So the key problem is a time conflict with another meeting. It must make you feel frustrated to try to do two things at once."

If the other person is evasive, unresponsive, or aggressive, you'll need to cycle through the steps again. Clearly describe what the other person is doing that is not acceptable; disclose how you feel; identify the effects; wait; then paraphrase and clarify as needed. A key goal of an assertive response is to seek an empathic connection between you and your partner. Paraphrasing feelings is a way of ensuring that both parties are connecting.

If you tend to withdraw from conflict, how can you become assertive? Visualizing can help. Think of a past situation in which you wished you had been more assertive and then mentally replay the situation, imagining what you might have said. Also practise verbalizing assertive statements. When you are able to be appropriately assertive, consciously congratulate yourself for sticking up for your rights. To sharpen your assertiveness skills, try the *Building Your Skills* box "How to Assert Yourself."

Building Your Skills | How to Assert Yourself

Working with a partner, describe a situation in which you could have been more assertive. Ask your partner to assume the role of the person toward whom you should have been more assertive. Now replay the situation, using the following skills:

1. *Describe:* Tell the other person that what he or she is doing bothers you. Describe rather than evaluate.
2. *Disclose:* Tell the other person how you feel. For example, "I feel X when you do Y."
3. *Identify effects:* Tell the other person the effects of his or her behaviour on you or your group. Be as clear and descriptive as you can.
4. *Wait:* After you have described, disclosed, and identified the effects, wait for a response.
5. *Paraphrase:* Use reflective listening skills, such as questioning, paraphrasing content, and paraphrasing feelings.

Observation of Assertiveness Skills

Ask your classmates to observe your role play and provide feedback, using the following checklist. When you have finished asserting your point of view, reverse roles.

_____ Clearly describes what the problem was
_____ Effectively discloses how he or she felt
_____ Clearly describes the effects of the behaviour
_____ Pauses or waits after describing the effects
_____ Uses effective questions to promote understanding
_____ Accurately paraphrases content
_____ Accurately paraphrases feelings
_____ Has good eye contact
_____ Leans forward while speaking
_____ Has an open body posture
_____ Has appropriate voice tone and quality

E-CONNECTIONS
Relating to Others | Using Words to Relate to Others Online

Today, people are relying more and more on electronically mediated communication (EMC) to "talk" to each other. Fifteen million Canadians log on to Facebook every month—that's half the population of Canada! And while the rest of the world has an average of 130 friends per user, Canadians have an average of 190 friends per user.

Not only do we connect online, but it's important to us to do so. In response to the statement "I feel addicted to Facebook," over one-third of the over 2850 students who responded to a survey indicated that they "agreed" or "strongly agreed." One survey respondent wrote "Facebook, I hate you!" in acknowledging the pervasive power it had over her life.[33]

Will the fact that we are using the written word in place of the spoken word to connect to others change the very nature of interpersonal relationships? In speculating about how our reliance on EMC will affect the way we use language and relate to others in the future, linguist Naomi Baron suggests the following consequences of our increased reliance on the written word:

- *Informality.* We will write more informally as we write more. What we write

to one another will continue to take the place of spoken messages, so our written messages will more closely resemble spoken messages.

- *Language Use.* We will become increasingly uncertain about how we use words, so we'll make up our own rules and not worry about precise language rules or usage in our informal text messages. As we tap out a quick text message, we may not be as careful or thoughtful about, for example, whether we hyphenate words or how we spell and use punctuation.

- *Writing's Influence on Talking.* The way we communicate in EMC contexts will influence how we communicate face to face. We'll use more abbreviations.

- *Word Control.* We will have more control over the messages we receive. Because we can often see who's texting, calling, or emailing us, we'll decide when, where, and even if we will receive messages. We will have what Baron calls greater "volume control" over the number of EMC words that reach us.

- *Written Culture.* We will increasingly become a "written culture" because of the power and importance of texting, instant messaging, and other ways of sharing written words.

- *More Relationships in Less Depth.* We'll know more people but less information about them. In an editorial in *The New York Times,* columnist Robert Wright noted, "Twenty years ago I rarely spoke by phone to more than five people in a day. Now I often send email to dozens of people a day. I have so many friends! Um, can you remind me of their names?"[34] In short, we know more people more shallowly.

- *Moment-to-Moment Contact.* Because we can be in touch with others in real time with our cell phones, text messages, and a variety of other tools, we will be able to experience what others are experiencing in real time. As Baron puts it, "When we are always on, we have the ability to live in other people's moments. Relationships can be maintained through running discourse rather than reflective synopsis. Absence may or may not make the heart grow fonder."[35]

APPLYING AN OTHER-ORIENTATION
to Enhancing Your Verbal Skills

The key to shared understanding is a focus on the needs, goals, and mindset of your communication partner. Throughout this chapter we have emphasized how to develop an other-oriented approach when communicating verbally. In focusing on others, keep the following principles in mind.

Meanings Are in People, Not in Words. Your communication partner creates meaning based on his or her own experiences. Don't assume that other people will always (or even usually) understand what you mean. Words are symbols, and the potential for misunderstanding them is high.

Meaning is fragile, so handle with care.

Words Have Power to Influence Others. Words have the power to determine how people view the world. They also affect thoughts and behaviours. Be mindful of the potency of words for influencing how others react. Words can trigger wars and negotiate peace; they affect how others react to us.

Speak to Others as They Would Like to Be Spoken To. It's not enough to consider how you would react to words and phrases you use; you need

to be tuned in to the kinds of messages another person might prefer. You may like "straight talk" and messages that are short and to the point. Your communication partner may prefer a softer tone and a more positive, supportive message than you need.

We're not suggesting that you should be a verbal chameleon and avoid asserting your own ideas and positions. We are suggesting that if you want to be heard and understood, thinking how others will interpret your message can enhance the communication process.

How Words Work (pages 127–130)

OBJECTIVE ❶ Describe the relationship between words and meaning.

Key Terms

symbols *127*

referents *127*

thought *127*

denotative meaning *128*

connotative meaning *128*

onomatopoeia *129*

symbolic interaction *130*

Critical Thinking Questions

1. How is language symbolic? How does the arbitrary nature of language and the naming of objects or experiences lead to misunderstandings?

2. How has culture affected your language? Do you use words that seem confusing to others? Have you been in a situation in which someone used a familiar word but with a different meaning than you were accustomed to? How did you resolve the misunderstanding?

Activities

Make a list of 10 to 15 familiar, everyday words and phrases (such as "home" or "online communication") and write their denotative and connotative meanings. Working in small groups, share your words with classmates and ask them to write down what the words mean to them. (Have them do the same with their own list of words.) Compare the connotative meanings. Are there differences in what a word means to different people? Is there a wide range of meanings? Can these differences be attributed to culture, gender, or differences in background and past experiences?

Web Resources

www.webopedia.com Uncertain about the meaning of a word that you find on the Internet? Look it up on the Webopedia. This site will help you interpret words that you don't understand.

The Power of Words (pages 130–134)

OBJECTIVE ❷ Identify how words influence our perceptions, thoughts, actions, relationships, and culture.

Key Terms

linguistic determinism *132*

linguistic relativity *132*

Sapir-Whorf hypothesis *132*

world view *133*

Critical Thinking Questions

1. Ethics: Do you think the use of profanity in everyday life is increasing? Have new communication technologies, including texting, blogging, IMing, and the like, contributed to this increase? Do mass media contribute to the increase? Can you think of examples? Do you think the media have relaxed their standards for allowing profanity? Explain.

2. Ethics: Make a list of euphemisms used in everyday speech as well as by politicians and other public figures. (Consider, for example, explanations of the Iraq War, discussions of recent elections, and terms used to describe the recession and economic solutions.) Is the use of these words and expressions appropriate? Do they deliberately mislead? Do they diminish the significance of a difficult situation such as economic woes (e.g., "downsizing") or war?

Activities

Collect print ads that feature catchy slogans or phrases. Make a list of other mass media ads (TV, radio, Internet, billboards, etc.) whose words or phrases grab your attention. Share the ads with your classmates and analyze as a group what makes the words or phrases powerful or memorable. Do the words influence your actions—for example, persuading you to do something or to buy a particular product? Explain.

Web Resources

http://faculty.washington.edu/ezent/el.htm At this site you'll learn tips about language and examples of good and bad uses of language. You'll be reminded that language reflects, reinforces, and shapes our perceptions of others.

Communication Barriers: Managing Misunderstandings (pages 134–140)

OBJECTIVE ❸ Identify word barriers and know how to manage them.

Key Terms

bypassing *134*

malapropism *134*

restricted code *135*

jargon *135*

allness statements *136*

indexing *136*

static evaluation *136*

polarization *137*

hate speech *137*

Critical Thinking Questions

1. Rephrase the following statements, using the skill of indexing:
   a. All politicians want power and control over others.
   b. All teachers are underpaid.
   c. All people from British Columbia like to brag about how beautiful their province is.

2. Ethics: Is it ethical to correct someone when he or she uses sexist language or makes a stereotyping remark about someone's race, gender, or sexual orientation? What if that person is your boss or your teacher? Explain your answer.

Activities

In small groups, brainstorm lists of "restricted code" words and/or jargon, including "textspeak" (abbreviations used in IMing and texting). Come up with as many words as you can. Share the lists that each group creates. Are the lists similar? Did classmates introduce you to words you hadn't known before? Do the restricted codes seem to suggest a particular group or culture? What do people in these subgroups have in common (for example, age, gender, ethnicity)?

Words of Support, How to Apologize, and How to Be Assertive

(pages 140–149)

OBJECTIVES **4** **5** **6** Understand how to use words to provide support and avoid defensiveness, how an apology can enhance the quality of interpersonal communication, and how appropriate assertiveness skills can enhance the quality of interpersonal communication.

Key Terms

extended "I" language *142*
elaborated code *144*
apology *145*

assertive *146*
aggressive *146*

Critical Thinking Questions

1. What is your reaction to the information presented in *eConnections: Relating to Others*? Do you find yourself texting, IMing, or communicating online more often than face to face these days? Do you feel that you have more friends because you use EMC? Are your relationships with these "friends" richer or more shallow than your face-to-face relationships? Explain.

2. Ethics: Is it ethical to mask your true feelings of anger and irritation with someone by using supportive statements or confirming statements when what you really want to do is tell the person off in no uncertain terms? Why or why not?

Activities

Assertiveness Practice: Working with a partner, describe a situation in which you could have been more assertive. Ask your partner to assume the role of the person toward whom you should have been more assertive. Now replay the situation, using the assertiveness skills described in the chapter. Ask your classmates to observe the role play and provide feedback, using the following checklist. When you have finished asserting your point of view, reverse roles with your partner.

____ Clearly describes the problem
____ Effectively discloses how he or she felt
____ Clearly describes the effects of the behaviour
____ Pauses or waits after describing the effects
____ Uses effective questions to promote understanding
____ Accurately paraphrases content
____ Accurately paraphrases feelings
____ Has good eye contact
____ Leans forward while speaking
____ Has an open body posture
____ Has appropriate voice tone and quality

Web Resources

www.vandruff.com/art_converse.html Are you a conversational terrorist, or do you know someone who is? In the article "Conversational Terrorism," you'll discover dos and don'ts for conversing with others and learn how to avoid terrorizing others when you talk with them.

7

Nonverbal Communication Skills

66 What you are speaks so loudly that I cannot hear what you say. 99 —Ralph Waldo Emerson

© Fotolia

OBJECTIVES	OUTLINE
❶ Explain why nonverbal communication is an important area of study.	Identifying the Importance of Nonverbal Communication
❷ Identify and describe eight nonverbal communication codes.	Understanding Nonverbal Communication Codes
❸ Enhance your skill in interpreting nonverbal messages.	How to Improve Your Skill in Interpreting Nonverbal Messages
❹ Enhance your skill in expressing nonverbal messages.	How to Improve Your Skill in Expressing Nonverbal Messages

D o you like to "people watch"? When you are sitting in a public place such as a shopping mall, an airport, or a bus stop, do you sometimes make assumptions about what other people might be like as you observe their comings and goings? Most of us are people watchers from time to time—we rely on nonverbal communication to help us make predictions about others. **Nonverbal communication** is behaviour other than written or spoken language that creates meaning. A person's tone of voice, eye contact, facial expressions, posture, movement, general appearance, use of personal space, manipulation of the communication environment, and a host of other nonverbal clues reveal how that person feels about others. All communication has both a content and a relationship dimension. Our nonverbal communication is a primary source of relationship cues.

In this chapter we will focus on how nonverbal communication affects the quality of our interpersonal relationships. Being able to interpret others' unspoken messages and appropriately express our own feelings through nonverbal communication are key components of being other-oriented. To help you become more skilled in both expressing and interpreting nonverbal messages, we'll discuss why nonverbal communication is important in establishing interpersonal relationships with others. We'll also note challenges in trying to accurately interpret the unspoken messages of others. After we discuss several nonverbal communication codes, we'll offer tips for helping you more accurately interpret nonverbal communication.

nonverbal communication. Behaviour other than written or spoken language that creates meaning for someone.

Identifying the Importance of Nonverbal Communication

Nonverbal communication is an ever-present form of human expression. If you are alive, chances are that people are making inferences about you based on your nonverbal behaviour. But are our people-watching guesses about others accurate? Sometimes yes, and sometimes no. This chapter is designed to help you increase your accuracy in evaluating the nonverbal messages of others. Just as you may inaccurately interpret these messages, other people may misjudge your own nonverbal cues. Because much of our nonverbal communication behaviour is unconscious, most of us have only a limited awareness or understanding of it. Let's begin by looking at the multiple reasons nonverbal communication is so important in the total interpersonal communication process.

Nonverbal Messages Are the Primary Way to Communicate Our Feelings and Attitudes

Amin knew that he was in trouble the moment he walked into the dining room. His wife, Sandra, gave him a steely stare. Her brow was furrowed and her arms were crossed. The table was set for eight, with candles burnt to nubs, an empty bottle of wine, and dirty plates at all but one place setting—his. Amin had forgotten the dinner party Sandra had planned, and he needed no words from her to sense the depth of her displeasure. Although Amin was momentarily in trouble for his forgetfulness, his ability to quickly read the nonverbal message in that situation will serve him well in the long run. Marriage partners who are skilled at interpreting the emotional meaning of a message are typically more satisfied in their marriages. After all, nonverbal communication is the primary way we communicate feelings, attitudes, and emotions.

Portrait artists pay close attention to nonverbal cues such as posture, facial expression, and gesture to capture their subjects' personalities. What do the nonverbal cues reveal about the woman in this Vincent van Gogh painting, *Portrait of Madame Ginoux (L'Arlésienne)*?

(© Scala/Art Resource, NY)

Nonverbal Messages Are Usually More Believable Than Verbal Messages

"Honey, do you love me?" asks Brenda.

"Of course I love you. Haven't I always told you that I love you?" mutters Jim, keeping his eyes on his iPad.

Brenda will probably not feel reassured by Jim's words. The contradiction between his spoken message of love and his nonverbal message of distraction and lack of interest will leave her wondering about his true feelings.

Actions speak louder than words. This expression became a cliché because it's true—nonverbal communication is more believable than verbal communication. Nonverbal messages are more difficult to fake. Most of us use the following cues, listed in order of most to least important, to help us discern when a person is lying:

- Greater time lag in response to a question

- Reduced eye contact

- Increased shifts in posture

- Unfilled pauses

- Less smiling

- Slower speech

- Higher pitch in voice

- More deliberate pronunciation and articulation of words

It is difficult to manipulate an array of nonverbal cues, so a skilled other-oriented observer can see when a person's true feelings leak out. The face, hands, and feet are key sources of nonverbal cues. Are you aware of what your fingers and toes are doing as you are reading this book? Even if we become experts at masking and manipulating our faces, we may first signal lack of interest or boredom with another person by finger wagging or toe wiggling, or we may twiddle a pen or pencil. When we become emotionally aroused, the pupils of our eyes dilate, and we may blush, sweat, or change our breathing patterns. Lie detector tests rely on these unconscious cues. A polygraph measures a person's heart and breathing rate, as well as the electrical resistance of the skin (called *galvanic skin response*), to determine whether he or she is giving truthful verbal responses.

Nonverbal Messages Work with Verbal Messages to Create Meaning

Although we rely heavily on nonverbal messages, they do not operate independently of spoken messages in our relationships. Instead, verbal and nonverbal cues work together in two primary ways to help us make sense of others' messages.

1. *Nonverbal cues help us manage verbal messages.* Specifically, our nonverbal cues can substitute for verbal messages, as well as repeat, contradict, or regulate what we say. When someone asks, "Which way did he go?", you can silently point to or look at the back door. In these instances, you are substituting nonverbal cues for a verbal message.

   You can also use nonverbal cues to repeat or reinforce your words. "Where is the library?" a student asks her professor. "Down that hall to the right and up the stairs," says the professor, pointing in the correct direction. The professor's pointing gesture repeats his verbal instruction and clarifies the message.

   "Sure, this is a good time to talk about our latest credit card statement," says Dave with a shaky voice, nervously looking at his watch and avoiding eye contact with his wife. In this instance, the nonverbal cues contradict the verbal ones, and as you learned earlier, the nonverbal message is almost always the one we believe.

   We also use nonverbal cues to regulate our participation in verbal exchanges. In most informal meetings, it is not appropriate or necessary to signal your desire to speak by raising your hand. Yet somehow you are able to signal to others when you'd like to speak and when you'd rather not talk. How does this happen? You use eye contact, raised eyebrows, an open mouth, or perhaps a single raised index finger to signal that you would like to make a point. If your colleagues do not see these signals, especially the eye contact, they may think you are not interested in talking.

2. *Nonverbal cues augment the emotional meaning of verbal messages.* Our unspoken cues accent and complement verbal messages to increase or decrease the emotional impact of what we say. "Unless we vote to increase our tax base," bellows a local politician while shaking his fist in the air to accentuate his message, "we will not have enough classroom space to educate our children!" A scolding mother's wagging finger and an angry supervisor's raised voice are both nonverbal cues that accent verbal messages.

Simultaneous and complementary verbal and nonverbal messages can also help colour the emotion we are expressing or the attitude we are conveying. The length of a hug while you tell your son you are proud of him provides additional information about the intensity of your pride. The firmness of your handshake when you greet a job interviewer can confirm your verbal claim that you are eager for employment.

People Respond and Adapt to Others Through Nonverbal Messages

You sense that your best friend is upset. Even though she doesn't tell you she's angry, you sense her mood by observing her grimacing facial expression and lack of direct eye contact with you. To help lighten the mood, you tell a joke. Many times every day, you "read" the nonverbal cues of others, even before they utter a word, to gain clues about what to say or how to react. Interpreting others' nonverbal messages helps us appropriately adapt our communication as we interact with them. **Interaction adaptation theory** describes how people adapt to the communication behaviour of others.

The theory holds that we respond not only to what people say but also to their nonverbal expressions to help us navigate through our interpersonal conversations each day. If, for example, your friend leans forward to tell a story, you may lean forward to listen. Or if during a meeting you sit with folded arms, unconvinced of what you are hearing, you may look around the conference table and find others with similarly folded arms. As if we were

BEING Other-ORIENTED

Although it may be tempting to look at one specific bit of nonverbal behaviour and reach a conclusion about someone's intentions, be cautious about taking a single cue out of context. Can you think of a situation in which someone thought they knew what you were thinking based on your nonverbal behaviour but they were wrong? What can you do to increase the accuracy of your own observations?

interaction adaptation theory. Theory suggesting that people interact with others by adapting to what others are doing.

part of an intricate dance, when we communicate, we relate to others by responding to their movements, eye contact, gestures, and other nonverbal cues.

Sometimes we relate by mirroring the posture or behaviour of others. Or we may find ourselves gesturing in sync with someone's vocal pattern. At times, you are conscious of such mirroring of behaviour, which is called **interactional synchrony**. At other times, you may not be aware that when your friend folds her arms while talking with you, you also fold your arms across your chest in a similar way. At a restaurant, you notice a couple who appear to be on a date. As they talk, they both lean forward toward each other. She crosses her legs; he crosses his legs. She touches her hair; he touches his hair. He tilts his head to the side; so does she. These unconscious gestures are signals of mutual interest and attraction, and are usually viewed as positive.

Nonverbal Communication Plays a Major Role in Interpersonal Relationships

As we learned in Chapter 1, communication is inescapable; and much of the meaning we communicate to others is based on nonverbal communications. Of course, the meaning that others interpret from your behaviour may not be the one you intended, and the inferences they draw based on nonverbal information may be right or wrong.

We learned in Chapter 3 that we begin making judgments about strangers just a fraction of a second after meeting them, based on nonverbal information. Within the first four minutes of interaction, we begin to draw conclusions about each other. Nonverbal cues are the ones that form first impressions, accurate or not.

Nonverbal expressions of support are important when providing comforting messages to others during times of stress and anxiety. Providing empathic, supportive facial expressions and vocal cues, hugs, and positive touch helps reduce stress and enhance a person's overall well-being.

Nonverbal cues are important not only when people initiate relationships but also as they maintain and develop mature relationships with others. In fact, the more intimate the relationship, the more people use and understand the nonverbal cues of their partners.

Long-married couples spend less time verbalizing their feelings and emotions to each other than they did when they were first dating; each learns how to interpret the other's subtle nonverbal cues. If your spouse is silent during dinner, you may know that she had a tough day and you should leave her alone and if your boyfriend is pacing back and forth when you arrive at his house, you know that he is nervous or anxious about something. In fact, all of us are more likely to use nonverbal cues to convey negative messages than to announce explicitly our dislike of something or someone. People also use nonverbal cues to signal changes in the level of satisfaction with a relationship. When we want to cool things off, we may start using a less vibrant tone of voice and cut back on eye contact and physical contact with our partner.

BEING Other-ORIENTED

The most powerful way to let someone know you care may be to express your support nonverbally rather than verbally. Think of a close friend or a family member. What nonverbal behaviours would best communicate support and empathy to that person?

interactional synchrony. The mirroring of each other's nonverbal behaviour by communication partners.

▶ RECAP Reasons to Study Nonverbal Communication

1. Nonverbal messages communicate our feelings and attitudes.
2. Nonverbal messages are usually more believable than verbal messages.
3. Nonverbal messages work with verbal messages to create meaning.
   - Nonverbal cues substitute for, repeat, contradict, or regulate verbal messages.
   - Nonverbal cues accent and complement emotional messages.
4. People respond and adapt to others through nonverbal messages.
5. Nonverbal messages play a major role in initiating, maintaining, and developing interpersonal relationships.

Culture

Research investigating nonverbal communication in a variety of cultures confirms that individuals interpret nonverbal messages from their unique cultural perspective. Note the following conclusions:

Facial Expressions

One research team found that some facial expressions, such as those conveying happiness, sadness, anger, disgust, and surprise, were the same in 68% to 92% of the cultures examined.[1] All humans probably share the same neuro-physiological basis for expressing emotions, but we learn different rules for sending and interpreting the expressions. For example, the Japanese culture does not reinforce the show of negative emotions; it is important for Japanese to "save face" and to help others save face as well.

Eye Contact

There seems to be more eye contact in interpersonal interactions between Arabs, South Americans, and Greeks than between people from other cultures. There is evidence that some black Americans look at others less often than white Americans do when sending and receiving messages. One of the most universal expressions among cultures appears to be the eyebrow flash (the sudden raising of the eyebrows when meeting someone or interacting with others).

Gestures

Hand and body gestures with the most shared meaning among Africans, North Americans, and South Americans include pointing, shrugging, head nodding, clapping, thumbs down, waving hello, and beckoning. There are, however, regional variations within cultures; it is not wise to assume that all people in a given culture share the same meaning for certain gestures. For example, the "okay" gesture

made by forming a circle with the thumb and finger has sexual connotations in some South American and Caribbean countries. In France, the okay sign means "worthless."

Space

Arabs, Latin Americans, and southern Europeans seem to stand closer to others than people from east and south Asia and northern Europe. If you have been to Britain, you know that people queue for buses in orderly straight lines. In France, however, queuing is less orderly and individuals are more likely to push forward to be the next customer or get the next seat on the bus. As with gestures, however, there are regional variations in spatial preferences.

Touch

Researchers have found that touch is something that is culturally based and learned. High-contact cultures are cultures in which people expect and value a higher degree of human touching than do people in other cultures. People from warmer climates tend to be from high-contact cultures—they prefer closer distances and expect more touching behaviour than people from cooler climates.[2] For example, people from Greece and Italy exhibit more touching behaviour than people from England, and South Americans initiate and receive more touching behaviour than North Americans.[3]

Gender

There is evidence that men and women display and interpret nonverbal cues differently.

Facial Expression

Research suggests that women smile more than men. It is also reported that women tend to be more emotionally expressive with their faces than men; this is perhaps related to the conclusion that women are more skilled at both displaying and interpreting facial expressions.

Eye Contact

Women usually use a more prolonged gaze than do men. Women, however, are less likely just to stare at someone; they break eye contact more frequently than men. In general, women receive more eye contact from others than do men.

Gestures and Posture

Overall, women appear to use fewer and less expansive gestures than men. Women are more likely, for example, to rest their hands on the arms of a chair while seated; men are more likely to gesture. Men and women position their legs differently: women cross their legs at the knees or ankles while men are more likely to sit with their legs apart.

Space

Men tend to prefer more space around them than do women. Women both approach and are approached more closely than men. And when conversing with others, women seem to prefer side-by-side interactions.

Touch

Men are more likely to initiate touch with others than are women. Women are touched more than men. Men and women also attribute different meaning to touch; women are more likely to associate touch with warmth and expressiveness than are men.

Vocal Cues

Vocal patterns may be more related to biological differences in the vocal register than other nonverbal behaviours. Women speak in both higher and softer tones than do men. Women use their voices to communicate a greater range of emotions than do men. Women are also more likely to raise their pitch when making statements; some people interpret the rising pattern (as in asking a question) as an indication of greater uncertainty.

Understanding Nonverbal Communication Codes

Keeping all these challenges in mind, we can begin looking at the categories of nonverbal information that researchers have studied: movement and gestures, eye contact, facial expressions, use of space and territory, touch, and personal appearance. Although we will concentrate on the codes that fall within these categories in mainstream Western culture, we will also try to look at codes for other cultures and subcultures.

Body Movement and Posture

In 1534, when French explorer Jacques Cartier and his men encountered the Mi'kmaq off the coast of Prince Edward Island, the two groups did not speak each other's language and therefore were forced to communicate through sign language. The Mi'kmaq signalled their willingness to trade through gestures, pointing, and hand waving. There is evidence that people have used gestures to communicate since ancient times—especially to bridge cultural and language differences. The first record of using sign language to communicate is found in Xenophon's *The March Up Country*, in which gestures were used to help the Greeks cross Asia Minor in about 400 BCE. Even when we do speak the same language as others, we use gestures to help us make our point.

Canadian Connections

Rules for Nonverbal Communication in Canada

What are the rules for nonverbal communication in Canada? In one "bible" of protocol for doing business in 60 different countries, readers are provided the following advice on nonverbal rules of behaviour with Canadians (note that this is not the complete list). This book was written in 1994. Do you see any changes in these rules or are they still the same now? Do you think the distinctions between French Canadians and British Canadians are fair reflections given the country's diversity today?

- In Canada, the standard greeting is a smile, often accompanied by a nod, wave, and/or verbal greeting.

- In business situations, a handshake is used upon greeting or introduction.

- Canadian businesspeople expect a firm handshake (web-to-web contact), direct eye contact, and an open, friendly manner. A weak handshake may be taken as a sign of weakness.

- Older men usually wait for women to offer their hand before shaking.

- French Canadians also have a fairly firm handshake, and they shake hands more often: upon greetings, introductions, and departures, even if the person has been greeted earlier that day.

- Good friends and family members sometimes embrace, especially among the French. A kissing of both cheeks may also occur, especially among the French.

- The standard distance between you and your conversation partner should be 60 cm. British Canadians are uncomfortable standing any closer to another person. French Canadians may stand slightly closer.

- Canadians, especially those of British descent, do not tend toward frequent or expansive gesturing.

- The backslap is a sign of close friendship among British Canadians. It is rarely used among French Canadians.

- Direct eye contact shows that you are sincere, although it should not be too intense. Some minorities look away to show respect.

- When sitting, Canadians often look very relaxed. Men may sit with the ankle of one leg on the knee of the other or prop their feet up on chairs or desks.

- In business situations, maintain good posture and a less casual pose.

- In most of Canada, to call the waiter or waitress over, briefly wave to get his or her attention. To call for the cheque, make a writing gesture. In Quebec, it is only necessary to nod the head backwards or to make a discreet wave of the hand.

Source: T. Morrison, W. A. Conaway, and G. A. Borden, *Kiss, Bow, or Shake Hands: How to Do Business in Sixty Different Countries* (Holbrook: Bob Adams, 1994). Printed with permission of Adams Media Corporation.

Kinesics is the study of human movement and gestures. We have long recognized that the movement and gestures we exhibit provide valuable information to others. Various scholars and researchers have proposed paradigms for analyzing and coding these movements and gestures, just as we do for spoken or written language.

One paradigm identifies four stages of "quasi-courtship behaviour." The first stage is courtship readiness. When we are attracted to someone, we may suck in our stomach, tense our muscles, and stand up straight. The second stage includes preening behaviours: we manipulate our appearance by combing our hair, applying makeup, straightening our tie, pulling up our socks, and double-checking our appearance in the mirror. In the third stage, we demonstrate positional cues, using our posture and body orientation to be seen and noticed by others.

Can you identify the quasi-courtship behaviour displayed by this couple?

(© Rido/Shutterstock)

One researcher found 52 gestures and nonverbal behaviours that women use to signal an interest in men. Among the most common unspoken flirting cues were smiling and surveying a crowded room with the eyes, and moving closer to the object of affection.[4] These cues intensify in the fourth stage of quasi-courtship behaviour, *appeals to invitation*, using close proximity, exposed skin, open body positions, and eye contact to signal availability and interest. Subjects in one study reported that they were aware of using all these techniques to promote an intimate relationship. In fact, we use these quasi-courtship behaviours to some extent in almost any situation in which we are trying to gain favourable attention from another.

Have you ever met someone and immediately labelled them as a "warm" person? What qualities did they exhibit that you associated with "warmth"? Chances are that they faced you directly, smiled frequently, made direct eye contact, and didn't fidget or make unnecessary hand gestures. People whom we label as "cold" tend to make less eye contact, smile less, fidget more, and turn away from their partners.

Albert Mehrabian has identified the nonverbal cues that contribute to perceptions of liking.[5] He found that an open body and arm position, a forward lean, and a more relaxed posture communicate liking. When we are attempting to persuade someone, we typically have more eye contact and a more direct body orientation; we are more likely to lean forward and closer to others.

Another team of researchers tried to classify movement and gestures according to their function. They identified five categories: emblems, illustrators, affect displays, regulators, and adaptors.[6]

Emblems. Nonverbal cues that have specific, generally understood meanings in a given culture and may actually substitute for a word or phrase are called **emblems**. When you are busy typing a report that is due the next day and your young son rushes in to ask for permission to buy a new computer game, you turn from your computer and hold up an open palm to indicate your desire for uninterrupted quiet. To communicate your enthusiastic enjoyment of a violin soloist at a concert, you applaud wildly. You want your children to stop talking while you are on the phone, so you put an index finger up to your pursed lips.

Illustrators. We frequently accompany a verbal message with **illustrators** that either contradict, accent, or complement the message. Slamming a book closed while sighing "I'm done with this!" or pounding the table while exclaiming "Listen—this is important!" are two examples of nonverbal behaviours that accent the verbal message. Typically, we use

kinesics. The study of human movement and gestures.

emblems. Nonverbal cues that have specific, generally understood meanings in a given culture and that may substitute for a word or phrase.

illustrators. Nonverbal behaviour that accompanies a verbal message and either contradicts, accents, or complements it.

nonverbal illustrators such as nods, pauses, or hand gestures at the beginning of clauses or phrases. Most of us use illustrators to help us communicate information about the size, shape, and spatial relationships of objects. When telling a friend about the fish you caught at the cottage, you hold your hands apart and say "It was this big!" Interestingly, you probably do the same while talking on the phone, even though your friend can't see you.

Affect Displays. Nonverbal movements and postures used to communicate emotion are called **affect displays**. As early as 1872, when Charles Darwin systematically studied the expression of emotion in both humans and animals, people recognized that nonverbal cues are the primary ways to communicate emotion. Our facial expressions, vocal cues, posture, and gestures convey the intensity of our emotions. If you are happy, for example, your face will reveal your joy to others, but the movement of your hands, the openness of your posture, and the speed with which you move will tell others *how* happy you are. Similarly, if you are feeling depressed, your face will probably reveal your sadness or dejection, while your slumped shoulders and lowered head will indicate the intensity of your despair. When we are feeling friendly, we use a soft tone of voice, an open smile, and a relaxed posture. When we feel neutral about an issue, we signal that feeling by putting little expression on our face or in our voice. When we feel hostile, we use a harsh voice, frown or grimace, and keep our posture tense and rigid.

Regulators. We use **regulators** to control the interaction or flow of communication between ourselves and another person. When we are eager to respond to a message, we make eye contact, raise our eyebrows, open our mouth, raise an index finger, and lean forward slightly. In a classroom, you may raise your hand to signal overtly that you want to talk. When you do not want to be part of the conversation or do not want to be called on in class, you do the opposite: avert your eyes, close your mouth, cross your arms, and lean back in your seat or away from the verbal action.

Adaptors. When we are cold, we reach for a sweater or wrap our arms around our chests to keep warm. When the temperature is 36°C, we fan ourselves to make our own breeze. These behaviours are examples of **adaptors**—nonverbal behaviours that help us to satisfy a personal need and adapt to the immediate situation. When you adjust your glasses, scratch a mosquito bite, or comb your hair, you are using movement to help you manage your personal needs and adapt to your surroundings—and you're communicating something about yourself to whoever may be present.

Understanding these five categories of nonverbal behaviour can help you understand interpersonal communication by giving you a new and more precise way to think about your own behaviour. By noting how often you use emblems instead of words to communicate a message, you can recognize how important emblems are in your relationships with others. The more you rely on emblems that have unique meanings for you and your partner, the more intimate the interpersonal relationship. Also, start to notice whether your nonverbal behaviour contradicts what you say. Monitoring your use of illustrators can help you determine whether you are sending mixed signals to others. Be aware of how you display affect. Knowing that your face and voice communicate emotion, and that posture and gesture indicate the intensity of your feelings, can help you understand how others make inferences about your feelings and attitudes. If other people have difficulty interpreting your emotional state, you may not be projecting your feelings nonverbally.

Since nonverbal cues can be ambiguous, it's not a good idea to use them to achieve a specific objective. However, as you have seen, people are more likely to respond in predictable ways if you use behaviours they can recognize and interpret easily.

affect displays. Nonverbal behaviour that communicates emotions.

regulators. Nonverbal messages that help control the interaction or level of communication among people.

adaptors. Nonverbal behaviours that help satisfy a personal need and help a person adapt or respond to the immediate situation.

RECAP Categories of Movement and Gestures

Category	Definition	Examples
Emblems	Behaviours that have specific, generally understood meaning	Raising a thumb to hitchhike
Illustrators	Cues that accompany verbal messages and provide meaning for the message	Pounding the podium to emphasize a point
Affect displays	Expressions of emotion	Hugging someone to express love
Regulators	Cues that control and manage the flow of communication between others	Looking at someone when you wish to speak
Adaptors	Behaviours that help you adapt to your environment	Scratching, combing your hair

Eye Contact

Whether you choose to look at someone or look away has an enormous impact on your relationship with that person. There are four main functions for eye contact in interpersonal interactions.

First, eye contact serves a *cognitive* function because it gives you information about another person's thought processes. For example, if your communication partner breaks eye contact after you ask him or her a question, you will know that he or she is probably thinking of something to say.

Second, we use eye contact to *monitor* the behaviour of others. We receive a major portion of the information we obtain through our eyes. We look at others to determine whether they are receptive to our messages.

Third, eye contact is one of the most powerful *regulatory* cues we use to signal when we want—or don't want—to talk. When you don't know the answer to a question your instructor asks in class, you probably look down and avoid meeting his or her eyes. When we do want to communicate with others, for example when we're standing in line at the coffee shop, we fix our eyes on the sales clerk to signal "My turn next. Please wait on me."

Finally, the area around our eyes serves an *expressive* function. The eyes have been called the "window to the soul" because they reveal our emotions to others. We may cry, blink, and widen or narrow our gaze to express our feelings.

When we do establish eye contact with others, it may seem that our gaze is constant; yet research suggests that we actually spend most of our time looking at something other than the person's eyes. One research team found that we focus on something else, including our partner's mouth, 57% of the time.[7] Not surprisingly then, facial expressions are another rich source of information in our communication with others.

ZITS © 2012 Zits Partnership, Dist. By King Features Syndicate.

Facial Expressions

You tell your parents that you will not be able to spend the holidays with them because you have decided to go skiing with your friends. You present your partner with a new abstract art painting that you would like to hang in your bedroom. As the personnel director reviews your résumé, you sit in silence across the desk from her or him. In each of these situations, you would be eagerly awaiting some reaction from the other person, and you would be scanning his or her face. Although we often try to manipulate our facial cues to project a premeditated feeling, our faces may still betray our true emotions to others.

To interpret our communication partner's facial expressions accurately, we need to put our other-orientation skills to work, focusing on what the other person may be thinking or feeling. It helps if we know the person well, can see his or her whole face, have plenty of time to watch it, and understand the situation that prompted the emotion. However, it is also helpful to know the cues for "reading" facial expressions.

Your face is versatile. According to one research team, it is capable of producing over 250 000 different expressions,[8] which, surprisingly, can be grouped under six primary emotional categories; the following list describes the changes that occur on our faces for each one.

Surprise: Wide-open eyes; raised and wrinkled brow; open mouth.

Fear: Open mouth; tense skin under the eyes; wrinkles in the centre of the forehead.

Disgust: Raised or curled upper lip; wrinkled nose; raised cheeks; lowered brow; lowered upper eyelid.

Anger: Tensed lower eyelid; either pursed lips or open mouth; lowered and wrinkled brow; staring eyes.

Happiness: Smiling; mouth may be open or closed; raised cheeks; wrinkles around lower eyelids.

Sadness: Lip may tremble; corners of the lips turn downward; corners of the upper eyelid may be raised.

The face can shift between the six categories rapidly, as is evident on the NASA videotape of activity inside Mission Control at the Johnson Space Center during the final minutes of the doomed flight of the space shuttle *Columbia* in February 2003. *New York Times* reporter John Schwartz describes how, though the voices of the mission controllers remained steady, their faces and body language showed a marked transition from the cool professionalism to wide-eyed alertness to dread and, finally, tears.[9]

Vocal Cues

Vocal cues are another category of nonverbal code that we respond to. Vocal cues communicate emotions and help us manage conversations. And even the lack of vocal cues communicates information.

Our Vocal Cues Communicate Emotions. Whether you are an infant or an adult, your voice is a primary tool for communicating information about the nature of relationships between you and others. We use our voices to present one message on the surface (with words) and usually a more accurate expression of our feelings with our vocal quality.

(© Pictorial Press Ltd/Alamy Stock Photo)

Say the following sentence out loud: "This looks great." Now say it sarcastically; you really don't think it looks great: "This looks great." Clearly, your vocal cues provide the real meaning.

When you express your ideas, your voice does most of the work in communicating your level of intimacy with others. The words you use may communicate explicit ideas and information, but it is your vocal cues that provide the primary relational cues, which truly indicate the degree of liking and trust that you feel toward others.

Some vocal expressions of emotion are easier to identify than others. Expressions of joy and anger are obvious ones, whereas shame and love are the most difficult emotions to identify based on vocal cues alone. We are also likely to confuse fear with nervousness, love with sadness, and pride with satisfaction.

Laughter is another vocal cue that you probably express every day. Your laugh not only reflects your emotional state; according to research, it also has a strong impact on the emotions of others. Laughter is contagious; when you laugh, you are expressing your emotions as well as increasing the likelihood that others will laugh as well.

Our voices also provide information about our self-confidence and our knowledge of the subject matter in our messages. Most of us would conclude that a speaker who mumbles, speaks slowly, consistently mispronounces words, and uses "uhs" and "ums" is less credible and persuasive than one who speaks clearly,

The face is an exhibit gallery for our emotions. The messages we convey through thousands of different expressions are usually more powerful and direct than verbal ones.

(© BananaStock/Thinkstock/Getty Images)

rapidly, and fluently. However, even though mispronunciations and vocalized pauses ("ums" and "ahs") seem to have a negative effect on credibility, they do not seem to be a major impediment to attitude change. People may, for example, think you are less knowledgeable if you stammer, but you may still be able to get your persuasive message across.

Our perception of others is influenced not only by "ums" and "ahs" but also by speaking rate. One team of researchers found that North Americans evaluated speakers with a moderate to slightly faster speaking rate as more "socially attractive" than speakers who had a slow rate of speech.[10] North American listeners also seem to prefer a speaking rate that is equal to or slightly faster than their own speaking rate.

Vocal Cues Help Us Manage Conversations. In addition to providing information about emotions, self-confidence, and knowledge, certain vocal cues, known as **backchannel cues**, serve a regulatory function in interpersonal situations, signalling when we want to talk and when we don't. When we are finished talking, we may lower the pitch of our final word. When we want to talk, we may start by interjecting sounds such as "I … I … I …" or "Ah … Ah … Ah …" to interrupt the speaker and grab the verbal ball. We also may use more cues, such as "Sure," "I understand," "Uh-huh," or "Okay," to signal that we understand the message of the other person and now we want to talk or end the conversation.

Our Use of Silence Speaks Volumes. Sometimes it is not what we say, or even how we say it, that communicates our feelings. Being silent may communicate volumes. Think of silence as the white spaces between and around the words on a page. Now think of a page with no white space at all—it would be quite difficult to decipher meaning from the black type.

backchannel cues. Nonverbal cues, typically vocal, that signal your wish to begin or end a conversation.

Personal Space

Imagine that you are sitting alone at a table for two in your local coffee shop. As you sit sipping your nonfat latte, you are startled when a complete stranger sits down at your table, directly across from you. With several empty tables available, you feel very uncomfortable that this unknown individual has invaded "your" area.

Normally, we do not think much about the rules we observe regarding personal space, but in fact, every culture has fairly rigid ways of regulating space in social interactions. Violations of these rules can be alarming and, as in the preceding scenario, even threatening. How close we are willing to get to others relates to how well we know them, as well as to considerations of power and status.

One of the pioneers in helping us understand the silent language of personal space was Edward T. Hall. His study of **proxemics** investigated how close or how far away we arrange ourselves around people and things.[11] Hall identified four spatial zones that we unconsciously define for ourselves, as shown in Figure 7.1. When we are between 0 and 0.5 metres (between 0 and 1.5 feet) from someone, we are occupying **intimate space**. This is the zone in which the most intimate interpersonal communication occurs. It is open only to those with whom we are well-acquainted, unless we are forced to stand in an elevator, a fast-food line, or some other crowded space.

The second zone, which ranges from about 0.5–1.5 metres (1.5 to 4 feet), is called **personal space**. Most of our conversations with family and friends occur in this zone. If someone we don't know well invades this space on purpose, we may feel uncomfortable.

Zone Three, called **social space**, ranges from 1.5 to 3.5 metres (4 to 12 feet). Most group interaction, as well as many of our professional relationships, takes place in this zone. The interaction tends to be more formal than that in the first two zones.

Public space, the fourth zone, begins at about 3.5 metres (12 feet). Interpersonal communication does not usually occur in this zone, and many public speakers and teachers position themselves even farther from their audience.

proxemics. The study of how close to or far away from people and objects we position ourselves.

intimate space. Zone One—space most often used for very personal or intimate communication, ranging from 0 to 0.5 metres (between 0 and 1.5 feet).

personal space. Zone Two—space most often used for conversation with family and friends, ranging from about 0.5 –1.5 metres (1.5 to 4 feet).

social space. Zone Three—space most often used for group discussion, ranging from 1.5 to 3.5 metres (4 to 12 feet).

public space. Zone Four—space most often used by public speakers or one speaking to many people, from 3.5 metres (12 feet) and beyond.

FIGURE 7.1

Edwin T. Hall's Four Zones of Space

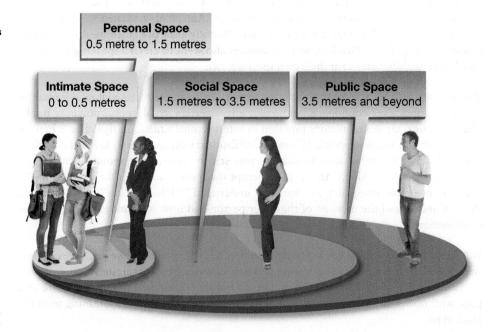

Personal Space 0.5 metre to 1.5 metres

Intimate Space 0 to 0.5 metres

Social Space 1.5 metres to 3.5 metres

Public Space 3.5 metres and beyond

The specific space that you and others choose depends on several variables. The more you like someone, the closer to them you will stand. We allow individuals with high status to surround themselves with more space than we allow for people with lower status. Large people also usually have more space around them than smaller people, and women stand closer to others than do men. All of us tend to stand closer to others in a large room than we do in a small room.

In a group, who's in charge, who's important, and who talks to whom are reflected by the spatial arrangement we self-select. The more dominant group members tend to select seats at the head of a table, while the shyer individuals often select a corner seat at a rectangular table.

▶ RECAP Edward T. Hall's Classification of Spatial Zones

Zone	Definition	Example
Zone One	Intimate space	0 to 0.5 metres (0 to 1.5 feet)
Zone Two	Personal space	0.5 to 1.5 metres (1.5 to 4 feet)
Zone Three	Social space	1.5 to 3.5 metres (4 to 12 feet)
Zone Four	Public space	3.5 metres (12 feet) and beyond

Territory. **Territoriality** is the study of how humans and animals use space and objects to communicate occupancy or ownership of space. You assumed "ownership" of the table in the coffee shop and the accompanying "right" to determine who sat with you because you and your latte were occupying the table. In addition to invading your personal space, the intrusive stranger broke the rules that govern territoriality.

We announce our ownership of space with **territorial markers**—things that signify that the area has been claimed—much as explorers once planted flags claiming uncharted land for their kings and queens. When you are studying at the library, for example, and need to get up and check a reference at the computer, you might leave behind a notebook or sweater. At resorts, people save beach and poolside chairs by placing towels on them to "claim" the chairs for the day. In rural areas, landowners post signs at the borders of their property to keep hunters off their territory. Signs, locks, electronic security systems, and other devices secure our home and office territories.

We also use markers to indicate where our space stops and someone else's starts. When someone sits too close, we may try to erect a physical barrier, such as a stack of books or a backpack or briefcase, or we might use our body as a shield by turning away. If the intruder does not get the hint, we may ultimately resort to words to announce that the space is occupied.

territoriality. The study of how animals and humans use space and objects to communicate occupancy or ownership of space.

territorial markers. Tangible objects that are used to signify that someone has claimed an area or space.

Touch

Standing elbow to elbow in a crowded elevator, you may find yourself in physical

"Well, are you going to invade my space or not?"

© Liza Donnelly

Clothes Affect Perceptions.
How is the superior status of senior-ranking RCMP officers conveyed through their orders of full dress?
(© RCMP/1995-041 (G))

contact with total strangers. As you stiffen your body and avert your eyes, a baffling sense of shame floods over you. If you are sitting at a conference table and you accidentally brush the toe of your shoe against your colleague's ankle, you may jerk away and may even blush or apologize. Why do we react this way to accidental touching? Normally, we touch to express intimacy. When intimacy is not our intended message, we instinctively react to modify the impression.

Countless studies have shown that intimate touching is vital to our personal development and well-being. Infants and children need it to confirm that they are valued and loved. Many hospitals invite volunteers in to hold and rock newborns whose mothers cannot do so themselves. Advocates of breastfeeding argue that the intimate touching it entails strengthens the bond between mother and child.

The amount of touch we need, tolerate, receive, and initiate depends on many factors. The amount and kind of touching you receive in your family is one big influence. If your mother or father greets you with hugs, caresses, and kisses, then you probably do this to others. If your family is less demonstrative, you may be restrained yourself. Most of us are more likely to touch people when we are feeling friendly, happy, or under other specific circumstances, such as sharing information, asking for a favour, sharing good news, or talking about intimate topics.

Appearance

In all our interactions with others, appearance counts. Our culture places a high value on weight, hairstyle, and clothes; these things are particularly important in the early stages of relationship development. Attractive females have an easier time persuading others than

Appearance Counts.
What role do you think appearance plays in the selection of television hosts?
(© WENN Ltd/Alamy Stock Photo)

do those who are perceived as less attractive. In general, we tend to think attractive people are more credible, happier, more popular, more sociable, and even more prosperous than less attractive people. And there is evidence that this might be true; the relationship between attractiveness and income has been established through research, with one study revealing that 68% of attractive adults were above the mean on occupational success—which included income—versus 32% of unattractive adults.[12]

The shape and size of your body also affects how others perceive you. Heavier and rounder individuals are often perceived to be older, more old-fashioned, more talkative, and more good-natured than thin people, who are perceived to be more ambitious, more suspicious of others, more uptight and tense, more negative, and less talkative. Muscular and athletically fit people are seen as better looking, taller, and more adventurous. These perceptions are, in fact, so common that they have become easily recognizable stereotypes on which casting directors for movies, TV shows, and plays rely in selecting actors and actresses.

Aside from keeping you warm and within the legal bounds of decency, your clothes also affect how others perceive you. The clothes you wear are a way of communicating to others how you want to be treated. In institutional settings, an individual's rank is typically denoted by his or her uniform, as with the orders of dress for the Royal Canadian Mounted Police. Although magazines are constantly giving prescriptions for ways to be attractive and stylish, there is no specific formula for dressing for success.

RECAP Codes of Nonverbal Communication

Movements and gestures	Communicate information, status, warmth, credibility, interest in others, attitudes, liking
Eye contact	Serves cognitive, monitoring, regulatory, and expressive functions
Facial expressions	Express emotions
Vocal cues	Communicate emotion through pitch, rate, volume, and quality, and modify the meaning of messages
Personal space	Provides information about status, power, and intimacy
Territory	Provides cues to use, ownership, or occupancy of space
Touch	Communicates intimacy, affection, or rejection
Appearance	Influences perceptions of credibility and attraction

How to Improve Your Skill in Interpreting Nonverbal Messages

How do you make sense out of the postures, movements, gestures, eye contact, facial expressions, uses of space and territory, touch, and appearance of others? Every one wants to know how to interpret these unspoken messages. Peter Collett, an internationally known nonverbal communication researcher, uses the analogy that nonverbal cues are like **tells** in the game of poker. A poker tell is a nonverbal cue that gives away what we are thinking and feeling—whether we're wearing a smirking smile about holding a good set of cards or frowning because we know we don't have a winning hand.[13] How do you interpret these tells? Although there are limitations to decoding the meaning in nonverbal cues, here are several strategies to help you improve your ability to interpret nonverbal messages.

Look for Dimensions of Meaning in Nonverbal Messages

Albert Mehrabian has found that we synthesize and interpret nonverbal cues along three primary dimensions: *immediacy, arousal,* and *dominance.*[14] These three dimensions provide a useful way to summarize how nonverbal cues may be interpreted.

Observe Immediacy Cues that Communicate Liking. Sometimes we are not able to put our finger on the precise reason we find a person likable or unlikable. Mehrabian believes that immediacy cues are a likely explanation. **Immediacy** cues are behaviours that communicate liking and engender feelings of pleasure. The principle underlying immediacy is simple: we move toward persons and things we like and avoid or move away from those we dislike. Immediacy cues increase our sensory awareness of others.

Our use of space and territory is not the only cue that contributes to positive or negative feelings. Mehrabian has noted several other nonverbal cues that increase immediacy. One of the most powerful is touch; others include a forward lean, increased eye contact, and an open body orientation. The meaning of these behaviours is usually implied rather than explicitly spelled out in words.

In brief, to communicate that we like someone, we use these cues:

Proximity:	Close, forward lean
Body orientation:	Direct, but could be side by side
Eye contact:	Eye contact and mutual eye contact
Facial expression:	Smiling

tell. A nonverbal cue, such as a facial expression, body posture, or eye behaviour, that gives away what we are thinking and feeling.

immediacy. The feelings of liking, pleasure, and closeness communicated by such nonverbal cues as eye contact, forward lean, touch, and open body orientation.

Metacommunication, as you recall from Chapter 1, is communication about communication—one channel of communication, such as nonverbal cues, provides information about another channel of communication, the words used. Because many, if not most, people communicate online using only text, it may seem odd to discuss the role of nonverbal communication as meta-messages when you tap out words to others. But even a lean communication medium such as instant messaging or email offers subtle (and sometimes not-so-subtle) nonverbal cues that provide meta-messages—information about the nature of your relationship with your communication partner.

Although electronically mediated communication (EMC) tends to emphasize content over relationship messages, relational cues are nonetheless present and provide meta-messages to others. Over time a considerable amount of relational metacommunication influences how you interact with others online. Understanding how nonverbal messages are evident in all forms of EMC, including text messages, can help you maintain an other-oriented perspective by interpreting the relational cues that are present. Here are several examples of how nonverbal messages, sometimes explicit yet often implicit, provide a meta-message when you relate to others online.

Emoticons Emoticons are used to express a range of emotions, from happiness :) to surprise :0, anger :<, and even flirtatious winks;). Even when used minimally, emoticons provide a shorthand way of expressing your feelings. Emoticons can also signal when you are

making a sarcastic remark, as when you write "I was thrilled to see her there :/." We use emoticons in text messages in places where we would pause or establish eye contact with others when talking face to face.

Punctuation An exclamation mark (!) provides a powerful emotional punch to whatever message you've expressed. Writing "Nice to hear from you!!" with a double exclamation mark upgrades a normal greeting to an enthusiastic declaration. Other punctuation marks also provide relational information: commas, colons, semicolons, and periods signal the language rhythm the writer had in mind as he or she was composing the message, just as our use of pauses does when we talk to others. A message dashed off with no punctuation communicates a meta-message of informality.

Capitalization Like the volume control on your TV, capitalization serves as a way to increase the volume of your message. Capitalizing letters has the same effect as shouting. When typed all in capital letters, the phrase "HEY, LET'S GET TO IT" communicates greater urgency that "Hey, let's get to it." Overuse of all capital letters would be like constantly raising your voice. So be careful to "shout" only when you need to add emphasis.

Message Length If you send someone a chatty, fairly long email message describing the details of your day and you get a short and simple reply that says "Thanks," the meta-message may be that your communication partner wasn't all that interested in you or your message. If

you send a lengthy message, you probably expect a long message in response.

Reciprocation or nonreciprocation of message length provides meta-message cues about interest in your message.

Response Time In addition to making inferences about how long a return message is, you will likely make inferences about how quickly you get a response. The shorter the response time, the more likely you will be to conclude that the other person is interested in the conversation. Of course, if you know the other person is not available when you send your message, a sluggish response time is understandable. But if you know the other person checks messages frequently or usually has his or her phone on, a long response time may signal a cooler, less-involved relationship.

Media Choice You send a meta-message to someone based on which communication medium you use. Canadian communication theorist Marshall McLuhan famously said, "The medium is the message." Your choice of whether to send a text message, make a phone call, or schedule a time to connect via webcam provides information about the relationship. A richer medium (such as a webcam session, which allows you to see images and converse in real time when immediate feedback is possible) signals that the message you wish to convey is relatively important.

Monitoring the way you encode EMC and the subtle relational cues you send can help ensure that the message you intended to express is the message received.

Gestures:	Head nods, movement
Posture:	Open, arms oriented toward others
Touch:	Cultural- and context-appropriate touch
Voice:	Higher pitch, upward pitch

arousal. The feelings of interest and excitement communicated by such nonverbal cues as vocal expression, facial expressions, and gestures.

Observe Arousal Cues That Communicate Responsiveness. The face, voice, and movement are primary indicators of **arousal**. If we see arousal cues, we conclude that another person is responsive to and interested in us. If the person acts in a passive or dull manner, we conclude that he or she is uninterested.

When you approach someone and ask whether he or she has a minute or two to talk, that person may signal interest with a change in facial expression and more animated vocal cues. People who are aroused and interested in you show animation in their face, voice, and gestures. Leaning forward, raising the eyebrows, and nodding the head are other cues that implicitly communicate arousal. Someone who says "Sure, I have time to talk with you" in a monotone and with a flat, expressionless face is communicating the opposite. If you are in class, slumped in your chair with your eyes closed, you are communicating to your professor that you are not interested in what she is saying. Think of arousal as an on–off switch. Sleeping is the ultimate switched-off state.

Observe Dominance Cues That Communicate Power. The third dimension of Mehrabian's framework for implicit cues communicates the balance of power in a relationship. **Dominance** cues communicate status, position, and importance.[15] A person of high status tends to have a relaxed body posture when interacting with a person of lower status. When you talk to a professor, he may lean back in his chair, cross one leg over the other, or exhibit other relaxed postures during the conversation. However, unless your professor is a colleague or a friend, you will maintain a relatively formal posture during your interaction in his office, perhaps even remaining standing.

Shaking hands is a centuries-old greeting or farewell ritual that communicates power or lack of it. People in leadership positions are more likely to be the ones who initiate a handshake than are non-leaders. The person who feels the most power in a relationship is more likely to shake hands with his or her palm facing down; a submissive handshake, according to Peter Collett, is offered with the palm facing up. Collett has meticulously analyzed handshakes of politicians and other leaders to reveal that the person who feels the most power literally takes the upper hand when shaking hands.[16]

Another dominance cue is the use of space. High-status individuals usually have more space around them; they have bigger offices and more "barriers" protecting them. A receptionist in an office is usually easily accessible, but to reach the president of the company, you may have to navigate through several corridors and past several administrative assistants and an executive assistant who are "guarding" the door.

Are most people aware of the power cues they express or receive from others? Your ability to detect nonverbal expressions of power may relate to whether you think you are powerful or not. One research team found that subordinates were better at interpreting power cues from their supervisors than supervisors were at interpreting power cues from their subordinates.[17] What this means is that if you think you have less power in a relationship, you are more likely to be aware of the more dominant power of others' nonverbal cues. If you think you do have power, you may be less sensitive to nonverbal expressions of power.

Other power cues that communicate feelings of dominance include the use of furniture, clothing, and locations. You study at a table in the library; the college president has a large private desk. You may wear jeans and a T-shirt to class; the president wears a business suit. Your residence room is tiny and closely surrounded by many others; the president's house is large, surrounded by a lush, landscaped garden in a prestigious neighbourhood. We use space, territory, posture, and artifacts such as clothing and furniture to signal feelings of dominance or submissiveness in the presence of others.

Research confirms that we have certain expectations about how people who are perceived to have power will behave nonverbally. People who are thought to have more power, for example, are thought to more freely express their anger and disgust than are people who have less power and status. The following nonverbal cues communicate dominance:

Use of Space:	Height (on a platform or standing)
	Facing a group
	More space surrounding a person

dominance. The feelings of power, status, and control communicated by such nonverbal cues as a relaxed posture, greater personal space, and protected personal space.

Eye Contact:	More when talking
	More when initially establishing dominance
	More when staring to establish power
Face:	No smile, frown
Touch:	Initiating touch
Voice:	Loud, low pitch, greater pitch range
	Slow, more interruptions, more talk
	Slight hesitation before speaking
Gesture:	Pointing at the other or at his or her property
Posture:	Standing, hands on hips, expanded chest, more relaxed

▶ RECAP Dimensions for Interpreting Nonverbal Behaviour

Dimension	Definition	Nonverbal Cues
Immediacy	Cues that communicate liking and pleasure	Eye contact, touch, forward lean, close distances
Arousal	Cues that communicate active interest and emotional involvement	Eye contact, varied vocal cues, animated facial expressions, forward lean, movement
Dominance	Cues that communicate status and power	Protected space, relaxed posture, status symbols

BEING **Other**-ORIENTED

The ability to accurately interpret the nonverbal expressions of others is both a natural talent and a skill that can be enhanced. How would you assess your own ability to accurately interpret the nonverbal messages of others, on a scale from 1 to 10, with 1 being low and 10 being high?

Use Effective Strategies for Interpreting Nonverbal Messages

In addition to looking for general patterns or dimensions of nonverbal behaviour, you can use several research-based strategies to increase your accuracy in interpreting nonverbal messages. These suggestions won't give you the ability to have 100 percent accuracy in decoding nonverbal cues, but they will help you enhance your "people watching" skill.

Consider Nonverbal Cues in Context. Just as quoting an expert out of context can change the meaning of a statement, trying to draw conclusions from an isolated behaviour or a single cue can lead to misinterpretations. Beware of looking at someone's folded arms and concluding that he or she does not like you or is not interested in what you are saying. It could be that the air conditioner is set too low and the person is just trying to keep warm.

Look for Clusters of Nonverbal Cues. Instead of focusing on a specific cue, look for corroborating cues that can lead to a more accurate conclusion about the meaning of a behaviour. Is the person making eye contact? Is he or she facing you? How far away is he or she standing from you?

Always consider nonverbal behaviours in conjunction with other nonverbal cues, the environment, and the person's verbal message.

Consider Past Experiences When Interpreting Nonverbal Cues. Familiarity may breed contempt, but it also increases our ability to interpret another's nonverbal behaviour. You may have learned, for example, that when your mother started crying when you played the piano, it meant she was proud of you, not melancholy. Family members can probably interpret one another's nonverbal cues more accurately than can those from outside the family. However, after knowing someone over a period of time, you begin to increase your sensitivity to certain glances, silences, movements, and vocal cues that might be overlooked or misunderstood by others.

Check Your Perceptions with Others. **Perception checking**, a key skill in interpreting messages, was discussed in Chapter 3. You can follow three steps to check your perception. First, observe and describe the nonverbal cues, making a point to note such variables as amount of eye contact, posture, use of gestures, facial expression, and tone of voice. Second, try to interpret what the individual is expressing through his or her nonverbal behaviour. Finally, check your perception by asking him or her if it is accurate. Of course, we are not suggesting that you need to go through life constantly checking everyone's nonverbal cues. Overusing this skill would be irritating to most people. We are suggesting, however, that when you are uncertain about how someone feels and it is important to know, a perception check may be in order. Consider this example:

Dana: Hi, Mom. I'm sorry Erik and I missed the family reunion last week. It's been a hectic week. The kids had something going on every night and we just needed to rest.

Muriel: [*frowns, has little eye contact, folds her arms, and uses a flat voice*] Oh, don't worry about it.

Dana: I know you said don't worry about it, Mom, but it looks like you're still upset. I know that look of yours. I also hear in your voice that you're not really pleased. Is it really okay, or are you still a little miffed?

Muriel: Well, yes, to be honest, Dad and I were really looking forward to getting all the kids together.

Dana: I'm sorry, Mom. We'll make an effort to be at the next one. Thanks for sharing with me how you really felt.

Addressing your question to a specific nonverbal cue will help you interpret your partner's behaviour in future interactions as well.

perception checking. The skill of asking someone whether your interpretation of his or her nonverbal behaviour is accurate.

▶ **RECAP**   **How to Check Your Perceptions of Others' Nonverbal Cues**

Steps	Consider
1. Observe their nonverbal behaviour.	Are they frowning?
	Do they have eye contact?
	Are their arms crossed?
	What is their tone of voice?
	What is their posture?
2. Form a mental impression of what you think they mean.	Are they happy, sad, angry?
	Is the nonverbal message contradicting the verbal message?
3. Ask questions to check whether your perceptions are accurate.	"Are you upset? You look angry."
	"Your expression and your voice suggest you don't believe me.
	"Do you think I'm lying?"
	"The look on your face tells me you really like it. Do you?"

Be Aware That the Nonverbal Expression of Emotion Is Contagious

Have you ever noticed that when you watch a funny movie, you are more likely to laugh out loud if other people around you are laughing? Or that when you are around people who are sad or remorseful, you are more likely to feel and express sadness? There's a reason why this happens: nonverbal emotional expressions are contagious. People often display the same emotions that a communication partner is displaying. According to **emotional contagion theory**, people tend to "catch" the emotions of others.

Interpersonal interactions can, then, affect your nonverbal expression of emotions. The ancient Roman orator Cicero knew this when he gave advice to public speakers. He said that if you want your audience to experience joy, you must be a joyful speaker. Or, if you want to communicate fear, then you should express fear when you speak. Knowing that you tend to catch or imitate the emotions of others can help you interpret your own nonverbal messages and those of others; you may be imitating the emotional expression of others around you.

Compare What You Expect to See with What You Actually Observe. We often interpret messages based on how we *expect* people to behave in a specific situation. Comparing what you expect to see with what you actually see and hear can increase your observation skill.

One theory that helps explain how and why we interpret nonverbal messages the way we do is called **expectancy violation theory**. Developed by Judee Burgoon and several of her colleagues, this theory suggests that each of us interacts with others with certain preconceived expectations about their behaviour.[18] Our expectations are based on our life experiences and our culture. The research conclusions that we've summarized in this book about when eye contact is likely to occur, when we'll probably smile or frown, or how most people express immediacy, dominance, or arousal are based on the general expectations

emotional contagion theory. Theory that emotional expression is contagious; people can "catch" emotions just by observing each other's emotional expressions.

expectancy violation theory. Theory that you interpret the messages of others based on how you expect others to behave.

Building Your Skills   **Practising Nonverbal Perception Checking**

We have identified several strategies to improve your skill at interpreting the nonverbal messages of others, including being able to check your perceptions of others. Accurately perceiving others gets to the heart of becoming other-oriented.

Look at the photographs to the right. First, note the nonverbal behaviour of the target person in the picture. Next, form a mental impression of what you think the other person is thinking and feeling. Finally, compose a perception-checking question that the other person in the photo could ask to confirm the target person's thoughts and feelings.

(© Monkey Business/Fotolia)

(© Hemera Technologies/PHOTOS. com/Thinkstock/Getty Images)

Photo 1

A. Describe the student's nonverbal behaviour.

B. What do you think the student is thinking and feeling?

C. What is a perception-checking question the teacher could ask her student?

Photo 2

A. Describe the customer's nonverbal behaviour.

B. What do you think the customer is thinking and feeling?

C. What is a perception-checking question the salesman could ask the customer?

TABLE 7.1	**Who's Telling the Truth? Differences Between Honest and Dishonest Communicators**	
Nonverbal Cue	**Honest Communicators . . .**	**Dishonest Communicators . . .**
Voice	Use fewer pauses when they talk.	Pause more; they are thinking about what "story" they want to give.
	Speak fluently, smoothly.	Use more nonfluencies ("ah," "er," "um").
	Speak at a normal speaking rate.	Speak a bit faster than normal.
Facial Expression	Smile genuinely and sincerely.	Display a plastered-on, phony smile.
		May smile a bit too long.
Gestures	Are less likely to play with objects as they speak.	Are more likely to play with objects (for example, twiddle a pencil).
	Use fewer gestures.	Use more gestures, more self-adaptors, touching their face and body, shrugging their shoulders.
	Are not likely to shift body weight.	Are more likely to shift their posture.
	Generally display less nervousness.	Display increased nervousness.
Eye Contact	Maintain normal eye contact—a steady, natural gaze.	May look away, maintain less direct eye contact.
	Have a normal eye-blink rate.	Have an increased eye-blink rate, a sign of increased anxiety.

Sources: Adapted from Dale Leathers, *Successful Nonverbal Communication* (New York: Macmillan, 1992), with supporting research from P. Ekman and W. Friesen, "Detecting Deception from the Body and Face," *Journal of Personality and Social Psychology,* 29 (1974): 288–98; M. Zuckerman, B. M. DePaulo, and R. Rosenthal, "Verbal and Nonverbal Communication of Deception," in *Advances in Experimental Social Psychology,* vol. 14, ed. L. Berkowitz (New York: Academic Press, 1981), 1–60.

we have when eye contact is likely to occur, when we'll probably smile or frown, or how most people express immediacy, dominance, or arousal are based on the general expectations we have about how other people behave. For example, most Westerners expect that when meeting a business colleague for the first time, a person will smile, extend a hand, say, "Hello, I'm…," and then say his or her name. If, instead, the person clasps two hands together and bows demurely without uttering a word, the nonverbal behaviour is not what we expect. This violation of our expectation would cause us to wonder what the "violator" of our expectations might mean by bowing instead of offering to shake our hand. When our expectations are violated, we may feel uncomfortable.

But when people behave nonverbally in ways that we may not expect, we adapt our behaviour, especially if we are other-oriented and skilled in responding to other people.[19] If your new business colleague greets you with a bow rather than a handshake, it is appropriate to offer a bow in return, rather than trying to shake the person's hand. So, we're constantly making observations and comparing what we expect with what we get, and then adapting our behaviour based on what happens. By being aware of your expectations and comparing what you expect to see with what you actually observe, you can increase your skill at being mindful when interpreting nonverbal tells.

Be Aware of Limitations When Interpreting Nonverbal Messages

Even though we have made great claims for the value of studying nonverbal behaviours and identified suggestions for interpreting nonverbal communication, it is not always easy to decipher unspoken messages. You have dictionaries to help interpret words, but there is no handy reference book to help you decode nonverbal cues. Although the term *body language* is often used in casual conversation, there is no universal or agreed-on interpretation for body movements or gestures. To help you with the decoding process, let's first look at some of the difficulties that hinder classification.

Nonverbal Messages Are Often Ambiguous. Most words carry a meaning that everyone who speaks the same language can recognize. But the meaning of nonverbal messages may be known only to the person displaying them. Perhaps even more importantly, that person may not intend for the behaviour to have any meaning at all. And some people have difficulty expressing their emotions nonverbally. They may have a frozen facial expression or a monotone voice. Or they may be teasing you, but their deadpan expressions lead you to believe that their negative comments are heartfelt. Often, it is difficult to draw meaningful conclusions about another person's behaviour, even if you know him or her quite well.

Nonverbal Messages Are Continuous. Words are discrete entities; they have a beginning and an end. You can circle the first word in this sentence and underline the last one. Nonverbal behaviours are not as easily dissected. Like the sweep of a second hand on a watch, many nonverbal behaviours are continuous. Some, such as a slap or a hand clap, have definite beginnings and endings. But more often than not, nonverbal behaviour unfolds without clearly defined starting and stopping points. Gestures, facial expressions, and even eye contact can flow from one situation to the next with seamless ease. Researchers have difficulty studying nonverbal cues because of this continuous stream, so be aware that trying to categorize and interpret them will be challenging as well.

Nonverbal Cues Are Multichanneled. Have you ever tried to watch two or three programs at once? Maybe you've had the hockey game playing on your family TV, while at the same time watching a YouTube video on your phone and catching up on a reality show on your iPad. As in that situation, nonverbal cues come at us simultaneously from a variety of sources. And just as you can really pay attention to only one program at a time—although you can move among them very rapidly—so, too, can you actually attend to only one nonverbal cue at a time.[20] Social psychologist Michael Argyle suspects that negative nonverbal messages (frowns, grimaces, lack of eye contact) command attention before positive messages when the two compete.[21] Moreover, if the nonverbal message contradicts the verbal message, then you may have trouble interpreting either one correctly.[22]

Nonverbal Interpretation Is Culture-Based. There is some evidence that humans from every culture smile when they are happy and frown when they are unhappy.[23] We also all raise, or flash, our eyebrows when meeting or greeting others, and young children in many cultures wave to signal that they want their mothers, raise their arms to be picked up, and suck their thumbs for comfort.[24] These common behaviours suggest that there is some underlying basis for expressing emotion. Yet each culture may develop unique rules for displaying and interpreting these gestures and expressions.

For example, unless you grew up there, you might be startled when on a visit to New Orleans you stumble on a handkerchief-waving, dancing, exuberantly singing crowd and discover that it is an African American jazz funeral. What to the uninformed may seem like disrespect for the dead, others recognize as a joyous send-off to a better world.

How to Improve Your Skill in Expressing Nonverbal Messages

Although we've offered recommendations about how to accurately interpret nonverbal cues, you may be asking yourself, "What can I do to express my feelings accurately to others using nonverbal cues?" Consider the following tips.

Be Mindful of Your Nonverbal Behaviour

Are you aware of your nonverbal behaviour at this moment? What is your facial expression communicating to others? Are you twiddling a pen or pencil? Are your hands and feet jiggling as you read these words? Even if you're not be aware of feeling anxious or nervous, your nonverbal behaviours may send those messages unless you're mindful of what you are doing. Being aware of your nonverbal behaviour is the first step in improving your skill in expressing your feelings to others. There is evidence that most people "leak" nonverbal cues—we can't completely control all aspects of our nonverbal behaviour, such as the size of the pupils in our eyes or our facial expressions. However, we can control many aspects of how we present ourselves to others. For example, now that you know the nonverbal behaviours that communicate liking, power, or interest, you can check to see if your behaviour matches your intentions.

There's another reason to be mindful of your nonverbal expressions: As we noted earlier, if your nonverbal message doesn't match your verbal message, it's your nonverbal message that will carry the most weight in influencing the meaning of the message. If your communication goal is to express an emotion, nurture a relationship, or provide support and encouragement, check to ensure that your nonverbal message is conveying the same sentiment you're expressing verbally. You can undermine your verbalized message with an out-of-synch or contradictory nonverbal message. So be aware of what your nonverbal message may be communicating to others.

Observe Others' Reactions to Your Nonverbal Behaviour

By being a keen observer of how other people respond to you, you can develop a greater understanding of how your behaviour affects others. For example, you may be in a good mood, but if others don't seem to be reacting positively to your positive feelings, take note of the reactions you're receiving. Are you doing something to trigger a negative reaction in others? Noting the amount and duration of eye contact you receive, the facial expressions of others with whom you interact, and even the openness of their body posture will provide clues to how other people are responding to your messages. Of course, their responses could be focused on something you've said rather than on your nonverbal behaviour. So it's especially useful to monitor how people are reacting to you when you're listening and not speaking.

Ask Others About Your Nonverbal Behaviour

It's good to have a close friend who can give you honest advice about the nonverbal impression you make on others. Just as you may ask a trusted confidant to give his or her reaction to what you're wearing, you can also ask people you trust for honest feedback about your nonverbal behaviour. Consider asking whether your actions fit your words and whether the feeling and overall mood you have is what you're communicating nonverbally. Asking for others' perception of your nonverbal behaviour—inviting perception checking—can help you evaluate your nonverbal behaviour.

Practise Your Nonverbal Behaviour

If you've taken a public speaking class, your instructor has undoubtedly encouraged you to practise your speech so as to polish your speech delivery. Maybe you videotaped your speech or even practised in front of a mirror to check your delivery. We're not suggesting that you rehearse "spontaneous" interpersonal conversations; that would cause you to sound stilted and artificial. But you can observe yourself on video to gain a sense of how others perceive you. If you think you need to polish your nonverbal social skills, you could consider practising greeting others or expressing both positive and negative emotions. Again, you need not develop a script and memorize your message, but using a video camera or even a mirror to practise facial expressions and informal gestures and observe your posture can give you some insight into how to enhance your nonverbal persona. Over 100 years ago, elocution teachers used charts and other drill and practice techniques to help their students practise how to walk, move, and express themselves. But we recommend that you approach practising nonverbal behaviour with a sense of play rather than as an assignment. Spending some time practising and experimenting with how you express yourself nonverbally can increase your awareness of how others see you.

APPLYING AN OTHER-ORIENTATION
to Nonverbal Communication

Nonverbal cues are the primary means by which we assess others' feelings and emotions. These cues also provide important information about the nature of the relationships you have with others. But because nonverbal messages are more ambiguous than verbal messages, your interpretation of someone's nonverbal behaviour may not always be accurate. One way to enhance your ability to interpret others' nonverbal communication is to be aware of someone's normal, baseline way of responding.

We noted, for example, that fidgeting fingers and tapping toes may be signs of inattention, frustration, or anxiety—but if you know that your communication partner *normally* fidgets or has a habit of tapping his fingers or wagging a pencil when listening, you have a baseline for interpreting the behaviour. "Oh," you may think, "he does that all the time. So he's not nervous. It's just a habit."

How do you develop a baseline for someone's normal nonverbal behaviour? You'll need to spend time with the other person. That's why we noted that the longer you know someone, the more accurately you can assess the meaning of the nonverbal messages. Perhaps a friend will say, "Oh, I'm really listening to you. I just fidget a lot." Or "I'm still interested in what you're saying; I'm just thinking." These statements give you perspective for interpreting the friend's behaviour. And over time, you can tell whether the person's interpretation of his or her own behaviour is accurate.

But most people don't verbalize their nonverbal behavioural norms or typical response patterns. So interpreting the nonverbal messages of others can be like testing a scientific hypothesis. You observe someone's behaviour and make a good guess about what the behaviour means. But you need a normal pattern of communication behaviour with which to compare the specific behaviour. Be patient: don't jump to conclusions about the meaning of a nonverbal behaviour based on a small sample of someone's behaviour. Knowing a person's normal, baseline nonverbal reactions will increase your accuracy in decoding that person's nonverbal messages.

Identifying the Importance of Nonverbal Communication

(pages 153–157)

OBJECTIVE ❶ Explain why nonverbal communication is an important area of study.

Key Terms

nonverbal
  communication *153*
interaction adaptation
  theory *155*

interactional synchrony *156*

Critical Thinking Questions

1. Consider a communication exchange you had recently. What nonverbal cues were present? What type of eye contact, body language, and facial expressions did you observe? Did you have difficulty interpreting the nonverbal cues of your communication partner(s)? Did the nonverbal cues communicate anything that was at odds with the spoken message? Explain.

2. Ethics: Is it appropriate to draw definitive conclusions about another's personality and attitudes based only on a reading of his or her nonverbal cues? Support your answer.

Activities

Over the next week, do some serious people watching. Spend some time observing people in a public place, such as a café or coffee shop, on campus, at a bus stop, or at the mall. Make an ongoing list of nonverbal behaviours you observe. Do these behaviours support the verbal messages you hear, such as greeting friends, asking for service, thanking someone, and the like? Are you able to notice whether any of these behaviours are ambiguous, continuous, or multichannelled? Do you observe gender and/or cultural differences in nonverbal behaviours? Discuss your findings with your classmates.

Web Resources

http://anthro.palomar.edu/language/language_6.htm Communication is far more than spoken or written words. At this site you can read the article "Hidden Aspects of Communication" to sharpen your skill in interpreting nonverbal cues.

Understanding Nonverbal Communication Codes (pages 158–167)

OBJECTIVE ❷ Identify and describe eight nonverbal communication codes.

Key Terms

kinesics *159*
emblems *159*
illustrators *159*
affect displays *160*
regulators *160*
adaptors *160*
backchannel cues *163*

proxemics *164*
intimate space *164*
personal space *164*
social space *164*
public space *164*
territoriality *165*
territorial markers *165*

Critical Thinking Questions

1. Consider some recent communication exchanges you had, either face to face or over the phone. How much information did you gather from your partner's vocal cues, including backchannel cues? Were you able to make inferences about your communication partner's mood and emotions just from the tone, pitch, rate, or quality of these vocal cues? Now compare these exchanges with some recent online communication you've had. Was it more difficult to make the same kinds of inferences about moods or emotions without vocal cues? Were there other ways in which emotions were communicated? Explain.

2. Ethics: Donald really wants to be hired as a salesperson. He hires a fashion consultant to recommend what he should wear and determine how he should look when he interviews for a job. In general, is it ethical to manipulate your appearance so that you can impress others?

Activities

Go on a nonverbal communication scavenger hunt. Observe your family members, classmates, and friends to find one or more of the following sets of nonverbal communicators:

a. Examples of emblems, illustrators, affect displays, regulators, and adaptors

b. Examples of how people use the four zones of personal space

c. Examples of the cognitive, monitoring, regulatory, and expressive functions of eye contact

d. Examples of emotions expressed by facial expressions or vocal cues

e. Examples of how people use touch to communicate

f. Examples of clothing or accessories that reveal intentions or personality traits

Web Resources

http://www.helpguide.org/mental/eq6_nonverbal_communication.htm This site defines nonverbal communication, explains why it is important, and offers tips for evaluating nonverbal signals.

How to Improve Your Skill in Interpreting and Expressing Nonverbal Messages (pages 167–176)

OBJECTIVES ❸❹ Enhance your skill in interpreting and expressing your nonverbal messages.

Key Terms

tell *167*

immediacy *167*

arousal *168*

dominance *169*

perception checking *171*

emotional contagion
   theory *172*

expectancy violation
   theory *172*

Critical Thinking Questions

1. Describe a situation in which you made eye contact with a stranger. Was it unpleasant or disturbing? Did the stranger's behaviour communicate interest or liking? How did you react? Explain.

2. Greg has been told that he sometimes comes across as cold, aloof, or standoffish. What could Greg do to communicate his desire to be warm and approachable?

3. Ethics: Is it ethical for salespeople, politicians, and others who wish to make a favourable impression to alter their nonverbal messages to get you to like them, vote for them, or buy their products? Explain.

Activities

Evaluate your classroom based on the nonverbal messages this learning space communicates. Consider the following questions:

- What does the furniture arrangement communicate about the likelihood for interaction with others?

- Based on the room arrangement, what cues provide information about who has the most power and influence in this space?

- What do the colours of the classroom communicate? For example, are they contemporary or old-fashioned? Are they conducive to learning? Do they affect interpersonal communication?

- What does research about zones of personal space reveal about interpersonal communication in the room?

- On a scale from 1 to 10 (with 1 being low and 10 being high), how would you evaluate the overall attractiveness of the furniture and room decor (posters, photos, other art)? How does the attractiveness (or lack of attractiveness) of the space influence interpersonal communication? How does it enhance or detract from learning?

- What other aspects of the room have an effect on interpersonal communication and/or learning?

Use the questions in the previous activity to evaluate another room where you spend a lot of time, such as the library or student centre, or a place where you typically study when you are not in class. Describe how the room's arrangement and overall appearance influence interpersonal communication as well as learning and studying.

Web Resources

www.academia.edu/425074/The_Nonverbal_Skills_You_Need _for_Successful_Negotiation This interesting article emphasizes the importance of nonverbal communication when negotiating with others, and suggests nonverbal cues that will help you project the image you want to project.

© COSPV/Shutterstock

8

Conflict Management Skills

66 Outside noisy, inside empty. 99 —Chinese Proverb

Eventually all relationships experience conflict. It's been estimated that people in a stable, romantic relationship experience a conflict episode about twice a week.[1] The longer you know someone, the greater the likelihood that you'll experience conflict with that person, simply because you spend time together and know more about each other. Since it is impossible to avoid all conflict, this chapter will explore some of the ways that you can best manage the inevitable conflict that occurs in your relationships with others.

Conflict management is not a single skill but a set of skills. However, managing conflict effectively involves more than learning simple techniques. The best route to success in resolving conflict effectively is to acquire knowledge about what conflict is, what makes it happen, and what we can do about it. We will begin by defining conflict, examining some of the myths about it, and focusing on some of its constructive functions. We will also discuss the relationship between conflict and power, and learn about some conflict management styles.

In addition, we will consider how learning about your typical style of managing conflict can give you insight into managing interpersonal differences. And finally, we will build on our discussions of listening skills and verbal and nonverbal communication in previous chapters to help you learn to manage the inevitable interpersonal conflicts that arise even in the best of relationships.

Conflict Defined?

A couple disagreeing about whether or not to adopt a pet; a student who thinks his professor has graded him unfairly; a boss frustrated with the performance of one of her employees. What do these three conflict scenarios have in common? In each case, both parties have different goals, needs, and experiences, and this incompatibility is at the root of all conflicts. But precisely what is conflict?

Interpersonal conflict, according to communication scholars William Wilmot and Joyce Hocker, includes four elements. It is (1) an expressed struggle (2) between at least two interdependent people (3) who perceive incompatible goals, scarce resources, or interference from others (4) and who are attempting to achieve specific goals.[2]

Conflict Elements

You probably don't need a textbook definition to determine whether you are experiencing conflict in a relationship. You know you're in conflict as you feel your emotions becoming aroused, as evidenced by an increased heart rate, muscle tension, and a raised voice. Still, looking at the elements of conflict can help you understand both why conflict occurs and how to manage it.

An Expressed Struggle. You typically don't know that someone is upset with you until he or she expresses displeasure with a remark or by a nonverbal behaviour such as a glare, a steely facial expression, or an emotion-laden tone of voice. The intensity of a conflict (as conveyed through the intensity of the emotion expressed) often correlates with the partners' perceptions of the importance of their unmet needs or goals. Sam Keltner developed the "struggle spectrum," shown in Figure 8.1, to describe conflicts ranging from mild differences to outright fights.[3] As conflict evolves in a relationship, it has the potential to escalate into

interpersonal conflict. An expressed struggle between at least two interdependent people who perceive incompatible goals, scarce resources, or interference in the achievement of their goals.

FIGURE 8.1

The Struggle Spectrum

Used by permission of the National Communication Association.

Mild Differences | Disagreement | Dispute | Campaign | Litigation | Fight

Canadian Connections | Family Violence in Canada

While we may think of ourselves as a non-violent society, the family home still represents one of the most violent places in our lives. According to the most recent report from Statistics Canada, *Family Violence in Canada: A Statistical Profile, 2010*, "Family violence—which includes a range of abusive behaviours that occur within relationships based on kinship, intimacy, dependency or trust—continues to be a disturbingly commonplace occurrence in lives of Canadians through all life stages."[4]

The report presents some disturbing statistics:

- In 2009, victims of spousal violence were less likely to report the incident to police than in 2004. Just under one-quarter (22%) of spousal violence

victims said that the incident came to the attention of the police, down slightly from 2004 (28%).

- Nearly 55 000 children and youth were the victims of a sexual offence or physical assault in 2009, about 3 in 10 of which were perpetrated by a family member.

- The 2009 spousal homicide rate remained stable for the third consecutive year. This follows nearly three decades of gradual decline. Women continue to be more likely than men to be victims of spousal homicide. In 2009, the rate of spousal homicide against women was about three times higher than that for men.

In addition to having been the victim of physical and sexual violence, many Canadians reported being the victim of emotional abuse. Emotional abuse includes such behaviours as rejecting (for example, refusing to acknowledge another person), degrading, terrorizing (for example, threatening to hurt a person or stalking), isolating, corrupting and exploiting, and denying emotional responsiveness (failing to be responsive to emotional needs). Emotional abuse often accompanies other forms of abuse, but it may also occur on its own.

In 2009, close to one in five Canadians (17%) said that they had experienced some form of emotional abuse in their current or previous relationship, with put-downs and name-calling being the most common form of abuse.

physical abuse, especially within our most intimate relationships. According to the 2009 General Social Survey (GSS), 6% of Canadians with a current or former spouse reported being the victim of spousal violence in the five years preceding the survey. Experts suggest that one reason violence occurs in so many relationships is that people don't have the skills to manage conflict by expressing their relational struggle effectively.[5] The *Canadian Connections* box examines violence in family relationships in Canada more closely.

At Least Two Interdependent People. By **interdependent**, we mean that what one person does or says affects the other. You are more likely to have conflict with people that you spend time with because you are connected to them in some way. Yes, you might have an emotional response to the driver who cuts you off in traffic, but the conflicts that weigh most heavily on us are those with people with whom we interact most frequently and with whom we have an emotional connection. And, as the old expression "it takes two to tango," suggests, it takes at least two people to have interpersonal conflict. You can certainly experience conflict within yourself, for example if you are torn between going out with your friends and studying for an important exam, but interpersonal conflict involves you and at least one other person.

Incompatible Goals, Scarce Resources, and Interference. Conflict often happens because two people want the same thing, but both can't have it; because what one person wants is the opposite of what the other wants; or because there aren't enough resources (time, money, or something else) to go around. Whether it's a battle between former spouses who both want custody of the children, or a conflict over whether you spend the holidays with your parents or with your partner's family, when there are conflicting or incompatible goals or insufficient resources, or when someone is blocking what you believe is rightfully yours, conflict happens.

Achieving a Goal. People in conflict both want something. As we noted, many conflicts occur because both people can't (or perceive that they can't) achieve their own goals. Therefore, understanding what the individuals want is an important step toward finding a

interdependent. Dependent on each other; one person's actions affect the other person.

way to manage the conflict. Most problems boil down to something you want more of or less of. Figuring out what you and the other person want more of or less of provides a starting point to getting to the end of conflict.

Conflict as a Process

Olivia was enjoying a second cup of coffee and listening to music while answering emails. All seemed well. Suddenly, for no apparent reason, her roommate Prianka stormed into the room and shouted, "I can't stand it anymore! We have to talk about who does what around here." Olivia was taken completely off guard. She had no idea her roommate was upset about the division of household chores. To her, this outburst seemed to come out of the blue; in reality, however, several events had led up to it.

Most relational disagreements have a source, a beginning, a middle, an end, and an aftermath.

Source: Prior Conditions. The first phase in the conflict process is the one that sets the stage for disagreement; it begins when you become aware that there are differences between you and another person. The differences may stem from role expectations, perceptions, goals, or resources. In the previous example, Prianka perceived that she and Olivia played different roles in caring for the household.

In interpersonal relationships, *many* potential sources of conflict may be smouldering below the surface. It may take some time before they flare up into overt conflict. Moreover, they may be compounded with other concerns, making them difficult to sort out. And it may not be just one conversation or issue that triggers conflict; multiple conflict "trip wires" may contribute to a conflict episode.

Beginning: Frustration Awareness. At this stage, at least one of you becomes aware that the differences in the relationship are increasingly problematic. You may begin to engage in self-talk, noting that something is wrong and creating frustration. Perhaps you realize that you won't be able to achieve an important goal or that someone else has resources you need to achieve it. Or you may become aware of differences in perceptions. Prianka knew that Olivia's family always spent their weekends relaxing. All the members of Prianka's family, in contrast, pitched in on weekends to get household chores done for the week. Prianka may have recognized that difference, even as her frustration level rose.

Becoming aware of differences in perception does not always lead to increased frustration. But when the differences interfere with something you want to accomplish, your frustration level rises. Prianka wanted to get the house clean so that she could turn her attention to studying for a test she had the next day. Olivia's apparent indifference to helping Prianka achieve that goal was a conflict trigger.

Middle: Active Conflict. When you bring your frustration to the attention of others, a conflict becomes an active, expressed struggle. If frustrations remain only as thoughts, the conflict is passive, not active. Active conflict does not necessarily mean that the differences are expressed with shouting or emotional intensity. An expression of disagreement may be either verbal or nonverbal. Calmly asking someone to change an attitude or behaviour to help you achieve your goal is a form of active conflict; so is kicking your brother under the table when he starts to reveal a secret to the rest of the family.

Olivia was not aware of the problem until Prianka stormed into the room demanding a renegotiation of roles. Prianka had been aware of her frustration for some time, yet had not acted on it. Many experts advocate not waiting until your frustration level escalates to peak intensity before you approach someone with your conflict. Unexpressed frustration tends to erupt like soda in a can that has just been shaken. Intense emotions can add to the difficulty of managing a conflict.

◢ RECAP | Understanding Conflict as a Process

Prior conditions stage	The stage is set for conflict because of differences in the individuals' actions or attitudes.
Frustration awareness stage	One individual becomes aware that the differences are problematic and becomes frustrated and angry.
Active conflict stage	The individuals communicate with each other about the differences; the conflict becomes an expressed struggle.
Resolution stage	The individuals begin seeking ways to manage the conflict.
Follow-up stage	The individuals check with themselves and each other to monitor whether both are satisfied with the resolution.

End: Resolution. When you begin to try to manage the conflict, you have arrived at the resolution stage. Of course, not all conflicts can be neatly resolved. Couples who divorce, business partners who dissolve their corporation, or roommates who go their separate ways have all found solutions, even though they may not be amicable ones.

After Prianka's outburst, she and Olivia were able to reach a workable compromise about the division of their household labour. Olivia agreed to clean the house every other week; Prianka promised not to expect her to do it on weekends.

Aftermath: Follow-Up. After a conflict has been resolved, the follow-up stage involves dealing with hurt feelings or managing simmering grudges, and checking with the other person to confirm that the conflict has not retreated into the frustration awareness stage. As we noted in Chapter 1, interpersonal relationships operate as transactive processes rather than as linear, step-by-step ones. Conflict does progress in stages, but you may need to resolve the same conflict again unless you confirm your understanding of the issues with your partner.

The Friday after their discussion, Olivia proudly showed off a spotless apartment to Prianka when she came home from class. Prianka responded with a grin and a quick hug, and privately resolved to get up early on Sunday morning so that she could go out to get Olivia a coffee and pastries before she woke up. This kind of mutual thoughtfulness exemplifies a successful follow-up in a conflict.

Understanding the stages of conflict can help you better manage the process. You'll also be in a better position to make the conflict a constructive rather than a destructive experience. Conflict is **constructive** if it helps build new insights and establishes new and beneficial patterns in a relationship. Conflict can focus attention on problems that may need solving, clarify situations that need changing, help you learn more about both yourself and your partner, and strengthen relationships by demonstrating that you can manage disagreements. Airing differences can lead to a more satisfying relationship in the long run.

Conflict can also be **destructive**. The sign of destructive conflict is a lack of flexibility in responding to others. Conflict can become destructive when people view their differences from a win–lose perspective, rather than looking for solutions that allow both individuals to gain. There is clearly a dark side to conflict. Cyberbullying, hate crimes, stalking, aggressive verbal abuse, and physical abuse are some of the potential negative effects of escalating, unmanaged conflict. In addition to emails and texts, Twitter, Facebook, Snapchat, Instagram, and YouTube make it easier to broadcast negative and destructive relational messages to more people at greater speed. A key purpose of this book, and specifically this chapter, is to identify sources of conflict *before* the relational

constructive conflict. Conflict that helps build new insights and establishes new patterns in a relationship.

destructive conflict. Conflict that dismantles rather than strengthens relationships.

Unresolved and poorly managed interpersonal conflict is a significant predictor of an unsatisfactory interpersonal relationship.
(© zulufoto/Shutterstock)

turbulence becomes destructive. The principles, strategies, and skills we offer won't eliminate conflict, but they can help you manage it when it occurs in both face-to-face and electronically mediated relationships.

Conflict Triggers

Researchers have found that just as conflict typically follows a predictable path as it evolves, there are also some common causes that trigger conflict. A **conflict trigger** is a perceived cause of conflict. What typically ticks people off? Here are some of the most common conflict triggers.

Criticism. Receiving criticism is one of the most frequently mentioned conflict triggers. Many people automatically interpret any criticism as a personal attack, and react by both becoming defensive and striking back at the other person with their own criticism or insults.

Feeling Entitled. If we believe we're entitled to something—whether "it" is a good grade in a class, a new car, or a relationship with someone—and we're denied getting what we think is ours, then conflict is a likely result.

Perceived Lack of Fairness. If we believe we have not been treated fairly or equitably, conflict is likely. "It's mine, not yours!" and "That's not fair!" are claims children make while playing with others in a sandbox; those same sentiments fuel conflict between adults, as well as international conflicts between nations.

More Perceived Costs Than Rewards. Another trigger for conflict escalation in a relationship occurs when one person feels that he or she is getting less out of the relationship than the other person. Over time, if the perceived burdens are greater than the joy of being in a relationship with someone, conflict ensues.

Different Perspectives. Researcher Lawrence Kurdek found that regardless of whether couples were heterosexual, gay, or lesbian, several topics or issues serve as conflict triggers: (1) power (who's in charge), (2) social issues (such as politics and religion), (3) personal flaws (such as use of drugs or alcohol, smoking, or laziness), (4) distrust (concern about whether one person is telling the truth), (5) intimacy (differences about the frequency and timing of sex), and (6) personal distance (as evidenced by the amount of time each person commits to the relationship).[6] (There are many other things that couples argue about, such as money, but money conflicts are often about power.) These "big six" appear to be common conflict themes across a wide variety of relationships.

Stress and Lack of Rest. When you are not at your physical best—when you're tired, stressed, or overworked—it may be wise to avoid situations that are likely to trigger disagreement. Before you know it, what you thought was just a casual remark can quickly escalate into conflict. The beginnings of vacations, when you and your friend, partner, or spouse may be at the peak of fatigue, are prime occasions for conflict. The end of a long workweek may also be a time when it doesn't take much to turn a casual conversation into a Friday-night fight. Not surprisingly, being under the influence of alcohol or other substances that impair judgment increases the chances that conflict will erupt.

conflict triggers. Common causes of interpersonal conflict.

Dialectical Tension. A **dialectical tension** stems from people's need or desire for two things at the same time. The tension results in uncertainty and discomfort with the relationship. Here are two classic dialectical tensions experienced by many relationships.

- *Wanting to be both separate and connected.* You may have a desire to be both separate from other people and connected to them at the same time; we want our freedom, but we also want the comfort, predictability, and convenience of having someone who is a consistent part of our life. This desire can cause conflict if, for example, you want more freedom in a relationship, but your partner wants to keep closer tabs on what you are doing and where you are. You may feel a personal dialectical tension because you want both things *at the same time*—to be close to the other person *and* to have your freedom.

- *Wanting to be both open and closed.* A second common dialectical tension is that we want and need various degrees of openness and closedness in our relationships. We want to share and disclose our thoughts and feelings, but we also want our privacy and secrecy.

The benefit of being aware of common conflict triggers is having the ability to spot them in your relationship before the conflict escalates into intractable tension that is more challenging to manage and threatens to end the relationship.

Conflict Myths

Although not all conflict is destructive to relationships, many cultures have taboos against displaying conflict in public. The prime experiences in life that shape how we learn to express and manage conflict occur in the families in which we grew up. According to one researcher, many of us were raised with four myths that contribute to our negative feelings about conflict.[7] Perhaps you were raised in a family that expressed conflict openly and often; still, learning about these common myths may help you understand the ways you or your partner responds emotionally to conflict.

dialectical tension. Tension arising from a person's need for two things at the same time.

Conflict Is Always a Sign of a Poor Interpersonal Relationship

It is an oversimplification to assume that all conflict is rooted in underlying relational problems. Conflict is a normal part of any interpersonal relationship. Although it is true that constant bickering and sniping can be a symptom of deeper problems, disagreements do not necessarily signal that the relationship is in trouble. Conflict in interpersonal relationships can play a constructive role in leading people to focus on issues that may need attention. The ebb and flow of interpersonal psychological intimacy and separation inevitably lead to some degree of conflict in any relationship. When conflict happens in one of your relationships, don't immediately assume that the relationship is doomed.

"How many miles before our next fight?"

Conflict Can Always Be Avoided

Many of us were taught early in our lives that conflict is undesirable and that we should eliminate it from our conversations and relationships. Yet conflict is normal, and arises in virtually every relationship. It's not the amount of conflict in a relationship; it's the way the partners manage it.

Conflict Always Occurs Because of Misunderstandings

"You just don't understand what my days are like. I need to go to sleep!" shouts Janice as she scoops up a pillow and blanket and stalks off to the living room. "Oh, yeah? Well, you don't understand what will happen if I don't get this budget in!" responds Ron, who is hunched over the desk in their bedroom. It is clear that Ron and Janice are having a conflict. They have identified the cause of their problem as a lack of understanding between them, but in reality they *do* understand each other. Ron knows that Janice wants to sleep; Janice knows he wants to stay up and work. Their problem is that they disagree about whose goal is more important. This disagreement, not lack of understanding, is the source of the conflict.

Conflict Can Always Be Resolved

Consultants, corporate training experts, and authors of self-help books often offer advice about how to resolve conflicts so that all will be well and harmony will prevail. However, not all differences can be resolved by listening harder or paraphrasing your partner's message. Some disagreements are so intense and the perceptions so fixed that individuals may have to agree to disagree and live with it.

> ▶ **RECAP** **Conflict Myths**
>
> | | |
> |---|---|
> | **Myth #1:** | Conflict is always a sign of a poor interpersonal relationship. |
> | **Myth #2:** | Conflict should always be avoided. |
> | **Myth #3:** | Conflict always occurs because of misunderstanding. |
> | **Myth #4:** | Conflict can always be resolved. |

Conflict Types

At some time or another, many close relationships go through a conflict phase. "We're always fighting," complains a newlywed, but if she were to analyze these fights, she would probably discover that the nature of the fights varied. One research duo found that most conflicts fit into three different categories: (1) **pseudo-conflict**—triggered by a lack of understanding; (2) **simple conflict**—stemming from different ideas, definitions, perceptions, or goals; and (3) **ego conflict**—when conflict gets personal.[8]

pseudo-conflict. Conflict triggered by a lack of understanding.

simple conflict. Conflict stemming from different ideas, definitions, perceptions, or goals.

ego conflict. Conflict involving personal attacks and emotional epithets.

Pseudo-Conflict: Misunderstandings

"Pseudo" means false or fake. Pseudo-conflict occurs when we simply miss the meaning in a message, but unless we clear up the misunderstanding by asking for more information, a real conflict might ensue. For example, you've arranged to meet a friend for lunch, but after waiting alone at your table for half an hour, you call your friend only to discover that she's been waiting at a restaurant across the street. Each of you is angry with the other for misunderstanding.

How can you avoid pseudo-conflict? A key strategy is to clarify the meaning of words and expressions that you don't understand. Keep the following strategies in mind to minimize misunderstandings before they occur:

- *Check your perceptions.* Ask to clarify what you don't understand; seek to determine whether your interpretation is the same as your partner's. For example, you could have asked, "So, we're meeting at the restaurant on the north side, right? The one we went to last time?"

- *Listen between the lines.* Look for puzzled or quizzical facial expressions on your partner. People may not voice their misunderstanding, but they may express their uncertainty nonverbally.

- *Establish a supportive rather than a defensive climate for conversation.* Avoid evaluating, controlling, using manipulative strategies, being aloof, acting superior, or rigidly asserting that you're always right. These classic behaviours are like pushing the button for increased defensiveness and misunderstanding.

ADAPTING TO DIFFERENCES
Understanding Others

Masculine and Feminine Conflict Styles

Research suggests that there are distinctions between so-called "feminine" and "masculine" styles of responding to conflict. Of course, individuals of either sex may employ some characteristics of both feminine and masculine styles. The feminine style is more likely to focus on relationship issues, whereas the masculine style typically focuses on tasks.[9] Those with the feminine style often interact with others to achieve intimacy and closeness, but those with the masculine style interact to get something done or to accomplish something apart from the relationship. When pursuing a goal, those employing a masculine style are often more aggressive and assertive than those employing a feminine style. The list below summarizes key differences that researchers have observed between feminine and masculine styles of responding to conflict.

Although these findings provide a starting point for analyzing our conflicts with members of the opposite sex, we caution against lapsing into "allness" statements such as "Oh, you're just like all women; that's why you disagree with me" or "You're just like all men; you never want to focus on how I feel." Even thinking in these ways can prevent you from listening to what your partner is saying. Also, although research has identified some gender-based differences in the way we manage conflict, some research studies suggest that the differences can, at times, be quite small. The context for the argument or the specific conflict trigger may be a more important factor than gender in shaping how we respond to and manage interpersonal conflict.

The most recent perspective on analyzing gender differences is called the partnership perspective. Rather than viewing gender differences as conflict between people who live on different planets, this perspective suggests that men and women are not locked into particular styles or approaches. The partnership approach emphasizes the importance of keeping channels open and avoiding the tendency to stereotype communication styles by gender.

Feminine Styles

- Are concerned with equity and caring; connect with and feel responsible to others
- Interact to achieve closeness and interdependence
- Attend to interpersonal dynamics to assess relationship's health
- Encourage mutual involvement
- Attribute crises to problems in the relationship
- Are concerned with the impact of the relationship on personal identity
- Often respond to conflict by focusing on the relationship

Masculine Styles

- Are concerned with equality of rights and fairness; adhere to abstract principles, rules
- Interact for instrumental purposes; seek autonomy and distance
- Are less aware of interpersonal dynamics
- Protect self-interest
- Attribute crises to problems external to the relationship
- Are neither self- nor relationship-centred
- Often respond to conflict by focusing on rules and being evasive until a unilateral decision is reached

Simple Conflict: Different Stands on the Issues

Simple conflict stems from differences in ideas, definitions, perceptions, or goals. You want to go to Lake Louise for your vacation; your partner wants to go to Quebec City. Your partner wants to fly; you would rather take the train. You understand each other, but you disagree.

A key to unravelling a simple conflict is to keep the conversation focused on the issues at hand so that the expression of differences does not deteriorate into a battle focusing on personalities.

To keep simple conflict from escalating into personal attacks, consider the following strategies:

- *Clarify your and your partner's understanding* of the issues and your partner's understanding of the source of the disagreement.

- *Keep the discussion focused* on facts and on the issue at hand rather than drifting back to past battles and unrelated personal grievances.

- *Look for more than just the initial solutions* that you and your partner bring to the discussion; generate many options.

- *Don't try to tackle too many issues at once.* Perform "issue triage"—identify the important issues and work on those.

- *Find the kernel of truth in what your partner may be saying.* Seek agreement where you can.

- *If tempers begin to flare and conflict is spiralling upward, cool off.* Come back to the discussion when you and your partner are fresh.

Ego Conflict: Conflict Gets Personal

Arguments that begin as pseudo- or simple conflicts can easily lapse into more vicious ego conflicts. And as each person in the conflict becomes more defensive about his or her position, the issues become more tangled. An argument can start with an offhand remark but can escalate into a major conflict because both participants began attacking each other and bringing up other sensitive issues instead of focusing on the original comment. Can you think of an example of an argument you had recently that escalated into an ego conflict?

If you find yourself involved in ego conflict, try to refrain from hurling personal attacks and emotional epithets back and forth. Instead, take turns expressing your feelings without interrupting each other, and then take time to cool off. It is difficult to use effective listening skills when your emotions are at a high pitch.

© Michael Maslin/Liza Donnelly

"Cool! My new cell phone allows me to see your angry face as well as hear your angry voice."

Here are additional strategies to consider when conflict becomes personal:

- *Try to steer the ego conflict back to simple conflict.* Stay focused on issues rather than personalities.

- *Make the issue a problem to be solved rather than a battle to be won.*

- *Write down what you want to say.* It may help you clarify your point, and you and your partner can develop your ideas without interruption. A note of caution: don't put angry personal attacks in writing. Make your written summary brief and rational rather than lengthy and emotional.

- *When things get personal, make a vow not to reciprocate.* Use the "I" messages that we talked about in Chapter 6 ("I feel uncomfortable and threatened when we yell at each other") rather than "you" messages ("You're so selfish" or "You never listen") to express how you are feeling.

- *Avoid contempt and sarcasm.* It may be tempting to roll your eyes and sarcastically say "Oh, that's brilliant" in response to something your partner has said, but expressing contempt through a sarcastic tone will not help solve the conflict, and will often escalate it.

Simple conflict can become ego conflict when communicating online, just as it can when communicating in person. See the *e-Connections* box to learn about managing conflict online.

▶ RECAP Types of Conflict

	Pseudo-Conflict	**Simple Conflict**	**Ego Conflict**
What It Is	Individuals misunderstand each other.	Individuals disagree over which action to pursue to achieve their goals.	Individuals feel personally attacked.
What to Do	Check your perceptions.	Clarify understanding.	Return to issues rather than personal attacks.
	Listen between the lines; look for nonverbal expressions of puzzlement.	Stay focused on facts and issues.	Talk about a problem to be solved rather than a fight to be won.
	Be supportive rather than defensive.	Generate many options rather than arguing over one or two.	Write down rational arguments to support your position.
	Listen actively.	Find the kernel of truth in what your partner is saying; emphasize where you agree.	Use "I" messages rather than "you" messages.

Conflict and Power

Often what we fight about is not what we're really fighting about. The topic of your argument may be anything from deciding which movie to see to something more significant, such as whether to have children. Yet underlying the surface issue may be a question about who has the power to make the decision. Comments during an argument like "Who made you the boss?" or "What gives you the right to make this decision?" indicate that underlying the conflict is an issue of power. Power and conflict go hand in hand, because people often use the sources of interpersonal power available to them to achieve their desired outcome when conflict occurs.

Underlying many interpersonal conflicts is the question of who has power to make decisions.
(© Ingram Publishing/Alamy Stock Photo)

Interpersonal power is the degree to which a person is able to influence or control his or her relational partner. During a conflict you may not even be aware of how you are drawing on the power you have, or that the other person is exerting power to influence you. Nonetheless, power issues are often the "back story" to the conflict. Understanding principles of power and sources of power can give you greater insight into how you are using power to influence others to achieve your goals and how others are seeking to influence or control you, especially during conflict.

Power Principles

Most of us probably don't like to think that other people have power over us, but power is a fundamental element of all our personal relationships. Understanding the role of power in our relations with others can help explain and predict our thoughts, emotions, and behaviours, especially during relational conflict.

Power Exists in All Relationships. Our definition of interpersonal communication that we presented in Chapter 1 suggests that *mutual influence* is an essential element any time you relate to others. When you talk, you are attempting to exert power over other people, if for no other purpose than to get them to listen to you. By definition, being in a relationship means letting someone have some influence on you *and* having influence on the other person.

Power Derives from the Ability to Meet a Person's Needs. If you can meet someone's need, then you have power. The degree to which one person can satisfy another person's interpersonal needs (for inclusion, control, and affection) as well as other needs (for food, clothing, safety, sex, money) represents the amount of power that person has.

In a **dependent relationship**, one person has a greater need for the partner to satisfy his or her needs; the power is out of balance and the person who depends on someone else to meet his or her needs has less power. The more we depend on one person to satisfy our needs, the more power that person has over us.

Both People in a Relationship Have Some Power. Although sometimes one person in a relationship has more power (influence) than the other, each person has some degree of power. When you were a child, your parents clearly had more power than you did; during conflicts, especially when you were quite young, they used their power to resolve conflicts in their favour. Now the power may be more balanced (or maybe not). When two people are satisfying each other's needs, they create an interdependent relationship; each person in the relationship has some amount of power over the other.

Power Is Circumstantial. Because our needs change, so does power. As you were growing up, you were very dependent on your parents and other adults. However, as you got older and developed skills, you no longer needed your parents to meet certain needs, and thus their power diminished. So the power balance ebbs and flows in a relationship over time and depending on circumstances.

Power Is Negotiated. Partners often negotiate which individual will have decision-making responsibility over what issues. But people can disagree as to who has power to do what. If one partner wants the power to control the TV remote and the other person also wants to have channel-changing power, conflict and tension are the result, unless some negotiation occurs. "Okay, you decide what we watch between 6:00 and 8:00 p.m. and I'll

interpersonal power. Degree to which a person is able to influence his or her partner.

dependent relationship. Relationship in which one partner has a greater need for the other to meet his or her needs.

control the remote the next two hours" may be one couple's way of negotiating the power. With power negotiated, the conflict is managed—unless one of the individuals wants to revisit who is in charge of the remote. If the negotiation is about something more weighty than who watches which TV program (such as sex, money, or children), the conflict can be more intense, and clearly more is at stake during the power negotiation.

Power to Persuade

When we have power, we may use it to manage conflict in order to achieve our goals and meet our needs using compliance-gaining strategies. **Compliance gaining** is taking actions in interpersonal relationships to gain something from our partners—to get others to comply with our goals. Compliance gaining is persuasion in an interpersonal context. We use communication to influence others by developing and applying compliance-gaining/persuasive strategies.

People's level of power affects what compliance-gaining strategies they employ. People with more power can be more efficient in gaining compliance by using simple, more direct (and sometimes inappropriate) strategies to accomplish their goals.[10] Those with less power need to carefully consider which strategies they can use that won't result in negative consequences. For example, telling your boss that you will quit if you don't have Friday night off might result in your no longer having a job. The appropriateness of compliance gaining varies according to our goals. For example, persuasive strategies involving either logic or emotion are seen as more effective in face-to-face interactions than in computer-mediated ones. Unlike in face to face conversation, electronically mediated communication is conducted through limited channels, as auditory, visual, nonverbal, and other cues are not available.[11] Communication scholar Kathy Kellerman compiled a list of 56 strategies that people might employ in trying to gain compliance (Table 8.1). Think about the last time you sought compliance from a friend, and see if you can identify the strategy or strategies you employed.

compliance gaining. Taking persuasive actions to get others to comply with our goals.

TABLE 8.1 Compliance-Gaining Strategies

Accuse	Comment	Hint	Protest
Acknowledge	Complain	Inform	Question
Advise	Compliment	Insist	Remark
Apologize	Confess	Insult	Report
Approve	Confirm	Joke	Reprimand
Argue	Criticize	Justify	Request
Ask	Demand	Offer	Ridicule
Assert	Disagree	Order	Suggest
Assure	Disclose	Permit	Summarize
Attack	Excuse	Plead	Tell
Blame	Explain	Point out	Thank
Boast	Forbid	Praise	Threaten
Challenge	Forgive	Prohibit	Vow
Claim	Give	Promise	Warn

Source: K. Kellerman, "A Goal-Directed Approach to Gaining Compliance: Relating Differences Among Goals to Differences in Behaviours.," *Communication Research* 31 (2004): 397–445.

Compliance-gaining strategies are responsive to the ongoing, transactive nature of interpersonal relationships. We plot strategies that develop over a number of interactions and modify them in accordance with others' responses. For example, before you ask to borrow money from your friend, you might first do a few favours for her during the day. Then if your friend says no to your request for a loan, you might remind her that she owes you for all you've done for her. If she still says no, you might offer to help her over the weekend with her class project. The type of relationship you have established with the other person will affect your strategy selection. Often, because of our power, we face little resistance from our partners to our requests, so we have no need for any compliance-gaining strategy.

Power Negotiation

If you realize that you don't have as much power as you'd like, you may want to renegotiate who has the power to do what in a relationship. Defining who has power can be a source of conflict in interpersonal relationships, potentially even bringing about the end of a relationship. When a partner abuses power, ending the relationship may be warranted. Ideally, partners negotiate a mutually acceptable and rewarding power relationship. To negotiate or renegotiate power in a relationship, consider the following strategies.

Assess Needs. The first step toward negotiating a satisfactory balance of power is to identify your needs and those of your partner. Knowing what you need and what the other person needs in the relationship can help you determine whether any negotiation or renegotiation of roles, responsibilities, and assumptions is warranted. Reflecting not just on your needs but also on the needs of the other person is an other-oriented strategy that can help you honestly and realistically start the negotiation process.

Identify Power-Based Conflicts. Examine your interpersonal conflicts for unresolved power issues. For example, in the first year of marriage, couples often argue about balancing job and family, about financial problems (including who spends money and on what), about the frequency of sexual relations, and about the division of household tasks. These problems involve issues of power, control, responsibility, and decision making. Such issues exist in other relationships as well. Examine your relationships for recurring patterns of conflict, and try to determine the role that power is playing. Conflicts can result from unacceptable imbalances of power (the feeling that one or the other partner has too much), from equal amounts of power (with each partner attempting to influence the other), or as a reaction to attempts to exert control or to dominate.

Discuss Power Issues Directly. If you're not talking about what the real, underlying issue may be during a conflict—the issue of power—the conflict is unlikely to be managed permanently. Identification of the unmet needs that are fuelling conflict should be followed up with conversation about who has, wants, and expects to have influence and control. But when talking about who has power and control in a relationship, it's vital to use the principles and skills of being supportive that we discussed in previous chapters, as well as effective listening and responding skills. Talking about who should have the power and influence in a relationship can be risky—like touching the third rail on a subway track that carries the electricity propelling the train. Some couples need a trained counsellor or therapist to help them work through issues of power in their relationships. The more intense the unmet need that is affecting the power imbalance, the greater the likelihood that help may be needed to address who has the influence in a specific situation.

Conflict Management Styles

What's your approach to managing interpersonal conflict: fight or flight? Do you tackle conflict head-on or seek ways to remove yourself from it? Most of us do not have a single way of dealing with differences, but we do have a tendency to manage conflict by following patterns we have used before. The pattern we choose depends on several factors: our personality, the individuals with whom we are in conflict, the time and place of the confrontation, and other situational factors. For example, if your boss gave you an order, you would respond differently from the way you would if your partner gave you an order.

One of several classifications systems for conflict is a five-style model based on the work of R. H. Kilmann and K. W. Thomas, which includes two primary dimensions: concern for others and concern for self.[12] These two dimensions result in five **conflict management styles**, shown in Figure 8.2. The five styles are (1) avoidance, (2) accommodation, (3) competition, (4) compromise, and (5) collaboration.

Avoidance

One approach to managing conflict is to back off and try to sidestep the conflict. Typical responses from someone who uses this style are "I don't want to talk about it," "It's not my problem," "Don't bother me with that now," or "I'm not interested in that." The **avoidance** style might indicate that a person has low concern for others as well as for himself or herself. This is sometimes called the "lose–lose" approach to conflict. The person using the avoiding conflict style wishes the problem or conflict would go away by itself and appears uninterested in managing it or in meeting the needs of the other person. People who avoid conflict may also just not like the hassle of dealing with a difficult, uncomfortable situation. Not dealing directly with conflict may also stem from being unassertive and unable to stand up for one's own rights.

People also avoid conflict sometimes because they don't want to hurt the feelings of others. There may be times when avoiding a major blow-up with someone is a wise strategy, but hoping the conflict will go away on its own is often not the best plan.

Evidence suggests that husbands are more likely to avoid confrontation as a way of managing conflict with their wives. One research team argues that males are likely

conflict management styles. The consistent patterns or approaches used to manage disagreements with others.

avoidance. Managing conflict by backing off and trying to sidestep it.

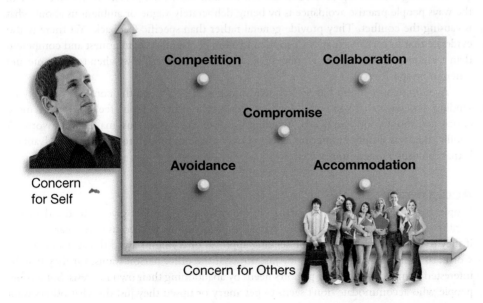

FIGURE 8.2

Conflict Management Styles

The five conflict management styles in relation to concern for others and concern for self.

to avoid conflict because of the way they process information, especially emotions.[13] Husbands may implicitly reason that it's better to keep quiet and avoid conflict than to speak up and try to sort things out; for them, the dissonance that results from speaking up is not worth the effort.

Research that looked at how parents and teenagers managed their conflict found that one of the least satisfying approaches to conflict management is the **demand-withdrawal pattern**; either the parent or the teenager makes a demand and the other person avoids conflict by changing the subject or walking away.[14] Researchers have found that making repeated demands that aren't directly addressed, while also hurling put-downs at each other, results in a more distressed parent–teenager relationship. If you see that you're in a demand-withdrawal pattern of conflict, try to change the tone of the interaction so that it becomes a conversation rather than a shouting match or a standoff in which you both just stop talking. Make it a goal to keep the conversation going rather than making a demand that results in the other person just walking away.

In some respects, avoiding conflict could be perceived as uncooperative. However, although it may not be cooperative, there are some advantages to avoiding conflict. It provides time for each person in the conflict to think about the issues, cool down, and ponder other approaches. If the conflict issue really is trivial or silly, it may be advantageous not to throttle up the tension.

Avoiding conflict can de-escalate the tension and allow each person to save face. One of the ways people practise avoidance is by being deliberately vague or ambiguous about what is causing the conflict. They provide general rather than specific feedback. Yet there is also evidence that in certain situations people find a direct response more honest and competent than a vague one. The trick is accurately reading a situation to know when to be vague and when to be specific.

Avoiding conflict also has several disadvantages. If you avoid the conflict, you may be sending a message that you really don't care about the other person's feelings; you're more concerned about your own needs. Avoiding the conflict may also just make things worse. A conflict that was simply simmering may boil over if it's not tended to. Another disadvantage is that the issue remains unresolved.

Accommodation

People who use the **accommodation** style of managing conflict give in to the demands of others. People may sometimes adopt an accommodation style because they fear rejection if they rock the boat. They may be seeking approval or trying to avoid threats to their self-worth; to avoid creating a scene, they just do what the other person wants. Or they may be interested in meeting the other person's needs by abandoning their own interests. Sometimes people who accommodate don't seem to get angry or upset; they just do what others want

demand-withdrawal pattern. Pattern in which one person makes a demand and the other person avoids conflict by changing the subject or walking away.

accommodation. Managing conflict by giving in to the demands of others.

them to do. However, in reality, they also accommodate to serve their own interests—to get people to like them. This conflict management style is sometimes called the "lose–win" approach. If you consistently accommodate, you sacrifice your own needs so that someone else can win the argument.

Using the accommodation style has several advantages. For one thing, it shows that you're reasonable and that you want to help. If the issue is a minor or trivial one, you may gain some credibility by just giving in this time. Of course, if you are wrong or have made a mistake, accommodation is an appropriate response.

There are disadvantages to accommodating, just as there are disadvantages to any conflict management style. Throughout this book, we've stressed the importance of becoming other-oriented. However, we've also noted that being other-oriented means considering the needs and position of the other person without necessarily doing what the other person wants. Sometimes a person may accommodate for self-protection rather than because he or she is genuinely interested in others. In the following exchange, note Luke's accommodation response to Jesse:

Jesse: Luke, I don't agree with you about how to approach the topic for our presentation. I think Professor Latham wants us to show the differences between these two theories rather than just summarize each of them.

Luke: Okay. Whatever you think is best. Let's do it your way.

Using the accommodation style can give the accommodator a false sense of security by producing a "pseudo-solution"—one that doesn't really solve anything but just postpones the effort of seeking a solution to the problem. And if you consistently accommodate, you may diminish your power to the extent that others take advantage of you; the next time a conflict arises, the expectation may be that you'll give in and the other person will get his or her way again. In addition, if you accommodate too quickly, you short-circuit the possibility of finding a creative solution that is to everyone's liking.

Competition

"You're wrong!" shouts Ed. "Here's how to get our project in on time. We can't waste time in the library. We just have to write up what we have."

"But Ed," notes Derek, "the assignment calls for us to have three library sources."

"No, we don't have time. Just do it," insists Ed.

Ed sees the issue as a competition that he must win.

Each of us has some need to control and also some need to be controlled by others, but people who have a **competition** conflict management style have a win–lose philosophy. They want to win at the expense of the other person, to claim victory over their opponents. They want to control others. They are typically not other-oriented; instead, they are focused on themselves.

People who compete often resort to blaming or seeking a scapegoat rather than assuming responsibility for a conflict. "I didn't do it," "Don't look at me," and "He made me do it" are typical blaming statements.

If these strategies do not work, people with a competitive style may try threats and warnings. Threats are actions that people can actually carry out. Warnings are negative prophecies they cannot actually control. The boyfriend who says "If you don't stop calling me names I'm going to leave you" has issued a threat; he has the power to leave. If he were to say "Don't call your parents names or they'll kick you out of the house," that would be a warning. In reality, he has no control over his partner's parents.

Obviously, threats are more powerful than warnings in changing behaviour, and then only if the other person would genuinely find the threatened actions punishing or disruptive.

competition. A conflict management style that stresses winning a conflict at the expense of the other person involved.

If a parent threatens to ground a child, the child will take the threat seriously only if he or she knows the parent will carry it out. If the parent has backed down in the past, the child will probably not pay much attention to the threat.

Is it ever appropriate to compete with others? Yes, if you believe that your position is clearly the best approach and that anything short of achieving your goal would be harmful to you and to others. In an election, someone will win and someone will lose; at the conclusion of a judicial trial, someone typically wins and someone loses. But even hard-fought elections and controversial trials have rules designed to maintain fairness for all involved in the conflict or decision. During often-emotional periods of competition, those involved nonetheless need to maintain an ethical concern for others.

Compromise

People who use the compromise style of managing conflict attempt to find a middle ground—a solution that somewhat meets the needs of all concerned. The word "somewhat" is important. Often when people compromise, no one gets precisely what he or she wants; each has to give up a bit of what he or she had hoped to get. When trying to craft a compromise, you're really expecting to lose something and win something simultaneously; you also expect your partner to lose and win. That's why the **compromise** style is called a "lose/win–lose/win" approach to conflict. As shown in Figure 8.2, when you compromise, you have some concern for others as well as some concern for yourself.

Compromise has some advantages. It can be a good thing if a quick resolution to the conflict is needed. To compromise reinforces the notion that all parties involved share in equal power. Compromise can also be useful if what is needed is a temporary solution, and it has the advantage of helping everyone save face because everyone wins at least something.

However, if compromising results in each person giving in but no person feeling pleased with the compromise, then a more collaborative approach to managing the conflict may be appropriate. Compromise can be tempting because it's easy, and while it's true that each party in the conflict may win with a compromise, the flip side is that each party also loses a bit. Finally, compromising just to make the conflict go away can be another way of avoiding underlying issues that may need to be discussed.

Collaboration

Collaborating involves having a high concern for both yourself and others. People who use a **collaboration** style of conflict management are more likely to view conflict as a set of problems to be solved than a game in which one person wins and another loses. Collaboration, which requires other-oriented strategies that foster a win–win climate, is based on the following principles offered by Harvard researchers Roger Fisher and William Ury:[15]

- *Separate the people from the problem.* Leave personal grievances out of the discussion; describe problems without making judgmental or evaluative statements about personalities.

- *Focus on shared interests.* Ask questions such as "What do we both want?," "What do we both value?," and "Where are we already agreeing?" to emphasize common interests, values, and goals.

- *Generate many options to solve the problem.* Use brainstorming and other techniques to generate alternative solutions. (You will learn more about problem-solving techniques later in this chapter.)

- *Base decisions on objective criteria.* Establish standards for an acceptable solution to a problem—these standards may involve cost, timing, and other factors. Suppose, for example, that you and your neighbour are discussing possible ways to stop another

---

BEING Other-ORIENTED

Collaboration would be impossible if you failed to consider the thoughts and feelings of the other person. What are ways to identify the interests you have in common? How can you determine where your goal overlaps with the other person's goal?

---

compromise. An attempt to find the middle ground in a conflict.

collaboration. Use of other-oriented strategies to manage a conflict to achieve a positive solution for all involved.

neighbour's dog from barking all night. You decide on these criteria: the solution must not harm the dog; it must be easy for the owner to implement; the owner must agree to it; it should not cost more than $50; and it must keep the dog from disturbing the sleep of others. Your neighbour suggests that maybe the dog can sleep in the owner's garage at night. This solution meets all but one of your criteria, so you call the owner, who agrees to put the dog in the garage by 10:00 p.m. Now everyone wins because the solution meets a sound, well-considered set of objective criteria.

The collaboration conflict management style is best used when those on all sides of the conflict need some new, fresh ideas. Using a collaborative approach also enhances commitment to the resolution of the conflict because all are involved in shaping the outcome. Collaborative approaches to managing conflict build rapport because everyone's concerns are at least noted, if not fully addressed. Finally, collaboration considers feelings and affirms the value of the interpersonal relationship.

It may sound as though collaboration is always the best approach to managing conflict. However, there are times when its disadvantages outweigh the advantages. One of the biggest disadvantages is the time, skill, patience, and energy required to manage conflict collaboratively. If a solution is needed quickly, other approaches such as compromise may be best.

So, which style of managing conflict is best? It depends on the outcome you seek, the amount of time you have, the quality of the relationship you have with the other people involved, and the amount of perceived power you and others have. Each style has advantages and disadvantages; no style has an inherent advantage all of the time.

The competent, other-oriented communicator consciously decides whether to compete, avoid, compromise, accommodate, or collaborate. Although collaboration seems to be the style preferred by most people, it, too, may not always be appropriate. Research suggests that what most people find most uncomfortable is either (1) no clear resolution to a conflict, (2) a conflict management process that is poorly managed, or (3) the avoidance of issues that they would like to discuss.[16] There is no single conflict management style that "works" in all situations. We do, however, strongly suggest that, when time and other factors permit, a collaborative (win–win) conflict management style is worth exploring. The conflict management skills presented at the end of this chapter are anchored in a collaborative approach to managing conflict.

RECAP Conflict Management Styles

	The person who uses this style . . .
Avoidance	Withdraws from conflict; tries to sidestep confrontation; finds conflict uncomfortable
	A lose–lose approach to conflict
Accommodation	Easily gives in to the demands of others; typically wants to be liked by others
	A lose–win approach to conflict
Competition	Dominates the discussion and wants to accomplish the goal even at the expense of others
	A win–lose approach to conflict
Compromise	Seeks the middle ground; will give up something to get something
	A lose/win–lose/win approach to conflict
Collaboration	Views conflict as a problem to be solved; negotiates to achieve a positive solution for all involved in the conflict
	A win–win approach to conflict

E-CONNECTIONS
Relating to Others
Managing Conflict Online

Conflict is inevitable, not only during our face-to-face interactions but also online. In fact, there are several reasons that conflict may be even more likely to occur when we communicate online:

Reduced Nonverbal Cues Because we may miss some of the subtle relational cues that exist in face-to-face situations, pseudo-conflict in cyberspace can escalate from a mere misunderstanding to substantive differences (simple conflict). And if those differences become personal (ego conflict), the conflict is much more difficult to unravel.

Haste Sometimes in our haste and informality, we tap out a message that is perfectly clear to us, but not to the recipient. Missed meaning because of a too-cryptic message often occurs online, and can lead to conflict.

Flaming Flaming occurs when someone sends an overly negative message that personally attacks someone else. The flamer can further intensify the negative message by "shouting" the message in ALL CAPITAL LETTERS. People are more likely to use flaming language online than when talking in person.

The Disinhibition Effect The tendency to escalate conflict online is called the **disinhibition effect**. Without another person physically in front of them, and with emotional tension rising, people tend to lash out; they lose some of their inhibitions, hence the term "disinhibition effect".

So, what should you do when you find yourself in an online conflict? Some of the same strategies that you would use when interacting in person can be useful, but there are other specific options to consider in cyberspace:

Take Time to Cool Off Because of the disinhibition effect, your first impulse may be to respond immediately with a reciprocal flaming message. While it may be cathartic to lash out in response to an unfair criticism or hurtful comment, escalating the conflict makes it more difficult to manage. Resist the temptation to "counterflame."

Move to a Richer Medium If you sense a conflict arising, consider moving the interaction to a more media-rich context. If it's possible, talk to your communication partner in person; if that's not possible, reach for the phone to talk in real time rather than asynchronously.

Make Sure You Understand the Issues Before Responding Before you write or say anything further, reread the previous messages. Try to assume the role of an impartial mediator. Rather than looking for ways to justify your actions or feelings, read the messages as if you were looking at the information for the first time.

Paraphrase Summarize, in your own words, what you understand your partner to be communicating. Then give the other person a chance to agree or disagree with your version. Don't make any further demands or requests until you're sure you understand the issues that are causing the controversy. Turn the conversation into one about clarification rather than about what you both want.

Use Repetition To enhance clarity and understanding of your message, you may need to repeat key points and summarize what you'd like to have happen during the conflict. Being more redundant when reinforcing what you want to occur in the conflict can be helpful to ensure that your key ideas are being understood. It's helpful to

slow the process down, especially when emotions may be running high; rather than piling on more details, make sure your essential points are clear.

Be Careful When Using Humour In face-to-face contexts, humour can help break the tension. But when you're with someone physically, you can more accurately read your partner's nonverbal behaviour to know when a joke is helping to reduce the tension and when it's not. Often what makes something funny is the timing of the joke's punch line, or the vocal or physical delivery of an intended humorous comment. Online, with limited nonverbal cues, what you think might reduce tension could escalate it.

Self Reflect Take a "time out" to analyze your emotional reactions. Why are you getting upset and angry? Understanding why you've become upset can help you understand how to begin managing the conflict.

Put Yourself In the Other Person's Position Use the other-oriented skill of decentring by asking yourself, "What was the other person thinking when he or she wrote that message?" Try to identify the thoughts that may have triggered the negative comments. Then, after considering the other person's thought process, empathize by asking yourself "What was the other person feeling?"

The bottom line is that conflict occurs both in person and online. Understanding that conflict may occur and rapidly escalate because of the nature of online communication, and implementing some of the suggestions presented here, may help you to cool a heated conflict and return your interaction to "room temperature."

flaming. Sending an overly negative online message that personally attacks another person.

disinhibition effect. The loss of inhibitions when interacting with someone online that leads to the tendency to escalate conflict.

Conflict Management Skills

For many people, learning to manage conflict is key to enhancing the quality of interpersonal relationships. Managing conflict, especially emotion-charged ego conflict, is not easy. The more stress and anxiety you feel at any given time, the more likely you are to experience conflict in your relationships with others. When you are under stress, it's more likely that conflict will become personal and degenerate into ego conflict. The opposite is also true: when you're rested and relaxed, you're less likely to experience conflict. However, even while relaxed and with a fully developed set of skills, don't expect to avoid conflict. Conflict happens. The following skills, previewed in our discussion of a collaborative approach to conflict, can help you generate options that promote understanding and provide a framework for collaboration.

Manage Your Emotions

You have a major group project at school with a deadline that is fast approaching. You email one of your group members to ask how he is progressing with his portion of the research, and three days later receive a reply that he hasn't started yet, as he's been busy with other things. You feel angry and frustrated. How should you respond? You may be tempted to write an angry reply, or to email your professor and complain.

Try to avoid taking action when you are in such a state. You may regret what you say, and you will probably escalate the conflict.

Often, the first sign that we are in a conflict situation is a feeling of anger, frustration, fear, or even sadness, which sweeps over us like an ocean wave. When we are emotionally charged, we experience physical changes as well: our heart pounds faster, our blood pressure rises, and our blood flows to our extremities, decreasing the blood supply to the problem-solving part of the brain. Such changes fuel our fight-or-flight responses. If we choose to stay, verbal or physical violence may erupt; if we flee from the conflict, we cannot resolve it. Until we can tone down our emotions (which does not mean eliminating them), we will find it difficult to apply other skills. Let's look at some additional specific strategies that you can draw on when an intense emotional response to conflict clouds your judgment and hampers your decision-making skills.

Be Aware That You Are Becoming Angry and Emotionally Volatile. One characteristic of people who "lose it" is that they let their emotions get the best of them. Before they know it, they are saying and doing things that they later regret. Unbridled and uncensored emotional outbursts rarely enhance the quality of an interpersonal relationship. An emotional purge may make you feel better, but your partner is likely to reciprocate, which will only escalate the conflict spiral.

Before that happens, become aware of what is happening to you. As we described earlier, your body will start to react to your emotions with an increased heart rate. Be sensitive to what is happening to you physically.

Seek to Understand Why You Are Angry and Emotional. Understanding what's behind your anger can help you manage it. Realize that it is normal and natural to be angry. It's a feeling everyone experiences. You need not feel guilty about it. Anger is often expressed as a defence when a person feels violated or is fearful of losing something important. Two powerful anger triggers are (1) feeling that you have not been treated fairly and (2) feeling entitled to something that you are being denied. Think about the last time you became very angry. Chances are your angry outburst stemmed from a sense that you were not treated fairly or that someone denied you something you were entitled to. Often there is a sense of righteous indignation when you are angry. You are being denied something you feel you should have.

Make a Conscious Decision About Whether to Express Your Anger. Rather than just letting anger and frustration build and erupt out of control, make a conscious choice about whether you should express your frustration and irritation. We're not denying that there are valid reasons for you to express anger and frustration, or suggesting that you should not express your feelings. Sometimes there is no way to let someone know how important an issue is to you other than by forcefully expressing your irritation or anger. As these lines from William Blake illustrate, sometimes the wisest strategy is to be honest with others and express how you feel:

I was angry with my friend:
I told my wrath, my wrath did end.
I was angry with my foe:
I told it not, my wrath did grow.

If you do decide to express your anger, don't lose control. Be direct and descriptive. The guidelines for listening and responding that we provided in Chapter 5 can serve you well. Keep your anger focused on issues rather than personalities.

Select a Mutually Acceptable Time and Place to Discuss a Conflict. If you are upset, or even tired, you are at risk for an emotionally charged shouting match. If you ambush someone with an angry attack, don't expect him or her to be in a productive frame of mind. Instead, give yourself time to cool off before you try to resolve a conflict. In the case of the group member who has not yet begun his part of the project, the best course of action would be to wait until your initial feelings of anger have subsided before contacting the individual and calmly and rationally explaining that his contribution is important to the project and that the entire group is counting on him. By that time you could gain control of your feelings and also think the issue through. Of course, sometimes issues need to be discussed on the spot; you may not have the luxury of waiting. However, whenever it is practical, make sure the other person is ready to receive you and your message.

Plan Your Message. If you are approaching someone to discuss a disagreement, take care to organize your message. Identify your goal and determine what outcome you would like; do not barge in and pour out your emotions.

Breathe. One of the simplest yet most effective ways to avoid overheating is to breathe. As you become aware that your emotions are starting to erupt, take a slow, deep breath. Then breathe again. This can help calm you and manage the physiological changes that adrenaline creates. Deep breathing—the prime strategy women use to manage the pain of childbirth—can be a powerful way to restore calmness to your spirit. Focusing on your breathing is also one of the primary methods of meditation. We're not suggesting that you hyperventilate, but taking deep, slow breaths that not only fill your upper lungs but move your diaphragm is an active strategy to help you regain rational control.

Monitor Nonverbal Messages. As you learned in Chapter 7, your actions play a key role in establishing the emotional climate in any relationship. Monitoring your nonverbal messages can help to de-escalate an emotionally charged situation. Speaking calmly, using direct eye contact, and maintaining a natural facial expression will signal that you wish to collaborate rather than control. Your nonverbal message should also support your verbal response. If you say you are listening to someone but you continue to read the paper or work on a report, you are communicating a lack of interest in the speaker and the message.

Avoid Personal Attacks, Name-Calling, and Emotional Overstatement. Using threats and derogatory names can turn a simple conflict into an ego conflict. When people feel attacked, they will respond by protecting themselves. Although you may feel hurt and angry,

BEING Other-ORIENTED

Saving face is giving the other person a way to maintain his or her dignity, even if his or her initial ideas and proposals are not accepted in the final resolution of a conflict. What strategies have you used to help others save face and maintain their personal dignity during conflict?

try to avoid exaggerating your emotions and hurling negative, personal comments at your partner. If you say you are irritated or annoyed rather than furious, you can still communicate your feelings, but you will take the sting out of your description. There's no need to be dishonest about how you are feeling; just don't overstate your emotions for dramatic effect. It may make you feel better, but it may make matters worse.

Also, avoid the bad habit of **gunny-sacking**. This occurs when you dredge up old problems and issues from the past, like pulling them out of an old bag or gunny sack, to use against your partner. Keep your focus on the issues at hand, not on old hurts. Gunnysacking usually succeeds only in increasing tension, escalating emotions, and reducing listening effectiveness.

Take Time to Establish Rapport. Taking time to establish a positive emotional climate can pay big dividends; this is especially important if you're not well acquainted with the person you're having the conflict with. Getting to know each other in a positive way can lead to a more satisfactory resolution to the conflict. Even if you know the other person well, take some time to build rapport. Chatting about such seemingly innocuous topics as the weather or local events can help break the ice and provide a basis for a more positive conversational climate. A positive emotional climate is especially important when trying to sort through vexing, conflict-producing issues.

Use Self-Talk. When Tom was chairing the committee meeting, Monique accused him of falsifying the attendance numbers at the last fine arts festival. Instead of lashing back at Monique, he paused, took a slow, deep breath and thought, "I'm tired. If I respond now, all we'll do is escalate this issue out of proportion." He then calmly told Monique that she did not have the correct information and that they would discuss this after the meeting. Perhaps you think that talking to yourself is an eccentricity. Nothing could be further from the truth. As you saw in Chapter 2, thoughts are directly linked to feelings, and the messages we tell ourselves play a major role in how we feel and respond to others. Ask yourself whether an emotional tirade and an escalating conflict will produce the results you want.

As you read the discussion about managing emotions, you may wonder if it's ever useful or productive to express negative emotions, especially anger, overtly when negotiating an issue. By expressing your irritation, you may motivate the other person to come up with better alternatives. In most cases, escalating emotional tension decreases the likelihood that the conflict will be managed smoothly and effectively. But sometimes, being honest in expressing your frustration may nudge things along in a productive way, especially if there are no good options to discuss.

Manage Information

Because uncertainty, misinformation, and misunderstanding are often by-products of conflict and disagreement, skills that promote mutual understanding are an important component of cooperative conflict management. Based on the describing, listening, and responding skills discussed in Chapter 5, the following specific suggestions can help you reduce uncertainty and enhance the quality of communication during conflict.

Clearly Describe the Conflict-Producing Events. Instead of just blurting out your complaints in random order, think of delivering a brief, well-organized mini-speech. Offer your perspective on what created the conflict, sequencing the events like a well-organized story. Describe the events dispassionately so that the other person shares your understanding of the problem. When Lise almost had a car accident, she came home and told her husband, "Last week you said you'd get the brakes fixed on the car. On

gunny-sacking. Dredging up old problems and issues from the past, like pulling them out of an old bag or gunny sack, to use against your partner.

Monday, when you still hadn't taken the car in, you said you'd do it on Wednesday. Now it's Friday and the brakes are in even worse shape. I had a close call this afternoon when the car almost wouldn't stop. We've got to get those brakes fixed before anyone drives that car again."

"Own" Your Statements by Using Descriptive "I" Language. "I feel upset when you post the week's volunteer schedule without first consulting with me," reveals Natasha. Her statement describes her feelings as her own. **"I" language** expresses how a speaker is feeling. The use of the word "I" conveys a willingness to "own" one's feelings and statements about them.

If Natasha had said, "You always prepare a schedule without telling anyone first. All of us who volunteer are mad about that," her statement would have had an accusatory sting. Beginning the statement with "you" sets the listener up for a defensive response. Also, notice that in the second statement, the speaker does not take responsibility for the anger; she suggests that it belongs to other unidentified people as well. If you narrow the issue down to a conflict between you and the other person, you put the conflict into a more manageable framework.

One final tip about using "I" messages: Monitor your **"but" messages**. What's a "but" message? It's a statement that makes it seem as though whatever you've said prior to the word "but" is not truly the way you feel. Here's an example: "I love you. I really love you. But I feel really frustrated when you leave your clothes lying on every chair." A "but" message diminishes the positive sentiment you expressed with your "I" language. We're not suggesting that you never say "but," only that you realize how the word may create noise for the listener; it may make your entire statement seem untrue.

Use Effective Listening Skills. Managing information is a two-way process. Whether you are describing a conflict situation to someone or that individual is bringing a conflict to your attention, good listening skills will be invaluable.

Give your full attention to the speaker and make a conscious point of tuning out your internal messages. Sometimes the best thing to do after describing the conflict-producing events is simply to wait for a response. If you don't stop talking and give the other person a chance to respond, he or she will feel frustrated, the emotional pitch will go up a notch, and it will become more difficult to reach an understanding.

Finally, do not just focus on the facts or details but analyze them so that you can understand the major point the speaker is making. Use your understanding of the details to interpret the speaker's major ideas. Remember to stay other-oriented and to "seek to understand rather than to be understood."[17]

Check Your Understanding of What Others Say and Do. Respond clearly and appropriately. Your response and that of your conflict partner will confirm that you have understood each other. Checking perceptions is vital when emotions run high.

If you are genuinely unsure about facts, issues, or major ideas addressed during a conflict, ask questions to help you sort through them instead of barging ahead with solutions. Then, summarize your understanding of the information; do not parrot the speaker's words or paraphrase every statement, but check key points to ensure that you have understood the message. Note how Kamal adeptly paraphrases to check his understanding:

Maggie: I don't like the conclusion you've written to the conference report. It doesn't mention anything about the ideas suggested at the symposium. I think you've also misinterpreted the CEO's key message.

Kamal: So, if I understand you, Maggie, you're saying the report missed some key information and may also include an inaccurate summary of the CEO's speech.

Maggie: Yes, Kamal. Those are the concerns I have.

"I" language. Statements that use the word "I" to express how a speaker is feeling.

"but" message. Statement using the word "but" that may communicate that whatever you've said prior to "but" is not really true.

Be Empathic

Understand others not only with your head but also with your heart. To truly understand another person, you need to do more than simply catch the meaning of his or her words; you need to put yourself in the person's place emotionally. What emotions is the other person feeling? Why is he or she experiencing these emotions? Throughout this book we have stressed the importance of becoming other-oriented. It's especially important to be other-oriented when you disagree with another person. Trying to understand what's behind your partner's emotions may give you the insight you need to reframe the conflict from your partner's point of view. With this other-oriented perspective, you may see new possibilities for managing the conflict.

Manage Goals

As we have seen, conflict is goal-driven. Both individuals involved in an interpersonal conflict want something, and for some reason, be it competition, scarce resources, or lack of understanding, the goals appear to be in conflict. To manage conflict, it is important to seek an accurate understanding of these goals and to identify where they overlap. Let's look at some specific strategies to help manage conflict by being aware of the other person's goals during conflict.

Identify Your Goal and Your Partner's Goal. After you describe, listen, and respond, your next task should be to identify what you would like to have happen. What is your goal? Most goal statements can be phrased in terms of wants or desires. Consider the following examples:

Problem	Goal
Your boss approaches you and wants you to work overtime; you need to pick up your son from daycare.	You want to leave work on time; your boss wants the work completed ASAP.
Your partner wants to sleep with the window open; you like a warm room and sleep better with the window closed.	You want a good night's rest; your partner wants a good night's rest.

Often, in conflicts, you will be balancing the achievement of your goal against the goal of maintaining your relationship with your partner. Eventually, you may decide that the latter goal is more important than the substantive conflict issue.

Next, it is useful to identify your partner's goal. In each of the problems listed above, you would need to know what the other person wants so that you can manage the conflict. Use effective describing, listening, and responding skills to determine what each of you wants and to verbalize your goals. Obviously, if you both keep your goals hidden, it will be difficult to manage the conflict.

Identify Where Your Goals and Your Partner's Goals Overlap. Armed with an understanding of what you want and what your partner wants, you can then determine whether the goals overlap. In the conflict over whether the window should be open or closed, the goal of both parties is the same: each wants a good night's sleep. Framing the problem as "how can we achieve our mutual goal," rather than arguing over whether the window should be open or closed, moves the discussion to a more productive level.

If you focus on shared interests (common goals) and develop objective, rather than subjective, criteria for the solution, there is hope for finding a resolution that will satisfy both parties.

BEING **Other**-ORIENTED

Being empathic is the core set of skills that allow you to be other-oriented. When you're involved in conflict with another person, what are the factors that hinder your ability to empathize with the other person? What actions and thoughts will enhance your skill in empathizing with another person?

Manage the Problem

If you can structure conflicts as problems to be solved (see Table 8.2 below) rather than battles to be won or lost, you are well on your way to seeking strategies to manage the issues that confront you and the other person involved in the conflict. Of course, as we have stressed earlier, not all conflicts can be resolved. However, approaching the core of a conflict as a problem to be managed can provide a constructive way of seeking resolution. Structuring a conflict as a problem also helps to manage the emotion and keeps the conversation focused on issues (simple conflict) rather than personalities (ego conflict).

There are many models of problem solving that can be used to arrive at a solution that everyone can live with in all kinds of conflicts. Most models rely on a set of defined steps that help clarify the problem, analyze the problem, generate and evaluate possible solutions, implement the chosen solution, and then evaluate the solution at a given date. These models can be found in business texts and counselling texts and are actively used by many organizations, such as the Ontario Provincial Police, and many corporations, such as IBM Canada. Here, we will focus on a very straightforward model: define the problem, analyze the problem's causes and effects, determine the goals, generate many possible solutions, and select a solution that best achieves the goals of the conflicting parties.

It's vital to be able to manage your emotions when you find yourself in an interpersonal conflict.
(© Comstock Images/Stockbyte/Getty Images)

Define the Problem. You can apply all the skills described so far to pursue a proven method for problem solving, which is shown in Table 8.2. First, *define the problem*. Most problems boil down to something you or your conflict partner want more or less of. For example, you may want more time, money, or freedom. Or you may want less interference, control, or criticism. To help you define the problem that is producing the conflict, renew your focus on your own and the other person's goals.[18] What do you want to happen, or not to happen?

Cara and Ian have been going out together for over a year. Lately, they have been fighting over small issues. They decide to spend some time talking about what is wrong and trying to understand each other. Rather than just dealing with symptoms (Cara complains that Ian snores at night), they keep talking until they get at the "real" or root problem. Cara wants to get married to Ian now. Ian wants to stay with Cara, but he wants to wait until he feels ready for marriage. He also wants to feel financially secure before he marries.

Analyze the Problem. Next, *analyze the problem*. To analyze is to break something down into its components. With the other party, begin by describing the conflict-producing events

TABLE 8.2	**Solving Problems: One Method of Organizing Problem-Solving Discussions**
1. Define the problem.	What is the issue?
2. Analyze the problem.	What are the causes, symptoms, effects, and obstacles?
3. Determine the goals.	What do you want? What does your partner want? How do the goals overlap?
4. Generate multiple solutions.	List many options rather than debating one or two strategies for achieving the goal.
5. Select the best solution and try it.	Eliminate options that are not mutually agreeable. If possible, take the best ideas from several generated to reach an amicable resolution.

in chronological order (see pages 182–184). Then, decide what type of conflict it is. If your analysis reveals it as a pseudo-conflict, keep on with the analysis process. Attempt to ferret out the rest of the symptoms, effects, and obstacles; decide whether the conflict stems from several sub-problems or from one major issue. As you proceed, you and the other party may decide that you need more information to help clarify the issues.

After some discussion, Cara and Ian analyze their problem. They realize they come from different family backgrounds and have different expectations about marriage. Cara's parents were high school sweethearts, were married when both were 18, and are still happily married after almost 25 years together. Ian's parents are older; they met after each of them had been divorced, and they married after a long, slow-paced relationship. Cara's and Ian's different frames of reference help explain their feelings about the timing of marriage.

Determine the Goals. The next step in managing the problem is to *determine your goals and your partner's goals* by following the information presented above on managing goals. Generate objective criteria for a solution using the previous guidelines about identifying your goals and your partner's goals. The more measurable, verifiable, and objective the criteria, the greater the likelihood that both parties will agree when the criteria have been met. Cara and Ian decide that, ultimately, they have the same goal—to get married. The issue boils down to timing. They decide to seek a course of action that will make them both feel secure.

Generate Multiple Solutions. Their next step is to *generate multiple solutions*. Simply understanding the issues and the causes, effects, symptoms, and history of a problem will not enable you to manage a conflict. It takes time and creativity to find mutually satisfactory solutions to most problems. It stands to reason that the more solutions you generate, the greater the probability that you can manage the conflict constructively. One way to generate options is through brainstorming. To use brainstorming, try the following suggestions:

1. Make sure the problem and the goals are clear to both of you.

2. Try to temporarily suspend judgment and evaluation.

3. Specify a certain time period for brainstorming.

4. Consider having each partner brainstorm ideas separately before a meeting, or write ideas down before verbalizing solutions.

5. Try to develop at least one unique or far-out idea. You can always tame wild ideas later.

6. Piggyback off the ideas of your partner. Encourage your partner to use or modify your ideas.

7. Write down all the ideas suggested.

8. Review each idea, noting ways to combine, eliminate, or extend them.

If the goal is to find the best way to manage the difficulty, it may take only one good idea to help move the conflict forward to a constructive resolution.

When they brainstorm, Cara and Ian generate the following options: save money for a year and then get married; take turns going to university; take turns working to support the family while the other gets a degree; get married now, get jobs and postpone university; get married now and take out student loans.

Select the Best Solution and Try It. Cara and Ian *select the best solution*. Sometimes, it may take several attempts at defining, analyzing, goal setting, and generating multiple ideas before a mutually agreeable solution emerges. It is always appropriate to recheck your understanding of the issues and goals. Cara and Ian decide to combine the best of several ideas. They agree to get engaged but not to set a date. Instead, they set a financial goal of $5000 in savings. When they reach that goal, they will set a wedding date. If they are both attending university, they will get part-time jobs so that they have income, and they will also apply for student loans.

If, after repeated attempts, you cannot arrive at a mutually acceptable solution, you may decide to keep trying. Or you may agree to take the issue to an impartial person who can help you identify conflict management strategies and solutions. At work, your immediate superior may be called in to help settle the matter. Or, occasionally, you may agree to disagree and drop it.

The goal of managing conflict is not just to solve a problem but to help manage relational issues with your partner, especially if your partner thinks he or she has "lost" the conflict. When seeking solutions to interpersonal problems, try to find ways for your partner to "win" while you also achieve your goal.

Building Your Skills | Communicating with Prickly People

Some people just seem to rub us the wrong way. They generate both friction and heat when we're trying to negotiate with them. In his popular book *Getting Past No,* William Ury suggests we try to change face-to-face confrontation into side-by-side problem solving.[19] Here are Ury's tips for managing conflict with difficult people, based on his review of negotiation literature.

- *Go to the Balcony.* "Going to the balcony" is a metaphor for taking a time out. Take a moment to excuse yourself to cool off when someone pushes your buttons. Staying on the "main stage" to keep banging out a solution may be counterproductive.
- *Step to the Side.* Rather than continuing to debate and refute every argument, step to the side by just asking questions and listening. Change the dynamic of the relationship from a confrontation to a conversation.
- *Change the Frame.* Reframe by trying to see more than an either/or way of managing the conflict. Try to see it from a third, fourth, or fifth point of view. Change your overall perspective for viewing the conflict by not being you: consider how someone else may view the issue.
- *Build a Golden Bridge.* To "build a golden bridge" is a metaphor for identifying ways to help the other person say yes by saving face. Find an alternative that allows the other person his or her dignity by using objective standards to find a solution.
- *Make It Hard to Say No.* Use information to educate rather than pummel the other person. As Ury puts it, bring people to their senses, not their knees. Help the other person understand the consequences of what he or she supports and the benefits of your alternatives.

Consider a conflict you've had with a prickly person that did not have a satisfying conclusion. How could you have implemented one or more of the five suggestions we've summarized

from Ury's research? If it were possible to have a "do over" with this difficult person, what would you do differently? Use the following worksheet to help you identify alternatives for dealing with the prickly person in the situation you have in mind.

Go to the Balcony. At what point in the conflict could you have suggested a cooling-off period?

_____

_____

Step to the Side. Instead of adding new ideas and arguments, when and how could you have stepped to the side to listen and paraphrase?

_____

_____

Change the Frame. How could you have changed the frame of the conflict? What would have been a different way of looking at the issue that created the conflict?

_____

_____

Build a Golden Bridge. What could you have done or said that would have helped the other person save face?

_____

_____

Make It Hard to Say No. What could you have said or done that would have helped the other person see the benefits of what you were proposing?

_____

_____

Source: Based on Getting past no: negotiating with difficult people by William Ury, Bantam Books 1991. © Steven A. Beebe.

APPLYING AN OTHER-ORIENTATION
to Conflict Management

To manage differences with others, consider the conflict-producing issue or issues from the other person's point of view. We don't claim that an other-orientation will resolve all conflicts. As we noted earlier, it's a myth that all conflict can be resolved. But being other-oriented is an important element in managing differences and disagreements. The following five strategies, drawn not only from this chapter but from the previous skill-development chapters, distill the essence of being other-oriented.

- *Stop.* Socially decentre by taking into account the other person's thoughts, feelings, values, culture, and perspective. Stop making your arguments and concentrate on your partner's points. How is your partner "making sense" out of what has happened to him or her?

- *Look.* Monitor your partner's emotions by observing his or her nonverbal messages. Look for emotional cues in your partner's face; observe posture and gestures to gauge the intensity of the feelings being expressed.

- *Listen.* Listen both for the details and for the main points; also listen for tone of voice. Focus on the overall story your partner is telling.

- *Imagine.* Imagine how you would feel if you were in your partner's place. Based on your knowledge of the person you're in conflict with, as well as of people in general, imagine the conflict from his or her point of view.

- *Question.* If you need more information about what a partner has experienced or if there is something you don't understand, gently ask appropriate questions.

- *Paraphrase.* To confirm your understanding of your partner's point of view, briefly summarize the essence of what you think your partner is thinking or feeling.

No checklist of skills will magically melt tensions resulting from long-standing or entrenched conflicts. But honestly trying to understand both a person's position and the emotion behind it is a good beginning to developing understanding—a prerequisite for managing differences.

Conflict Defined, Conflict Myths, and Conflict Types (pages 180–189)

OBJECTIVES ❶ ❷ ❸ Define interpersonal conflict, identify commonly held myths about interpersonal conflict, and compare and contrast three types of interpersonal conflict.

Key Terms

interpersonal conflict *180*   dialectical tension *185*
interdependent *181*   pseudo-conflict *186*
constructive conflict *183*   simple conflict *186*
destructive conflict *183*   ego conflict *186*
conflict triggers *184*

Critical Thinking Questions

1. Think of a recent communication exchange with a friend, spouse, classmate, or co-worker that began as a seemingly casual conversation but escalated into a conflict. Can you identify a reason for this, such as one or both of you feeling tired, stressed, or anxious? Is there anything you could have done to avoid the conflict? What cues might you each have looked for to understand the other's mood?

2. Melissa and Jake always seem to end up making personal attacks and calling each other names when they get into a disagreement. What type of conflict are they experiencing when they do this, and how can they avoid it?

3. Ethics: Is it ethical to mask your true emotions in order to get along with others? Is honesty in a relationship always the best policy? Explain your response.

Activities

Based on the discussion of conflict presented on pages 182–184, think of a recent conflict you had with someone or a conflict that is still ongoing. To help you better understand and manage the process, answer the following questions:

Prior Conditions Stage

- What were the prior conditions that led to the conflict?
- How long were some of the prior conditions simmering in the background?

Frustration Awareness Stage

- When did you become aware that you were frustrated and that your needs weren't being met or that there was an issue to resolve?
- When did you perceive that the other person was aware that a conflict might exist?

Active Conflict Stage

- What caused the conflict to move from frustration to active conflict?
- What type of conflict was (is) it—pseudo-conflict, simple conflict, or ego conflict?

Resolution Stage

- What conflict management skills did you use (or are you and the other person using) to manage emotions, information, goals, or the problem?
- What conflict management skills could you have used, but didn't?

Follow-Up Stage

- Has the conflict been truly managed and resolved, or not? What leads you to that conclusion?
- Did you or the other person explicitly indicate that the conflict is over?

Web Resources

www.cios.org/encyclopedia/conflict/index.htm This conflict management site provides an introduction to the study of conflict management through links that explain why the study of conflict is important, key elements of conflict, the nature of conflict and conflict variables, and skills for conflict managers, and offers a self-test to check your conflict management understanding.

Conflict and Power (pages 189–192)

OBJECTIVE ❹ Describe the relationship between conflict and power.

Key Terms

interpersonal power *190*   compliance gaining *191*
dependent relationship *190*

Critical Thinking Questions

1. Examine several recent interpersonal conflicts for unresolved power issues. (For example, consider conflicts that have focused on managing money, household tasks, or intimacy.) What role did power play in the conflict? Does one of you have more power over the other? How might you renegotiate that power imbalance?

2. Ethics: Are certain types of power more ethical to use during a conflict than others? Explain your answer, describing conditions that would justify the use of certain types of power.

Activities

Statements About Conflict: Read each statement once, and on a separate piece of paper, indicate whether you agree (A) or disagree (D) with each statement. Take five or six minutes to do this.

1. Most people find an argument interesting and exciting.
2. In most conflicts, someone must win and someone must lose. That's the way conflict is.
3. The best way to handle a conflict is simply to let everyone cool off.
4. Most people get upset at a person who disagrees with them.
5. If people spend enough time together, they will find something to disagree about and will eventually become upset with each other.
6. Conflicts can be solved if people just take the time to listen to one another.
7. If you disagree with someone, it is usually better to keep quiet than to express your personal opinion.
8. To compromise is to take the easy way out of conflict.
9. Some people produce more conflict and tension than others. These people should be restricted from working with others.

After you have indicated whether you agree or disagree with the statements, ask a good friend, roommate, family member, or romantic partner to read each statement and indicate whether he or she agrees or disagrees. Compare answers and discuss the results. Use this activity as a way of identifying underlying assumptions that you and the other person have about conflict. You could also do this activity in a small group. After comparing responses with others in the group, the entire group could seek to develop a consensus about each statement. If conflict occurs about a specific statement, use the principles of conflict management that are presented in the chapter to assist you in managing the disagreement.

Web Resources

http://www.humanresourcesiq.com/hr-talent-management/articles/10 -ways-to-manage-emotions-during-conflict-in-the Visit this site to learn tips and strategies for controlling your emotions during workplace conflicts.

Conflict Management Styles and Skills (pages 193–207)

OBJECTIVES **5** **6** Describe five conflict management styles, and identify and use conflict management skills to help manage emotions, information, goals, and problems when attempting to resolve interpersonal differences.

Key Terms

conflict management styles *193*
avoidance *193*
demand-withdrawal pattern *194*
accommodation *194*
competition *195*

compromise *196*
collaboration *196*
flaming *198*
disinhibition effect *198*
gunny-sacking *201*
"I" language *202*
"but" message *202*

Critical Thinking Questions

1. Richard has an explosive temper. He consistently receives poor performance evaluations at work because he lashes out at those who disagree with him. What is his conflict management style? What strategies might help him manage his emotional outbursts?
2. Have you experienced the disinhibition effect when communicating with others online? Was this in response to a blatantly negative message? Or was it your perception that you were being attacked? What was the result? How did you respond? What strategies could you have employed to avoid a conflict?

Activities

Over the next week or so, keep a list of every conflict you observe or are involved in. Make a note of what the conflict was about, whether there were underlying power issues (that you could detect), whether the conflict was resolved satisfactorily for both parties, and if so, what strategies and skills were employed. Could you indentify a specific conflict management style? If the conflict involved you, did you use the style you typically use? Why or why not? Discuss your findings with your classmates.

Web Resources

www.etu.org.za/toolbox/docs/building/conflict.html This site explores conflict management and how organizations use conflict management to achieve their goals. The site also touches on how to identify signs and stages of conflict as well as how to manage and resolve conflict situations.

9

Understanding Interpersonal Relationships

© StockLite/Shutterstock

❝ You can hardly make a friend in a year, but you can lose one in an hour. ❞ —Chinese Proverb

OBJECTIVES

1. Define interpersonal relationships and identify some ways to distinguish among them.

2. Identify and differentiate between short-term initial attraction and long-term maintenance attraction.

3. Identify and describe the stages of relational escalation and de-escalation.

4. Describe the main components of three theories that explain relational development.

OUTLINE

Interpersonal Relationships Defined

Genesis of Interpersonal Relationships: Attraction

Stages of Interpersonal Relationship Development

Theories of Interpersonal Relationship Development

Pat: Hi, aren't you in my communication course?

Jinping: Oh yeah, I've seen you across the room.

Pat: What do you think about the course so far?

Jinping: It's okay, but I feel a little intimidated by some of the class activities.

Pat: I know what you mean. It gets kind of scary to talk about yourself in front of everyone else.

Jinping: Yeah. Plus some of the stuff you hear. I was paired up with this one student the other day who started talking about being arrested last year on a drug charge.

Pat: Really? I bet I know who that is. I don't think you have to worry about it.

Jinping: Don't mention that I said anything.

Pat: It's okay. I know that guy, and he just likes to act big.

This interaction between Pat and Jinping illustrates the reciprocal nature of interpersonal communication and interpersonal relationships. As you learned in Chapter 1, interpersonal relationships are connections that we develop with other people as a direct result of our interpersonal communication with them. The character and quality of interpersonal communication is affected, in turn, by the nature of the relationship.

The conversation between Pat and Jinping begins with a casual acknowledgment but quickly proceeds to a higher level of intimacy. Jinping confides in Pat. Pat, an other-oriented listener, offers confirmation and support; this response encourages Jinping to confide even more. In this brief encounter, Pat and Jinping have laid the groundwork for transforming their casual acquaintanceship into a more intimate relationship.

The first eight chapters of this book covered skills that contribute to managing your interpersonal relationships. Now we turn to examining the nature of those relationships and how those skills can be applied to developing, maintaining, and terminating them. In this chapter we examine the nature of interpersonal relationships and the principles of how relationships work, including two relationship development theories.

relationship. Connection we establish when we communicate with another person.

interpersonal relationship. Those connections we make with other people through interpersonal communication.

Interpersonal Relationships Defined

In Chapter 1, we defined a **relationship** as a connection you establish when you communicate with another person. Every time you engage in interpersonal communication, you are in a relationship, but it is only through ongoing, recurring interactions that you develop interpersonal relationships. An **interpersonal relationship** is a perception shared by two people of an ongoing connection that results in the development of relational expectations and varies in interpersonal intimacy. Let's first consider the four elements that constitute this definition: shared perception, ongoing connection, relational expectations, and interpersonal intimacy. We'll then consider the impact of circumstance, choice, and power in defining the nature of interpersonal relationships.

Shared Perception

To be in an interpersonal relationship, both individuals must share a perception that they have an ongoing relationship. Sometimes, only one person believes there is a relationship—a belief that, at the extreme,

In an intimate, trusting relationship, we can feel safe in telling our deepest secrets to another person.
(© Tom McCarthy/PhotoEdit, Inc.)

might lead to obsessive behaviour or stalking. However, even when each partner recognizes that he or she has a relationship, that doesn't necessarily mean that both partners think of the relationship in the same way. Discrepancies in the perceptions of the relationship can be a source of interpersonal conflict, requiring heart-to-heart talks about each person's wants and relational expectations. Generally, the greater the similarity in partners' perceptions of their relationship, the stronger their relationship will be.

Ongoing Connection

The second component of the definition, an ongoing connection, means that the interpersonal relationship is a process. The *Harry Potter* books and films provide good examples of the process nature of relationships. The relationships among the three main characters—Harry, Hermione, and Ron—evolve and change as they share experiences and learn more about each other. Processes are also irreversible—once something is done, it can't be undone (unless by some wizard's magic). For example, you can't take back an argument you've had in a relationship. While you can be forgiven, the argument will always have an impact on the partners and the relationship.

Relational Expectations

As you continue to interact and develop your relationships, you also form relational expectations. Any time you interact with someone you bring a set of preformed expectations based on your socialization and experiences; however, as you develop an interpersonal relationship, you and your partner establish expectations specific to that relationship. Think about the expectations that you have of your friends and that they have of you. For example, you might have a friend with whom you primarily play video games; thus, you know what your time together will be like, how you'll talk, what you'll talk about, etc. These expectations are part of the relationship process and are continually developing and changing. Sometimes the expectations are violated, which can create turmoil in the relationship. For example, if you're used to getting daily text messages from a friend and you suddenly start getting messages only once or twice a week, it creates relational uncertainty which can lead to stress and conflict.

Interpersonal Intimacy

Interpersonal intimacy is the degree to which relational partners mutually confirm and accept each other's sense of self. As self-disclosure and closeness increase, partners become more and more dependent upon each other to provide this confirmation. We are also able to relax more and be ourselves. In the most intimate relationships, our partners know our strengths and our weaknesses but still accept us; we don't have to hide our flaws or fear rejection.

interpersonal intimacy. The degree to which a person's sense of self is accepted and confirmed by another person in a relationship.

Think about the range of interpersonal relationships you have. You should be able to classify them according to their level of interpersonal intimacy (level of self-disclosure and confirmation of your self). Figure 9.1 orders the types of interpersonal relationships according

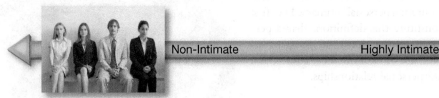 

Non-Intimate   Highly Intimate

Stranger ⟷ Acquaintance ⟷ Casual Friend ⟷ Friend ⟷ Close Friend ⟷ Best Friend/Spouse

FIGURE 9.1

Continuum of Interpersonal Intimacy and Relationships

© Steven A. Beebe

to their relative intimacy. Our closest relationships play important roles in helping us confirm our value. And although we depend on them less, even casual relationships confirm our value; we look for others to implicitly (and sometimes explicitly) tell us that they like who we are. As interpersonal intimacy increases, we are more and more able to just be ourselves and still feel accepted. In the most intimate relationships, our partners know our strengths and our weaknesses but still accept us; they love us in spite of our flaws—we reach a point where we don't have to hide our flaws or fear rejection because of those flaws.

We communicate our sense of intimacy to others both directly, through our words, and indirectly, through actions. We might directly tell another person how we feel about him or her and how much we value the relationship, or we might choose an indirect way of expressing interpersonal intimacy, by, for instance, disclosing highly personal information. We also might use nonverbal cues, such as close physical proximity, eye contact, tone of voice, touch, and time spent interacting. The choice to become intimate distinguishes some relationships from others that exist only because of circumstance.

Circumstance or Choice

Relationships of circumstance form not because we choose them, but simply because our lives overlap with others' in some way. Relationships with family members, teachers, classmates, and co-workers fall into this category. In contrast, relationships that we seek out and intentionally develop are **relationships of choice**. These relationships might include those with friends, lovers, spouses, and counsellors. Of course, these categories are not mutually exclusive. Relationships of circumstance can also be relationships of choice: Your brother, sister, or work colleague can also be your best friend, and a classmate could become a romantic partner, and eventually, a spouse.

We act and communicate differently in the two types of relationships because the stakes are different. The effect of the same behaviour on different relationships can be dramatic. If we act in foolish or inappropriate ways, our friends might end the relationships. If we act the same way within the confines of our family, our relatives may not like us much, but we will still remain family.

In some sense, all relationships begin by circumstance; through circumstance, we first become aware of another person. What we learn as a result of circumstance serves as the basis for our interpersonal attraction toward the other person and determines whether we then establish a relationship of choice. Part of that movement from circumstance to choice involves negotiating how decision making and power will be managed within the relationship.

Power

Relationships can also be categorized according to the way partners share power or decision-making responsibilities—the relative power role that each partner plays. Relationships require merging needs and styles, negotiating how decisions are made that affect both partners, and managing inevitable interpersonal conflicts. Failure to agree on roles can lead to instability, and attempts to change an agreed-on definition of the roles can meet resistance. Nonetheless, decision-making and power-sharing roles are continually tweaked. Think about how each of the following descriptions of power sharing applies to your relationships with friends, family, classmates, and co-workers and to the conflicts that arise in these relationships.

In a **complementary relationship**, one partner usually dominates or makes most of the decisions. Maybe one person likes to talk and the other likes to listen; one person likes to decide on what movies to watch and the other will watch anything. As a child, your relationship with your parents was probably complementary—they made the decisions. As you grew older, those roles were renegotiated, and that renegotiation might have been accompanied by some conflict. People in complementary relationships experience relatively few decision-making conflicts, because one partner readily defers to the other.

relationships of circumstance. Interpersonal relationships that exist because of life circumstances (who our family members are, where we work or study, etc.).

relationships of choice. Interpersonal relationships we choose to initiate, maintain, or terminate.

complementary relationship. Relationship in which power is divided unevenly, with one partner dominating and the other submitting.

© Randy Glasbergen.
www.glasbergen.com

© Randy Glasbergen / glasbergen.com

GLASBERGEN

"For a good relationship, I need someone who shares the same taste in music, movies, and TV...so I've started dating my iPod."

In a **symmetrical relationship**, both partners behave toward power in the same way, either both wanting power or both avoiding it. A **competitive symmetrical relationship** exists when both people vie for power and control of decision making. For example, each partner wants to play a different video game, and neither one wants to give in to the other. Equality of power is likely to result in more overt attempts at control than occur when one partner has more power than the other. Effective management of decision making requires strong conflict management skills. When neither partner wants to take control or make decisions, a **submissive symmetrical relationship** is created. Because neither partner feels comfortable imposing his or her will on the other, often both partners flounder, unable to make a decision or to act. Perhaps both people want to play a video game, but neither wants to declare which video game the other should have to play.

In reflecting on your current relationships, you might find that few seem to fit the descriptions of complementary or symmetrical. Instead, most of your relationships are probably **parallel relationships** involving a shifting back and forth of the power between the partners, depending on the situation. You might defer the video game selection to your friend Adam who knows about every video game ever made. On the other hand, Adam defers to you to decide where to get pizza. Establishing this arrangement with Adam might have involved initial conflict until you both felt comfortable with your roles. What happens when you and Adam decide to go out? Who decides where you're going? Parallel relationships often involve continual negotiation of who has decision-making power over which issues. These changes often occur in concert with movement from one stage of the relationship to another.

Genesis of Interpersonal Relationships: Attraction

Attraction is the starting point of all interpersonal relationships. **Interpersonal attraction** is the degree to which you want to form or maintain an interpersonal relationship. The attraction that moves relationships of circumstance to relationships of choice differs sometimes from the type of attraction that sustains relationships once they are formed. **Short-term initial attraction** is the degree to which you sense a potential for developing an interpersonal relationship. For example, you might find one of your classmates (relationship of circumstance) to be physically attractive, but never move to introduce yourself. Despite the short-term initial attraction, you might decide there is little potential for developing a relationship. However, as you walk out of the class, you might strike up a conversation with another classmate about an upcoming concert by one of your favourite bands, which happens to be this classmate's favourite as well.

You decide it would be fun to go together. Over time, you discover lots of areas of compatibility and attraction that serve as the foundation for a long-term friendship. **Long-term maintenance attraction** is the level of liking or positive feelings that motivate us to maintain or escalate a relationship. Through interpersonal communication, self-disclosure, and continued interactions, we learn information about others that either fosters or diminishes our long-term maintenance attraction to them.

symmetrical relationship. Relationship in which both partners behave toward power in the same way, either both wanting power or both avoiding it.

competitive symmetrical relationship. Relationship in which both people vie for power and control of decision making.

submissive symmetrical relationship. Relationship in which neither partner wants to take control or make decisions.

parallel relationships. Relationships in which power shifts back and forth between the partners, depending on the situation.

interpersonal attraction. Degree to which you are motivated to form or maintain an interpersonal relationship.

short-term initial attraction. Degree to which you sense a potential for an interpersonal relationship.

long-term maintenance attraction. A liking or positive feeling that motivates you to sustain a relationship.

Both types of attraction involve assessing and acting on the potential value of a relationship. We try to determine how promising, viable, and rewarding the relationship might be and continue to make such assessments throughout the course of the relationship. Over time, our assessments may change. In the romantic comedy *Crazy, Stupid, Love*, a young law student, played by Emma Stone, initially rejects the advances of a slick, handsome womanizer, played by Ryan Gosling, who tries to pick her up in a bar. Although she is physically attracted to him, she turns him down, assuming he is cold and shallow. However, when she does relent and go home with him, they stay up all night, just talking, and form a close emotional connection that leads to a loving relationship.

Like these film characters, most of us begin predicting outcome values in initial interactions and continually modify our predictions as we learn more about the other person. We pursue attractions beyond the initial interaction stage if we think they can yield positive outcomes, and generally avoid or terminate relationships for which we predict negative outcomes.

Over time, our assessment of the potential value of a relationship may change, as in the movie *Crazy, Stupid, Love*, in which a shallow physical attraction eventually transforms into a warm and loving relationship.
(© Photos 12/Alamy Stock Photo)

Of particular interest is the role interpersonal communication plays in attraction. Attraction and interpersonal communication are interdependent; that is, each affects the other. Short-term initial attraction acts as the impetus to communicate interpersonally—it prompts us to interact with others. The resulting interpersonal communication provides additional information that might contribute to long-term maintenance attraction. While several factors act to increase our likelihood of actually talking to another person, it is what occurs during those interactions that really determines whether we remain attracted to the person.

Factors Leading to Short-Term Initial Attraction

You enter a room filled with people you don't know and proceed to the area where beverages are being served. As you stand there looking around the room, whom do you talk to? Whom do you approach? To whom are you attracted? Two factors particularly affect us in such situations: proximity and physical appearance.

Proximity. You are probably going to start talking to whoever is standing closest to you. Similarly, you are more likely to form relationships with classmates sitting on either side of you than with someone seated at the opposite end of the room. This is partly because physical **proximity** increases communication opportunities. Any circumstance that increases the possibilities for interacting is also likely to increase attraction.

Physical Appearance. As you stand in the room full of people, you are also likely to approach people because of their physical appearance. **Physical appearance**, a form of nonverbal communication, provides us with information that helps us make some decision about how promising a relationship might be. It acts as a filter to reduce relationship

proximity. Physical nearness to another that promotes communication and thus attraction.

physical appearance. Nonverbal cues that allow us to assess relationship potential.

possibilities. If everyone in the room were 20 years older than you, except for one person on the other side of the room, whom would you approach for conversation? Similarity with another person creates an attraction because we assume the other person will have values and interests similar to ours. We use physical appearance to make predictions about who is most likely to reciprocate our overtures for conversation—that is, who is most likely to have something in common with us. Whether a relationship grows depends on what happens in the initial interaction and subsequent interactions.

Still, you have probably found that even if you and another person are of a similar age, culture, or race, you won't continue a relationship if you don't have much else in common. That's one reason why physical appearance is not a strong factor for long-term maintenance attraction. Sexual attraction also influences interest in forming relationships. At the most basic level, people might seek partners for physical affection and sexual gratification, to meet sexual needs. In short-term sexual relationships, physical appearance tends to be more important than in long-term romantic relationships. However, in the process of meeting sexual needs, people may develop long-term relationships.

Sources of Both Initial and Long-Term Attraction

Some qualities serve both to lead us to initiate interactions and to sustain attraction as the relationship develops. These qualities are generally readily visible on first meeting another person and increase as we gather more information about the other person.

We are attracted to people on the basis of similarity—we like people whose interests, personalities, values, and backgrounds are similar to our own.
(© Hetizia/Fotolia)

Credibility, Competence, and Intelligence. Credibility, competence, and intelligence are related personal qualities that, in and of themselves, evoke attraction. Most of us are attracted to individuals who seem competent. We like those who are sure of themselves, but not full of themselves. We assume they are competent if they seem skilled, knowledgeable, and experienced. Intelligence and competence are more important predictors of initial attraction in eventual romantic relationships than in friendships. We find people credible if they display a blend of enthusiasm, trustworthiness, competence, and power.

Self-Disclosure and Reciprocation of Liking. While providing negative or intimate information about ourselves too early might have a negative impact on a developing relationship, a certain amount of openness and self-disclosure increases attraction. Similarly, an open display of attraction or liking for another person can result in a reciprocation of that attraction: we like those who like us. As relationships progress from initiation to intimacy, further openness increases attraction. Self-disclosure has a positive impact on liking between strangers and an even greater impact in more developed relationships. In addition, our attraction to another person increases our tendency to self-disclose.

Reciprocation of liking means that we like those who like us. One way to get other people to reciprocate liking, particularly in romantic relationships, is to show that we like them. In a study in which participants were instructed to display liking, the frequency of their smiles, intensity of gaze, proximity during a conversation, forward leaning, and pitch variations correlated with their partners' reports of social attraction.[1]

Similarities. In general, we are attracted to people whose personalities, values, upbringing, personal experiences, attitudes, and interests are similar to ours. We seek them out through shared activities. You may, for example, join a campus environmental group because you know the members share your interest in the environment. Within the group, you would be

reciprocation of liking.
Liking those who like us.

ADAPTING TO DIFFERENCES
Understanding Others | Cultural Differences in Self-Disclosure

The social penetration model suggests that self-disclosure can be described by both breadth—the number of topics we discuss—and depth—the level of intimacy we establish with others. Do cultural differences affect how much we disclose to one another? Several researchers suggest that the answer is yes. People's cultural backgrounds affect both the kinds of things they reveal and the intimacy of the information about themselves they share with others. Intercultural communication scholar William Gudykunst found that North Americans are more likely than Japanese to reveal more personal and intimate information about themselves to people whom they consider close friends.[1] Self-disclosure researcher Mie Kito found the same thing; Japanese students disclosed less about themselves than did students from North America.[2] Both Japanese and American students disclosed more about themselves in romantic relationships than with their friends. Americans were more likely than the Japanese to talk about their sex lives, dating patterns, and love interests and to reveal their emotions. A researcher investigating Korean communication patterns found that North Americans tended to disclose more than Koreans about their marital status, sexual morality, and use of birth control.[3] But Koreans were more likely than Americans to talk about issues related to education and family rules.

What are the larger implications of these studies? Simply this: The amount of self-disclosure that is considered appropriate is learned; the level of self-disclosure with which we are comfortable varies from culture to culture. Cultural norms influence how much we reveal about ourselves.

1. W. B. Gudykunst and T. Nishida, "Social Penetration in Japanese and American Close Friendships," in *Communication Yearbook 7*, edited by R. N. Bostrom (Beverly Hills, CA: Sage, 1963), 592–611.

2. M. Kito, "Self-Disclosure in Romantic Relationships and Friendships Among American and Japanese College Students, *The Journal of Social Psychology* 145 (2005): 127–40.

3. J. C. Korn, "Friendship Formation and Development in Two Cultures: Universal Constructs in the United States and Korea," in *Interpersonal Communication in Friend and Mate Relationships*, edited by A. M. Nicotera (Albany: State State University of New York Press, 1993), 61–78.

especially attracted to those who have a similar sense of humour, who share the same attitudes on certain issues, or who enjoy some of the other activities that you enjoy. Similarly, joining a Facebook group or posting on an online discussion board could lead to online friendships with individuals who share your interests.

In the initial stages of a relationship, we try to emphasize positive information about ourselves to create a positive and attractive image. We reveal those aspects of ourselves that we believe we have in common with the other person, and the other person does the same. You save your revelations about important attitudes and issues for a later stage in the relational development process. Attitude similarity is more likely to be a source of long-term maintenance attraction than of short-term initial attraction. Similarity of interests and leisure activities appears more important in same-sex friendships than in opposite-sex relationships.

Similarities are viewed as positive because they give people something in common to talk about, making interactions comfortable and communication effective. Similarities are also viewed as positive because they represent sources of shared fun and pleasure as well as a basis for social and emotional support. However, it's also important to recognize that similarities can have a downside. Associating only with people who are exactly like ourselves can get boring, while being exposed to the opinions and experiences of people who differ from us can challenge us to expand our horizons.

Differences and Complementary Needs. "Vive la différence!" "Opposites attract." "Variety is the spice of life." Such phrases reflect a positive attitude toward differences. One reason we are drawn to people who are different from us is that we learn and grow by such exposure. People who are different from us expose us to new ideas, activities, and perspectives, and prompt self-assessment. However, differences can also lead to points of conflict and hamper our ability to effectively communicate.

Differences can lead to long-term maintenance attraction when we find a person whose strengths complement our weaknesses. People in a relationship have **complementary needs** when each partner contributes something to the relationship that the other partner needs. We can view a pair of individuals as a team in which each person complements the

complementary needs.
Needs that match, with each partner contributing something to the relationship that the other partner needs.

Canadian Connections

Are People Who Live Alone Lonelier Than People Who Live with a Spouse or Partner?

Do people who are married or living with a partner have more friends and acquaintances than single people? Do they have better-quality social networks? Are people who live alone more likely to experience feelings of "social loneliness" than those who are living in a couple? A 2011 article in *Canadian Social Trends* attempts to answer these questions, using data on social networks from Statistics Canada's 2008 General Social Survey (GSS).

The article compares the personal networks of adults between the ages of 25 and 64 who live alone to those of adults living in a couple. Various aspects of personal networks are taken into consideration, including the number of people in the network, the frequency of face-to-face and telephone contact, and the feeling of social loneliness.

- According to the 2008 GSS, which collected data from approximately 20 000 Canadians aged 15 and over, people who live alone are less likely than those living in a couple to say that they felt "close" to a significant number of their relatives (i.e., that they felt they could speak freely with them and call on them for help). The article reports that 70% of participants in the study who live alone said that they

felt close to three or more relatives, compared with 81% of those living in a couple. In addition, many people living in a couple have close ties to their spouse or partner's family network as well as their own, giving them more opportunities for developing meaningful relationships with relatives.

- In 2008 there was little difference between the number of close friends reported by people living alone and those of people living in a couple. In both groups, 55% had between three and eight close friends. However, people living alone report fewer acquaintances than people living with a partner. Acquaintances are important because they help reduce social isolation and may provide more focused or specialized assistance in times of need. According to the GSS, 44% of those living alone had 20 or more acquaintances, compared with 52% of those living in a couple. People living alone were also slightly more likely to have a small number of acquaintances, suggesting that having a spouse or partner may increase a person's likelihood of meeting new people.

- The researchers combined data on the number of close relatives, close friends, and acquaintances in order to measure the overall size of personal networks. The results show that 31% of those living alone had a small overall network, compared with 21% of those living alone; additionally, 25% of those living in a couple had a very large overall network, compared with 16% of those living alone.

- Interestingly, both groups were satisfied with their frequency of contact; approximately 85% of both those living alone and those living in a couple said that they were satisfied with how frequently they were in contact with relatives, friends, and acquaintances.

In summary, the personal networks of people living alone are different from those of people living with a spouse or partner. Those living alone have fewer close ties with relatives and fewer acquaintances. However, those living alone had similar numbers of close friends to those living in a couple. Still, when the data is combined, people living alone are more likely to have poor-quality personal networks and to experience a strong feeling of social loneliness than people living in a couple.

other. Perhaps you're not very good at making decisions about what to do for fun on the weekend. You might form a complementary relationship with someone who always plans and does exciting things on weekends. The bottom line in terms of power in relationships is that there are no "perfect" matches, only degrees of compatibility relative to needs.

Short-term initial attraction gets relationships started, but the process of changing to long-term maintenance attraction involves working through a series of stages, each reflecting changes in attraction, self-disclosure, and intimacy. The remainder of this chapter focuses on the nature of those stages and on theories that explain how and why interpersonal attraction and intimacy increase and decrease.

Stages of Interpersonal Relationship Development

relational development.
Movement of a relationship from one stage to another, either toward or away from greater intimacy.

Although researchers use different terms and different numbers of stages, all agree that **relational development** proceeds in discernible stages. The stage we are in affects our interpersonal communication, and our interpersonal communication is the tool we use

RECAP Genesis of Interpersonal Relationships: Attraction

Interpersonal attraction	Degree to which you want to form or maintain an interpersonal relationship
Short-term initial attraction	Degree to which you sense potential for developing a relationship
Long-term maintenance attraction	Level of liking or positive feelings motivating you to maintain or escalate a relationship
Factors Leading to Short-Term Initial Attraction	
Proximity	Physical nearness to someone that promotes communication and thus attraction
Physical appearance	Nonverbal cues that allow us to assess relationship potential
Factors Leading to Both Short-Term Initial Attraction and Long-Term Maintenance Attraction	
Credibility, competence, and intelligence	Personal qualities that in and of themselves evoke attraction
Self-disclosure and reciprocation of liking	Openness; attraction toward a person who seems attracted to you
Similarity	Comparable personalities, values, upbringing, personal experiences, attitudes, and interests
Differences and complementary needs	Appreciation of diversity; matching needs

to move ourselves from stage to stage. Individuals in an intimate stage discuss topics and display nonverbal behaviours that do not appear in the early stages of a relationship. Outsiders can usually tell what stage a relationship is in by observing the interpersonal communication.

You can think of the stages, from first meeting to intimacy, as the floors in a high-rise building. Relational development is like an elevator that stops at every floor. As you get to each floor, you might get off and wander around for a while before taking the elevator to the next floor (see Figure 9.2). Each time you get on, you don't know how many floors up the elevator will take you, or how long you will stay at any given floor. In fact, sometimes you never get back on the elevator, electing instead to stay at a particular stage of relational development. But sometimes we move quickly from floor to floor toward intimacy. Part of the time you share this elevator with your partner, and the two of you make decisions about how far up you will go on the elevator, how long to stay at each floor, and when and whether to ride the elevator down.

FIGURE 9.2

Model of Relational Development

© Steven A. Beebe

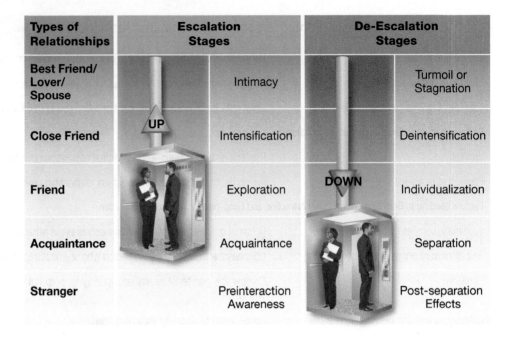

Types of Relationships	Escalation Stages		De-Escalation Stages	
Best Friend/ Lover/ Spouse		Intimacy		Turmoil or Stagnation
Close Friend	UP	Intensification		Deintensification
Friend		Exploration	DOWN	Individualization
Acquaintance		Acquaintance		Separation
Stranger		Preinteraction Awareness		Post-separation Effects

Just as there are lights on a panel to let you know the elevator has moved from one floor to another, markers, or turning points, signal a move from one stage to another in a relationship. **Turning points** are specific events or interactions that are associated with positive or negative changes in a relationship. A first meeting, first date, first fight, first road trip together, first time having sex, first time saying "I love you" and first time meeting a partner's family might all be turning points that indicate a relationship is moving forward. Turning points may violate expectations, which might also increase our uncertainty. One way to clarify the violation and reduce uncertainty is to discuss these turning points with our partner. One pair of researchers found that 55% of the time, turning points inspired a discussion about the nature of the relationship.[2] Such discussion helps the partners reach mutual agreement about the definition of the relationship.

Turning points can be divided into two types. **Causal turning points** are events that directly affect the relationship. Your relationships are filled with such turning points, moving you closer or further apart. Finding out that your friend has told you a significant lie might cause you to terminate the relationship. Because the event caused a change in the relationship, it is a causal turning point. On the other hand, receiving and accepting an invitation from a friend to visit his or her family for the first time is a **reflective turning point**, because it signals that a change has occurred in the definition of the relationship. The invitation and acceptance don't cause a change, but rather *reflect* a change in how you and your friend perceive the relationship.

Relational Escalation

Relational escalation is the movement of a relationship toward greater intimacy. This movement usually goes through a series of discernible stages: preinteraction awareness, acquaintance, exploration, intensification, and intimacy. Movement from one stage to another represents an increase in the amount of intimacy between two people. Each stage is accompanied by specific communication patterns, turning points, and relational expectations.

turning point. Specific event or interaction associated with a positive or negative change in a relationship.

causal turning point. Event that brings about a change in a relationship.

reflective turning point. Event that signals a change in the way a relationship is defined.

relational escalation. Movement of a relationship toward intimacy through five stages: preinteraction awareness, acquaintance, exploration, intensification, and intimacy.

Preinteraction Awareness. As you can see in the model in Figure 9.2, the first floor is the *preinteraction awareness stage*. At this stage, you might observe someone or even talk with others about him or her without having any direct interaction. Gaining information about others without directly interacting with them is a *passive strategy.* Through your passive observations, you form an initial impression. You might not move beyond the preinteraction awareness stage if that impression is not favourable or the circumstances aren't right. During the preinteraction awareness stage, one person might signal his or her openness to being approached by the other; but these cues, such as smiling or eye contact, can be misread. Such misreadings might result in failure at the next stage.

Acquaintance. On the basis of the impression you formed in the preinteraction awareness stage, you might decide to interact with the other person. Sometimes circumstances lead to immediate interaction, and there is little or no preinteraction awareness. In either case, the very first interaction is a turning point that begins the *acquaintance stage,* in which conversations stick to safe and superficial topics and you present a "public self" to the other person. There are actually two sub-stages in the acquaintance stage: introductions and casual banter. In the **introductions** sub-stage, we tell each other our names and share basic demographic information—where we're from, what we do, and so on. In this sub-stage, the interaction is typically routine—partners usually spend the first four minutes asking each other various standard questions. Except for those of us who are forgetful or who don't pay attention, we introduce ourselves to another person only once. Once we have made his or her acquaintance, we can interact without having to introduce ourselves again.

The second sub-stage is **casual banter**, talking about impersonal topics with little or no self-disclosure. You might engage only in introductions, or move from introductions to casual banter, or engage only in casual banter without even going through introductions. You've probably experienced this sub-stage in classrooms many times, as you make the acquaintance of a classmate sitting next to you, skipping introductions and just talking about casual topics. Subsequent interactions in the acquaintance stage involve continuing casual banter—discussing the weather, current events, daily news, or some common experience (what happened in class today, how the company picnic went, and the like). Many of our relationships never move beyond this stage.

introductions. Sub-stage of the acquaintance stage of relationship development, in which interaction is routine and basic information is shared.

casual banter. Sub-stage of the acquaintance stage of relationship development, in which impersonal topics are discussed but very limited personal information is shared.

Exploration. If you and your partner decide to go to the next floor, *exploration,* you will begin to share more in-depth information about yourselves. But you will have little physical contact, maintain your social distance, and limit the amount of time you spend together. This stage can occur in conjunction with the acquaintance stage. During this stage, communication becomes easier, and a large amount of low-risk disclosure occurs. Exploration entails the kind of conversation that might occur when you go out to get a bite to eat with a co-worker whom you know only casually. If your conversation includes sharing more personal information about yourselves, such as your interests and hobbies, where you grew up, what your families were like, or similar personal information, then you are in the exploration stage.

Intensification. If you proceed to the *intensification stage,* you will start to depend on each other for self-confirmation and engage in more risky self-disclosure. You will spend more time together, increase the variety of activities you share, adopt a more personal physical distance, engage in more physical contact, and personalize your language. Also, you may often discuss and redefine the relationship in this stage, perhaps

As couples proceed from exploration to intensification, they have more physical contact and begin sharing more activities and confidences.
(© logoboom/Shutterstock)

putting a turning-point label on yourselves, such as "going steady," "good buddies," or "best friends." Other turning points associated with this stage include decisions to date each other exclusively, to become roommates, or to spend time with each other's families.

Intimacy. The "top floor" in the relational high-rise is the *intimacy stage*. In this stage, the two partners turn to each other for confirmation and acceptance of their self-concepts. Their communication is highly personalized and synchronized. They talk about anything and everything. There is a free flow of information and intimate self-disclosure. There is a commitment to maintaining the relationship that might even be formalized through marriage or some other agreement. Partners incorporate more of their own language code (nicknames, inside jokes, and special words) and use fewer words to communicate, relying more on nonverbal cues. They have increased understanding of each other's words and nonverbal cues. Their roles and the relationship are discussed and more clearly defined. Physical contact increases, and their physical distance during conversations decreases. Reaching this stage takes time—time to build trust, time to share personal information, time to observe each other in various situations, and time to build a commitment and an emotional bond.

Relational De-Escalation

Relational de-escalation is the movement that occurs when a relationship decreases in intimacy or comes to an end. The process of ending a relationship is not as simple as going down the same elevator you came up on; it is not a reversal of the relationship formation process. Relational de-escalation can also involve only one or two of the stages. For example, a relationship might move from being one between good friends to a more casual friendship. A **post-intimacy relationship** occurs when partners de-escalate from the intimate stage but still maintain a relationship. A couple might decide they like each other as friends but no longer want a romantic or exclusive relationship; thus, they de-escalate and maintain the relationship at the intensification or exploratory stage. Our model identifies five stages of relational de-escalation: turmoil or stagnation, deintensification, individualization, separation, and post-separation.

Turmoil or Stagnation. When an intimate relationship is not going well, it usually enters the stage of either *turmoil* or *stagnation*. Turmoil involves an increase in conflict, as one or both partners tend to find more faults in the other. The definition of the relationship seems to lose its clarity, and mutual acceptance declines. The communication climate is tense, and exchanges are difficult.

Stagnation occurs when the relationship loses its vitality and the partners become complacent. Communication and physical contact between the partners decrease; they spend less time together, but do not necessarily fight. Partners in a stagnating relationship tend to go through the motions of an intimate relationship without the commitment; they simply follow their established relational routines.

As with the up elevator, individuals can stop at this point on the down elevator and decide to quit descending. The relationship can remain in turmoil or stagnate for a long time, or the individuals can repair, redefine, or revitalize the relationship and return to intimacy.

Deintensification. If the turmoil or stagnation continues, however, the individuals might move to the *deintensification stage*, decreasing their interactions; increasing their physical, emotional, and psychological distance; and decreasing their dependence on the other for self-confirmation. They might discuss the definition of their relationship, question its future, and assess each partner's level of satisfaction or dissatisfaction. The relationship can be

relational de-escalation.
Movement of a relationship away from intimacy through five stages: turmoil or stagnation, deintensification, individualization, separation, and post-separation.

post-intimacy relationship.
Formerly intimate relationship that is maintained at a less intimate stage.

Building Your Skills | Graphing Your Relationship Changes

Think of an interpersonal relationship you have had for at least a year. On the graph, plot the development of that relationship from stage to stage, indicating the relative amount of time you spent in each stage. You can also indicate whether you backed up to a previous stage at any point.

If possible, have your relational partner create a similar graph, and compare your perceptions of how the relationship has developed. What differences are there and why?

You also might want to compare your graph with those of classmates to see how different relationships develop. What can you tell from the graphs about the nature of their relationships?

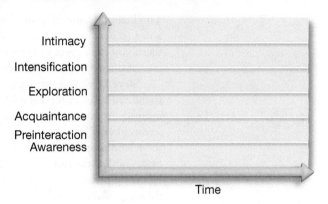

repaired and the individuals can move back to intensification and intimacy, but that is more difficult to accomplish at this stage.

Individualization. On the next floor down, the *individualization stage,* the partners tend to define their lives more as individuals and less as a couple. Neither views the other as a partner or significant other anymore. Interactions are limited. The perspective changes from "we" and "us" to "you" and "me," and property is defined in terms of "mine" or "yours" rather than "ours." Both partners turn to others for confirmation of their self-concepts.

Separation. In the *separation stage,* individuals make an intentional decision to eliminate or minimize further interpersonal interaction. If they share custody of children, attend mutual family gatherings, or work in the same office, the nature of their interactions will change. They will divide property, resources, and friends. For relationships that never went beyond exploration or intensification, however, the negotiation is often relatively painless. One study of post-dissolution romantic relationships found four specific patterns of commitment changes after a breakup: a *linear process,* in which commitment remained the same; a *relational decline* (the most common), in which commitment continued to decline over time; *upward relational progression,* in which commitment actually increased (perhaps re-escalating the relationship); and *turbulent relational progression,* in which the commitment went up and down several times.[3]

When intimates separate, their extensive personal knowledge about each other often makes any future interaction—now limited to casual banter—awkward and uncomfortable. Over time, of course, each partner knows less about who the other person has become. For example, even after spending just a few years away from your high school friends, you might have difficulty interacting with them because your knowledge of one another is out of date.

Post-Separation Effects. Although interaction may cease altogether, the effect of the relationship is not over. The bottom floor on the down elevator, where you remain, is the *post-separation stage.* This floor represents the lasting effects the relationship has on your self and, therefore, on your other interactions and relationships. In this final stage of terminating relationships, we create a public statement for people who ask why we broke up and also come to grips with losing the relationship. Sometimes our sense of self gets battered during the final stages of a relationship, and we have to work hard to regain a healthy sense of self.

BEING Other-ORIENTED

Relationships involve continual negotiation of the movement toward or away from intimacy. One partner often moves toward or away from intimacy before the other catches up. Not knowing what stage your partner is in creates discontent and conflict. Think about a relationship you have that has recently become closer. Who sees the relationship as closer, you or your partner? Does your partner also recognize this difference? How do you think your partner feels about it?

Theories of Interpersonal Relationship Development

Think about some of your closer relationships. How did you move from being acquaintances to being close friends? The model of relational stages provides a description of the stages you can expect to experience as you move through interpersonal relationships. However, it doesn't explain what motivates people to move from one stage to another.

Steve Duck suggests we go through a process of "**filtering**," in which a potential close friend must pass criteria at each stage of relational development.[4] In essence, a move toward intimacy from one stage to the next means that a person has passed through another, finer screen filter. These screens represent decision points in which we make some assessment of the relationship and decide how we want to proceed. We can choose to escalate, maintain, or de-escalate the relationship. Three theories reflect the kind of decision making that might be taking place: social exchange theory, relational dialectics theory, and social penetration theory (self-disclosure).

Social Exchange Theory

You've probably been in a difficult relationship where you have asked yourself, "Is this relationship really worth it?" At one time or another we all ask ourselves whether the rewards we are gaining from a particular relationship are worth the costs—the trouble or expense necessary to sustain the relationship. **Social exchange theory** asserts that we base relational decisions on getting the greatest amount of reward with the least amount of cost.[5] Relational rewards include friendship and love, fun, and laughter, money or favours, support and assistance, and confirmation of our value. Costs include loss of time, freedom, money, and self-esteem, and can even include psychological or physical abuse.

One factor we assess in deciding whether to pursue a relationship is the *magnitude* of the rewards and costs—the relative size of how much you put into and get out of a relationship. Another factor is how the rewards compare to the costs—the *ratio*. A relationship with high rewards (magnitude) might not be worth maintaining if the costs are also high (producing a low ratio). Perhaps you have a friend who is a lot of fun to be with, but you always have to pay that person's way, making the relationship cost as much as it rewards. On the other hand, you might enjoy your relationship with a co-worker because you have fun working together (reward) and the relationship costs you little. Rewards and costs affect our decisions to escalate, maintain, or terminate a relationship.

Relationships can be evaluated in terms of immediate, forecasted, and cumulative costs and rewards. **Immediate costs and rewards** occur in a relationship at the present moment in time. Think about a relationship that you are in and consider how much you put into it, and how much you get out of it. **Forecasted costs and rewards** are based on projection or prediction. We make guesses about the potential or future outlook of a relationship. When you meet someone for the first time, you make a judgement about whether a relationship with this person would be rewarding. You also use forecasting to decide whether to remain in existing relationships during troubled times (when costs escalate or rewards deteriorate). You don't immediately abandon long-term relationships at the first sign of trouble if you believe that things will improve. For example, you can tolerate the increased costs associated with a roommate who's intolerable to live with during finals week because you know once finals are done, those costs will be gone and the relationship will be rewarding again.

Another reason why people remain in ongoing relationships during periods of low immediate rewards has to do with cumulative costs and rewards. **Cumulative costs and rewards** represent the total costs and rewards accrued over the duration of the relationship. Just as you put money in savings when you have more income than expenses, you

filtering. Process of reducing partners moving to each stage by applying selection criteria.

social exchange theory. A theory that claims people make decisions on the basis of assessing and comparing the costs and rewards of a decision.

immediate costs and rewards. Those costs and rewards that are associated with a relationship at the present moment.

forecasted costs and rewards. The costs and rewards of a relationship that an individual assumes will occur on the basis of projection and prediction.

cumulative costs and rewards. The total costs and rewards accrued during the duration of a relationship.

can also build up a relational savings account from extra rewards. You can then draw on that savings account when immediate costs escalate. But if those costs continue for a long time, you may interact less and eventually end the relationship as the accumulated rewards are exhausted. If, over a year, you developed a friendship that included a lot of great times and those great times stopped, you'd probably hang on to the friendship for a while but eventually let it fade away.

People seem to construct templates in their minds for what relationships should be like. **Expected costs and rewards** represent expectations and ideals about how rewarding a relationship should be relative to its costs. We have a model of the ideal friend, the ideal lover, the ideal co-worker, and so on. We use the expected costs and rewards associated with these ideals to assess current relationships. We might abandon a relationship if we don't think it matches or has the potential to match our ideal. In essence, we set standards or criteria for our relationships by which we assess the desirability of a given relationship. Like Duck's filtering process, ideal images allow you to sort through relationships and focus on those that are closest to or exceed your ideal. The major difficulty associated with such comparisons rests in setting reasonable standards or ideals. For example, some parents avoid arguing in front of their children, creating an expectation in their children that a happy marriage is conflict free. As adults, the children might evaluate their own marriages as unsuccessful for failing to achieve this ideal. If you find that you are continually unable to find relationships that measure up to your ideals, you may need to reassess your expected rewards and costs.

Finally, we compare the rewards and costs of our current relationships with those we forecast for other potential relationships. We reduce our time spent with one friend when we believe we can have a more rewarding relationship with another person. We will move quickly to terminate a relationship if it falls below our expectations and if we think we have an opportunity to develop a new relationship that has the potential to exceed all our expectations. We try to spend the most time in those relationships that have the best relative outcomes. All these comparisons work together. We compare our current relationships with previous ones, with our ideals, and with potential ones.

expected costs and rewards. Expectation of how much reward we should get from a given relationship in comparison with its costs.

relational dialectics theory. A theory that says relational development occurs in conjunction with various tensions that exist in all relationships, particularly connectedness versus autonomy, predictability versus novelty, and openness versus closedness.

Relational Dialectics Theory

As illustrated in Figure 9.3, interpersonal relationships are erratic and non-linear; we become closer, then we drift farther apart, only to become close once again. **Relational dialectics theory** views relationship development as the management of the tensions that pull us in two directions at the same time.

FIGURE 9.3

Sample Relational Development Graph

© Steven A. Beebe

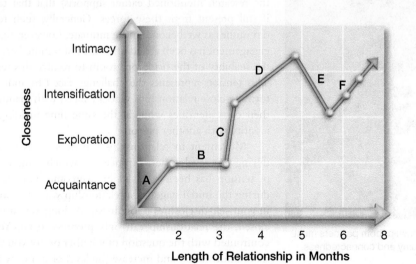

Identifying Dialectical Tensions. Researcher Leslie Baxter has identified three dialectical tensions that have been widely used in interpersonal research.[6]

- *Connectedness versus autonomy.* We desire to connect with others and to become interdependent while at the same time having a desire to remain autonomous and independent. In one study of married couples, these desires to be connected and autonomous were found to be the most frequently occurring of the dialectical tensions.[7]

- *Predictability versus novelty (certainty versus uncertainty).* Knowing what to expect and being able to predict the world around us helps us reduce the tension that occurs from uncertainty. At the same time, we get bored by constant repetition and routine and therefore are attracted to novelty and the unexpected. Relationships that fall into routines may be comfortable, but they also suffer from a need for freshness.

- *Openness versus closedness.* We wish we could disclose information to others and to have those we are attracted to disclose to us. One ideal we seem to have in relationships is the ability to be totally open with our partners. However, we also value our privacy and feel a desire to hold back information. This tension was identified in the study of married couples mentioned earlier as the most important of the three tensions, although it did not occur as often as the other two tensions.

Dialectical Tensions and Relationships. According to relational dialectics theory, each pair of tensions is present in every relationship, but the impact of each changes as a relationship progresses. Movement in relationships can be seen as a shift that occurs in the relative pull of one tension. For example, when you begin developing a new friendship, one issue you have to address is whether you want to give up some of your autonomy (freedom to do your own things) in order to spend time with this other person (connectedness). Notice how this is similar to social exchange theory in that you weigh costs (giving up autonomy) against rewards (becoming connected).

Forces of autonomy and connectedness can both be found even in close relationships. Even though long-married couples have usually settled the issues of interdependence versus independence, relational dialectics theory asserts (and the research mentioned earlier supports) that that tension is still present from these forces. Generally, such tension diminishes as we become more intimate; however, many an engagement has been called off at the last minute because of the inability of the bride or groom to resolve this tension. This tension represents the challenge faced by individuals forming close relationships who are faced with maintaining their own identities while at the same time melding their identity with another person.

Movement in relationships can be seen as moments during the developmental process in which some element of tension has been resolved or overcome. For example, during the initial stages of a relationship you are restrained in your self-disclosures (closedness). As long as you remain closed, the relationship can only progress so far. You are confronted with the question of whether or not you should share information and increase the level of intimacy in the

When a couple commits to a relationship, both partners must find a new balance between autonomy and connectedness.
(© Don Smetzer/PhotoEdit, Inc.)

Many of the principles and rules that guide our self-disclosure in face-to-face (FtF) interactions apply as well to electronically mediated communication (EMC). However, blogs, Facebook and LinkedIn pages, Internet forums, and Twitter provide different contexts for your decisions about what to share with both strangers and friends. Research suggests that we disclose more quickly in Internet interactions than in FtF ones because of anonymity, the lack of "gating features" or filters such as shyness or weak social skills, little expectation of actually meeting or sustaining a relationship, and the

perception of similarity fostered by messaging in a forum devoted to a shared interest (e.g., groups discussing Aston Martins, quilting, hockey, or *The Bachelor*).[8] Interestingly, research found that people reveal more of their "true self" (the parts of their self they would like others to know but don't show) when interacting with strangers online than when interacting FtF.[9] Think about your own FtF and online interactions with others. Have you shared parts of yourself online that you'd like to share in your FtF interactions but don't? What things have your friends posted on social network pages (such

as photos or results of personal surveys) that you've seen as almost too personal or disclosing? Sometimes the blogs, tweets, and text messages from friends might tell you more than you really want to know. Another research study found that in same-sex friendships, students who reported being the most comfortable self-disclosing online communicated with their friends more online and less in FtF interactions compared with those who were less comfortable self-disclosing.[10] For some, seeking support or discussing difficult issues appears to be easier to do online.

relationship. Tension exists until you make your decision. Once you have decided, some of the tension is relieved. Thus, if you decide on more openness, the reduction in tension is accompanied by a change in the relationship—a turning point.

Still, tensions remain, and we often decide to back away from intimacy as another way of managing them. Rather than a straight, linear progression toward intimacy, the management of dialectical tensions results in relationships moving up a stage or two, then down a stage or more, and back up again as partners negotiate the tensions. One study found that over half of the friendships studied progressed through a cycle of development, deterioration, and then development again, with each change being signalled by a turning point.[11]

Self-Disclosure and Social Penetration Theory

You probably recall from Chapter 2 that *self-disclosure* occurs when we purposefully provide information to others about ourselves that they would not learn if we did not tell them. Your Facebook page, Instagram pictures, and Twitter posts reflect a form of self-disclosure, allowing large numbers of people, including strangers, access to your personal information. As relationships develop, we might use electronically mediated communication to self-disclose further. In this chapter, self-disclosure is examined as an important part of the process of developing relationships. In fact, it is so important that social psychologists Irwin Altman and Dalmas Taylor built a theory based on it.[12] The main premise of their **social penetration theory** is that the movement toward intimacy is connected to increased breadth and depth of self-disclosing, as reflected in their model (Figure 9.4).

Understanding the Social Penetration Model. The **social penetration model** starts with a circle that represents all the potential information about yourself that you could disclose to someone (see Figure 9.4, circle A). This circle is divided into many pieces like a pie, with each piece representing a particular aspect of your "self," like hobbies, religious beliefs, interests, and fears. These many pieces represent the **breadth** of available about you.

social penetration theory.
Theory of relational development that posits that increases in intimacy are connected to increases in self-disclosure.

social penetration model.
A model of the self that reflects both the breadth and the depth of information that can potentially be disclosed.

breadth. The various pieces of self, like hobbies, beliefs, family, school, and fears that can be potentially disclosed.

FIGURE 9.4
Social Penetration Model
© Steven A. Beebe

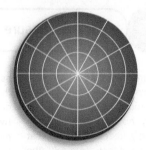

A
Your "self" with all its various dimensions. The wedges represent the breadth of your "self," and the rings represent depth.

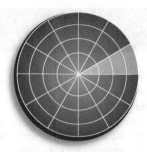

B
A limited relationship in which one dimension of your "self" has been disclosed to another person.

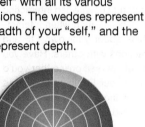

C
A relationship with greater breadth than B but with no intimacy.

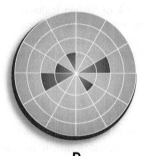

D
A highly intimate, close relationship in which there has been extensive breadth and depth of disclosure.

The concentric circles in the pie represent the depth of information you could disclose. By **depth**, we mean how personal or intimate the information is; telling your friend about your fear of elevators is more intimate than telling someone that your favorite flavour of ice cream is vanilla. In this way, social penetration is like an onion, where each layer of the onion is peeled away as you move toward the onion core. The centre circle represents this core, the most personal, intimate information about you. Each of your relationships involves social penetration, or the extent to which others learn intimate information (depth) as well as the number of different pieces of information they learn (breadth). The shading on circle B shows a relationship with one aspect revealed but with a high degree of penetration/depth. Can you think of a relationship that you have that fits this pattern—someone that knows a lot about only one aspect of your life—a co-worker, classmate, doctor? In circle C, more pieces of the pie are shaded, but the information is all fairly safe, superficial information about you, such as where you went to school, your hometown, or your major in college or university. These would be the kind of disclosures associated with a new friendship. Circle D represents almost complete social penetration, the kind achieved in an intimate, well-developed relationship in which a large amount of self-disclosure has occurred.

Enhancing Intimacy by Self-Disclosing over Time. According to social penetration theory, it is through the process of revealing information that it becomes possible for relationships to become more intimate. In an intimate friendship, we become aware of things about our friends that few, if any other people may know. Simply disclosing information about yourself is no guarantee that your relationship will become intimate (with *intimate* here referring to both greater depth and greater breadth of self-disclosure).[13] As we mutually

depth. How personal or intimate the information is that might be disclosed.

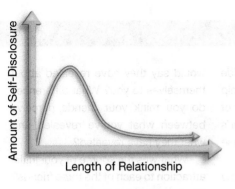

Graph A

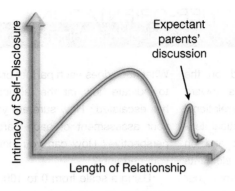

Graph B

FIGURE 9.5

Self-Disclosure and Relational Development

© Steven A. Beebe

self-disclose, we often discover incompatibilities or even negative information, which may lead to relational de-escalation.

Typically, a large *amount* of low-risk self-disclosure takes place in the early stages of relational development, and that amount decreases as the relationship becomes more and more intimate (Figure 9.5, Graph A). There is only so much information to share about ourselves, so the amount of disclosure slows down as the relationship continues, assuming the partners have remained open. While the amount decreases, the *intimacy* (depth) of our disclosures, which are limited initially, increases as the relationship escalates (Figure 9.5, Graph B)—but that too eventually decreases after we have shared most of our intimate information. However, the pattern of the amount and intimacy of disclosure is often not as neat as the two graphs indicate. Relationships experience periods of marked increases and decreases in the amount and intimacy of self-disclosure, reflecting some change in the relationship. Even long-term relationships can experience dramatic increases and decreases in disclosure; for example, first time expectant parents are likely to disclose their intimate fears and expectations about child rearing (as shown on the graph).

Interpersonal relationships cannot achieve intimacy without self-disclosure. Without true self-disclosure, we form only superficial relationships. You can confirm another person's self-concept, and have your self-concept confirmed, only if both you and your partner have revealed yourselves to each other—you have both self-disclosed.

RECAP   Theories of Interpersonal Relationship Development

Theory	Definition	Application
Social Exchange Theory	People make relational decisions based on getting the greatest amount of reward with the least amount of cost.	You break up a long-distance relationship because the expense (driving time, cell phone bills) seems greater than what is gained from the relationship (fun, support).
Relational Dialectics Theory	Relational development involves managing the tensions that result from opposing forces pulling toward two directions at the same time.	The time you spend with your new romantic partner is taking away time from your other friends. You must decide how to deal with your desire to be in the romantic relationship and still maintain your friendships.
Social Penetration Theory	Movement toward intimacy is connected to the breadth and depth of self-disclosure.	Your casual relationship with a roommate centres primarily on rent, shared bills, and housecleaning. One night your roommate shares the news that his parents are getting a divorce. You listen empathically as he shares his thoughts and feelings, sharing similar information when appropriate. From that point on, your relationship becomes closer and more intimate.

APPLYING AN OTHER-ORIENTATION
to Understanding Interpersonal Relationships

This chapter has focused on the movement of relationships toward and away from intimacy; on relational costs and rewards, dialectical tensions, and self-disclosure; and on attraction. These relational elements were discussed primarily from your perspective—the rewards you may perceive, the tensions you experience, and your attraction to others. But reflecting from time to time on these elements from your relational partners' points of view can enhance these relationships. Why not start right now? Take a moment to identify a specific close friend of the same sex, a friend of the opposite sex, and a casual friend.

In what stage of development is each relationship, and how far along that stage is it? How does your perception compare with where each of your partners sees the relationship? What cues does each partner provide to indicate how far the relationship has escalated? How sure are you of your assessment of each partner's perspective? How can you increase your certainty?

Using a scale from 0 to 100, how rewarding would you say each relationship is? How costly? Consider whether each of your three friends sees the relationship as more or less rewarding than you do. Does each see the relationship as more costly or less costly than you do?

How comfortable are you with the current balance between connectedness and autonomy in each relationship? How comfortable is each of your three friends?

What percentage (from 0% to 100%) of your "self" have you disclosed to each of your three friends? How much do you think your friends would say they have revealed about themselves to you? What differences do you think your friends perceive between what you've revealed and what they have revealed?

What was the source of your initial attraction to each of the three friends? What was the basis of each person's attraction to you? What is your long-term maintenance attraction to each person based on? What continues their attraction toward you?

Rarely do two people view their relationship in exactly the same way. If you didn't find any significant discrepancies between your views and your friends' views, you might be missing some information. Look for additional cues that might help you more completely understand your friends' perspectives, or consider sharing your views while seeking theirs.

Interpersonal Relationships Defined (pages 211–214)

OBJECTIVE ❶ Define interpersonal relationships and identify some ways to distinguish among them.

Key Terms

relationship *211*

interpersonal relationship *211*

interpersonal intimacy *212*

relationships of circumstance *213*

relationships of choice *213*

complementary relationship *213*

symmetrical relationship *214*

competitive symmetrical relationship *214*

submissive symmetrical relationship *214*

parallel relationships *214*

Critical Thinking Questions

1. Identify qualities beyond those cited in the text's definition of an interpersonal relationship that vary among your relationships.

2. Identify some advantages and disadvantages associated with each type of power relationship.

3. Ethics: To what degree can an individual pursue changing a relationship of circumstance into a relationship of choice if the other person rejects the initial attempt to change the relationship? What options does the person who rejects the continued attempts to change the relationship have?

Activities

Create two columns on a piece of paper. In the first column, write the names of three individuals with whom you have different relationships (for example, a parent, best friend, co-worker). Using a scale of 1 (low) to 5 (high), indicate the degree to which each person likes to be in control and make decisions when you're together. In the second column, indicate the degree to which you like to be in control and make decisions when you're with each person.

Web Resources

http://www.managementstudyguide.com/interpersonal-relationship -skills.htm This site explains several skills that will help you build healthy interpersonal relationships with co-workers.

Genesis of Interpersonal Relationships: Attraction (pages 214–218)

OBJECTIVE ❷ Identify and differentiate between short-term initial attraction and long-term maintenance attraction.

Key Terms

interpersonal attraction *214*

short-term initial attraction *214*

long-term maintenance attraction *214*

proximity *215*

physical appearance *215*

reciprocation of liking *216*

complementary needs *217*

Critical Thinking Questions

1. Under what circumstances is it appropriate to act on your initial short-term attraction toward another person? Under what circumstances is it inappropriate?

2. Which source of attraction is probably the most important for sustaining a long-term relationship? Why? Which is least important? Why?

Activities

Make a list with two columns of names: people you regard as casual friends and those you regard as close friends. Identify what attracts you to the people on your list. Compare your ideas of what attracts you to casual friends and close friends with the ideas of other students. How does your list reflect the categories of attraction identified in the text?

Web Resources

http://rozenbergquarterly.com/attraction-and-relationships-the-journey -from-initial-attachments-to-romantic-love/ This essay explores the stages that lead to romantic love.

Stages of Interpersonal Relationship Development (pages 218–223)

OBJECTIVE ❸ Identify and describe the stages of relational escalation and de-escalation.

Key Terms

relational development *218*

turning point *220*

causal turning point *220*

reflective turning point *220*

relational escalation *220*

introductions *221*

casual banter *221*

relational de-escalation *222*

post-intimacy relationship *222*

Critical Thinking Questions

1. Think about three relationships you have that have remained in the exploration or intensification stage. What has prevented the relationships from escalating to the next stage? Why have you sustained the relationships?

2. Ethics: If two people have agreed to maintain a relationship below the highest level in the model of relational stages

(the intimacy stage), is it ethical for one of the people to nonetheless continually try to move the relationship to the intimacy stage?

Activities

Brainstorm some of the turning points you have experienced in both the escalation and de-escalation of your relationships. Identify the relational stages in which the turning points occurred. Identify whether each turning point is a causal or a reflective one. How significant an impact are turning points in your development of relationships?

Web Resources

www.uclarelationshipinstitute.org/d/our-philosophy_main This site, sponsored by the UCLA Relationship Institute, explores the issues associated with the different stages of intimate interpersonal relationships, including advice and resources for new couples, established couples, new parents, and unhappy couples.

Theories of Interpersonal Relationship Development (pages 224–230)

OBJECTIVE 4 Describe the main components of three theories that explain relational development.

Key Terms

filtering *224*
social exchange theory *224*
immediate costs and
  rewards *224*
forecasted costs and
  rewards *224*
cumulative costs and
  rewards *224*

expected costs and
  rewards *225*
relational dialectics
  theory *225*
social penetration theory *227*
social penetration model *227*
breadth *227*
depth *228*

Critical Thinking Questions

1. Explain (a) how social exchange theory relates to relational dialectics theory, (b) how social exchange theory relates to social penetration theory, and (c) how relational dialectics theory relates to social penetration theory and to self-disclosure.

2. Ethics: How ethical is it to intentionally increase the cost and reduce the rewards for a relational partner as a strategy for ending the relationship?

Activities

Make a list of 10 pieces of information about yourself that vary in how intimate or risky the information is (its depth). Put (+) next to those you know are appropriate to disclose to a fellow student you have just met. Put (−) next to those you know are inappropriate and (?) next to those you are unsure about. Under what circumstances might the pieces of information you marked with (−) or (?) be appropriate to disclose? Your disclosures should match your level of trust in the other person. Remember that how much and what you disclose will be taken by the other person as statement of how you feel about the relationship—your level of disclosure should match your relational feelings.

Web Resources

www.queendom.com/tests/access_page/index.htm?idRegTest=716 This is a self-test that assesses your willingness to self-disclose to others. The questions themselves provide a good source for personal reflection.

© auremar/Fotolia

10

Managing Relationship Challenges

66 Love begins with a smile, grows with a kiss, and ends with a teardrop. 99 —Anonymous

Charise:	I heard you went to the new Will Smith movie last night.
Simon:	Yeah, it was pretty good.
Charise:	I thought we agreed to go see it together?
Simon:	Oh, sorry. I forgot; besides, you were busy anyway.
Charise:	Don't lie. You didn't forget—you just didn't want to go with me.
Simon:	Hey, wait a minute. It's no big deal. It was just a movie.
Charise:	Who'd you go with?
Simon:	A gang of us from work went.
Charise:	Who?
Simon:	Just some people from work.
Charise:	You're a liar! I heard it was just you and some girl.

Throughout this book you have read about various factors that can impede effective interpersonal communication: language misunderstandings, biased perceptions, misinterpretation of nonverbal cues, weak listening skills, destructive conflict styles, and inappropriate self-disclosures. All of these factors can negatively affect interpersonal relationships. The above exchange between Charise and Simon reflects another set of issues that are covered in this chapter. Simon has obviously broken a promise he made to Charise about seeing a movie together, which places a strain on the relationship. Simon compounds the problem by being deceptive, but Charise calls him on it. Unlike the specific conflicts that you read about in Chapter 8, the challenges covered in this chapter reflect systemic relational issues. Interpersonal communication also has a dark side, in that it can be used in ways that are detrimental to others. These include being deceitful, as Simon is, and saying things that hurt other people's feelings, as Charise does. These relationship challenges and the darker aspects of interpersonal communication can contribute to relational de-escalation and termination.

Relationship Challenges

The movement toward an intimate relationship doesn't always go smoothly. Chapter 9 described some general expectations about how relationships develop, and you have your own additional set of expectations about relationships, but what happens when you encounter the unexpected? Any relationship can be challenged by one partner's failure to meet the other's expectations (a failure event), by attempts to maintain a relationship over long distances, or by social biases against certain types of relationships. Overcoming each of these challenges requires strong resolve and commitment by the relationship partners.

Violations of Relational Expectations
Just as relational expectations are part of the definition of relationships, violations of those expectations are an unavoidable part of relationship development.

Understanding Violations of Relational Expectations. Violations of relationship expectations can be classified according to the nature and origin of the expectations, as well as the severity of the transgression.

Socially Based Expectations. You develop sets of socially based relational expectations specific to given types of relationships, including expectations about their rewards and costs.

You have sets of expectations for what a best friend should be, what a romantic partner or spouse should be like, how rewarding a relationship with an opposite-sex friend should be, and so on. Violations of these expectations arouse uncertainty and produce emotional reactions such as hurt and anger.[1] You might assess a relationship in light of your expectations and decide to de-escalate or terminate the relationship. Or you might modify your expectations so that you no longer consider the event to be a violation. For example, if you held the expectation that friends lend other friends money but your friends kept turning down your requests, you might stop seeing money lending as a quality of friendship. Finally, you might decide to discuss the violation of the expectation with the other person in an attempt to persuade him or her to change. How you manage relational violations affects the health of the relationship.

Relationship-Specific Expectations. You and your partners also develop shared sets of expectations and understandings that are specific to each relationship. These understandings can be either implicit or explicit. *Implicit understandings* represent an unspoken compact between the partners about the relationship and each other. *Explicit understandings* are stated compacts and agreements. Violations of both types of understandings arouse uncertainty and evoke various responses. For example, your roommate agrees to clean up the apartment over the weekend (an explicit understanding) and then fails to do so. Your friend says he'll meet you at the restaurant at 7:00 (an explicit understanding) but doesn't show up until 8:00. Some very personal information that you shared with only one other person (an implicit understanding) suddenly becomes common knowledge among your other friends. These are called **failure events**—violations of understandings that occur between people in interpersonal relationships. Effective management of a failure event can lead to a clearer understanding of both the expectations and the relationship.

Severity. Failure events and transgressions can be thought of as occurring along a continuum of severity, with those that are least severe often being ignored altogether. At the more severe end of the continuum would be transgressive behaviours such as unfaithfulness in romantic relationships, which might include spending time with another person, breaking a promise, flirting, betraying a trust or confidence, or keeping secrets from the partner. The most severe violations can have a traumatic impact on a relationship. Because a defining characteristic of intimate romantic relationships is often sexual fidelity, cheating on one's partner is considered a severe moral transgression and often leads to the termination of the relationship. We don't all assess the severity of a violation in the same way; we might see flirting as a minor failure event while our partner views it as severe.

You can strengthen your relationships by being other-centred. Discuss your expectations and violations with your partner to improve your understanding of how he or she perceives these violations.

Responding with Discussion. The process of addressing failure events often follows the reproach–account pattern, in which both partners must make a number of decisions. The first decision is whether a failure event has actually occurred. This may be easier to determine with moral transgressions, because we expect partners to know what is appropriate, given the culture's inherent moral code. If the transgression is not a moral one, had both parties agreed to a specific rule or expectation? Did both parties understand the rule? Was the rule appropriate, applicable, and accepted?

After answering these questions, both parties must decide whether to discuss the failure. If we don't care that much about the relationship or the issue, we might opt to ignore the failure, deciding it is not worth the effort. The decision to complain to or reproach a partner should be motivated by a desire to clarify relational expectations or to avoid the failure event in the future by modifying the partner's behaviours.[2] A **reproach** is a message

failure events. Violations of understandings between people in interpersonal relationships.

reproach. A message that a failure event has occurred.

that a failure event has occurred. Reproaches are usually direct statements, but they can also be conveyed indirectly through hints or nonverbal messages. For example, if you are upset that a close friend forgot your birthday, you might act cold and distant. Reproaches range from *mitigating* (mild) to *aggravating* (threatening and severe). For example, if your friend forgets to return a book she borrowed, you might offer a mitigating reproach such as "Hey, Nadia, I was wondering if you were done with that book I loaned you?" On the other hand, "Remind me to never loan you a book again, Nadia; you are obviously irresponsible" is an aggravating reproach.

What would you say to each reproach if you were Nadia? Which reproach would make you more likely to apologize? Which would you be more likely to ignore? The nature of the reproach affects the response, or the **account**. Accounts can also be initiated without a reproach, simply because a person knows he or she has failed to live up to an expectation. Self-initiated accounts are more likely to evoke a favourable reaction from a partner than are accounts given in response to reproaches. Apologizing as you arrive late at a friend's house for dinner is more likely to appease the irritated friend than acting as though you've done nothing wrong or apologizing only *after* being reproached. The accounts people offer typically take one of five forms:

- *Apologies* include admission that the failure event occurred, acceptance of responsibility, and expression of regret.

- *Excuses* include admission that the failure event occurred, along with an assertion that nothing could have been done to prevent the failure.

- *Justifications* involve accepting responsibility for the event but redefining the event as not a failure.

- *Denials* are statements that the failure event never took place.

- *Absence of an account,* or *silence,* involves ignoring a reproach or refusing to address it.

In developing your account, honestly and objectively consider how much you are to blame. Adopt an other-oriented perspective by considering the reproacher's objectives, desires, and feelings so that you can understand his or her reason for reproaching you. Regardless of the legitimacy of the reproach, the person's feelings and reactions are real, and you must determine the most effective manner in which to address them. Sometimes simply admitting your failure and making a genuine effort to correct it is the best response.

Once they receive an account, reproachers must decide whether they find the account acceptable and can consider the issue resolved. When accounts are rejected, account givers often provide another account. However, rejection of accounts can escalate the failure event into an interpersonal conflict. Management of the conflict requires the skills and strategies discussed in Chapter 8.

Responding with Forgiveness. Forgiveness of a failure event or interpersonal transgression was defined by respondents in one study as a process involving accepting the event, moving on, coming to terms, getting over it, letting go of negative feelings and grudges, and continuing the relationship.[3] Intimate relationships rarely survive interpersonal transgressions that are not forgiven. Communication scholars Vincent Waldron and Douglas Kelley suggest taking these seven steps to achieve forgiveness.[4]

1. *Confront the transgression:* The failure event and hurt must be acknowledged by both partners.

2. *Manage emotion:* Emotions must be acknowledged, expressed, and accepted by both partners.

account. Response to a reproach.

3. *Engage in sense making:* Both partners need to understand and empathize. Ideally, the wounded partner feels what the transgressor felt and understands the reasons for the transgression.

4. *Seek forgiveness:* The transgressor requests forgiveness, offers an apology, expresses regret, and acknowledges the other's hurt.

5. *Grant forgiveness:* Forgiveness can be immediate or conditional. To manage the wounded partner's anguish, granting forgiveness can be viewed as a gift or a show of mercy.

6. *Negotiate values and rules.* Both partners need to clarify, negotiate, and renew commitment to relevant relational rules and morals.

7. *Transition, monitor, maintain, or renegotiate.* Time is needed to re-establish trust while readjusting to the pre-transgression state. Continue review and renegotiation of rules as needed.

"I don't want your apology -- I want you to be sorry."

Each step addresses an important part of the forgiveness process, and some can be further broken down. Whether forgiveness is achieved is ultimately dependent on such factors as personality (including the ability to empathize), the quality of the relationship, the nature of the transgression (its severity), and the perceived intention and selfishness of the transgressor.

Responding with Retaliation. Instead of a reproach, failure events might be met with retaliation. Retaliation involves an attempt to hurt the partner in response to the hurt she or he has caused—to "even the score." For example, an act of infidelity can motivate a partner to even the score by also being unfaithful. We might want our partner to feel the same degree of hurt that we felt, thus creating a sense of equity and balance. We might also retaliate to convey how hurt we are, to regain some power, and to discourage future transgressions. Retaliation behaviours can include aggressive communication (yelling, accusing, and sarcasm); active distancing (giving the partner the silent treatment or withholding affection); manipulation attempts (evoking the transgressor's jealousy or guilt, or testing his or her loyalty); contacting a rival; and violence.

Physical Separation and Distance

The mobility of today's population means that we are often moving away or being separated for a time from people with whom we have formed interpersonal relationships. We tend to think of long-distance relationships primarily as dating relationships. However, you probably have or will have long-distance relationships with your parents, spouse, children, siblings, and other family members; with friends; and even with co-workers or clients. Each long-distance relationship requires specific maintenance strategies in order to be successfully managed. In addition, more people are meeting and developing long-distance relationships online. Long-distance relationships vary in terms of expected length of separation, length of time between face-to-face visits, and the actual distance between the partners.

The Nature of the Separation. How often partners are able to get together face to face also determines the impact of the physical distance. Think about your own experience of being in a long-distance relationship: Was it the number of kilometres between you or the frequency

Technology and social media make it easier for couples in long-distance relationships to communicate effectively.
(© bloomua/Shutterstock)

of getting together that had the most impact? Today, the impact of physical separation is lessened by technology and social media. Couples can share their thoughts and feelings through email, texting, and Facebook, and they can even communicate "face to face" through the use of applications such as Skype and FaceTime.

Costs and Rewards. In Chapter 9, social exchange theory (analysis of rewards and costs) was used to explain our decision to escalate or de-escalate a relationship. It also offers a way to analyze the survival of long-distance relationships. Distance introduces added costs to maintaining a relationship, including actual monetary costs such as long-distance phone charges and expenses involved in commuting (for gasoline, airline tickets, food), as well as the expenditure of time spent commuting to see a partner and the disruption of normal routines (leaving less time available for other activities). These costs are weighed against the benefits or rewards of the relationship. The rewards depend on what you are seeking in the relationship. Obviously, if you are looking for a relationship that meets physical needs and need for affection, a permanent long-distance relationship would probably be unsatisfactory. On the other hand, if your need is for a confidant and you don't require face-to-face interactions, a long-distance arrangement might be acceptable. Or, if you perceive the costs as investments rather than losses, you might sustain your commitment to the relationship.[5] Some relationships continue for a lifetime, even with little face-to-face time, because the rewards of interacting far exceed any costs.

Tensions Created by Long-Distance Relationships. Tensions sometimes arise when one person is trying to maintain both long-distance relationships and proximal relationships. For example, the autonomy that a long-distance relationship affords provides more time for proximal relationships with others. Visits by long-distance partners can put strains on proximal partners if the two sets of friends don't get along, or if they vie for the mutual friend's time together during those visits. Long-distance couples also create tensions by over-planning their time together so that they don't feel they've wasted their time.

Minimizing idealization and maintaining communication are probably the most important factors in sustaining strong relationships, even over long distances. The more open and honest you can keep the communication, the more similar your long-distance relationships will be to proximal ones.

Relationships That Challenge Social Norms

Each culture establishes certain norms about what are appropriate and inappropriate relationships, based on social values, biases, and prejudices. Among the types of relationships often discouraged are those between people of different races, religions, or ethnicities. In addition, many societies have social mores against romantic relationships between individuals who differ significantly in age or who are of the same sex. When norms are violated, partners face social pressure to conform or risk being ostracized. Fortunately, norms change, and in Canada the number of relational restrictions have decreased in the last 30 years; nonetheless, developing any of these types of relationships still presents challenges.

Partners in intercultural relationships face the challenge of communicating and interacting effectively, as discussed in Chapter 4. They may also confront bias against the relationship itself. One aspect of many of these relationships is the clash between in-groups and out-groups. The social or cultural group that one identifies as belonging to is referred to as one's **in-group**;

in-group. A social or cultural group to which one identifies as belonging.

Building Your Skills   Forgiveness

How forgiving a person are you? The following scale was developed to assess forgiving personalities. Be honest and objective in assessing your own behaviours. Indicate the degree to which you agree or disagree with each of the statements using the following scale:

1 _ _ _ _ _ _ _ _ _ _ _ _ 2 _ _ _ _ _ _ _ _ _ 3 _ _ _ _ _ _ _ _ _ _ 4 _ _ _ _ _ _ _ _ _ _ 5 _ _ _ _ _ _ _ _ _ 6 _ _ _ _ _ _ _ _ 7

Strongly Disagree   **Neutral/Mixed**   **Strongly Agree**

_____ 1A. I can forgive a friend for almost anything.

_____ 2A. I try to forgive others even when they don't feel guilty for what they did.

_____ 3A. I can usually forgive and forget an insult.

_____ 4A. I have always forgiven those who have hurt me.

_____ 5A. I am a forgiving person.

_____ Total of A items

_____ 1B. People close to me probably think I hold a grudge too long.

_____ 2B. If someone treats me badly, I treat him or her the same.

_____ 3B. I feel bitter about many of my relationships.

_____ 4B. Even after I forgive someone, things often come back to me that I resent.

_____ 5B. There are some things for which I would never forgive even a loved one.

_____ Total of B items

(A Total) _____ minus (–) (B Total)_____ = _____

The possible totals on this scale range from +30 to –30, with 0 being the midpoint. The more positive your total, the more likely you are to be a forgiving person. Examine your lower scores for the A items. Which ones could be improved? Examine your higher scores for the B items. What can you do to change those?

Source: Republished with permission of John Wiley & Sons, Inc., from J. W. Berry, E. Worthington, L. O'Connor, L. Parrott, and N. Wade, "Forgiveness, Vengeful Rumination and Affective Traits", *Journal of Personality,* 73 (2005): 183–225; permission conveyed through Copyright Clearance Center, Inc.

these can include ethnic groups, religious groups, and cliques or groups of friends. People are considered part of an in-group whenever they view themselves as such. Those who are not part of this group are part of an **out-group**.

Those outside a norm-challenging relationship might see the relationship as a threat to their respective race or ethnic group (whether they are part of the in-group or the out-group). The more different the interloper is perceived to be, the greater the threat and negative reactions.[6] For example, Catholics might feel more hostility toward a Jewish-Catholic couple than toward a Lutheran-Catholic one. Those outside the relationship have difficulty understanding the attraction between the partners and might minimize it as simply motivated by the appeal of "forbidden fruit." In contrast, those in the relationship obviously have a different perspective. They can see their differences as an opportunity to learn both about others and about themselves; and they focus on the similarities in their values and personal characteristics rather than on differences.

Romantic gay and lesbian relationships are increasingly accepted in Canada. According to the 2011 census, there are 64 575 same-sex couples in Canada, up 42.4% over 2006 and almost double the total in 2001. Of those, 21 015 were

In 2003, Ontario's Michael Stark and Michael Leshner became the first same-sex couple in Canada to legally marry. They were named the Canadian Newsmakers of the Year by *Time* magazine.
(© Michael Stuparyk/GetStock.com)

out-group. A social or cultural group different from one's own.

Building Your Skills   Friends with a Difference

Think of someone you know from each of the following group: (a) someone at least 10 years older than you are; (b) someone from a country where people speak a different language than you do; (c) someone of a different sexual orientation; (d) someone of a different race; (e) someone of a different religion.

1. With which of these people is communication easiest? Why?

2. With which of these people is communication hardest? Why?

3. How do family and friends react to this relationship? Why?

4. How have differences affected your interpersonal communication in each friendship?

5. How does this friendship compare with friendships with those who are similar to you?

married couples. On July 20, 2005, Canada became the first North American country to legalize same-sex marriage nationwide. The 2011 census—the first to capture five years of data after same-sex marriage was legalized in Canada in 2005—shows that the number of same-sex married couples nearly tripled between 2006 and 2011, rising from 7500 to 21 000.[7]

The Dark Side of Interpersonal Communication and Relationships

The "dark side" of interpersonal communication is the use of interpersonal communication in damaging, unethical ways. Throughout the text we have focused primarily on how interpersonal communication can be used for developing fulfilling relationships, for managing conflict cooperatively, for improving relationships, and for helping you meet your interpersonal needs. However, interpersonal communication can also be used to deceive and hurt people. Regrettably, the dark side of interpersonal communication and relationships is more prevalent than you might think; for example, studies focusing on deception have found that it is pervasive in interpersonal interactions.[8] There is a dark side to relationships as well, including obsessive relational intrusion, stalking, jealousy, and relational violence.

Deception

You wake up to discover you've overslept, but because an absence would hurt your grade, you come to class late and tell the instructor that you had car trouble. Your roommate is going on a date wearing an outfit that you think is nice—but not on her; when asked what you think, you say "I've always liked that outfit," omitting the fact that you don't think it suits her. You are developing a close physical relationship with someone but choose not to disclose the number or extent of your previous sexual relationships.

Each of these scenarios represents a situation in which there is deception, but the impact and seriousness of the deceptions differ. One way to assess the seriousness is to ask yourself, "What would happen if the other person discovered my deception?" Your instructor and your roommate might be upset, but deceiving them would probably not have the same impact as falsely declaring your love or not disclosing your sexual activity to a partner. Communication scholar Mark Knapp divides lies into two categories: low-stake lies and high-stake lies.[9] The size of the stake represents how much might be gained by the deception and how much would be lost if the lie were detected. The lie to the instructor, the roommate, and one's Facebook friends are low-stake lies, while not revealing previous sexual activity might be considered a high-stake lie.

Interpersonal deception theory, as developed by Judee Burgoon and David Buller, is an explanation of deception and detection as processes affected by the transactional nature of interpersonal interactions.[10] A number of factors influence the process, including the context, the relationship, communication skills, suspicion, and expectations. Individuals intentionally and strategically manipulate information to achieve some goal; their audience listens and evaluates the truthfulness of the information. In other words, one person tries to get away with a lie and the other person decides whether to believe it or not. To avoid being caught, deceivers need to implement effective deception strategies and monitor listeners' responses. Listeners might accept the deception without pause, express skepticism, or blatantly challenge the deception. Each listener reaction lets the deceiver know his or her next course of action. Think about the last time you deceived someone. To what degree did you alter your strategy because of the context, the relationship, or the likely suspicion of your partner? When a listener questions your statements, you might act indignant, restate your claim more forcefully, or add more convincing evidence. Of course, you might also come clean and admit your lie.

Creating a deceptive Facebook profile might not be as serious as deceiving your parents about what websites you visit.
(© Blue Moon Stock/Superstock)

Deception by Omission (Concealment). Deception by omission (concealment) involves intentionally holding back some of the information another person has requested or that you are expected to share. For example, your parents ask where you were last night, and you reply that you went to the movies. While that is true, you don't tell your parents that you also went to a party at a friend's house afterward. You have not "lied," but you have been deceptive. Determining whether an omission is deceptive depends on the intention of the deceiver. What was your reason for omitting the information about the party? Were you attempting to avoid your parents' response, or did you simply forget?

We can also present information and leave out information so as to intentionally mislead the listener. For example, telling your roommate "I've always liked that outfit" is intended to create the impression that you think the outfit is attractive on her. This deception provides you some protection if you are later called to task by your roommate for not saying the outfit looked bad. You can reply, "I never said it looked good on you." Despite your claim, your roommate would know your intention was to deceive. These types of omissions are sometimes called "half-truths," because the statements themselves are truthful, but they are not the complete truth.

Another form of deception by omission demonstrates how deceptions can be failure events. You may fail to share information that you know you should provide to another person because of relational expectations. For example, knowing that your best friend's fiancée has been having an affair but not telling your friend about it is deception by omission. Your friend's discovery that you didn't share the information is likely to create a conflict, because he will no doubt believe you owed it to him to share your "secret." Deception by omission can undermine decision making; for example, not disclosing sexual history prevents one's partner from making informed decisions about the level of risk he or she might be encountering.[11] While omitting information is not usually considered as grievous as falsifying information,[12] when the omitted information is important, omission is viewed as just as deceptive as falsifying.[13]

Deception by Commission. Deception by commission is the deliberate presentation of false information—lying. Among the types of deception by commission are white lies,

interpersonal deception theory. An explanation of deception and detection as processes affected by the transactional nature of interpersonal interactions.

deception by omission (concealment). Intentionally holding back some of the information another person has requested or that you are expected to share.

deception by commission. Deliberate presentation of false information.

© Roy Delgado/CartoonStock

"Give it to me straight, Doc - unless a lie would be better."

exaggeration or embellishment, and bald-faced lies. **White lies** typically involve only a slight degree of falsification that has a minimal consequence. Calling these deceptions "white lies" seems to make us feel a little less guilty. Your listing on Facebook of bands as favourites when they are not would probably be considered a white lie. Sometimes we use **exaggeration**— "stretching the truth" or embellishing the facts. Telling someone you were at the library for a couple of hours when it was only 20 minutes is an exaggeration, and a lie. Most of us have stories we've told over and over that continue to become more embellished as we tell them. **Baldfaced lies** are outright falsifications of information intended to deceive the listener. Baldfaced lies have more impact on the behaviour of those who hear them than white lies or exaggeration. The emotional impact of such deception is related to the importance of the relationship, the importance of the information, and the importance of honesty to the people involved. The potential negative impacts explain why we are less likely to lie to our best friends than we are to strangers.

Reasons for Deception. While there are a variety of reasons people are deceptive, those reasons can be placed into two general categories: altruistic and self-serving. Altruistic motivation is a common reason we lie to a close friend. Our concerns about hurting other people may lead us to lie to protect them—for example, not telling a roommate her outfit is unbecoming. On the other hand, we might deceive others because we either gain personally through the deception or avoid some undesirable consequence. Not being truthful with the instructor about why you were late to class is an attempt to avoid a negative consequence. In general, we lie more to strangers and acquaintances than to friends, and those lies are more likely to be for personal gain or exploitation, whereas relatively more of our lies to friends are altruistic or other-centred.[14] The two categories of altruistic and self-serving lies include a number of specific reasons for deception.

1. *To gain resources.* Deception might help you acquire material resources, such as money or property. You might also use deception to achieve intangible goals, such as fostering a relationship or bolstering your self-esteem. Perhaps you intend the bands you falsely list as favourites on Facebook to make you more attractive.

2. *To avoid harm or loss of resources.* Deception may be used to prevent another person's negative reaction or to protect resources. For example, if an angry friend suspected you had broken her computer, you might lie if you were afraid she would damage something of yours in retaliation or that she would ask you to pay for repairs. Or you might avoid having to give up your free time by lying to a friend about not being able to help her move over the weekend.

3. *To protect one's self-image.* Most people attempt to present or maintain a certain image that they think others will find desirable, and people will lie if they fear their actions undermine that image. For instance, you might always be late for appointments, but

white lies. Deception by commission involving only a slight degree of falsification that has a minimal consequence.

exaggeration. Deception by commission involving "stretching the truth" or embellishing the facts.

baldfaced lies. Deception by commission involving outright falsification of information intended to deceive the listener.

you don't want people to think you are habitually late, so you lie about what made you late.

4. *For entertainment.* Teasing can be a form of deception if we tell other people things that aren't true. "I heard that Billy has a crush on you—not!" The reason for this kind of deception is to laugh at the other person's reaction.

5. *To protect another person's resources, self-image, or safety.* If you believe that certain information is harmful to another person, you might choose to keep it secret or to falsify it. In lying to protect friends from what you view as "harmful truths," you need to be honest with yourself about whether your deception is really for their benefit. Is saying "I love you" when you don't really love someone a way to avoid hurting the person— or is it a way to avoid facing conflict and threats to your resources?

Effects of Deception. While at times deception seems to be acceptable because of the benefits it provides, it can obviously also cause harm, and there are fundamental ethical questions about dishonesty. Harm can be the direct result of the deception, or it can result when deception is detected or uncovered. Here are some of the more obvious ways deception can be harmful:

1. *Leading to incorrect decisions or actions.* If false information is used in decision making, then a person may take the wrong course of action.

2. *Harming relationships.* A significant impact of deception is to harm relationships, particularly if the deception is detected; it might even lead to termination of the relationship.

3. *Loss of trust.* Trust is a fundamental element of relationships, and once deception has been detected in a relationship, it may be hard for partners to regain trust. Repeated deception and detection may result in one person assuming that anything the other person says is a lie.

4. *Harming innocent bystanders.* Lies often have a ripple effect, whereby other people (innocent bystanders) are harmed.

5. *Additional harm.* Other negative consequences of deception include punishment, embarrassment, a guilty conscience, and a damaged reputation.[15]

The closer the relationship, the more effective people become at recognizing their partners' deceptions. However, expressing suspicion can also signal inherent distrust in a partner. Interestingly, the closer the relationship, the more people know what cues their partners are suspicious of, and therefore the better equipped they are to adapt and avoid detection of their deception. Deception occurs in all our relationships. We are both instigators and recipients of deception. Ethically, you should strive for honest relationships, and it would be nice to believe you could be totally honest all the time. However, honesty can be harmful too, so you are faced with weighing the harms of honesty against the harms of deception. The survival of your interpersonal relationships depends on your ability to effectively manage the challenge of deception.

Communication That Hurts Feelings

When people discover that they have been deceived, they usually feel betrayed, foolish, angry, and/or hurt. But deception is only one way in which we hurt people's feelings. As we discussed earlier, the truth can hurt, too. One of the more powerful aspects of language is that it

What we say and how we say it can hurt other people's feelings, especially those of family members or romantic partners.
(© Gary Conner/PhotoEdit)

active verbal responses. Reactive statements made in response to a hurtful message.

acquiescent responses. Crying, conceding, or apologizing in response to a hurtful message.

invulnerable responses. Ignoring, laughing, or being silent in response to a hurtful message.

envy. A feeling of discontent arising from a desire for something someone else has.

jealousy. Reaction to the threat of losing a valued relationship.

cognitive jealousy. Thoughts about the loss of a partner, reflections on decreases in the partner's time for the other, and analyses of behaviours or occurrences deemed suspicious.

emotional or affective jealousy. Feelings of anger, hurt, distrust, worry, or concern aroused by the threat of losing a relationship.

behavioural jealousy. Actions taken to monitor or alter a partner's jealousy-evoking activity.

can be used to cause emotional pain. We can be hurt by insults, criticism, or teasing about our appearance, personality, intelligence, abilities, ethnicity, relationships, or sexual behaviour.

Disconfirming responses (discussed in Chapter 5) are one type of message that hurts listeners by undermining their sense of self-esteem, even when that is not the speaker's intention. When we receive a hurtful message, such as a disconfirming response, we try to determine the speaker's intention. The intention affects how hurt we feel. A heartfelt apology can help alleviate another person's hurt when we've said something casually that had an unintended effect: "I'm sorry, I didn't mean it the way it sounded."

Research by Anita Vangelisti and Linda Crumley identified three general categories of reactions to messages that hurt.[16] The first category, **active verbal responses**, includes reactive statements made by the hurt person, such as counterattacks, self-defence statements, sarcastic comments, and demands for explanations. The second category includes crying, conceding, or apologizing, which are considered **acquiescent responses**. Finally, **invulnerable responses** such as ignoring the message, laughing, or being silent are attempts to show that the message did not hurt. Of course, in addition to responding verbally, we are also reacting emotionally, such as by displaying anger after being criticized.[17]

Among their other findings on hurtful messages, Vangelisti and Crumley found that people are more hurt by messages from family members than from nonfamily members and that romantic relationships are more damaged by hurtful messages than either family or nonromantic, nonfamily relationships.[18] In romantic relationships, honest but hurtful messages about the relationship were found to be more hurtful than messages about a person's personality, appearance, or behaviours.[19] Such relationally oriented messages tended to threaten receivers' face, probably because such statements implied the potential loss of the relationship.[20] How the message is conveyed also affects its impact, with harsh, abrasive messages creating greater hurt.[21]

Hurtful messages are probably unavoidable in interpersonal relationships, but how you respond to and manage the impact of those messages affects the level of satisfaction and happiness you feel in your relationships. When you are the recipient of a hurtful message, you should let the speaker know that your feelings are hurt and ask the person to clarify the reasons for making such a statement. The speaker might not realize that the message was hurtful.

A strong other-orientation is needed to monitor the impact of your messages on other people. Generally, your understanding of the other person can help you select the best strategy for presenting a potentially hurtful message and the best time to deliver the message.

Jealousy is a feeling that arises when we fear a relationship is in doubt, and the feeling can lead to jealous behaviour.

(© Mircea Netval/Shutterstock)

Jealousy

If you have ever wished that you drove as nice a car or received grades as high as those of one of your classmates, then you have experienced envy. **Envy** is a discontented feeling that arises from a desire for something someone else has. But if you have been upset because one of your good friends was spending more time working than hanging out with you, or because your boyfriend or girlfriend showed interest in another person, then you have experienced jealousy. **Jealousy** is a reaction to the threat of losing a valued relationship.[22] The future of the relationship is in doubt and the partner's loyalty is questioned.[23] Jealousy manifests itself in our thoughts, feelings, and behaviours. **Cognitive jealousy** includes thoughts about the loss of your partner, reflections on decreases in your partner's time with you, and analyses of behaviours or occurrences deemed suspicious. **Emotional or affective jealousy** includes the feelings of anger, hurt, distrust, worry, or concern aroused by the threat of losing the relationship. **Behavioural jealousy** represents actions taken to monitor or alter a partner's jealousy-evoking activity, such as watching your partner obsessively at social gatherings, telling a partner to stop flirting, or secretly checking a partner's texts, emails, or Facebook posts.

Sometimes concern about loss of the relationship arises because of the presence of a third party, but it can also result from outside factors that jeopardize the relationship—the partner turning to others for advice, loss of influence over the partner to someone else, or a partner's spending more time on hobbies, school, or work. Jealousy presents a paradox in that, on one hand, it represents a strong display of interest and love, but on the other hand, it represents paranoia and lack of trust.[24] Sometimes people are flattered by another's jealousy and even seek to evoke it to confirm the value of a relationship. At other times, jealousy is seen as a statement of possessiveness and restriction. Interestingly, the two partners in a relationship usually have contrasting emotional reactions to the jealousy. For the person feeling jealous, the potential loss of the relationship creates fear, anger, and sadness.[25] The person's partner might also feel fearful and angry, but may also feel a wide variety of other emotions, including being amused, flattered, mistrustful, baffled, condescending, upset, or put off.

Using Jealousy as a Tactic. You can probably think of several TV shows or movies in which one character tries to make some other character jealous. The reasons for evoking jealousy are primarily for relational rewards (such as to test the strength of the relationship, to bolster one's self-esteem, or to improve the relationship) or to gain relational revenge (teaching the partner a lesson or punishing the partner).[26] Among the tactics people use to make another person jealous are "distancing" (being too busy to get together; excluding the other from plans, activities, and other friends; or ignoring the other person); "flirtation facade" (sending oneself flowers, posting pictures of oneself with others on social media, or expressing attraction to or sexual interest in another); and "relational alternatives" (letting your partner know you are thinking about other relationships by talking about past relationships, present relationships, or other people).[27]

The use of jealousy as a tactic to improve a relationship by getting the partner to pay more attention to you or display greater commitment is risky. Discovering that you intentionally evoked his or her jealousy could be viewed by your partner as manipulative and create defensiveness (as discussed in Chapter 6).

Managing Jealousy. Concern about the possible loss of or a significant change in a relationship is neither inappropriate nor unusual. For example, the discovery or assumption that a friend is spending more time on some other interest implicitly disconfirms us—the object of the friend's attention is more important than we are. While one person might simply accept the situation, another person might feel jealousy. The arousal of jealousy suggests a need for more information. Directly discussing the situation with the partner and asking for an explanation tends to evoke a more positive response than spying or seeking information from a third party.[28] A jealous partner must decide whether to even raise the issue, depending on whether he or she is interested in relational repair. How someone expresses feelings of jealousy directly affects the partner's response. Calmly expressing feelings, presenting oneself in a positive manner, and expressing caring are viewed more positively than displays of violence, being insulting or threatening, or confronting a rival.[29] Expressing jealousy arouses uncertainty about the jealous partner, particularly when the jealousy is expressed indirectly through crying or acting hurt or depressed.[30]

Unwanted Attention

When a person we are attracted to is no longer attracted to us, most of us move on. Our dependence on a partner in a close relationship might lead us to express some resistance to his or her decision to terminate the relationship, but eventually we accept the decision. Unfortunately, some individuals do not give up when another person fails to reciprocate their attraction, has no interest in a relationship, or desires to terminate a relationship. These

A person who feels stalked experiences concern for her or his personal safety and fear of unwelcome intrusions.
(© Brand X/Superstock)

individuals might engage in obsessive behaviours, trying to form or to continue a relationship. In some instances, such pursuit is simply annoying, but at its extreme, it arouses well-founded fears for personal safety.

Obsessive relational intrusion (ORI) is the term used by communication scholars William Cupach and Brian Spitzberg to describe situations in which a stranger or acquaintance who desires or assumes a close relationship with another person repeatedly invades the other person's privacy.[31] In other words, someone wants a relationship with someone else who doesn't. Unlike stalking, ORI is usually annoying and frustrating but not threatening.[32] Obsessive relational intrusion is marked by such behaviours as unregulated self-disclosing; trying to get the other person to disclose; offering unwanted gifts, notes, calls, and other expressions of affection; arranging coincidental meetings; and expressing a desire for physical contact.[33]

There is a fine line between trying to hang on to or pursue a relationship and becoming obsessive. With ORI, normal relationship development behaviours become exaggerated and are pursued obsessively, making the change from non-intrusive to intrusive difficult to pinpoint.[34] Thus, it is the repeated and sustained display of these behaviours after rejection that indicates ORI. In addition, we often negotiate relationships through indirect and implicit ways, increasing the likelihood that one partner will misunderstand the other's intentions and interest. For instance, the ambiguity of non-verbal messages could cause your smile to be seen as an invitation for interaction rather than as a general expression of your happy mood, leading someone, even a stranger, to initiate an unwanted approach and attempt to establish a relationship. Confusion about relational goals and definitions can lead your partner to think the relationship is more intimate than you do. Such confusion can result in intrusions on your privacy. Clearly discuss your goals, interests, and desires, as well as the nature of the relationship to help clarify these confusions, and seek understanding of your partner's perspective.

Stalking involves repeated, unwelcome intrusions that create concern for personal safety and fear in the target.[35] It can be thought of as an extreme form of ORI, though sometimes stalking is motivated by revenge and not the pursuit of a relationship.[36] Stalking is an instance of the dark side of interpersonal communication, in which unwanted communication—in the form of phone calls, texts, social media postings, face-to-face meetings, letters, and emails—is used to instill fear. Stalking appears more prevalent on college and university campuses than among the general public; studies show that almost 30% of males and females surveyed feel they have been stalked.[37] Possible reasons for this prevalence are the lack of social and relational skills in young adults and the close proximity and sharing of space that occur on college and university campuses.

Unfortunately, there is no absolutely safe and effective way to end such behaviours, but Spitzberg and Cupach offer three recommendations for addressing ORI and stalking, based on advice from other scholars and professionals:[38]

1. *Harden the target.* "Hardening the target" involves making it harder for someone to contact you or invade your space. For example, you might change your phone number, rent a post office mail box, change locks, eliminate access information on Facebook, and/or install a security system.

2. *Keep others apprised.* You should inform family, friends, co-workers, employers, school administrators, and law enforcement officials of your situation. Also, consider informing

obsessive relational intrusion (ORI). Repeated invasion of a person's privacy by a stranger or acquaintance who desires or assumes a close relationship.

stalking. Repeated, unwelcome intrusions that create concern for personal safety and fear in the target.

Electronically mediated communication (EMC) has many positive benefits, as we've noted: EMC allows us to quickly and easily stay in touch with our friends, colleagues, family members, and other people we love. But EMC messages can have a dark side. If personal or private information about you becomes known to others, it can be used to embarrass you or create significant negative financial consequences. And spending too much time in EMC can have a negative impact on your face-to-face relationships.

We may easily forget that some emails and social media posts can be viewed by other people. This means that information about you can be accessed not just by family members or potential employers, but also by people with darker motivations, which is why there is a growing concern about teenagers and young adults posting information on social media sites, as well as circulating cell phone pictures and videos.

Online harassment can come from people you know well, people you know only slightly, or complete strangers. After ending a relationship, a person might be subjected to repeated unwanted phone calls, text messages, or posts on their Facebook wall from the former partner.

These unwanted messages might simply be pleas for reconciliation, or they might involve threats of relational violence. Other disturbing uses of EMC include circulating intimate, private, or false information (including photos) about an individual sending viruses or hacking into other people's computers; and posing as someone else online.

Recently, Canadians were shocked by the suicides of two young girls who had been the victims of "cyberbullying." In 2012, 15-year-old Amanda Todd, of British Columbia, was found dead after being bullied and physically assaulted after she was blackmailed into exposing her breasts online via webcam. Less than one year later, 17-year-old Rehtaeh Parsons, of Nova Scotia, hanged herself after months of bullying and harassment related to the online circulation of sexually explicit photos and video of her alleged gang rape.

The best way to handle online harassment and bullying is to be smart about how you use EMC. Here are some tips to consider:

- Use an alias and not your real name when posting in online forums.

- Limit the amount of personal information you include in your social networking profiles.

- Be smart about the passwords you use; nonsense combinations are best, since hackers have software that allows them to test long lists of actual words.

- Be cautious about the photos that you share online, and be aware when others may be photographing you. Ask your friends not to share photos online without your permission.

- If you are faced with EMC harassment, provide a clear and assertive statement that you do *not* want to be contacted, and keep copies of any messages you receive.

- Inform your Internet service provider, and consider changing your Internet address or service provider.

- Since many of these harassing behaviours are illegal, it may also be appropriate to report the incidents to law enforcement agencies. See the *Canadian Connections* box in this chapter for more details.

---

people in other places you frequent (a gym, grocery store, restaurant, or bar). Let everyone know that you don't want contact with the person and provide photos of the person if possible.

3. *Avoid.* After telling the intruder or stalker to leave you alone, you should avoid any further contact. Don't answer calls, don't respond to emails or texts, ignore any approaches the person might make—don't interact. Your actions need to support your insistence that the relationship is over.

In terms of privacy, electronically mediated communication allows users some protection of privacy. Fifty-eight percent of social network users report setting their main profile to private, with women being more private (67 percent) than men (48 percent).[39] Younger users and women are more active than their counterparts in unfriending others, deleting comments, and untagging photos—thus increasing their control of privacy.[40] However, 48 percent of all users indicate difficulty in managing the privacy controls. And people to whom we give access can still engage in surveillance, ranging from checking in on us to obsessively monitoring our Facebook page, online postings, pictures, and so on.[41] In addition to invading our privacy, such surveillance can arouse jealousy and conflict in a romantic partner who is upset by the messages or photos posted on your page.

Relational Violence

Relational violence can occur in any relationship—with a spouse, a dating partner, children, family members, friends, or co-workers. Unlike acts of violence against unknown individuals, relational violence occurs within the context of an ongoing relationship and is sometimes a defining characteristic or dynamic of the relationship.[42]

The term *violence* often connotes physical harm inflicted on another person, but we will use the term **relational violence** to refer to the full range of destructive behaviours aimed at other people, including aggressiveness, threats, violent acts, and verbal, psychological, and physical abuse. At the extreme, relational violence involves forceful acts against another person. But hitting your fist through a plaster wall in rage during an argument is certainly a violent act, even though the partner is not directly abused. The act still instills fear, and the violence it represents can escalate.

Sociologist Michael Johnson separates partner violence into three types:[43]

1. *Intimate terrorism:* Using violence to control or dominate

2. *Violent resistance:* Meeting attempts at control with a violent response

3. *Situational couple violence:* Responding with violence to a specific relational conflict or tension

Males are responsible for almost all intimate terrorism, females for violent resistance, and both men and women engage in situational couple violence, which is probably the most frequently occurring form of relational violence.[44] The presence of intimate terrorism will most likely lead to the abused partner's leaving the relationship, whereas incidents of situational couple violence are usually not so severe as to end the relationship.[45]

Sadly, acts of relational violence are a form of communication—the dark side of communication. Acts of relational violence communicate anger, frustration, lack of control, and disregard for a partner and the relationship, while instilling fear and engendering retaliation, counterattacks, and subversion. The results of a study of males participating in a domestic violence program found that compared with nonviolent males, violent males engaged in more name calling, criticizing, blaming, swearing, ridiculing, and mutual verbal aggression with their partners.[46] Patterns of negative communication, ineffective conflict management and problem-solving skills, and lack of good argumentation skills all appear to contribute to an individual's propensity for relational violence. Avoiding relational violence is a strong reason for improving interpersonal communication skills. Relational violence is never acceptable,

relational violence. Range of destructive behaviours aimed at other people, including aggressiveness, threats, violent acts, and verbal, psychological, or physical abuse.

▶ RECAP   The Dark Side of Interpersonal Communication and Relationships

Deception	Using communication to deceive through false or misleading information.
Deception by Omission	Holding back information so as to leave an incorrect impression with a listener.
Deception by Commission	Deliberately presenting false information in such forms as white lies, exaggeration, or baldfaced lies.
Communication That Hurts Feelings	Causing pain to others either intentionally or unintentionally, by such means as offering unwelcome or negative information or criticizing traits or abilities.
Obsessive Relational Intrusion	Repeatedly invading a person's privacy out of a desire for or assumption of a close relationship with the other person.
Stalking	Making repeated, unwelcome intrusions that create concern for personal safety and fear in the target.
Jealousy	Reacting to the threat of losing a valued relationship.
Relational Violence	Engaging in a range of destructive behaviours aimed at other people, including aggression, threats, violent acts, and verbal, psychological, and physical abuse.

nor is it the fault of the victim; do not accept relational violence as a condition of your relationships. If you find yourself either the victim or the perpetrator of relational violence, you should seek professional help. An online search will direct you to numerous help agencies.

Relationship De-Escalation and Termination

All relationships experience challenges, ranging from minor ones such as petty fighting when you are tired to major ones such as lying, jealousy, and cheating in a romantic relationship. The inability to effectively manage relational challenges can contribute to the de-escalation or even termination of a relationship. For example, how likely would you be to continue a relationship after discovering that your partner had deceived you? Once a deception has been uncovered, relationships are more likely to be terminated when the offender can be avoided and there is a lack of overall communication.[47] When you pick up signals of relational problems, you have three choices: you can wait and see what happens, make a decision to redefine or end the relationship, or try to repair the relationship.

Signs of Relationship Problems

Part of effective relationship management involves being sensitive to cues that signal relational problems or change. As the *Understanding Diversity* box "Gender and Ending Relationships" indicates, women usually sense trouble in a relationship earlier than do men—but what exactly do they sense? Because each stage in a relationship has unique communication qualities, specific verbal and nonverbal cues can tip us off when a relationship begins to de-escalate.[48] There is a decrease in touching and physical contact (including less sexual activity), physical proximity, eye contact, smiling, vocal variety in the voice, and ease of interaction. In addition, there is a decrease in the amount of time spent together, an increase in time between interactions, and more separation of possessions. The interactions become less personal, and so does the language.

John Gottman, who studied couples for over 20 years, identified four categories of communication behaviour that indicate increasing problems in a marriage.[49] These behaviours undermine effective communication between couples and can lead to the end of the relationship. The first warning sign is criticism of, or attacks on, the other person's personality. The second sign is the display of contempt through insults and psychological abuse. The third sign is defensive behaviour such as denying responsibility, making excuses, whining, and counter-complaining. The final communication behaviour that undermines a marriage is stonewalling, in which the partners withdraw, quit responding to each other, and become minimally engaged in the relationship. Among the four, stonewalling is the single best predictor of divorce. If all four signs are consistently present, there is a 94% chance that

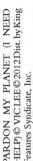

PARDON MY PLANET (I NEED HELP) © VIC LEE © 2012 Dist. by King Features Syndicate, Inc.

IT'S NOT YOU, IT'S ME. I HAVE HORRIBLE TASTE IN MEN.

Is Cyberbullying Against the Law?

(© Comstock Images/Stockbyte/Getty Images)

It is an offence under Canada's *Criminal Code* to share intimate images of a person without the consent of the person in the image. This offence came into force on March 10, 2015. This law applies to everyone, not just people under 18. The purpose of this offence is to protect the privacy a person has in his or her nudity or sexual activity.

With digital technology rapidly changing, there has been an increase of cyberbullying in the form of distributing intimate or sexual images without the consent of the person in the photo or video.

This type of behaviour can occur in a variety of situations. Often it appears to be a form of revenge: a person has willingly shared an intimate image of himself or herself with a boyfriend or girlfriend, and when the relationship ends, the partner may distribute those photos in what is sometimes called 'revenge porn.'

Whatever the motivation, the impact of this kind of cyberbullying can be devastating to a person's self-esteem, reputation and mental health. In some cases, these acts may have played a part in teens taking their own lives.

Judges now have the authority to order the removal of intimate images from the Internet if the images were posted without the consent of the person or persons in the image.

Anyone convicted of distributing an intimate image without consent could face serious legal consequences. For example:

- they could be imprisoned for up to five years;
- their computer, cell phone or other device used to share the image could be seized; and
- they could be ordered to reimburse the victim for costs incurred in

removing the intimate image from the Internet or elsewhere.

An "intimate image" is defined as an image that depicts a person engaged in explicit sexual activity or that depicts a sexual organ, anal region, or breast. Furthermore, the image would have to be one where there person depicted had a reasonable expectation of privacy at the time of the recording and had not relinquished his or her privacy interest at the time of the offence.

Other laws related to cyberbullying

Several other *Criminal Code* offences also deal with bullying, including cyberbullying. Depending on the exact nature of the behaviour, the following current offences could be charged:

- Criminal harassment
- Uttering threats
- Intimidation
- Mischief in relation to data
- Unauthorized use of computer
- Identity fraud
- Extortion
- False messages, indecent or harassing telephone calls
- Counselling suicide
- Incitement of hatred
- Defamatory libel

Source: What are the potential legal consequences of cyberbullying? Public Safety Canada. Retreived from http://www.getcybersafe.gc.ca/cnt/cbrbllng/prnts/lgl-cnsqncs-en.aspx#a04.

the couple will eventually divorce.[50] Most couples experience some of these behaviours, but happy couples develop effective communication patterns to overcome them.

Repair and Rejuvenation of Relationships

Repairing a relationship involves applying all the maintenance skills we talked about earlier. Some of the strategies for dealing with conflict that you learned in Chapter 8 will also help you. Underlying the success of any repair effort, however, is the degree to which both partners want to keep the relationship going. The nature of the problem, the stage of the relationship, and the commitment and motivation of the partners all affect the success of repair efforts. There is no single quick solution to relational problems because so many factors influence each one. You need to focus on the specific concerns, needs, and issues that underlie the problem, then adapt specific strategies to resolve it. Professional counselling may be an important option.

ADAPTING TO DIFFERENCES
Understanding Others

Men's and Women's Responses to Relationship Challenges

Men and women differ when it comes to dating and marital breakups. Women tend to be stronger monitors of the relationship, so they usually detect trouble before men do. Women's sensitivity to the health of the relationship may be one factor that makes them more likely to initiate the termination of a relationship as well.[1] However, when some men want out of a relationship, they engage in behaviours that women find totally unacceptable. This allows both partners to feel as if they were the ones who initiated the breakup and therefore lets them "save face."

Relationship-ending problems are sometimes associated with behaviours that appear early in a relationship. Marriages in which the men avoid interaction by stonewalling and responding defensively to complaints are more likely to end in divorce.[2]

In one study of divorce, men tended to see the later part of the process as more difficult, whereas the women said the period before the decision to divorce was more difficult. In addition, two-thirds of the women were likely to discuss marital problems with their children as compared with only one-fourth of the men; and men were twice as likely to say that no one helped them during the worst part of the process.[3]

During de-escalation, couples tend to use fewer intimate terms; they use less present tense and more past tense; make fewer references to their future in the relationship; use more qualified language ("maybe," "whatever," "we'll see"); make fewer evaluative statements; and spend less time discussing any given topic. They fight more, and they disclose less. If one person becomes less open about discussing attitudes, feelings, thoughts, and other personal issues, he or she is probably signalling a desire to terminate, or at least redefine, the relationship. Can you pick up the signals of the couple's difficulty reflected in the picture on page 252?

Notes:
1. S. W. Duck, *Understanding Relationships* (New York: Guilford Press, 1991).
2. J. M. Gottman and S. Carrere, "Why Can't Men and Women Get Along? Developmental Roots and Marital Inequities," in *Communication and Relational Maintenance*, ed. D. J. Canary and L. Stafford (San Diego: Academic Press, 1991), 203–229.
3. G. O. Hagestad and M. A. Smyer, "Dissolving Long-Term Relationships: Patterns of Divorcing in Middle Age," in *Personal Relationships 4: Dissolving Personal Relationships*, ed. S. Duck (London: Academic Press, 1982), 155–188.

What if it is your partner who wants to end the relationship? There is no pat answer for addressing this situation. If a friend stops calling or visiting, should you just assume the relationship is over and leave it alone, or should you call and ask what's up? People lose contact for myriad reasons. Sometimes it is beneficial to ask an individual directly if he or she is breaking off the relationship, although such direct requests place your self-concept on the line. How should you react if your friend confirms a desire to end the relationship? If possible, try to have a focused discussion on what has contributed to his or her decision. You might get information you need to repair the relationship. Or you might gain information that will help you in future relationships.

Another response to signs of relationship disintegration is to rejuvenate the relationship—to put new life back in it. The ability to rejuvenate a relationship depends on the degree to which partners recognize the reasons for relational decay and the level of their interest in rejuvenating the relationship. When only one partner wishes to rejuvenate the relationship, the first task becomes convincing the uninterested partner of the value of doing so. Sometimes, if the de-escalation is caused by specific behavioural problems of one partner, then commitment to changing those behaviours is one avenue for re-energizing the relationship. Because the problem behaviour represents a failure event, the partner might have to provide an account, admit failure, and ask for forgiveness. In general, rejuvenation is usually conducted through implicit moves rather than direct discussion.[51] In other words, we change our behaviours or engage in positive behaviours that we hope our partner will recognize as an effort on our part to improve the relationship. Think about times when you have made a change or put forth extra effort for friends or family members to help reduce relational tension—cutting back on your use of swear words you know your mother dislikes, studying more, doing the dishes without being asked, washing your father's car, or baking your friend some cookies. However, another problem might arise if the partner fails to recognize that you've made such efforts. Has this happened to you?

Not recognizing your effort can be another failure event: "I can't believe you didn't say anything about my doing the dishes for you." Not all efforts are implicit; having a serious relational talk, reconnecting after separating (reconciliation), accepting or forgiving a partner's transgression, and seeking outside help are other ways people report rejuvenating their relationships.[52]

The Decision to End a Relationship

If you do choose to reduce the level of intimacy in the relationship, consider your goals. Do you want to continue the relationship at a less intimate level, or terminate it altogether? Do you care enough about the other person to want to preserve his or her self-esteem? Are you aware of the costs involved in ending the relationship? There is no one correct or best way to end a relationship. Ending relationships is not something you can practise to improve. However, you can practise the effective relational management skills such as decentring and empathy, adaptation, and compliance gaining. These skills will also help you in ending relationships.

We rely on our social networks for support and self-confirmation when an intimate relationship comes to an end. Advice about how to handle the loss of a close relationship is plentiful, but each person must find a way to compensate for the loss of intimacy and companionship. The loss of an important relationship hurts, but it need not put us out of commission if we make the most of our friends and family.

The de-escalation and termination of a relationship are not inherently bad. Not all relationships are meant to endure. Ending a relationship can be a healthy move if the relationship is harmful, or if it no longer provides confirmation of the self or satisfies interpersonal needs; it also can open the door to new relationships. Sometimes we choose not to end a relationship but rather to de-escalate to a less intimate stage where there is a better balance between benefits and costs.

Breaking up an intimate relationship is hard because of the degree to which we become dependent on the other person to confirm our sense of self. When a relationship ends, we may feel as if we need to redefine who we are. The most satisfying breakups are those that confirm both partners' worth rather than degrade it. "I just can't be what you want me to be," "I'll always love you but …," and "You're a very special person, but I need other things in life" are all examples of statements that do not destroy self-esteem.

The process of ending a relationship is considerably different depending on whether only one party wants out of the relationship (unilateral) or both are agreeable to it (bilateral).[53] In a **bilateral dissolution**, both parties are predisposed to ending the relationship; they simply need to sort out details such as timing, dividing possessions, and defining conditions for the contact after the breakup. In a **unilateral dissolution**, the person who wants to end the relationship must choose a strategy (see pages 254–256) to get his or her partner to agree to the dissolution. Sometimes, however, people simply walk out of a relationship.

How Relationships End

A declining relationship usually follows one of several paths. Sometimes a relationship loses energy and runs down like a dying battery. Instead of a single event that causes the breakup, the relationship **fades away**—the two partners just drift further and further apart. They spend less time together, let more time go by between interactions, and stop disclosing much about themselves. You've probably had a number of friendships that ended this way—perhaps long-distance relationships. Because long-distance relationships require a great deal of effort to maintain, a move away can easily decrease the level of intimacy between two people.

bilateral dissolution. Ending a relationship when both parties are agreeable.

unilateral dissolution. Ending a relationship when only one party is agreeable.

fading away. Ending a relationship by slowly drifting apart.

Partners may experience one of three types of relationship termination: fading away, where the partners drift slowly apart; sudden death, where separation is immediate; or incrementalism, where the conflicts gradually build until they reach the breaking point.

(© jcjgphotography/Shutterstock)

Some relationships end in "sudden death."[54] As the name suggests, **sudden death** moves straight to separation. One partner might move away or die, or, more frequently, a single precipitating event such as infidelity, breaking a confidence, a major conflict, or some other major role violation precipitates the breakup. Sudden death is like taking an express elevator from a top floor to the basement.

Between fading away and sudden death lies incrementalism. **Incrementalism** is the process by which conflicts and problems continue to accumulate in the relationship until they reach a critical mass that leads to the breakup; the relationship becomes intolerable or, from a social exchange perspective, too costly. "It just got to a point where it wasn't worth it anymore" and "It got to the point where all we did was fight all the time" are typical statements about incremental endings.

Reasons for De-Escalating and Ending Relationships

When a relationship comes to an end, we often ask ourselves, "What happened?" "Why did the relationship come to an end?" We engage in this "post-mortem" regardless of whether we or our partner initiated the breakup. If our partner initiated the breakup and did not provide adequate explanations, we are left to wonder and guess about what happened. We may continue behaviours that undermine future relationships because we failed to understand how we contributed to the termination of the present relationship.

According to researcher Michael Cody, students' assessments of what caused their intimate heterosexual relationships to break up can be put into three categories.[55] "Faults" were cited as the number-one cause. These are personality traits or behaviours in one partner that the other partner dislikes. The number-two cause, "unwillingness to compromise," represents a variety of failings on the part of one or both partners, including failure to put enough effort into the relationship, a decrease in effort, or failure to make concessions for the good of the relationship. The final cause, "feeling constrained," reflects one partner's desire to be free of the commitments and constraints of a relationship. However, a variety of other elements can contribute to the breakup of both romantic and non romantic relationships, including loss of interest in the other person, desire for independence, and conflicting attitudes about issues affecting the relationship, such as values, sexual conduct, marriage, and infidelity.

Just as there are behavioural rules for making and maintaining friends, there are behaviours that, if you pursue them, will almost certainly cost you a friendship. Listed in order of offensiveness, they are as follows.[56]

1. Acting jealous or being critical of your relationship

2. Discussing with others what your friend said in confidence

3. Not volunteering help in time of need

4. Not trusting or confiding in your friend

5. Criticizing your friend in public

6. Not showing positive regard for your friend

7. Not standing up for your friend in his or her absence

8. Not being tolerant of your friend's other friends

9. Not showing emotional support

10. Nagging your friend

Friendships differ from romantic relationships in many ways, including the reasons for relational disintegration. When one researcher asked individuals to identify why their same-sex friendships ended, first on the list was physical separation.[57] Second, respondents

sudden death. Ending a relationship abruptly and without preparation.

incrementalism. Ending a relationship when conflicts and problems finally reach a critical mass.

reported that new friends replaced old friends as circumstances changed. Third, people often just grow to dislike a characteristic of the friend's behaviour or personality. Finally, one friend's dating activity or romantic relationships can interfere with and contribute to the decay of a friendship. It should come as no surprise that casual friendships are more likely to end than are those between close or intimate friends. Close friendships are better able to withstand change, uncertainty, and separation.

A Model of Ending Relationships

Steve Duck developed a model to show stages in the ending of a relationship.[58] First one partner reaches some threshold of dissatisfaction that prompts him or her to consider ending the relationship. Having passed this threshold, the person enters an **intrapsychic phase**, in which he or she privately evaluates the partner's behaviours, often focusing on the reasons mentioned earlier to justify withdrawing. Social exchange theory predicts that in this phase, the person will assess the relationship's costs and rewards and will be inclined to termi-nate the relationship if he or she finds it no longer "profitable."[59] We might still remain in an unprofitable relationship if there is a reservoir of profits to offset the current costs. How-ever, as with a savings account, there is only so much we can withdraw before we have to close the account or end the relationship. We might also remain in an unprofitable relation-ship if we predict that the relationship will become profitable again.

From time to time, we all become frustrated with a relationship—and for some of us, the frustration may become severe enough that we consider terminating but without proceeding further than this phase. However, we might "leak" our thoughts and feelings through our communication, displaying such emotions as hostility, anxiety, stress, or guilt. We might decide to confide in a third party about our dissatisfaction. We might consider various strategies for ending the relationship.

At some point, we might decide to move from our private internal contemplations about the relationship to confronting our partner. This is the **dyadic phase** in the model. If our partner feels challenged and intimidated by our desire to end the relationship, we might have to justify our thoughts and feelings. Our partner might also criticize our behaviour and identify our failings. He or she might raise issues that cause us to re-evaluate the relation-ship, our partner, and the costs of dissolving the relationship. We might decide instead to work on improving and repairing the relationship.

If we decide to end the relationship, we enter the **social phase** and begin making the information public. Sometimes a person's social network will mobilize to preserve the rela-tionship. Friends might act as mediators, encouraging reconciliation and suggesting ways to repair the relationship. Of course, friends can also reinforce a decision to separate. Rumours and stories about what happened and what is happening can fuel bad feelings and hasten the end of the relationship.

In the **grave-dressing phase**, one or both partners may attempt to "place flowers on the grave" of their relationship to cover up the hurt and pain associated with its death. They need a public story that they can share with others about what happened: "We still love each other; we just decided we needed more in our lives." However, personal accounts of breakups often place blame on the other partner: "I knew he had his faults, but he thought he could change, and he just wasn't able to." During this phase, our friends encourage us to get back into social activities; they might even try to fix us up with dates. Most importantly, we go through an internal stage in which we try to accept the end of the relationship and let go of feelings of guilt, failure, and blame.

Strategies for Ending Relationships

When the vitality in long-term relationships fades away over a period of years, the individu-als move slowly through the de-escalation stages before finally going their separate ways.

intrapsychic phase. The first phase in relationship termination when an individual engages in an internal evaluation of the partner.

dyadic phase. The second phase in relationship termination when the individual discusses termination with the partner.

social phase. The third phase in relationship termination in which members of the social network around both parties are informed of and become involved in the termination process.

grave-dressing phase. The final phase in relationship termination when the partners generate public explanations and move past the relationship.

Brand-new relationships are far more likely to end abruptly. The more established the relationship, the longer and more complex the ending.

However, no matter what stage a relationship is in, partners use both direct and indirect strategies when they wish to end it. **Indirect termination strategies** represent attempts to break up a relationship without explicitly stating the desire to do so. **Direct termination strategies** involve explicit statements. The strategy that a person chooses will depend on the level of intimacy in the relationship, the level of desire to help the partner save face, the degree of urgency for terminating the relationship, and the person's interpersonal skills.

Indirect Termination Strategies. One researcher identifies three strategies that people use to disengage indirectly: withdrawal, pseudo–de-escalation, and cost escalation. *Withdrawal* involves reducing the amount of contact and interaction without any explanation.[60] This strategy is the most dissatisfying for the other partner.[61] Withdrawal represents an attempt to avoid a confrontational scene and to save face.

In *pseudo–de-escalation*, one partner claims that he or she wants to redefine the relationship at a lower level of intimacy, but in reality, he or she wants to end the relationship. Statements such as "Let's just be friends" or "I think of you more as a sister" might be sincere, or they might reflect an unspoken desire to disengage completely. When both parties want to end the relationship, they sometimes use mutual pseudo–de-escalation and enter into a false agreement to reduce the level of intimacy as they move to disengagement.

Cost escalation is an attempt to increase the costs associated with the relationship to encourage the other person to terminate it. A dissatisfied partner might ask for an inordinate amount of the other person's time, pick fights, criticize the other person, or violate relational rules.

Direct Termination Strategies. The same researcher also identified four direct strategies that we use to terminate relationships: negative identity management, justification, de-escalation, and positive tone.[62] *Negative identity management* is a direct statement of the desire to terminate the relationship. It does not take into account the other's feelings, and it might even include criticisms. "I want out of our relationship," "I just can't stand to be around you anymore," and "I'm no longer happy in this relationship and I want to date other people" reflect negative identity management.

Justification is a clear statement of the desire to end the relationship accompanied by an honest explanation of the reasons. Justification statements may still hurt the other person's feelings: "I've found someone else who I want to spend more time with and who makes me happy," or "I feel as if I've grown a great deal and you haven't." A person who uses justification does not fault the other person, and he or she makes some attempt to protect both parties' sense of self. One researcher found that most people on the receiving end like this strategy best.[63]

De-escalation is an honest statement of a desire to redefine the relationship at a lower level of intimacy or to move toward ending the relationship. One partner might ask for a trial separation so that both people can explore other opportunities and gain a clearer understanding of their needs:[64] "Neither of us seems to be that happy with the relationship right now, so I think we should cool it for a while and see what happens."

Positive tone is the direct strategy that is most sensitive to the other person's sense of self. This strategy can seem almost contradictory because the initiator tries to affirm the other's personal qualities and worth at the same time that he or she calls a halt to the relationship. "I love you; I just can't live with you," "I'm really sorry I've got to break off the relationship," and "You really are a wonderful person; you're just not the one for me" are examples of positive-tone statements.

indirect termination strategies. Attempts to break up a relationship without explicitly stating the desire to do so.

direct termination strategies. Explicit statements of a desire to break up a relationship.

▶ RECAP Strategies for Ending Relationships

	Term	Explanation
How Relationships End	Fading away	The relationship dissolves slowly as intimacy declines.
	Sudden death	The relationship ends abruptly, usually in response to some precipitating event.
	Incrementalism	Relational conflicts and problems accumulate until they become intolerable and the relationship ends.
Indirect Termination Strategies	Withdrawal	One person reduces the amount of contact, without any explanation.
	Pseudo–de-escalation	A desire for less intimacy is claimed when the person really just wants out.
	Cost escalation	One partner increases relational costs to encourage the other to end the relationship.
Direct Termination Strategies	Negative identity management	A desire to end the relationship is stated directly, without concern for the other person's feelings.
	Justification	A desire to end the relationship is stated directly but with an explanation of the reasons.
	De-escalation	A desire to lower the level of intimacy or move toward termination is stated.
	Positive tone	A desire to end the relationship is stated directly with affirmation of the other person's value.

Recovery Strategies

Our identities are often tied to our relationships, and the more intimate the relationship, the more our identity is likely to be threatened if the relationship ends. Letting go of a close relationship is not easy, and the accompanying grief and pain can be debilitating. However, maintaining positive self-esteem and being able to nurture other relationships requires engaging in effective post-dissolution recovery. Relationship researcher Ann Weber created a list of strategies to help address the grief and loss of non-marital breakups.[65] The following strategies are adapted from her list:

1. *Express your emotions.* You need to vent your feelings, if not to your "ex," then to a sympathetic listener, in a journal, or in some other forum. (There are even websites where you can share your story.)

2. *Figure out what happened.* Understanding what occurred in the relationship is one way to get a handle on your current emotions. You need to accept the reasons for the breakup and work toward acceptance.

3. *Realize, don't idealize.* We sometimes view the end of a relationship as the death of a dream. In order to deal with a loss more realistically, Weber suggests mentally reviewing your partner's flaws.

4. *Prepare to feel better.* You might be surprised to find yourself feeling relief and joy. Finding the humour and irony in the breakup can help you cope with the grief. There's a funny side to most situations; we need to be able to joke and laugh about the situation with our friends.

5. *Expect to heal.* Some of the hardest words to accept from others are "It will get better." Although we may not want to believe it, we do recover from injuries, and breakups are a type of injury.

6. *Talk to others.* Isolation is usually not a very healthy way to handle grief. Friends expect to provide comfort by listening to you discuss your feelings. The more open and honest you can be in sharing your thoughts and feelings, the faster you will heal. Don't be afraid to be direct in explaining to friends what you want or need from them; they can't read your mind.

7. *Get some perspective.* This strategy involves a little bit of wallowing in your misery by reading stories, seeing movies, or listening to songs about other people's experiences in breaking up. These can help you put your own situation into perspective.

8. *Be ready for further punishment, or maybe reward.* Weber suggests that once you've gone through the above strategies, it's time to explore potential relationships. Learn from your past experiences, hang on to pleasant memories, and move forward.

Facing the end of a relationship that has meant a great deal to us is one of the more difficult experiences we face in our social lives. The more intimate and involved we become, the more heartbreaking the end. However, as the advice just presented suggests, there is life after the breakup of a relationship, and it is important to go through a recovery cycle that includes accepting the breakup, accepting the pain, realizing that you still have value and worth, and then moving. Of course, all of this is easy to say and much more difficult to accomplish—which is one reason we should not isolate ourselves but lean on other interpersonal relationships and family members to help us cope. Regrettably, relationships do come to an end, but just as we develop skills in initiating relationships, we can develop the ability to cope effectively with their termination.

APPLYING AN OTHER-ORIENTATION
to Relationship Challenges

Most of the challenges discussed in this chapter can be managed more effectively if you apply an other-orientation, whether you are the perpetrator or the victim. You can use other-orientation to mediate your relationship challenges in several ways.

Avoiding or Minimizing Relational Challenges. An other-orientation might lead you to *not* engage in a behaviour that could result in some harm or stress for your partner. Consider a recent failure event or interpersonal transgression that you committed. If you had considered your partner's feelings and response beforehand, would you still have committed the violation? Such pre-emptive other-orientation can lead us to alter what we say or do—or avoid saying or doing it at all—thus avoiding hurtful messages or deception.

Selecting Appropriate Repair Strategies. Perhaps you have considered your partner's reaction but engaged in a failure event anyway. Intentionality makes it more difficult to achieve forgiveness or ameliorate hurt feelings. Nonetheless, by socially decentring, you anticipate your partner's thoughts and feelings about your transgression, helping you plan an appropriate repair strategy. For example, you are better able to choose between offering a simple apology or making significant reparations to restore the relationship.

Appreciating Your Partner's Reactions to Challenges. By social decentring, you can better understand your partner's reactions to relationship challenges. For example, suppose your girlfriend or boyfriend returns after a semester studying abroad and acts distant and even belligerent toward you after you introduce the new friends you've made. Your other-orientation would help you appreciate how your partner is affected by the change from a long-distance relationship back to a proximal one and understand why your partner feels jealous of your new friendships.

Managing Relational Termination. Being other-oriented can make de-escalating or terminating a relationship more difficult, because of an increased sensitivity to what your partner might feel about your decision.

You might avoid or delay ending the relationship because you know how it will hurt the other person. On the other hand, maintaining a relationship when you no longer care about someone in the same way is a form of deception. The challenge is to use your understanding of the other to develop an approach that minimizes the hurt and best protects your partner's face, such as developing a direct, positive-tone strategy.

Forgiving. As the recipient of a partner's interpersonal transgression, deception, hurtful message, or decision to de-escalate or terminate the relationship, you might find that an other-orientation can contribute to healing and even to forgiving your partner. Suppose you know that your partner's need to be independent is greater than his or her desire for an intimate relationship. If so, it should be easier to come to terms with the end of the relationship than if you failed to recognize this need. Forgiving does not mean ignoring what occurred or excusing your partner. But your own mental health is generally improved by forgiving.

Source: Reproduced by permission of SAGE Publications Ltd., London, Los Angeles, New Delhi, Singapore and Washington DC, from L. K. Guerrero & G. F. Bachman, Forgiveness and Forgiving Communication in Dating Relationships: An Expectancy-Investment Explanation, *Journal of Social and Personal Relationships* 27 (2010): 801–23, Copyright (© SAGE Publications Ltd, 2010).

Relationship Challenges
(pages 234–240)

OBJECTIVE ❶ Identify and explain the challenges that individuals involved in interpersonal relationships must navigate to be successful.

Key Terms

failure events *235*

reproach *235*

account *236*

in-group *238*

out-group *239*

Critical Thinking Questions

1. James was supposed to help clean up the apartment on Saturday, but he was gone all day. His roommate reproached him when he returned. Create three accounts James could provide that differ in terms of how likely they are to make the situation worse.

2. Jack and Jill are in an exclusive romantic relationship, but because they attend different schools, they are living 600 kilometres apart. Things have not been going very smoothly recently, and Jill has gone out with a guy from her school a few times without telling Jack. Is Jill's behaviour ethical?

3. Ethics: You are having lunch with a close friend when you both observe an interracial couple sitting down to eat. Your friend makes a highly derogatory comment about the couple that offends you. What should you do? What will you do? Why?

Activities

1. Consider two recent failure events you created where the other person reproached you, one that you handled well, and one that escalated to conflict. What factors contributed to the different outcomes? What did you do differently in the two events? What could you have done more effectively in the second failure event?

2. Think about an existing situation in your life where someone has upset you or not met your expectations, and you have not forgiven him or her. What impact is not forgiving the person having on you? What's in the way of your forgiving the person? What can you do to reach forgiveness?

Web Resources

www.soc.ucsb.edu/sexinfo/article/long-distance-relationships This site provides tips and connections to other sites addressing the challenges of long-distance relationships.

The Dark Side of Interpersonal Communication and Relationships
(pages 240–249)

OBJECTIVE ❷ Describe the issues that constitute the dark side of interpersonal communication and those that constitute the dark side of interpersonal relationships.

Key Terms

interpersonal deception theory *241*

deception by omission (concealment) *241*

deception by commission *241*

white lies *242*

exaggeration *242*

baldfaced lies *242*

active verbal responses *244*

acquiescent responses *244*

invulnerable responses *244*

envy *244*

jealousy *244*

cognitive jealousy *244*

emotional or affective jealousy *244*

behavioural jealousy *244*

obsessive relational intrusion (ORI) *246*

stalking *246*

relational violence *248*

Critical Thinking Questions

1. What factors would influence your reaction to the discovery that another person had deceived you?

2. Under what circumstances is it okay for you to be deceptive? Under what circumstances is it okay for your friends to lie to you?

3. Ethics: You suspect that a male friend is engaging in obsessive relational intrusion toward his former girlfriend. What obligation do you have to act on this? What would you do? What if your friend were a woman obsessively intruding on a former boyfriend?

Activities

Indicate with a check mark whether you have ever engaged in any of the following behaviours, and then decide if your behaviour might be consider stalking. Compare your responses with those of your classmates and discuss.

_____ a. Asking someone for a date, even after being told no.

_____ b. Giving someone flowers, even though he or she doesn't want them.

_____ c. Sending text messages without signing them.

_____ d. Calling a person just to hear his or her voice on the answering machine, but not leaving a message.

_____ e. Calling someone even though you know the person doesn't want to talk to you.

_____ f. Following another person around to see where he or she goes.

_____ g. Asking someone's friend for personal information about that person.

_____ h. Taking a class just because a particular person will be there.

_____ i. Following someone in your car from a store to his or her home without his or her knowledge.

Web Resources

http://cpancf.com/articles_files/jealousyinrelationships.asp This article, by a licensed psychologist, differentiates between normal and abnormal jealousy in intimate relationships.

www.loveisnotabuse.com This site, sponsored by Fifth and Pacific, provides detailed information about and analysis of the problem of abuse and suggests action steps.

www.domesticviolenceinfo.ca/article/warning-signs-of-abuse-139.asp This site provides information about the warning signs of domestic abuse, myths and facts about domestic abuse, and resources for getting help.

Relationship De-Escalation and Termination (pages 249–258)

OBJECTIVE ❸ Explain the process of relational de-escalation and termination, including strategies for terminating and recovering.

Key Terms

bilateral dissolution *252*
unilateral dissolution *252*
fading away *252*
sudden death *253*
incrementalism *253*
intrapsychic phase *254*
dyadic phase *254*

social phase *254*
grave-dressing phase *254*
indirect termination
   strategies *255*
direct termination
   strategies *255*

Critical Thinking Questions

1. How do you know when it is time to get out of a relationship?

2. Think of a romantic relationship that you chose to end. How well does Duck's model of relationship dissolution fit your experience? What happened that is not reflected in his model?

3. Ethics: Under what circumstances is it ethical for someone to use sudden death withdrawal as a strategy for ending an intimate relationship? Under what circumstances would this behaviour be unethical?

Activities

Identify two relationships that you ended and two relationships that the other person ended. In each case, try to determine which of the indirect or direct strategies were used. What differences were there in how the relationships ended? What effects do you think the choice of strategy had on you and your partner? What strategies did you use to recover from the breakup? Which was the most helpful? Least helpful? What other strategies for recovery have you used that helped?

Survey your friends to find out how they have ended close relationships and how they recovered from the termination of a close relationship. Try to identify the termination and recovery strategies they seem to have used.

Web Resources

http://www.lifehack.org/articles/communication/8-signs-its-time-end-the-relationship.html This site lists eight signs that it might be time to end a relationship.

www.askmen.com/dating/heidi_100/112_dating_girl.html This site, primarily aimed at men, provides articles on a wide variety of topics, including breaking up and recovering from breakups.

http://breakup-songs.com This site lists titles and lyrics of songs about breaking up.

© Scott Griessel/Fotolia

11

Interpersonal Relationships at Home and at Work

66 A family in harmony will prosper in everything. 99

—Chinese Proverb

Think about the progression of relationships throughout your life: for the vast majority of us, it both starts and ends with family. You are born or adopted into a family—your first relationships are likely to be with your mother, father, siblings, grandparents, aunts and uncles, and cousins. Most of these relationships will continue into your adult years. Outside the family, you form other important relationships, including friendships, romantic relationships, and relationships with your co-workers.

This chapter focuses on some of the most important categories of relationships, from family relationships, which are usually relationships of circumstance, to friendships and romantic relationships, which are relationships of choice, and finally to work relationships, which can be a combination of the two.

Interpersonal Relationships at Home

At one time, almost two-thirds of families generally consisted of a working father, a stay-at-home mother, and at least two biological children. Today, very few families fit that description. Divorce, single-parent families, same-sex couples, mothers with careers outside the home, the longer wait to start families, and increasing mobility have all dramatically altered the very nature of Canadian families and rapidly led to increasingly diverse family structures.

According to Statistics Canada's 2011 General Social Survey, approximately five million Canadians reported having separated or divorced within the last 20 years. Of those, 38% had a child together at the time of their separation or divorce, with 24% having at least one child aged 18 or younger. Therefore, in 2011, approximately 1.2 million Canadian parents were separated or divorced from their child's other parent.[1]

While families have changed, so has communication within the family. The way family members interact with one another has been altered by a variety of social influences. Most research on family communication tends to be descriptive; it describes how different types of families interact. We can offer suggestions on how to improve or enhance communication in families, but there is no single best way to communicate in families. Each family faces unique challenges for understanding and improving communication.

Like many other entities covered in this text, families are dynamic and changing. Because the members of a family get older, roles and relationships change over time. As well, families add and lose members: as new children are born, or as a family member moves out of the home, the dynamics of the family also change. Families reflect our increasing cultural diversity, often blending two or more cultures to make their own unique culture. Ultimately, what is true of a family at one moment of time may not hold true later. By now you have already experienced the kinds of change that take place in families as you have gone from being completely dependent on your parents to becoming more independent. As you get older, you may discover that your relationship with your parents changes still more as you begin providing care for them. As you consider your own family experiences and apply the principles we discuss in this chapter, remember above all to continually monitor your family relationships and adapt accordingly.

Family Defined

You might think that because families are basic to human existence, there's no need for a formal definition of a family—but definitions have been attempted, and there has been considerable controversy as to what constitutes a family. Traditional definitions focus on the roles of husbands, wives, and children who all live together under one roof. Here is one definition written by sociologist George Murdock in 1949:

> The family is a social group characterized by common residence, economic cooperation, and reproduction. It includes adults of both sexes, at least two of whom maintain a socially approved sexual relationship, and one or more children, of one's own or adopted, of the sexually cohabiting adults.[2]

Other definitions of family de-emphasize the traditional roles of mother, father, and children, placing more emphasis on interpersonal relationships and personal commitment. For example, Statistics Canada states that a "census family" consists of a married couple (with or without children), a common-law couple (with or without children), or a lone parent of any marital status, with at least one child. A couple may be of opposite sex or same sex. Families with children are further classified as "intact" (in which all children are the biological or adopted children of both spouses), or a "stepfamily" (in which there is at least one biological or adopted child of only one married spouse or common-law partner, whose birth or adoption preceded the current relationship).[3]

The Vanier Institute of the Family defines family as

> any combination of two or more persons who are bound together over time by ties of mutual consent, birth and/or adoption or placement and who, together, assume responsibilities for variant combinations of some of the following:
>
> - Physical maintenance and care of group members
> - Addition of new members through procreation or adoption
> - Socialization of children
> - Social control of members
> - Production, consumption, distribution of goods and services, and
> - Affective nurturance—love[4]

For our purposes in this chapter, we synthesize these various perspectives and include both heterosexual and homosexual couples or families to define the **family** as a self-defined unit made up of any number of persons who live or have lived in relationship with one another over time in a common living space, and who are usually, but not always, united by marriage and kinship.

Family Types

The definition of *family* embraces a variety of types, and the type of family people are part of has a significant effect on the roles, relationships, and communication of the family members. As you consider some major family types, keep in mind that even within each type, there are variations. For example, a family consisting of a single mother raising two sons will have different dynamics than one composed of a single father raising two daughters.

A **natural or nuclear family** consists of a mother, a father, and their biological children. Changes in culture, values, economics, and other factors have rendered this once most traditional family type no longer typical. Today, such a family is sometimes called an *idealized natural family.*

The increasingly common **blended family** consists of two adults and one or more children who come together as a result of divorce, separation, death, or adoption. The children are the offspring of other biological parents or of just one of the adults who are raising them. Blended families represent a multitude of possible relationship combinations.

family. Unit made up of any number of persons who live or have lived in relationship with one another over time in a common living space and who are usually, but not always, united by marriage and kinship.

natural or nuclear family. Mother, father, and their biological children.

blended family. Two adults and their children. Because of divorce, separation, death, or adoption, the children may be the biological offspring of other parents, or of just one of the adults who is raising them.

Extended families, blended families, and single-parent families all involve unique relationships and communication patterns.

(© Tetra Images/Getty Images)

single-parent family. One parent and one or more children whom he or she is raising.

extended family. Family unit including relatives such as aunts, uncles, cousins, or grandparents, and/or unrelated persons who are part of a family unit.

family of origin. Family in which a person is raised.

circumplex model of family interaction. Model of the relationships among family adaptability, cohesion, and communication.

The **single-parent family** is self-explanatory. This type of family has one parent and at least one child. Divorce, unmarried parents, separation, desertion, and death make single-parent families the fastest growing type of family unit in North America today.

The **extended family** typically refers to the relatives—aunts, uncles, cousins, or grandparents—who are part of the family unit. Some extended families also include individuals who are not related by marriage or kinship but are treated like family.

The term **family of origin** refers to the family in which you were raised, no matter what type it is. It is in your family of origin that you learned the rules and skills of interpersonal communication and developed your basic assumptions about relationships. You may have been raised in more than one family of origin, due to divorce and remarriage.

Families come in all sizes and forms. A gay or lesbian couple may decide to live together and form a family and raise a child or children. Since 2001, in recognition of diversity in families, Statistics Canada has included same-sex couples in its census statistics. At the heart of our definition of a family is the concept that it includes people who live in close relationship with one another. A family is a family if the people in it think of themselves as a family.

Two Models of Family Interaction

Regardless of the type of family you have, communication plays a major role in determining the quality of family life. As shown in Figure 11.1, one research team found that over 86% of the families who reported family difficulty and stress said that communication was the key source of the problem.[5] Psychologist Howard Markman found that the more positively premarital couples rated their communication with their partner, the more satisfied they were with their marriage relationships more than five years later.[6]

Circumplex Model. The **circumplex model of family interaction** was developed to explain the dynamics of both effective function and dysfunction within family systems.[7] The model's three basic dimensions are adaptability, cohesion, and communication. Complete

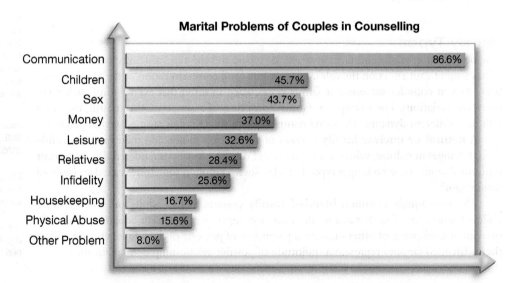

Marital Problems of Couples in Counselling

Communication	86.6%
Children	45.7%
Sex	43.7%
Money	37.0%
Leisure	32.6%
Relatives	28.4%
Infidelity	25.6%
Housekeeping	16.7%
Physical Abuse	15.6%
Other Problem	8.0%

FIGURE 11.1

Sources of Family Difficulties

© Steven A. Beebe

Building Your Skills — Identifying Your Family System

Choose the statement from each set of four that best describes the behaviour typical of your family.

Level of Cohesion

1a. There is little closeness in my family. We are all pretty independent of each other. None of us has any really strong feelings of attachment to the family, and once the kids get to move out, there's not much drive to stay connected with the family.

b. There is some closeness in my family and some interdependence, but not much—mainly we each do our own thing. The family usually gets together just for special occasions.

c. My family is connected to each other, but we also have our independence. We get together at times besides just the holidays. There are feelings of loyalty to the family and we are pretty close to each other.

d. My family is very close-knit and tight. We depend a lot on each other. We are always doing things together. There is nothing family members wouldn't do for each other. My family members feel a need for each other.

Level of Adaptability

2a. Family members come and go to the dinner table as they see fit. There are few rules about how to behave at the dinner table. My parents don't have a particular role at dinner.

b. There are a few rules that govern dinner table behaviour. My mom and dad are about equal in terms of who says what the kids should do, but the kids get a lot of say in what happens and how things are done. Both parents play a similar role.

c. In my family, usually my mom/dad makes most of the decisions, and my dad/mom goes along with that. The kids get to have some input about what happens. We usually get together for dinner and have a set of rules to follow.

d. Only one parent in my family makes the decisions and the other parent follows along. There are a lot of rules about how the kids should behave. At dinner, there are a number of rules that we follow and roles that we play—who clears the dishes, the proper way to ask for things, etc.

Take out a piece of paper, draw a line across the top, and label it "Cohesion." At even intervals, write 1a, 1b, 1c, and 1d. Next, draw a line down the left-hand side of the page and label it "Adaptability." At even intervals, write 2a, 2b, 2c, and 2d. Now, determine where the statement you chose from the first set fits along the Cohesion continuum; then locate your choice from the second set on the Adaptability continuum. Draw a vertical line down from the point you marked on the Cohesion continuum; draw a horizontal line to the right from the point you marked on the Adaptability continuum. Where the lines intersect gives a rough idea of what your family might be like in terms of its cohesion and adaptability. According to the circumplex model of family interaction, the further the point of intersection is to the left, the more separated or even disengaged your family is, while the further the point is to the right, the more connected or even enmeshed your family is. The further the point of intersection is toward the bottom of the page, the more structured or even rigid your family is, while the further the point is toward the top of the page, the more flexible or even chaotic your family is.

---

the *Building Your Skills* questions about family systems to find out how these dimensions apply to your family. **Adaptability**, which ranges from chaotic to rigid, is the family's ability to modify and respond to changes in its own power structure and roles. For some families, tradition, stability, and historical perspective are important to a sense of comfort and well-being. Other families that are less tradition-bound are better able to adapt to new circumstances.

The term **cohesion** refers to the emotional bonding and feelings of togetherness that families experience. Family cohesion ranges from excessively tight, or enmeshed, to disengaged. Because family systems are dynamic, families usually move back and forth along the continuum from disengaged to enmeshed.

The third key element in the model—and the most critical one—is communication. Through communication, families can adapt to change (or not) and maintain either enmeshed or disengaged relationships, or even something in between. Communication determines how cohesive and adaptable families are. Communication keeps the family operating as a system. The nature of the communication in the family has a direct impact on the development of family members' interpersonal communication skills. For example, one study found that ability to self-disclose, offer emotional support, and manage conflicts among friends and romantic partners was related to being raised in a family that supported learning

adaptability. A family's ability to modify and respond to changes in the family's power structure and roles.

cohesion. The emotional bonding and feelings of togetherness that families experience.

about a diverse world and sharing opinions without fear of condemnation (a family high in flexibility and cohesion).[8] How has your family background shaped your interpersonal communication?

The circumplex model helps explain relationships among family cohesiveness, adaptability, and communication at different stages of family development. In general, families with balanced levels of cohesion and adaptability function better across the entire family life cycle than do those at the extremes of these dimensions. A balanced family has a moderate amount of cohesion and adaptability—represented by the centre circle on the model. Balanced families can often adapt better to changing circumstances and manage stressful periods, such as the children's adolescence. Not surprisingly, these balanced families usually have better communication skills.

As we have already emphasized, however, research suggests that *there is no single best way to be a family*. At some stages of family life, the ideal of the balanced family may not apply. Older couples, for example, seem to operate more effectively when there is more rigid structure and a lower level of cohesiveness. Families with young children seem to function well with high levels of both cohesion and adaptability. Only one thing is constant as we go through family life: effective communication skills play an important role in helping families change their levels of cohesiveness or adaptability. These skills include active listening, problem solving, empathy, and being supportive. Dysfunctional families—those that are unable to adapt or alter their levels of cohesion—invariably display poor communication skills. Family members blame others for problems, criticize one another, and listen poorly.

Family Communication Patterns Model. The early work of media researchers who examined families' orientation toward discussing world issues became the foundation of a theory by family communication scholars Mary Ann Fitzpatrick, L. David Ritchie, and Ascan Koerner. This theory classifies families based on family members' openness to talking with each other. The **family communication patterns model** is based on the idea that communication in families can be described in terms of two dimensions: the level of conversation, which is the degree to which family members are encouraged to discuss any topic; and the level of conformity, which is the degree to which the family emphasizes embracing the same values, attitudes, and beliefs.[9] Families with a strong conversation orientation engage in frequent discussions, all family members share their thoughts and feelings, and they all share in decision making. Families strong on conformity seek homogeneity, harmony, avoidance of conflict, and obedience to elders. Families range from strong to weak in their conversation and conformity orientations, as shown in the two-dimensional model in Figure 11.2. The intersection of the two dimensions produces four types of families, each type with its own unique communication patterns. As you read about each type, think which one best describes your family's communication pattern.

Consensual families possess a high orientation toward both conversation and conformity. Parents encourage children to talk, but the children are expected to accept their parents' explanations and values as the parents make the decisions. In essence, children must give in to whatever their parents say, which undoubtedly creates stress for the children. As a matter of fact, a lot of negative feelings get expressed in consensual families, and such families rely heavily on external social support.

Pluralistic families possess a high conversation orientation and a low conformity orientation. These families have very open, unrestrained conversations; they emphasize talking without a concern for conforming. Parents do not try to control their children's thinking, but they do expect quality arguments and support. Family members do not express many negative feelings, and hostility levels are low, probably because family members are free to discuss

family communication patterns model. A model of family communication based on two dimensions: conversation and conformity.

consensual families. Families with a high orientation toward both conversation and conformity.

pluralistic families. Families with a high orientation toward conversation but a low orientation toward conformity.

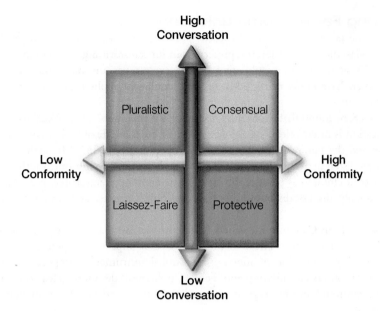

FIGURE 11.2

Model of Family Communication Patterns

© Steven A. Beebe

conflicts and are not pressured to conform. Pluralistic families have the most positive family relationships among the four family types.

Protective families possess a low conversation orientation and a high orientation toward conformity. Parents wield their authority in decision making and expect obedience without discussions or explanations. Because harmony, agreement, and conformity are the goals, conflict is discouraged, and without conflict experience, family members are actually ill equipped to manage conflict in the outside world. The lack of conflict management skills leads members of protective families to experience higher levels of hostile feelings, more venting of those feelings, and short emotional outbursts.

Finally, **laissez-faire families** possess a low orientation toward both conversation and conformity. These families tend to have few interactions on only a few topics. Parents support individual decision making but do not take much interest in the decisions. This pattern eventually undermines the children's confidence in their own decision-making abilities. Conflicts are infrequent, as is venting of negative feelings, since there is little reason for hostility and little investment in the relationships—children feel disassociated from the family.

The communication patterns in a family have a direct impact on both the well-being of family members and the development of interpersonal communication skills. One group of reviewers who analyzed research on family communication patterns discovered that the conversation orientation related more to positive psychosocial factors (self-esteem, mental and physical health, closeness, and relational satisfaction) than did the conformity orientation.[10] In essence, open communication appears to be one of the most significant and positive communication dynamics a family can adopt. Coming from a family with a strong conversation orientation relates to strong relationship maintenance skills, which in turn create more closeness in friendships.[11] Conformity, on the other, hand appears to reduce the flexibility and spontaneity underlying effective relationship maintenance skills.[12]

The family communication patterns model is not a complete picture of complex family dynamics, but it does provide a foundation for an understanding of healthy family communication patterns.

protective families. Families with a low orientation toward conversation but a high orientation toward conformity.

laissez-faire families. Families with a low orientation toward both conversation and conformity.

Improving Family Communication

Wouldn't it be fantastic if you could learn special techniques guaranteed to enrich your family life? Alas, there are no surefire prescriptions for transforming your family system into one that a TV sitcom family would envy. Instead, we can pass on some skills and principles that researchers have either observed in healthy families or applied successfully to improve dysfunctional ones.

Virginia Satir found that, in healthy families, "the members' sense of self-worth is high; communication is direct, clear, specific, and honest; rules are flexible, humane, and subject to change; and the family's links to society are open and hopeful."[13] In such families, she notes, people listen actively; they look at one another, not through one another or at the floor; they treat children as people; they touch one another affectionately regardless of age; and they openly discuss disappointments, fears, hurts, angers, and criticism, as well as joys and achievements.[14]

In a study, John Caughlin identified 10 factors that were associated with families that had good communication.[15] Those factors, in order of impact, are openness, maintaining structural stability, expression of affection, emotional/instrumental support, mind-reading (knowing what others are thinking and feeling), politeness, discipline (clear rules and consequences), humour/sarcasm, regular routine interaction, and avoidance of personal and hurtful topics.

After reviewing several research studies, family communication scholars Kathleen Galvin and Bernard Brommel identified eight qualities exhibited by functional families: interactions are patterned and understood; there is more compassion and less cruelty; problems are addressed to the person who created them—other family members are not scapegoated; there is self-restraint; boundaries about safe territories and roles are clear; life includes joy and humour; misperceptions are minimal; and positive interactions outweigh negative ones.[16]

Of the qualities identified in these two studies, how many are present in your family? Which qualities do you think your family could use more of?

Not all of the qualities identified above specifically involve communication, though all are certainly affected by and affect communication. The following sections explore some of the skills and strategies you can follow to improve your family communication.

Take Time to Talk About Relationships and Feelings. Healthy families talk. The quantity of communication depends on family members' needs, expectations, personalities, careers, and activities. However, the talking extends beyond idle chatter to focus on issues that help the family adapt to change and maintain a sense of cohesiveness.

Often, because of the crush of everyday responsibilities and tasks, family members may lapse into talking only about the task-oriented, mundane aspects of making life work: housecleaning, grocery shopping, errand running, and other uninspiring topics. Healthy families communicate about much more: their relationships, how they are feeling, and how others are feeling. They make time to converse, no matter how busy they are. They have an other-orientation in these conversations, instead of focusing on themselves. In addition, they enjoy each other and don't take themselves too seriously. If you haven't done so recently, try to talk to your family members about how they really are and share information about yourself.

Listen Actively and Clarify the Meaning of Messages. Because talking about relationships is important in healthy families, it is not surprising that effective listening is also important. In the often stressful context of family life, good listening skills are essential.

Good listening requires an other-orientation. In Chapter 5 we presented fundamental skills for listening and responding to messages. Family members will communicate with greater accuracy if they learn to stop, look, and listen. *Stop:* minimize mental and outside distractions; don't try to carry on a conversation over a TV blaring, a video game bleeping,

BEING **Other**-ORIENTED

Mind-reading is identified as a factor that contributes to good communication in a family. The ability of family members to know what other members are thinking and feeling means they can more effectively adapt. How well do members of your family read each other's minds? How does this ability, or the lack of it, affect your overall family communication? What is needed to improve this ability in your family?

or a stereo's distracting rhythmic pulse. *Look:* constantly monitor the rich meaning in non-verbal messages; remember that the face and voice are prime sources for revealing emotional meaning, and that body posture and gestures provide clues about the intensity of an emotion. *Listen:* focus on both details and major ideas. Asking appropriate follow-up questions and reflecting content and feelings are other vital skills for clarifying the meaning of messages. Remember the importance of checking your perceptions about the meaning of nonverbal messages.

Support and Encourage One Another. A smoothly functioning family can be a supportive, encouraging sanctuary from everyday stresses. Through communication, people can let others know that they support and value them. Satir suggests that many, if not most, sources of dysfunction in families are related to feelings of low self-worth.[17] Healthy families take time to nurture one another, express confirming messages, and take a genuine interest in each person's unique contributions to the family. Researchers have found that supportive messages—those that offer praise, approval, help, and affection—can lead to higher self-esteem in children, more conformity to the wishes of the parent, higher moral standards, and less aggressive and anti-social behaviour.[18] Jane Howard, who travelled extensively in search of a "good family," found that "good" families have a sense of valuing and supporting each other.[19] How can you let your family members know you value and support them?

Use Productive Strategies for Managing Conflict, Stress, and Change. In 2013, police reported 87 820 incidents of family violence in Canada, with spousal violence being the most common (48%) and parental violence the next most common (17%).[20]

Abuse and violence are the extreme examples of what happens when people fail to resolve conflicts in a collaborative manner. Husbands and wives must learn to handle conflict in constructive ways and to manage their conflicts with their children similarly.

John Gottman has developed a set of suggestions for handling conflict between couples, some of which apply equally well to parent–child and sibling conflicts.[21] Many of his suggestions reflect recommendations made in Chapter 8 on managing conflict. Gottman suggests picking your battles carefully, scheduling the discussion, employing a structure (build an agenda, persuade and argue, resolve), and moderating your emotions. In dealing with your partner, acknowledge his or her viewpoint before presenting your own, trust your partner, communicate non-defensively, and provide comfort and positive reinforcement. Conflict might be tempered by enhancing the romance and finding enjoyment in the relationship. He further suggests taking stock of the relationship and knowing when to seek help or to end the relationship.

No list of dos and don'ts will help you manage all differences in a family relationship. The suggestions offered here provide only a starting point. As we have emphasized, you will need to adapt these skills and suggestions to the context of your unique family system, but research consistently shows that listening skills and empathy are strong predictors of family satisfaction.

RECAP How to Improve Family Relationships

Take time to talk about relationships and feelings.

- Be other-oriented in your focus.
- Don't take yourself too seriously.

Listen and clarify the meaning of messages.

- Stop, look, and listen.
- Check your interpretation of messages.

Support and encourage one another.

- Use confirming messages.
- Be selective in disclosing your feelings.

Use productive strategies for managing conflict, stress, and change.

- Watch for communication warning signs.
- Learn to renegotiate role conflicts.

Specific Family Relationships

Most of you will choose a life partner and/or get married at some point in your life, and many of you will become parents. Most of you had a relationship with your parents or other adults that greatly influenced your development through childhood. And many of you grew up with at least one younger or older sibling. These relationships are the most

---

E-CONNECTIONS
Relating to Others   **Networked Families**

Technology has had a tremendous effect on families. Here are a few facts from the 2008 Pew Internet & American Life Project concerning the impact of technology on families:

- Compared with single adults or other family types, families with children at home have the highest percentage (94%) of ownership of home computers; 58% have more than one computer.

- Sixty-five percent of families with a mother, father, and a child between 7 and 17 years old living at home report that all members of the family use the computer(s).

- Eighty-nine percent of families with children between 7 and 17 have multiple cell phones, and in 57% of those families the children have their own cell phones.

- Families with more than one cell phone, as well as families with more than one computer, are less likely to have dinner together and are less satisfied with family time. In those families, both parents are more likely to be working, providing the funds and creating the need for technology, but reducing available time (though parents tend to cut back more

on leisure time than on family time). Still, 51% have dinner together every day.

- How does the Internet affect family leisure time activities? Internet users were just as likely to socialize in person with family and friends as non-Internet users. However, 25% of adults report that their Internet use has decreased their TV viewing.

- Spouses who both have cell phones are more likely to contact each other daily to say hello and chat (70%), as well as to coordinate their schedules (64%), compared with other couples (54% and 47%, respectively).

- Among couples with children between 7 and 17 years old, 42% contact the children by cell phone every day, 35% by landline phone, 7% by text message, and 1% by instant message or social network pages.

- Fifty-seven percent of couples with children under 18 share equally in contacting the children; for 36%, the mother is the primary communicator; and for 6%, the primary communicator is the father.

- The Internet and cell phones were seen as increasing the quality of

communication with family members who do not reside with them by 53% of respondents, and increasing the quality of communication with those who did reside with them by 47% of the respondents. A decrease in quality was reported by less than 4% of respondents.

How much do the results of the Pew survey reflect your family? Since you were probably raised with computers and cell phones in your household from an early age, you might not be able to appreciate how their introduction changed communication in your family. Nonetheless, you should be able to identify some of their impact. How often do you email, text-message, or call your parents? Your siblings? Other relatives? How often do they contact you? How does electronically mediated communication (EMC) affect interactions in your household when you are home? When you have your own family, will you set guidelines for your children regarding their use of the Internet or cell phones?

Source: Based on B. Wellman, A. Smith, A. T. Wells, and T. L. M. Kennedy, "Networked Families," Pew Internet & American Life Project, October 19, 2008. © Steven A. Beebe.

common ones that constitute family relationships. One feature you probably recognize about your own family relationships is how they have changed and continue to change. Your current relationships with your parents and siblings are considerably different from when you were a pre-adolescent. Your relationship with your spouse will also change over the course of your marriage, as will your relationships with your own children. All our family relationships are important to us because, among other things, they affect our self-concept and sense of self-worth.

Committed Partners. What drives people to form a lifelong commitment to a partner? What is it that makes such a commitment so appealing? Many people seek commitment as a precursor to having children and forming a nuclear family. And marriage represents the ultimate intimate, romantic relationship to which we vow lifelong commitment. Formal recognition and cultural approval of one's relationship through the ritual of marriage adds additional meaning and challenges to the relationship. Gaining public and legal recognition is one reason why some gay and lesbian committed partners seek the right to marry.

Many gays and lesbians seek public and legal recognition of their relationships in the form of marriage.

(© BananaStock/Thinkstock/Getty Images)

Marriage has other significant benefits. On average, married people live longer than unmarried ones, for a variety of reasons. One reason is that marriage has generally been linked to psychological well-being. One study found that spouses in marriages that weren't completely satisfying still enjoyed some psychological well-being if they had positive relationships with other family members and a best friend.[22] Nevertheless, those positive relationships were not enough to overcome the negative impact of a poor-quality marriage, demonstrating that although friends contribute to our daily well-being, marriage maintains our overall well-being.[23]

Most of us take the commitment of marriage very seriously. When two people enter into marriage, they spend a lot of time defining their roles and working through the trials of cohabitation. The nature of their relationship depends on a variety of factors, such as how they distribute power and make decisions (symmetric, complementary, or parallel) and what roles they each assume. Despite the variety of differences, couples can be classified according to how the partners communicate with one another.

Researcher Mary Anne Fitzpatrick identified four types of married couples found in North American society: traditional, independent, separate, and mixed.[24] According to Fitzpatrick, **traditional couples** are interdependent, exhibit a lot of sharing and companionship, follow a daily routine, are not assertive, have conflicts, emphasize stability over spontaneity, and follow traditional community customs (such as the wife taking the husband's last name). **Independent couples** share and exhibit companionship but allow each other individual space; they believe the relationship should not limit their individual freedoms. They are psychologically interdependent but have a hard time matching schedules, and they also engage in conflict. **Separate couples** hold somewhat opposing values: on the one hand, they support traditional marriage and family values; on the other hand, they stress the individual over the couple. They have low interdependence and avoid conflict. This means that by maintaining their autonomy, they display less companionship and sharing than the other couple types, but they still try to keep a daily routine. In each of the preceding three types of married couples, both the wife and the husband share the same perspective about the nature of their relationship. When the husband and the wife have divergent perspectives on their roles, they are a **mixed couple** (the fourth type).

You might be wondering what it takes to ensure that you have a happy marriage. A number of factors affect marital satisfaction: approaches to conflict management, level of uncertainty, power, equity, decision-making patterns, sexual activity, empathy, age,

traditional couples. Married partners who are interdependent and who exhibit a lot of sharing and companionship.

independent couples. Married partners who exhibit sharing and companionship and are psychologically interdependent but allow each other individual space.

separate couples. Married partners who support the notion of marriage and family but stress the individual over the couple.

mixed couples. Married couples in which the husband and wife each adopt a different perspective (traditional, independent, separate) on the marriage.

education, social status, presence of children, similarities, differences, marital expectations, and, of course, communication. The complexity of the factors that lead to marital satisfaction has prevented the identification of a definitive set of skills or behaviours. Generally, research has done a better job of explaining what will lead to the failure of a marriage than what will ensure its success. Chapter 10 lists the four communication markers identified by marriage researcher John Gottman as highly predictive of divorce: criticism, contempt, defensive behaviours, and stonewalling. But the absence of these behaviours does not ensure happiness. What is known is that the behaviours Gottman identified—poor communication in general and the inability to manage conflict constructively—are likely to lead to dissatisfaction, dysfunction, and/or relational termination.

If you are good at communicating and managing conflict, will you have a happy marriage? Not necessarily. Communicating does not guarantee increased happiness; you might not like what you hear. Good communication just means openly sharing more information—information that has the potential to have a positive or negative effect, depending on what you learn. Hearing your spouse's constant complaints about family members, financial issues, personal distress, doubts about the marriage, or desires to engage in activities you dislike might reduce your relational satisfaction. Nonetheless, the negative impact of *not* communicating seems much greater than the negative impact of communicating. Partners should strive to establish effective communication and use that communication to honestly share and explore each other's expectations.

Parents and Children. A great deal of research has been done on the nature of the interaction between parents and their children. Most studies focus on identifying the most effective ways for parents to communicate with their children or describing the nature of parent–child interactions. And some studies have examined the impact of a parent's communication on the development of the child's communication skills as an adult. Your parents have affected your interpersonal communication development in three ways: by interacting with you, by providing instruction about communication rules and principles, and by engaging in communication that you observed.

Children Learn Through Interacting. The way your parents interacted with you affects your behaviour and attitudes, although the effect is not always straightforward. One study found that grade 7 children's views on openness in sharing thoughts and feelings were similar to the views of their mothers, and their views on conformity and authority were similar to those of their fathers. By the grade 11, however, children's views on openness matched those of their fathers, whereas their views on conformity matched those of their mothers.[25]

Children Learn Through Instruction. Your parents affected your communication development by providing you with specific instructions. They overtly conveyed such communication rules as not to interrupt others, to be polite, and to maintain eye contact when talking.

Children Learn Through Observation. Your communication behaviours are also affected by observing your parents' interactions, notably, your parents' approaches to handling conflict. Observing destructive and hostile conflicts between parents can lead children to adopt similar styles in marriage. Similarly, your observations of how your parents interacted with their friends and co-workers and their interactions with strangers all served as potential models for your own communication behaviours. Parents who engage in ego conflicts, gunny-sacking, and other destructive conflict behaviours can either instill those styles in their children or instill a fear of conflict, leading children to avoid or accommodate. Parents who avoid conflict or who hide their conflict interactions from their children might be teaching their children to repress conflict issues or creating an expectation of a conflict-free marriage. On the other hand, children who observe their parents managing conflicts constructively are more prosocial—considerate, empathic, cooperative, and sharing.

Each parent has his or her own communication strengths and weaknesses. Since interpersonal relationships are transactional, it is the combination of both parents' communication styles that affects your communication development. Take a moment to consider how each of your parents or other significant relatives has had an impact on your communication behaviour. To what degree have they shaped your response to interpersonal conflict? How have they affected your ability to express caring, love, warmth, and affection? What impact have they had on your listening skills, respect for others, and openness? Some of your communication behaviours might not match those of your parents because you developed them as a reaction to your parents' patterns. For example, your dislike for your parents' aggressiveness might lead you to be passive. Finally, some of your qualities might not be learned at all but are communibiological—passed down genetically. Nonetheless, when you have your own children, be sensitive to the impact of how you communicate with them and with those around you on the development of their communication skills.

Siblings. Although relationships with brothers and sisters tend to be the most enduring relationships in our lives, generalizing about communication between siblings is difficult, because so many factors influence the nature of the relationships, including the sex, age, and number of siblings. Overall, however, we are motivated to communicate with our siblings because of feelings of intimacy—a desire to sustain the relationship, to keep in touch, to show caring and concern, and to encourage. Sibling communication between the ages of 18 and 34 differs from such communication during later years because we are more motivated to do something with our siblings, get something from them, escape from doing something else, accomplish things together, get information, or simply continue a routine or habit.[26] Besides changes in our motives, additional changes occur as we move through the three stages of sibling relationships: childhood and adolescence, early and middle adulthood, and late adulthood and old age.[27] During the first stage, siblings live together, engage in daily interactions, compete for and share resources (like bedrooms and bathrooms), and probably face greater demands and more pressing tasks than in the latter stages. During the early and middle adulthood stage, siblings begin independent lives, starting their own nuclear families and pursuing careers. Sibling interactions become voluntary and perhaps more intermittent, due to such factors as geographic distance. In the late adulthood stage, siblings retire and their children are grown up, so siblings once again turn to each other. Siblings often provide important sources of support to one another as they cope with the aging and deaths of parents.

BEING Other-ORIENTED

Despite being raised under the same roof, siblings differ due to a variety of factors ranging from communibiology to birth order. What experiences have your siblings had that differ from yours (being born first or last, having to move when they were in high school)? How have those experiences affected them? How are their values and beliefs similar to or different from yours? Why?

Interpersonal Relationships at Work

Organizations look for employees who can relate effectively to other people—bosses, subordinates, peers, and clients. All the skills you have been studying throughout this text can improve your effectiveness in organizational relationships. As shown in the *Canadian Connections* box, interpersonal communication skills rank high on the list of essential workplace skills. Note that skills such as working with a team, joint planning, and making decisions with others all require your ability to communicate effectively at the interpersonal level.

After you graduate, the workplace becomes a major source for developing interpersonal relationships. You make friends with the people with whom you work. You will socialize on the job with various people from the organization and may socialize with them outside of work. Your interactions in the workplace typically vary according to their degree of task versus social orientation. This variation is the source of both personal satisfaction and conflict. Conflicts arise when job-related decisions affect personal relationships, and vice versa. As a manager, you might become friends with some of your subordinates, but if the work performance of one of those subordinates falls below a satisfactory level, the friendship could

Canadian Connections — Soft Skills in the Workplace

What soft skills will Canadians need to work in a global economy? In other words, what skills, abilities, and knowledge will employers be seeking as they hire new workers in the next several years? A document developed by the Corporate Council of Education, a program of the National Business and Education Centre of the Conference Board of Canada, outlines the foundation skills for employability. The Corporate Council encompasses representation from numerous Canadian companies, including Air Canada, Bell Canada, General Motors of Canada Limited, IBM Canada, Nortel, Shell Canada Limited, and Xerox Canada Limited, to name a few. The following is a summary of these skills. Note that many of the skills require interpersonal skills and the ability to communicate effectively.

Employability Skills 2000+

The skills you need to enter, stay in, and progress in the world of work—whether you work on your own or as a part of a team. These skills can also be applied and used beyond the workplace in a range of daily activities.

Fundamental Skills

The skills needed as a base for further development

You will be better prepared to progress in the world of work when you can:

Communicate

- read and understand information presented in a variety of forms (e.g., words, graphs, charts, diagrams)
- write and speak so that others pay attention and understand
- listen and ask questions to understand and appreciate the points of view of others
- share information using a range of information and communications technologies (e.g., voice, email, computers)
- use relevant scientific, technological, and mathematical knowledge and skills to explain or clarify ideas

Manage Information

- locate, gather, and organize information using appropriate technology and information systems
- access, analyze, and apply knowledge and skills from various disciplines (e.g., the arts, languages, science, technology, mathematics, social sciences, and the humanities)

Use Numbers

- decide what needs to be measured or calculated
- observe and record data using appropriate methods, tools, and technology
- make estimates and verify calculations

Think and Solve Problems

- assess situations and identify problems
- seek different points of view and evaluate them based on facts
- recognize the human, interpersonal, technical, scientific, and mathematical dimensions of a problem
- identify the root cause of a problem; be creative and innovative in exploring possible solutions
- readily use science, technology, and mathematics as ways to think, gain, and share knowledge, solve problems, and make decisions
- evaluate solutions
- make recommendations or decisions, implement solutions, check to see if a solution works, and act on opportunities for improvement

Personal Management Skills

The personal skills, attitudes, and behaviours that drive one's potential for growth

You will be able to offer yourself greater possibilities for achievement when you can:

Demonstrate Positive Attitudes and Behaviours

- feel good about yourself and be confident
- deal with people, problems, and situations with honesty, integrity, and personal ethics
- recognize your own and other people's good efforts
- take care of your personal health
- show interest, initiative, and effort

Be Responsible

- set goals and priorities by balancing work and personal life
- plan and manage time, money, and other resources to achieve goals
- assess, weigh, and manage risk
- be accountable for your actions and the actions of your group
- be socially responsible and contribute to your community

Be Adaptable

- work independently or as a part of a team
- carry out multiple tasks or projects
- be innovative and resourceful: identify and suggest alternative ways to achieve goals and get the job done
- be open and respond constructively to change
- learn from your mistakes and accept feedback
- cope with uncertainty

Learn Continuously

- be willing to continuously learn and grow
- assess personal strengths and areas for development
- set your own learning goals
- identify and access learning sources and opportunities
- plan for and achieve your learning goals

Work Safely

- be aware of personal and group health and safety practices and procedures, and act in accordance with them

Teamwork Skills

The skills and attributes needed to contribute productively

You will be better prepared to add value to the outcomes of a task, project, or team when you can:

Work with Others

- understand and work within the dynamics of a group
- ensure that a team's purpose and objectives are clear
- be flexible: respect and be open to and supportive of the thoughts, opinions, and contributions of others
- recognize and respect people's diversity, individual differences, and perspectives
- accept and provide feedback in a constructive and considerate manner

- contribute to a team by sharing information and expertise
- lead or support when appropriate, motivating a group for high performance
- understand the role of conflict in a group to reach solutions
- manage and resolve conflict when appropriate

Participate in Projects and Tasks

- plan, design, or carry out a project or task from start to finish with well-defined objectives and outcomes

- develop a plan, seek feedback, test, revise, and implement
- work to agreed quality standards and specifications
- select and use appropriate tools and technology for a task or project
- adapt to changing requirements and information
- continuously monitor the success of a project or task and identify ways to improve

Source: "Employability Skills 2000+" brochure. Ottawa: Conference Board of Canada, 2000. Printed with permission of Conference Board of Canada.

interfere with your ability to address that problem. Many companies used to have policies prohibiting socializing among employees; however, such policies created strong dissatisfaction and discontent. Organizational policies that nurture relationships among employees build camaraderie and a supportive work atmosphere.

Workplace Friendships

TV shows set in the workplace, such as *30 Rock, The Office, Brooklyn Nine-Nine,* and *Parks and Recreation,* often find humour in workplace relationships, including the shifting friendships among coworkers. As these shows often illustrate, workplace friendships can develop with anyone in an organization, though generally friendship is most likely between co-workers who are at the same status level. However, friendships also develop between supervisors and subordinates, between employees and clients, and between members of totally different departments within an organization. Friendships at work are like any other relationships in terms of relational dimensions and development. The initial development of workplace friendships occurs for a variety of reasons, such as proximity, sharing tasks, sharing a similar life event, or perceiving similar interests. As a relationship develops, the changes identified are similar to those typically found in any developing friendship—easier and more flexible communication, increased self-disclosing, more frequent interactions, more socializing, and increased discussion of both work problems and non-work topics.

Interpersonal communication skills help us in our interactions with co-workers. Developing satisfying interpersonal relationships in an organization is often a rewarding part of a job.
(© Golden Pixels/Shutterstock)

Workplace friendships might be limited to a particular context: perhaps you have a colleague you eat lunch with regularly, or you develop a friendship with someone working on a shared project, and the friendship ends when the project is complete. Outside of the workplace, friendships often find us associating with other people who are similar in age, status, and the like; however, workplace friendships often involve people who differ in age or status. For example, you may find yourself becoming friends with a supervisor or subordinate who is considerably older or younger than you. Having a friend of the opposite sex may be more likely at work than it is outside work, where such relationships might be expected to become romantic or might threaten existing intimate relationships.

Workplace friendships enhance an organization's communication network by increasing the flow and openness of information. Just as outside friendships provide us with support and resources, so do workplace friendships. Workplace friends are in a position to

BEING Other-ORIENTED

The same workplace friendship can have different values for each partner. These differences can be the source of conflict and even harassment. What values or functions have you sought in a recent workplace friendship? What would your friend say you wanted out of the friendship? What values or functions did your friend see in the relationship? If you've had a workplace friendship end, what would your former friend say were the reasons it ended?

understand and appreciate our organizational complaints and related frustrations. Friends help friends and, in an organization, that can mean lending a hand, providing information, being an ally, or providing material support.

Just as with any friendship, those at work can deteriorate and end. However, unlike other friendships, we often continue in relationships of circumstance as co-workers, superiors, or subordinates. Some reasons for the deterioration of workplace friendships are personality issues, interference of one friend's personal life in work, problems created by different expectations for friend and work roles, promotion of one person to a position of authority over the other, and betrayal of trust. How do you go about ending workplace friendships? Some of the strategies for ending relationships discussed in Chapter 10 also apply to workplace friendships. Specific indirect strategies for the workplace include keeping all conversations focused on work topics; nonverbally distancing from the other through the use of a disapproving tone and facial expressions; escalating the cost of maintaining the friendship by being more independent or making more demands; and avoiding socializing outside the workplace.[28] When all else fails, some of our students have reported quitting their jobs to end a workplace relationship. The ability to redefine a friendship as only a work-based relationship requires strong relationship management skills to minimize the stress and potential resentfulness felt by a co-worker or a subordinate.

Workplace Romances

The workplace actually provides an opportune arena for the development of intimate relationships because of the convenience and exposure to a wide pool of potential partners. Many people find their future spouses in the workplace. A 2009 Valentine's Day national survey for Careerbuilder.com found that 31% of workers surveyed had married a person they dated at work. Some companies even hire married couples because they see a value in having both partners working for the same company. In contrast, some companies have policies prohibiting dating a co-worker—but how can a policy prevent people from becoming attracted? In the workplace, you interact with people in a safe and defined context that affords the opportunity to learn about others and share information about yourself. Trust evolves, similarities are discovered, attraction develops, and the interactions move toward more intimacy. In general, dating in the workplace is not particularly problematic when those involved work in different units or when there are no direct job-related power issues.

The values and functions associated with friendships also apply to romantic relationships. Workplace romantic partners share organizational, professional, and personal information, provide emotional comfort and understanding, and offer assistance on tasks. Workplace romances can energize the partners as well as their work associates, as they all share the joy and excitement of the relationship, which bolsters workplace morale.

However, there are significant challenges associated with workplace romances. For example, dating among members of the same unit can be a problem if it interferes with the ability of the couple to perform their jobs. If you are involved in such a situation, your interactions with your partner at work need to remain professional. Co-workers are sometimes uncomfortable around romantic partners and may worry about inappropriate sharing of information, unequal work distribution, or other potential problems. The most significant problems in workplace romances occur when the relationship is between a boss and his or her employee. The employee might feel coerced into the romantic relationship, which constitutes **sexual harassment**. Even if the superior does not threaten or show favouritism to the subordinate, the subordinate could believe that rejecting the superior's advances would be professionally detrimental. This type of sexual harassment is usually referred to as **quid pro quo**, a Latin phrase that basically means "You do something for me and I'll do something for you." A supervisor who says or implies "Have sex with me or your job will be in jeopardy" or "If you want this promotion, you should have sex with me" is obviously using

sexual harassment. Unwanted sexually oriented behaviour in the workplace that results in discomfort and/or interference with the job.

quid pro quo. Latin phrase that can be used to describe a type of sexual harassment. The phrase roughly means "You do something for me and I'll do something for you."

ADAPTING TO DIFFERENCES
Understanding Diversity

Male and Female Interactions in the Workplace

The following six scenarios reflect some of the general ways men and women differ in their approach to communication in the workplace. These scenarios are based on North American stereotypes about men and women in the workplace. As you read each one, see if the description of your sex's approach actually reflects how you behave. Also think about the degree to which you believe the stereotype presented for the opposite sex. The author of these scenarios does a good job of taking an other-oriented approach to helping improve communication, and the principles she offers apply regardless of the sex of those involved.

Power Plays

Her way: Women tend to ask lots of questions before beginning work.

His way: Men simply roll up their sleeves.

The result: Men assume women aren't up to the job. If they were competent, reason men, then women wouldn't be asking so many questions. But in fact, women typically verify and validate data before starting tasks, sometimes to improve their performance. If you're a male boss, listen to the questions women ask. Sometimes, these may add information or clarify things for everyone.

The reverse scenario is that men hate to ask for directions (big news, right?). But women assume that if men don't ask questions, they must know enough to complete a job. That's often not the case. For women bosses, it's a good idea to verify that men have enough knowledge to complete a task. Oversee the work in the early phases or offer help without being asked.

Picture Imperfect

Her way: Women frequently use anecdotes or illustrations about home or relationships.

His way: Men rely on metaphors about sports or war.

The result: Dialogue can hit a dead end. Women often do not follow the touchdown, full-court-press images, and vice versa. Don't simply gender-reverse images to communicate. Instead, consider your audience and use gender-neutral images (of nature, movies, or weather, for example). Or use images you like, but with an explanation of what you mean.

Command Conflicts

Her way: Growing up, girls tend to establish relationships.

His way: Boys usually vie for leadership.

The result: Men and women impose authority differently. "Women tend to be more collaborative in the workplace, putting relationships first," says Roz Usheroff, a business trainer and author of *Customize Your Career.* "Men routinely challenge and expect to be challenged." Each often finds the other's style ineffective or insulting. To jump the divide, borrow a bit from the other's style. Men can try a more collaborative approach. Women need to take over more often.

Detailed Disputes

Her way: Women like to tell and hear stories, including stories about trials and errors, turnings and returnings.

His way: Men "cut to the chase."

The result: Each sex becomes too impatient to hear the other. "Women push for details generally for three reasons: to show concern, to vicariously participate in an experience or conversation, and to verify assumptions," says Dianna Booher, author of *Communicate with Confidence.* "Men tend to gather details just long enough to get the big-picture message and then dump them as trivial."

Again, each sex can benefit from the other's behaviour. Men ought to explain their thinking and not simply jump to conclusions. Women need to get to the bottom line more quickly.

Emotional Exchanges

Her way: She tends to treat male colleagues as she would her husband or boyfriend.

His way: He often handles women associates as he would his wife or girlfriend.

The result: Subtle and tricky gender miscommunication. Typically, men and women bring into the office some version of the sexual dynamics they have at home. We also gravitate to workplace confidants, mentors, or employees who resemble the intimates in our personal lives, especially spouses. If you're in some kind of standoff or you feel as though he or she "doesn't understand" you, take a break to think it through. Make sure you're not importing a personal issue into the workplace environment.

Decision Drivers

Her way: Women are generally more comfortable talking about their feelings.

His way: Men prefer to dwell on the facts and skip the feelings.

The result: Communication trouble. Every communication has both an intellectual and an emotional component; misunderstanding arises when we ignore one of the two dimensions. A man can acknowledge the emotional dimension: "I know this is a difficult conversation for you. It's difficult for me, too." A woman might dial down emotional intensity by increasing her focus on problem analysis: "I think there are three pieces to the issues we've been discussing."

The definition of a diverse work force, of course, is an environment where people accept differences rather than deny them. If we pay attention to gender differences, we just might untangle the gender communications knots—and get the job done faster, too.

Source: Written by Joanna Krotz for Microsoft Small Business Center website. Printed by permission of Joanna Krotz.

his or her power as a boss to gain sexual favours in exchange for something the employee wants. To avoid these situations, organizations often develop extensive sexual harassment policies. You should learn the policies of any organization where you are employed and assert your rights if you find yourself being sexually harassed.

Upward Communication: Talking with Your Boss

Upward communication involves the flow of communication from subordinates up to superiors. The only person in an organization who does not communicate upward is the boss, president, or chief executive officer (CEO), though even they usually answer to a governing board or to shareholders. Although today's organizational emphasis on quality encourages communication from lower levels to higher levels, effective upward communication is still far from the norm. Many employees fear that their candid comments will not be well received. Others may wonder, "Why bother?" If managers offer no incentive for sharing information up the line, it is unlikely that their subordinates will make the effort.

If there is little upward communication, the organization may be in a precarious situation. Those lower down in the organization are often the ones who make contact with the customer, make the product, or work most closely with the development and delivery of the product or service; they hear feedback about the product's virtues and problems. If supervisors remain unaware of these problems, productivity or quality may suffer. In addition, if employees have no opportunities to share problems and complaints with their boss, their frustration level may be dangerously high. Upward communication helps managers deal quickly with problems and hear suggestions for improving processes and procedures. One pair of researchers suggests that subordinates can "manage up" by being sensitive to the needs of supervisors.[29] If you know what your boss's most important goals are, along with his or her strengths, weaknesses, and preferred working style, you will be in a good position to establish a more meaningful relationship that will benefit both of you.

This process of managing might be mediated by how influential subordinates perceive their superiors to be. In 1952, an organizational researcher discovered that subordinates were more satisfied in their jobs when they felt their immediate supervisor had influence on decisions made at higher levels.[30] This is called the Pelz effect, after its discoverer, Donald Pelz. Subsequent research by organizational communication scholar Fred Japlin found that when subordinates perceived their supervisors as supportive, the Pelz effect was particularly strong in creating a sense of openness and satisfaction.[31] Having a supportive and influential superior enhances communication because employees are more open to sharing information.

Downward Communication: Talking with Your Subordinates

Downward communication refers to the flow of information from those higher up in an organization to those of lower rank. It can happen via memo, newsletter, poster, or email—or, of course, face to face. Most downward communication consists of instruction about how to do a job, rationales for doing things, statements about organizational policies and procedures, feedback about job performance, and information that helps develop the mission or vision of the organization.

What is the best way to communicate with employees: in writing or face to face? It depends on the situation. Often the best method is oral, with a written follow-up or email. If you need immediate employee action, face-to-face communication followed by a written reminder is the most effective (sending only a written memo is the least effective). However, if you are communicating about long-term actions, a written message is the most effective. Certain situations, such as reprimanding an employee or settling a dispute, are best handled in face-to-face interactions rather than through the use of any written messages.

upward communication.
Communication that flows from subordinates to superiors.

downward communication.
Communication that flows from superiors to subordinates.

The best managers take care to develop and send ethical, other-oriented messages. Then they follow up to ensure that the receiver understood the message and that it achieved its intended effect. Managers need to be especially other-oriented when they are sharing sensitive information or broaching personal topics.

As mentioned earlier, behaviours by supervisors that involve using power against subordinates for sexual favours constitute sexual harassment. However, supervisors also have a responsibility to eliminate a second type of sexual harassment that represents another dark side of interpersonal communication: a hostile environment. An employee in a **hostile environment** feels his or her rights are being violated because of working conditions or offensive behaviour on the part of other workers. Telling lewd or obscene stories or jokes about members of the opposite sex, using degrading terms to describe women or men, or displaying risqué photographs of nude or seminude people can contribute to a hostile working environment. For example, one female firefighter in British Columbia allegedly found pornographic pictures on her bed; this was one among many reported incidents in the department. After many years of harassment, she went public with her complaints.[32] A supervisor who either creates or fails to change work situations that are threatening to a subordinate is a party to sexual harassment. Jokes are not innocent and pictures are not "all in fun" if they make an employee feel degraded. Supervisors must adopt an other-oriented approach with respect to this issue; it is the receiver, not the sender, of the message who determines whether the behaviour is hostile. Wise supervisors do not wait for a problem to occur. They take a proactive approach, offering all workers seminars on how to avoid engaging in sexually offensive behaviour and explicitly discussing what workers should do if they become the victims of sexual harassment.

Horizontal Communication: Talking with Your Colleagues

Horizontal communication refers to communication among co-workers at the same level within an organization. In larger organizations, you may talk with other workers in different departments or divisions who perform similar jobs at a similar level; that, too, is horizontal communication. Most often you communicate with your colleagues to coordinate job tasks, share plans and information, solve problems, make sure you understand job procedures, manage conflict, or get a bit of emotional support on the job.

Information travels through a workplace the way gossip travels through "the grapevine." Sometimes errors creep into workplace information that is spread this way. Although grapevine errors can cause problems for an organization, most continue to encourage co-worker communication because it enhances teamwork and allows the work group to develop a certain degree of independence. Some organizations even try to formalize horizontal communication by forming quality circles, or groups of employees who meet together on a regular basis. These groups usually talk about such issues as how to improve the quality of services or products, reduce mistakes, lower costs, improve safety, or develop better ways of working together. This active participation in the work process encourages workers to do a better job. Moreover, the training they receive through participation in these groups—in group problem solving, decision-making skills, listening, relating, speaking, and managing conflict—applies to other areas of their work as well.

Outward Communication: Talking with Your Customers

Increasingly, successful organizations are those that are other-oriented; they focus on the needs of those they serve through **outward communication**. That is, rather than relying solely on the judgments of their corporate executives, they are spending time and money to find out what the *customer* perceives as quality. They are also training their staff to develop more empathy, better listening skills, and more awareness of nonverbal messages from customers.

hostile environment. Type of sexual harassment in which an employee's rights are threatened through offensive working conditions or behaviour on the part of other workers.

horizontal communication. Communication among colleagues or co-workers at the same level within an organization.

outward communication. Communication that flows to those outside an organization (such as customers).

Building Your Skills   Other-Orientation at Home and at Work

Throughout this text, we have advocated taking an other-oriented approach to interpersonal communication. There are times when taking an other-oriented perspective or being empathic could be disadvantageous if you ignore your own needs, values, or priorities. Look at the following situations and consider how being other-centred might be counterproductive or lead to poor decisions. How can you be other-centred and still make good decisions in each situation?

- You receive a call from the middle-school principal that your grade 7 son is being suspended for two days for fighting with another student. Because you are other-centred, you

understand that your son is very self-conscious about being overweight, and the other kids make fun of him for it. He's also been struggling with his studies because he has a hard time concentrating and reading material. He has low self-esteem and does not feel that other kids like him.

- You are a manager and one of your subordinates is increasingly late, misses deadlines and appointments, and is turning in poor work. Taking an other-centred approach, you come to realize that this employee is facing a divorce, has a child who was recently arrested, and is suffering from panic attacks.

APPLYING AN OTHER-ORIENTATION
to Family and Workplace Relationships

Your parents will probably like this part of the text if the other-orientation exercise described below results in increased appreciation for them on your part. For you, the benefit is a better understanding of arguably the most influential family members in your life: your parents.

Effective other-orientation requires a consideration of your parents' backgrounds: their treatment as children by their own parents, siblings, and other relatives; their educational and work experiences; and finally, the community and historical era in which they were raised. Imagine that you are writing a biography of your parents. Ask them about their upbringing, their childhood experiences, their education, their friends, their challenges—doing so, of course, while using your best listening skills. Talk to your uncles, aunts, grandparents, parents' friends, or older siblings to gain a more complete perspective on your parents. Socially decentre by putting yourself in their situation, imagining what it would have been like to grow up as they did, to work and raise a family. The goal of such reflections is to understand your parents' behaviours and the choices

they have made in creating a family and raising you.

Adopting an other-orientation puts you in a position to better understand those with whom you interact so that you more effectively manage those relationships and ultimately accomplish your personal goals. Applying an other-orientation to your understanding of co-workers, managers, subordinates, and clients can enhance your workplace effectiveness. One of our colleagues used to announce to his large lecture classes that the key to succeeding in his class was to figure out what he wanted and to give it to him—a pretty simple application of an other-orientation. Similarly, by figuring out what your boss, employees, or clients want, you are in a better position to adapt. Unlike the lecture situation, however, you do have options about how to respond in the workplace. For example, knowing that an employee is having difficulty at home with his family doesn't mean you simply give the person lots of time off, since you also have a responsibility to the company to ensure that various jobs get done. In some ways, this is a situation in which being

empathetic can mean that a manager's decision making is more difficult.

In business negotiation simulations with MBA students, those who thought about the interests and goals of their counterparts (perspective taking) gained more benefits for themselves and the counterparts than did those who were concerned with the others' feelings (empathy) or those who negotiated without considering either.[33] Empathy was less effective and sometimes even detrimental to gaining benefits for the negotiators. However, since empathy creates the greatest satisfaction for the other person, the positive relationship it builds could be beneficial in future interactions.[34]

These findings suggest that considering the other person's perspective can help you develop creative solutions that take into account both your goals and the goals of your partners (a principle of collaborative conflict management). Given that many of your organizational relationships will be long-term, showing empathy can help establish trust and satisfaction for others, but perspective taking is also needed to help ensure that both parties benefit.

Interpersonal Relationships at Home (pages 262-273)

OBJECTIVE ❶ Identify and describe the types of families, the models used to describe family interactions, and the ways to improve family communications.

Key Terms

family *263*

natural or nuclear family *263*

blended family *263*

single-parent family *264*

extended family *264*

family of origin *264*

circumplex model of family interaction *264*

adaptability *265*

cohesion *265*

family communication patterns model *266*

consensual families *266*

pluralistic families *266*

protective families *267*

laissez-faire families *267*

traditional couples *271*

independent couples *271*

separate couples *271*

mixed couples *271*

Critical Thinking Questions

1. Do you think the institution of the family is deteriorating, or is it just changing? Support your answer.

2. Family communication changes throughout the life of the family: the married couple has a certain communication style that changes with the arrival of the first child and subsequent children. How might changes over the lifetime of a typical family cause it to evolve from one type of family to another in each of the two models of family communication?

3. Ethics: Is it ethical to withhold thoughts and feelings from family members? Should family members always "tell it like it is"? Should parents encourage their children to tell everything they know and feel?

Activities

What are your attitudes about families? Indicate whether you agree or disagree with the following statements. Talk to other class members and find out which items you agree and disagree on. Try to find reasons for differences of opinion. Decide together how you might reword statements to make ones on which you'd both agree.

____1. Most family members know how to communicate effectively; they just don't take the time to practise what they know.

____2. Family conflict is a symptom rather than a cause of deteriorating family relationships.

____3. Family conflict is harmful to family harmony, and conflict should be avoided at all costs.

____4. Most family conflict occurs because we don't understand the other family member; we fail to communicate effectively.

____5. Families function best if there is one leader of the family.

____6. Ineffective communication is the single most important cause of family conflict, divorce, and family tension.

____7. Nonverbal communication (facial expression, eye contact, tone of voice, posture, and so on) is more important than verbal communication; what you do is more important than what you say.

____8. It is sometimes necessary to ignore the feelings of others in order to reach a family decision.

____9. The best way to love your spouse is to care more for your partner than you care for yourself.

____10. Generally speaking, the quality of family life is deteriorating today.

____11. There is one best approach or set of rules and principles that will ensure an effectively functioning family.

Do a family inventory: Assess your own family's communication behaviour using the list of qualities of healthy families on page 268 and the skills and strategies for improving family communication. Which qualities are (were) strongest? Which need(ed) the most improvement? When you get married and have children, what qualities do you feel will be most important for your family to have? How will you accomplish that?

Some people develop relationships of choice with their family members. In groups of five or six, identify someone who has developed such a relationship with (a) a sibling, (b) a parent, and (c) another relative. Discuss why some students have developed friendships with these family members and why other students have not. Explore how these relationships are likely to change over the next 10 to 20 years.

Web Resources

www.youtube.com Conduct a search by entering "John Gottmann." You'll find several videos in which the noted marriage researcher talks about marriage.

Interpersonal Relationships at Work (pages 273–280)

OBJECTIVES ❷ ❸ Describe the values and functions of workplace friendships, and the types of formal relationships and communication in the workplace, and the unique values and challenges associated with romantic relationships in the workplace.

Key Terms

sexual harassment *276*

quid pro quo *276*

upward communication *278*

downward communication *278*

hostile environment *279*

horizontal communication *279*

outward communication *279*

Critical Thinking Questions

1. In what ways are workplace friendships different from friendships outside the workplace? In what ways are they similar? Which kind of relationship is more challenging to maintain? Why?

2. Jerry is president of an IT company. He has a sense that his managers are not tapping the wealth of ideas and suggestions that lower-level employees might have for improving productivity. What specific strategies could Jerry implement to improve upward communication?

3. Ethics: You've become very attracted to one of your subordinates with whom you get along with very well. You work well together and have had lunch and drinks together. You suggest pursuing a romantic relationship, but the subordinate feels that this would create conflict of interest. If you really think this could be a special long-term relationship, should you continue to convince the subordinate, or return to a purely professional relationship? Why?

4. Ethics: Clayton has email service at work but not at home. Is it ethical for Clayton to use the computer at work on company time to send and receive email messages from his brother three or four times a week?

Activities

What values or functions of a workplace friendship are most important to you? Make a list and compare it with those of your classmates.

You believe your boss is treating you unfairly because you have not responded to what you interpreted as romantic overtures (though no explicit request for a date or affection has ever been made). How can you best address this issue?

Think about the best manager or supervisor you have worked for or observed. Make a list of the qualities that you think made this manager so effective. Think about the worst manager or supervisor you've worked for or observed. Make a list of the qualities that made the manager so ineffective. Compare your lists with those of your classmates and identify the five best and five worst qualities. To what degree does communication play a role in these qualities?

Web Resources

www.workrelationships.com/site/quiz This 15-item quiz, the Appropriate Workplace Behaviour Test, is designed to test your knowledge of ethical relational behaviour in the workplace.

www.uky.edu/~drlane/orgcomm/325ch11.ppt#263,7 This site offers a PowerPoint presentation on workplace relationship challenges.

Chapter 1

1. "Solitary Confinement Should Be Banned in Most Cases, UN Expert Says," UN News Centre (October 18, 2011), http://www.un.org/apps/news/story.asp?NewsID=40097

2. J. T. Masterson, S. A. Beebe, and N. H. Watson, *Invitation to Effective Speech Communication* (Glenview, IL: Scott, Foresman, 1989).

3. W. Carl and S. Duck, "How to Do Things with Relationships … and How Relationships Do Things with Us," *Communication Yearbook*, 28 (2004): 1–35.

4. M. Buber, *I and Thou* (New York: Scribner's, 1958); also see M. Buber, *Between Man and Man* (New York: Macmillan, 1965). For a detailed discussion of perspectives on interpersonal communication and relationship development, see G. H. Stamp, "A Qualitatively Constructed Interpersonal Communication Model: A Grounded Theory Analysis," *Human Communication Research*, 25(4) (June 1999): 531–547; J. P. Dillard, D. H. Solomon, and M. T. Palmer, "Structuring the Concept of Relational Communication," *Communication Monographs*, 66 (March 1999): 49–65.

5. D. Yankelovich, *The Magic of Dialogue: Transforming Conflict into Cooperation* (New York: Simon & Schuster, 1999); for an excellent discussion of dialogue, also see S. W. Littlejohn and K. Domenici, *Engaging Communication in Conflict: Systemic Practice* (Thousand Oaks, CA: Sage, 2001), 25–51.

6. Buber, *I and Thou*.

7. V. Satir, *Peoplemaking* (Palo Alto, CA: Science and Behavior Books, 1972); J.B. Miller and P.A. deWinstanley, "The Role of Interpersonal Competence in Memory for Conversation," *Personality and Social Psychology Bulletin* 28 (January 2002): 78–89.

8. A. Astin, *What Matters in College? Four Critical Years Revisited* (San Francisco: Jossey-Bass, 1993).

9. Conference Board of Canada, *Employability Skills 2000+* (Ottawa: Conference Board of Canada, 2000), www.conferenceboard.ca

10. M. Argyle, *The Psychology of Happiness* (London: Routledge, 2001).

11. L. Chalmers and A. Milan, "Marital Satisfaction During the Retirement Years," *Canadian Social Trends* (Spring 2005), Statistics Canada Catalogue No. 11-008.

12. M. Argyle, *The Psychology of Interpersonal Behaviour* (London: Penguin, 1983).

13. Canadian Mental Health Association (Vancouver), "Understanding Depression" (October 1995).

14. Sherry Turkle, TED Talk, March 2012on.ted.com/Turkle. Accessed April 5, 2012.

15. http://www.emarketer.com/Article/Twitter-Trails-Facebook-by-Long-Shot-Canada/1011972#sthash.vDcoqxIP.dpuf

16. CRTC, Communications Monitoring Report, 2015 http://www.crtc.gc.ca/eng/publications/reports/PolicyMonitoring/2015/cmr.htm

17. Cisco, VNI Mobile Forecast Highlights, 2014-2019 http://www.cisco.com/assets/sol/sp/vni/forecast_highlights_mobile/index.html#~Country

18. D. Knox, V. Daniels, L. Sturdivant, and M. E. Zusman, "College Student Use of the Internet for Mate Selection," *College Student Journal*, 35 (March 2001): 158.

19. http://www.huffingtonpost.com/james-parsons/facebooks-war-continues-against-fake-profiles-and-bots_b_6914282.html

20. K. M. Cornetto, "Suspicion in Cyberspace: Deception and Detection in the Context of Internet Relay Chat Rooms," paper presented at the annual meeting of the National Communication Association, Chicago (November 1999).

21. J. B. Walther, B. Van Der Heide, S.-Y. Kim, D. Westerman, and S. T. Tong, "The Role of Friends' Appearance and Behavior on Evaluations of Individuals on Facebook: Are We Known by the Company We Keep?" *Human Communication Research*, 34 (2008): 28–49; also see N. S. Baron, *Always On; Language in an Online and Mobile World* (Oxford: Oxford University Press, 2008), 64–70; N. Chesley, "Blurring Boundaries? Linking Technology Use, Spillover, Individual Distress, and Family Satisfaction," *Journal of Marriage and Family,* 67 (December 2005): 1237–1248; D. K.-S. Chan and G. H.-L. Cheng, "A Comparison of Offline and Online Friendship Qualities at Different Stages of Relationship Development," *Journal of Social and Personal Relationships*, 21 (2004): 305–320; R. R. Provine, R. J. Spencer, and D. L. Mandell, "Emotional Expression Online: Emoticons Punctuate Website Text Message," *Journal of Language and Social Psychology* 26 (2007): 299-307."

22. J. Shuler, "E-mail Communication and Relationships," in *The Psychology of Cyberspace* (August 1998), www.rider.edu/users/suler/psycyber/psycyber.html

23. Amanda Frank, "Fired over Facebook Comments," http://career-advice.monster.ca/in-the-workplace/leaving-a-job/firedover-facebook-comments-canada/article.aspx

24. Elizabeth Bromstein, "14 Canadians who were fired for social media posts," Workopolis, May 15, 2015 04:15 pm http://www.workopolis.com/content/advice/article/14-canadians-who-were-fired-for-social-media-posts/

25. "Editorial: The danger of using Twitter," *Chicago Tribune*, December 24, 2013 http://articles.chicagotribune.com/2013-12-24/opinion/ct-twitter-regret-edit-1224-jm-20131224_1_tweet-twitter-users-twitterverse

26. R. Kraut, S. Kiesler, B. Boneva, J. Cummings, V. Helgeson, and A. Crawford, "Internet Paradox Revisited," *Journal of Social Issues*, 58 (2002): 49–74; P. E. N. Howard, L. Raine, and S. Jones, "Days and Nights on the Internet: The Impact of a Diffusing Technology," *American Behavioral Scientist*, 45 (2001): 383–404.

27. Pew Internet & American Life Project, "September 2005 Daily Tracking Survey/Online Dating Extension," http://www.pewinternet.org/pdfs/Online_Dating_Questions.pdf

28. L. C. Tidwell and J. B. Walther, "Computer-Mediated Communication Effects on Disclosure, Impressions, and Interpersonal Evaluations: Getting to Know One Another a Bit at a Time," *Human Communication Research* 28 (July 2002): 317–348.

29. N. S. Baron, *Always On: Language in an Online and Mobile World.* (Oxford: Oxford University Press, 2008), 27.

30. I. Sproull and S. Kiesler, "Reducing Social Context Cues: Electronic Mail in Organizational Communication," *Management Science*, 32 (1986): 1492–1513.

31. L. K. Trevino, R. L. Draft, and R. H. Lengel, "Understanding Managers' Media Choices: A Symbolic Interactionist Perspective," in *Organizations and Communication Technology*, edited by J. Fulk and C. Steinfield (Newbury Park, CA: Sage, 1990), 71–74.

32. W. S. Sanders, "Uncertainty Reduction and Information-Seeking Strategies on Facebook," paper presented to the National Communication Association, San Diego, CA (November 2008).

33. J. B. Walther and L. Tidwell, "When Is Mediated Communication Not Interpersonal?" in K. Galvin and P. Cooper, *Making Connections* (Los Angeles: Roxbury Press, 1996).

34. T. Pearce, "How Much Does Your Teen Text? Try 4,050 Times a Month," *The Globe and Mail Online*, October 15, 2010, http://www.theglobeandmail.com/life/the-hotbutton/how-much-does-your-teen-text-try-4050-times-amonth/article1759423

35. As cited by D. Crystal, *txtng: The gr8 db8* (New York: Oxford University Press, 2008).

36. Crystal, *txtng: The gr8 db8*, 42.

37. A. Kingston and A. Ballingall, "Public Display of Disaffection," *Maclean's*, 124(36) (September 19, 2011): 57–58.

38. "Text Messaging," Emily Post, http://www.emilypost.com/home-and-family-life/133-college-andbeyond/391-text-messaging

39. B. Zuckerman, "Ryan Reynolds," *People*, 75 (25) (June 27, 2011), http://www.people.com/people/archive/article/0,20505409,00.html

40. See D. Barnlund, *Interpersonal Communication: Survey and Studies* (Boston: Houghton Mifflin, 1968).

41. O. Wiio, *Wiio's Laws—and Some Others* (Espoo, Finland: WelinGoos, 1978).

42. S. B. Shimanoff, *Communication Rules: Theory and Research* (Beverly Hills: Sage, 1980).

43. M. Argyle, M. Hendershot, and A. Furnham, "The Rules of Social Relationships," *British Journal of Social Psychology,* 24 (1985): 125–139.

44. For a discussion of criticism of the communibiological approach, see C. M. Condit, "Culture and Biology in Human Communication: Toward a Multi-causal Model," *Communication Education*, 49(1) (January 2000): 7–24.

45. J. Hakansson and H. Montgomery, "Empathy as an Interpersonal Phenomenon," *Journal of Social and Personal Relationships*, 20 (2003): 267–284; Y. Nakatani, "The Effects of Awareness-Raising Training on Oral Communication Strategy Use," *The Modern Language Journal*, 89 (2005): 76–91.

46. J. M. Twenge, *Generation Me: Why Today's Young Americans Are More Confident, Assertive, Entitled—and More Miserable Than Ever Before* (New York: Free Press, 2006), 69.

47. M. V. Redmond, "Adaptation in Everyday Interactions," paper presented at the annual meeting of the Chicago: National Communication Association (November 1997).

48. F. Maina, "Culturally Relevant Pedagogy: First Nations Education in Canada", *The Canadian Journal of Native Studies*, 17(2) (1991): 293–314.

Chapter 2

1. K. Horney, *Neurosis and Human Growth* (New York: W. W. Norton, 1950), 17.

2. R. A. Baron and D. Byrne, *Social Psychology* (Boston: Allyn & Bacon, 2003).

3. E. Goffman, *The Presentation of Self in Everyday Life* (Garden City, NY: Doubleday, Anchor, 1959).

Also see E. Goffman, *Frame Analysis: An Essay on the Organization of Experience*, p. 508 (Cambridge, MA: Harvard University Press, 1974).

4. W. James, *The Principles of Psychology* (New York: Holt, 1890).

5. C. H. Cooley, *Human Nature and the Social Order* (New York: Scribner's, 1902).

6. J. Poisson, "Footloose and Gender-Free: Toronto Couple Believe Children Should Make Their Own Decisions, Including Whether to Tell People If They Are a Boy or a Girl," *Toronto Star*, May 21, 2011, A.26.

7. This adaptation of S. L. Bem's work is from R. M. Berko, L. B. Rosenfeld, and L. A. Samovar, *Connecting: A Culture-Sensitive Approach to Interpersonal Communication Competency* (Fort Worth, TX: Harcourt, Brace, 1994).

8. B. Marcus, F. Machilek, and A. Schütz, "Personality in Cyberspace: Personal Web Sites as Media for Personality Expressions and Impressions," *Journal of Personality and Social Psychology*, 90(6) (2006): 1014–1031; J. B. Walther, B. Van Der Heide, S. Y. Kim, D. Westerman, and S. T. Tong, "The Role of Friends' Appearance and Behavior on Evaluations of Individuals on Facebook: Are We Known by the Company We Keep?" *Human Communication Research*, 34 (2008): 28–49.

9. L. C. Tidwell and J. B. Walther, "Computer-Mediated Communication Effects on Disclosure, Impressions, and Interpersonal Evaluations: Getting to Know One Another a Bit at a Time," *Human Communication Research*, 28 (July 2002): 317–348.

10. B. Cornwell and D. C. Lundgren, "Love on the Internet: Involvement and Misrepresentation in Romantic Relationships in Cyberspace vs. Realspace," *Computers in Human Behavior*, 17 (2001): 197–211.

11. D. Knox, V. Daniels, L. Sturdivant, and M. E. Zusman, "College Student Use of the Internet for Mate Selection," *College Student Journal*, 35 (March 2001): 158.

12. M. K. Matsuba, "Searching for Self and Relationships Online," *CyberPsychology & Behavior*, 3 (2006): 275–284.

13. L. A. Lefton, *Psychology* (Boston: Allyn & Bacon, 2000).

14. For research supporting the five major personality traits see: R. R. McCrae and P. T. Costa, "Validation of the Five-Factor Model of Personality Across Instruments and Observers," *Journal of Personality and Social Psychology* 52 (1987): 81–90; S. V. Paunonen and M. S. Ashton, "Big Five Factors and Facets and the Prediction of Behavior," *Journal of Personality & Social Psychology* 81 (2001): 524–39; H. E. Cattell, "The Original Big Five: A Historical Perspective," *European Review of Applied Psychology* (1996): 5–14.

15. S. Booth-Butterfield, "Instructional Interventions for Situational Anxiety and Avoidance," *Communication Education*, 37 (1988): 214–223.

16. J. C. McCroskey and V. P. Richmond, *Fundamentals of Human Communication: An Interpersonal Perspective* (Prospect Heights, IL: Waveland Press, 1996).

17. Booth-Butterfield, "Instructional Interventions."

18. P. Zimbardo, *Shyness, What It Is, What to Do About It* (Reading, MA: Addison-Wesley, 1977).

19. F. E. X. Dance and C. Larson, *The Functions of Human Communication* (New York: Holt, Rinehart & Winston, 1976), 141.

20. G. H. Mead, *Mind, Self and Society* (Chicago: University of Chicago Press, 1934).

21. A. A. Milne, *The House at Pooh Corner*, Methuen and Co, 1928.

22. Summarized by D. E. Hamachek, *Encounters with the Self* (New York: Holt, Rinehart & Winston, 1982), 3–5; R. B. Adler and N. Towne (eds.), *Looking Out/Looking In* (Fort Worth, TX: Harcourt, Brace, Jovanovich, 1993). Also see C. R. Berger, "Self-Conception and Social Information Processing," in *Personality and Interpersonal Communication*, edited by J. C. McCroskey and J. A. Daly (Newbury Park, CA: Sage, 1987), 275–303.

23. Hamachek, *Encounters with the Self*; Berger, "Self-Conception and Social Information Processing."

24. W. C. Schutz, *FIRO: A Three-Dimensional Theory of Interpersonal Behavior* (New York: Holt, Rinehart & Winston, 1958).

25. V. J. Derlega, B. A. Winstead, A. Mathews, and A. L. Braitman, "Why Does Someone Reveal Highly Personal Information? Attributions For and Against Self-Disclosure in Close Relationships," *Communication Research Reports* 25, no. 2 (May 2008): 115–30.

26. Dindia, "Self-Disclosure Research."

27. J. P. Forgas, "Affective Influence on Self-Disclosure: Mood Effects on the Intimacy and Reciprocity of Disclosing Personal Information," *Journal of Personality and Social Psychology* 100, no. 3 (2011): 449–61.

28. B. J. Bond, "He Posted, She Posted: Gender Differences in Self-Disclosure on Social Network Sites," *Rocky Mountain Communication Review* 6, no. 2 (October 2009): 29–37.

29. B. J. Bond, "He Posted, She Posted," 29.

30. Adapted from W. Ham, *Man's Living Religions* (Independence, MO: Herald Publishing House, 1966), 39–40.

31. S. Petronio, *Boundaries of Privacy: Dialectics of Disclosure* (Albany: State University of New York Press, 2000).

Chapter 3

1. M. Gladwell, *Blink: The Power of Thinking Without Thinking* (New York: Little, Brown, 2005).

2. G. A. Kelly, *The Psychology of Personal Constructs* (New York: Norton, 1995).

3. S. Utz, "Show Me Your Friends and I Will Tell You What Type of Person You Are: How One's Profile, Number of Friends, and Type of Friends Influence Impression Formation on Social Networking Sites," *Journal of Computer-Mediated Communication* 15 (2010): 314–35.

4. S. D. Gosling, D. Gaddis, and S. Vazire, "Personality Impressions Based on Facebook Profiles," In *Proceedings of the International Conference on Weblogs and Social Media* (Boulder, CO, March 26–28, 2007).

5. S. T. Tong, B. Van Der Heide, L. Langwell, and J. B. Walther, "Too Much of a Good Thing? The Relationship Between Number of Friends and Interpersonal Impressions on Facebook," *Journal of Computer-Mediated Communication* 13 (2008): 531–49.

6. S. Asch, "Forming Impressions of Personality," *Journal of Abnormal and Social Psychology*, 41 (1946): 258–290.

7. F. Heider, *The Psychology of Interpersonal Relations* (New York: Wiley, 1958).

8. A. L. Vangelisti and S. L. Young, "When Words Hurt: The Effects of Perceived Intentionality on Interpersonal Relationships," *Journal of Social and Personal Relationships*, 17 (2000): 393–424.

9. G. W. F. Hegel, *Phenomenology of Mind* (Germany: Wurzburg & Bamburg, 1807).

10. R. M. Kowalski, S. Walker, R. Wilkinson, A. Queen, and B. Sharpe, "Lying, Cheating, Complaining, and Other Aversive Interpersonal Behaviors: A Narrative Examination of the Darker Side of Relationships," *Journal of Social and Personal Relationships*, 20 (2003): 472–490.

11. P. Cateora and J. Hess, *International Marketing* (Homewood, IL: Irwin, 1979), 89, as discussed by L. A. Samovar and R. E. Porter, *Communication Between Cultures* (Belmont, CA: Wadsworth, 2001), 52.

12. Asch, "Forming Impressions of Personality."

13. E. Goffman, *The Presentation of Self in Everyday Life* (Garden City, NY: Doubleday, Anchor, 1959).

Chapter 4

1. J. Gray, *Men Are from Mars, Women Are from Venus* (New York: HarperCollins, 1992).

2. J. T. Wood, "A Critical Response to John Gray's Mars and Venus Portrayals of Men and Women," *Southern Communication Journal*, 67 (2002): 201–211.

3. D. Tannen, *You Just Don't Understand* (New York: William Morrow, 1990).

4. P. Gibson, "Gay Male and Lesbian Youth Suicide," *Report of the Secretary's Task Force on Youth Suicide*, edited by M. R. Feinleib (Washington, DC: U.S. Department of Health and Human Services, January 1989).

5. *Random House Webster's Unabridged Dictionary* (New York: Random House, 1998), 1590.

6. B. J. Allen, *Differences Matter: Communicating Social Identity* (Long Grove, IL: Waveland, 2004), 68.

7. J. Montepare, E. Koff, D. Zaitchik, and M. Albert, "The Use of Body Movements and Gestures as Cues to Emotions in Younger and Older Adults," *Journal of Nonverbal Behavior*, 23 (Summer 1999): 133–152.

8. N. Howe and W. Strauss, *Millennials Rising: The Next Great Generation* (New York: Vintage, 2000).

9. Howe and Strauss, *Millennials Rising*.

10. H. Karp, C. Fuller, and D. Sirias, *Bridging the Boomer Xer Gap: Creating Authentic Teams for High Performance at Work* (Palo Alto, CA: Davies-Black, 2002).

11. M. Argyle, *The Psychology of Social Class* (London: Routledge, 1994).

12. B. J. Allen, *Difference Matters: Communicating Social Identity* (Long Grove, IL: Waveland, 2004), 113.

13. G. Hofstede, *Culture's Consequences: International Differences in Work-Related Values* (Beverly Hills, CA: Sage, 1980).

14. R. Shuter and S. Chattopadhyay, "Emerging Interpersonal Norms of Text Messaging in India and the United States," *Journal of Intercultural Communication Research* 39, no. 2 (July 2010): 123–47.

15. P. Cateora and J. Hess, *International Marketing* (Homewood, IL: Irwin, 1979), 89, as discussed by L. A. Samovar and R. E. Porter, *Communication Between Cultures* (Belmont, CA: Wadsworth, 1991), 52.

16. E. T. Hall, *Beyond Culture* (Garden City, NY: Doubleday, 1976).

17. Peter Coy, "The Future of Work," *Business Week* (August 20 and 27, 2007), p. 43.

18. R. E. Axtell, *Do's and Taboos of Hosting International Visitors* (New York: John Wiley & Sons, 1989), 118.

19. S. Kamekar, M. B. Kolsawalla, and T. Mazareth, "Occupational Prestige as a Function of Occupant's Gender," *Journal of Applied Social Psychology*, 19 (1988): 681–688.

20. D. E. Brown, "Human Universals and Their Implications," in *Being Humans: Anthropological Universality and Particularity in Transdisciplinary Perspectives*, edited by N. Roughley (New York: Walter de Gruyter, 2000), 156–174. For an applied discussion of these universals, see Steven Pinker, *The Blank Slate: The Modern Denial of Human Nature* (London: Penguin, 2002).

21. S. Pinker, "The Moral Instinct," *The New York Times Magazine* (January 13, 2008): 36–42.

22. Pinker, "The Moral Instinct," 36.

23. F. L. Casmir, "Foundations for the Study of Intercultural Communication Based on a Third-Culture Building Model," *International Journal of Intercultural Relations*, 23 (1999): 91–116; also see S. DeTurk, "Intercultural Empathy: Myth, Competency, or Possibility for Alliance Building?" *Communication Education*, 50 (October 2001): 374–384.

24. B. J. Broome, "Building Shared Meaning: Implications of a Relational Approach to Empathy for Teaching Intercultural Communication," Human Communication Research 1 (1975): 99–125."

25. W. B. Gudykunst and Y. Kim, *Communicating with Strangers* (New York: Random House, 1984); Gudykunst, *Bridging Differences*.

26. D. Matsumoto, S. Nakagawa, and S. H. Yoo, "Culture, Emotion Regulation, and Adjustment," *Journal of Personality and Social Psychology* 94, no. 6 (2008): 925–937.

27. M. J. Bennett, "Overcoming the Golden Rule: Sympathy and Empathy," in *Communication Yearbook 3*, edited by D. Nimmo (Beverly Hills, CA: Sage, 1979), 407–422.

28. Bennett, "Overcoming the Golden Rule."

Chapter 5

1. H. J. M. Nouwen, *Bread for the Journey* (San Francisco: HarperCollins, 1997), entry for March 11.

2. L. Cooper and T. Buchanan, "Listening Competency on Campus: A Psychometric Analysis of Student Learning," *The International Journal of Listening*, 24 (2010): 141–63.

3. D. Worthington, G. D. Bodie, and C. Gearhart, "The Listening Styles Profile Revised (LSP-R): A Scale Revision and Validation," paper presented at the Eastern Communication Association, Arlington, VA (2011).

4. D. Bodie and D. L. Worthington, "Revisiting the Listening Styles Profile (LSP-16): A Confirmatory Factor Analytic Approach to Scale Validation and Reliability Estimation," *International Journal of Listening* 24.2 (2010): 69–88.

5. D. L. Worthington, "Exploring the Relationship Between Listening Style Preference and Personality," *International Journal of Listening* 17 (2003): 68–87; D. L. Worthington, "Exploring Jurors' Listening Processes: The Effect of Listening Style Preference on Juror Decision Making," *International Journal of Listening* 17 (2003): 20–37.

6. J. B. Weaver III and M. Kirtley, "Listening Styles and Empathy," *Southern Communication Journal 2* (1995): 131–41.

7. Worthington, "Exploring the Relationship Between Listening Style Preference and Personality."

8. Worthington, "Exploring Jurors' Listening Processes: The Effect of Listening Style Preference on Juror Decision Making."

9. L. Sargent and J. B. Weaver, "Correlates Between Communication Apprehension and Listening Style Preferences," *Communication Research Reports* 14 (1997): 74–78.

10. D. Tannen, *You Just Don't Understand* (New York: William Morrow, 1990).

11. O. E. Rankis, *The Effects of Message Structure, Sexual Gender, and Verbal Organizing Ability upon Learning Message Information* (doctoral dissertation, Ohio University, 1981); C. H. Weaver, *Human Listening: Process and Behavior* (New York: Bobbs-Merrill, 1972); R. D. Halley, "Distractibility of Males and Females in Competing Aural Message Situations: A Research Note," *Human Communication Research*, 2 (1975): 79–82; S. A. Beebe and J. T. Masterson, *Family Talk: Interpersonal Communication in the Family* (New York: Random House, 1986); J. Lurito, "Listening and Gender," paper presented to the Radiological Society of North America, Chicago (2000), as cited by L. Tanner, "Listening Study Finds Difference in the Sexes," *Austin-American Statesman*, November 29, 2000: A11.

12. S. L. Sargent and J. B. Weaver III, "Listening Styles: Sex Differences in Perceptions of Self and Others," *International Journal of Listening*, 17 (2003): 5–18.

13. ABC News, *20/20*, January 12, 1998, featuring the research of communication researcher Kittie Watson.

14. J. T. Wood, "A Critical Response to John Gray's Mars and Venus Portrayals of Men and Women," *Southern Communication Journal*, 67 (2002): 201–211.

15. The Canadian Press, Cellphones in Class Could Be Useful: McGuinty," (September 15, 2010).

16. "Teens Say Cellphones Distracting in Class," Parentcentral.ca (February 24, 2011).

17. D. Carnegie, *How to Win Friends and Influence People* (New York: Holiday House, 1937).

18. K. Acheson, "Silence as Gesture: Rethinking the Nature of Communicative Silence," *Communication Theory* 18 (2008): 535–55.

19. K. K. Halone and L. L. Pecchioni, "Relational Listening: A Grounded Theoretical Model," *Communication Reports*, 14 (2001): 59–71.

20. K. Ruyter and M. G. M. Wetzels, "The Impact of Perceived Listening Behavior in Voice-to-Voice Service Encounters," *Journal of Service Research*, 2 (February 2000): 276–284.

21. M. V. Redmond, "The Functions of Empathy (Decentering) in Human Relations," *Human Relationships* 42 (1993): 593–606; also see M. V. Redmond, "A Multidimensional Theory and Measure of Social Decentering," *Journal of Research in Personality* 19 (1995): 35–58. For an excellent discussion of the role of emotions in establishing empathy, see D. Golem, *Emotional Intelligence* (New York: Bantam, 1995).

22. D. L. Rehling, "Compassionate Listening: A Framework for Listening to the Seriously Ill," *The International Journal of Listening* 22 (2008): 83–89.

23. For an excellent review of research about expressing affection and empathy, see K. Floyd, *Communicating Affection: Interpersonal Behavior and Social Context* (Cambridge, England: Cambridge University Press, 2006); also see K. Floyd and M. T. Morman, "Affection Received from Fathers as a Predictor of Men's Affection with Their Own Sons: Tests of the Modeling and Compensation Hypotheses." *Communication Monographs* 67, no. 4 (2000): 347–61.

24. Floyd, *Communicating Affection*.

25. S. Gilbert, "Self-Disclosure, Intimacy, and Communication in Families," *Family Coordinator*, 25(3) (1976): 221–231.

26. E. Sieburg and C. Larson, "Dimensions of Interpersonal Response," paper delivered at the annual conference of the International Communication

Association, Phoenix, Arizona (April 1971); K. Ellis, "Perceived Teacher Confirmation: The Development and Validation of an Instrument and Two Studies of the Relationship to Cognitive and Affective Learning," *Human Communication Research*, 26 (2000): 264–291.

27. R. Boulton, *People Skills* (New York: Simon & Shuster, 1979). We also acknowledge others who have presented excellent applications of listening and responding skills in interpersonal and group contexts: D. A. Romig and L. J. Romig, *Structured Teamwork Guide* (Austin, TX: Performance Resources, 1990); S. Deep and L. Sussman, *Smart Moves* (Reading, MA: Addison-Wesley, 1990); P. R. Scholtes, *The Team Handbook* (Madison, WI: Joiner Associates, 1992); Hargie, Sanders, and Dickson, *Social Skills*; S.W. Littlejohn and K. Domenici, *Engaging Communication in Conflict; Systemic Practice* (Thousand Oaks, CA: Sage, 2001).

Chapter 6

1. B. Spitzberg and J. P. Dillard, "Social Skills and Communication," in *Interpersonal Communication Research: Advances Through Meta-Analysis*, edited by M. Allen, R. W. Preiss, B. M. Gayle, and N. Burrell (Mahwah, NJ: Erlbaum, 2002), 89–107.

2. K. Kellermann and N. A. Palomares, "Topical Profiling: Emergent, Co-occurring, and Relationally Defining Topics in Talk," *Journal of Language and Social Psychology*, 23 (2004): 308–337.

3. C. K. Ogden and I. A. Richards, *The Meaning of Meaning* (London: Kegan, Paul Trench, Trubner, 1923).

4. *The American Heritage Dictionary of the English Language* (Boston: Houghton Mifflin, 1969), 1162.

5. See G. H. Mead, *Mind, Self and Society* (Chicago: University of Chicago Press, 1934); H. Blumer, *Symbolic Interactionism: Perspective and Method* (Englewood Cliffs, NJ: Prentice Hall, 1969).

6. A. Korzybski, *Science and Sanity* (Lancaster, PA: Science Press, 1941).

7. G. Gusdorff, *Speaking* (Evanston, IL: Northwestern University Press, 1965), 9.

8. C. S. Areni and J. R. Sparks, "Language Power and Persuasion," *Psychology & Marketing* 22 (2005): 507–25.

9. B. L. Whorf, "Science and Linguistics," in *Language, Thought and Reality*, edited by J. B. Carroll (Cambridge, MA: MIT Press, 1956): 207. This discussion of the Sapir-Whorf hypothesis is based on D. Crystal, *The Cambridge Encyclopedia of Language* (Cambridge, UK: Cambridge University Press, 1997).

10. We thank one of our anonymous reviewers for this example.

11. W. Johnson, *People in Quandaries* (New York: Harper & Row, 1946).

12. S. Duck, "Talking Relationships into Being," *Journal of Social and Personal Relationships*, 12 (1995): 535–540.

13. J. K. Alberts, C. G. Yoshimura, M. Rabby, and R. Loschiavo, "Mapping the Topography of Couples' Daily Conversation," *Journal of Social and Personal Relationships*, 22 (2005): 299–322.

14. Heraclitus, Fragment 41, quoted by Plato in *Cratylus*.

15. Associated Press. "'Canuck' No Slur, Editor Rehired," *Peterborough Examiner*, February 28, 1999, B1.

16. D. Yankelovich, *The Magic of Dialogue: Transforming Conflict into Cooperation* (New York: Simon & Shuster, 1999).

17. J. Gray, *Men Are from Mars, Women Are from Venus* (New York: HarperCollins, 1992).

18. J. T. Wood, "A Critical Response to John Gray's Mars and Venus Portrayals of Men and Women," *The Southern Communication Journal* 67 (2002): 201–11.

19. J. Wood, *Gendered Lives: Communication, Gender, and Culture,* (Mason, OH: Cengage Learning, 2008).

20. V. B. Harper, Jr., "Differences Between Males and Females Concerning Perceived Electronic Mail Appropriateness," *The Quarterly Review of Distance Education* 9, no. 3 (2008): 311–16.

21. A. Colley and Z. Todd, "Gender-Linked Differences in the Style and Content of E-Mails to Friends," *Journal of Language and Social Psychology* 21 (2002): 380–92.

22. A. C. Knupsky and N. M. Hagy-Bell, "Dear Professor: The Influence of Recipient Sex and Status on Personalization and Politeness in E-Mail," *Journal of Language and Social Psychology* 30, no. 1 (2011): 103–13.

23. J. Wood, *Gendered Lives.*

24. J. Wood, *Gendered Lives.*

25. M. R. Mehl, S. Vazire, N. Ramirez-Esparza, R. Slatcher, and J. W. Pennebaker, "Are Women Really More Talkative Than Men?" *Science* 317, no. 5834 (2007): 82.

26. A. Mulac, "The Gender-Linked Language Effect: Do Language Differences Really Make A Difference?" In *Sex Differences and Similarities in Communication: Critical Essays and Empirical Investigations of Sex and Gender in Interaction,* edited by D. J. Canary and K. Dindia (Mahwah, NJ: Erlbaum, 1998), 127–55.

27. Tannen, *You Just Don't Understand.*

28. J.R. Gibb, "Defensive Communication," *Journal of Communication,* 11 (1961): 141–148. Also see R. Boulton, *People Skills* (New York: Simon & Shuster, 1979), 14–26; O. Hargie, C. Sanders, and D. Dickson, "Social Skills," in *Interpersonal Communication* (London: Routledge, 1994); O. Hargie (Ed.), *The Handbook of Communication Skills* (London: Routledge, 1997); S. W. Littlejohn and K. Domenici, *Engaging Communication in Conflict* (Thousand Oaks, CA: Sage, 2001).

29. A. M. Bippus, "Recipients' Criteria for Evaluating the Skillfulness of Comforting Communication and the Outcomes of Comforting Communication," *Communication Monographs,* 68 (2001): 301–313.

30. K. Ohbuchi, M. Kameda, and N. Agarie, "Apology as Aggression Control: Its Role in Mediating Appraisal of and Response to Harm," *Journal of Personality and Social Psychology,* 56 (1989): 219–227.

31. J. R. Meyer and K. Rothenberg, "Repairing Regretted Messages: Effects of Emotional State, Relationship Type, and Seriousness of Offense," *Communication Research Reports,* 21 (2005): 348–356.

32. D. Cloven and M. E. Roloff, "The Chilling Effect of Aggressive Potential on the Expression of Complaints in Intimate Relationships," *Communication Monographs,* 60 (1993): 199–219.

33. V. Boogart, "Discovering the Social Impacts of Facebook on a College Campus" (master's thesis, Kansas State University, 2006), 38, as cited in N. S. Baron, *Always On; Language in an Online and Mobile World* (Oxford: Oxford University Press, 2008), 97.

34. R. Wright, "E-mail and Prozac," *The New York Times*, April 17, 2007, A23.

35. Baron, *Always On,* 226.

Chapter 7

1. Several studies offer evidence of the universality of facial expressions. See P. Ekman, "Strong Evidence for Universals in Facial Expressions: A Reply to Russell's Mistaken Critique," *Psychological Bulletin*, 115 (1994): 268–287; Ekman and Friesen, "Constants Across Culture in the Face and Emotion," *Journal of Personality and Social Psychology*, Vol 17(2), Feb 1971, 124–129; *Facial Action Coding System: Investigator's Guide* (Palo Alto, CA: Consulting Psychologists Press, 1978); P. Ekman and W. Friesen, "A New Pan-cultural Facial Expression of Emotion," *Motivation & Emotion*, 10 (1986): 159–168; P. Ekman, E. R. Sorenson, and W. Friesen, "Pancultural Elements in Facial Displays of Emotion," *Science,* 164 (1969): 86–88; D. Matsumoto, "Scalar Ratings of Contempt Expressions," *Journal of Nonverbal Behavior,* 29 (2005): 91–104.

2. C. Beaulieu, "Intercultural Study of Personal Space: A Case Study." *Journal of Applied Social Psychology*, 34(4) (2004): 794–805.

3. For a review of culture and touch, see R. Dibiase and J. Gunnoe, "Gender and Cultural Differences in Touching Behavior," *The Journal of Social Psychology,* 144(1) (2004): 49–62.

4. M. Moore, *Journal of Ethology and Sociology* (Summer 1994); also see D. Knox and K. Wilson, "Dating Behaviours of University Students," *Family Relations,* 30 (1981): 255–258.

5. A. Mehrabian, *Silent Messages* (Belmont, CA: Wadsworth, 1972), 108.

6. P. Ekman and W. V. Friesen, "The Repertoire of Nonverbal Behaviour: Categories, Origins, Usage and Coding," *Semiotica*, 1 (1969): 49–98.

7. P. Ekman, W. V. Friesen, and S. S. Tomkins, "Facial Affect Scoring Technique: A First Validity Study," *Semiotica*, 3 (1971): 37–58; P. Ekman and W. V. Friesen, *Unmasking the Face* (Englewood Cliffs, NJ: Prentice-Hall, 1975).

8. Ekman and Friesen, *Unmasking the Face*; Ekman, Friesen, and Tomkins, "Facial Affect Scoring Technique."

9. J. Schwartz, "NASA Official Says He Held Out Hope in Final Moments," *New York Times*, February 15, 2003, A14.

10. R. L. Street, R. M. Brady, and W. B. Putman, "The Influence of Speech Rate Stereotypes and Rate Similarity on Listeners' Evaluations of Speakers," *Journal of Language and Social Psychology*, 2 (1983): 37–56.

11. E. T. Hall, *The Hidden Dimension* (Garden City, NY: Doubleday, 1966).

12. J. H. Langlois, L. Kalakanis, A. J. Rubenstein, A. Larson, M. Hallam, and M. Smoot, "Maxims or Myths of Beauty? A Meta-analytic and Theoretical Review," *Psychological Bulletin* 126 (2000): 390–423.

13. P. Collett, *The Book of Tells* (London: Doubleday, 2003).

14. A. Mehrabian, *Nonverbal Communication* (Chicago: Aldine Atherton, 1972).

15. K. J. Tusing and J. P. Dillard, "The Sounds of Dominance: Vocal Precursors of Perceived Dominance During Interpersonal Influence," *Human Communication Research*, 26 (January 2000): 148–171.

16. Collett, *The Book of Tells*.

17. J. A. Hall, J. C. Rosip, L. Smith LeBeau, T. G. Horgan, and J. D. Carter, "Attributing the Sources of Accuracy in Unequal-Power Dyadic Communication: Who Is Better and Why?" *Journal of Experimental Social Psychology*, 41 (2005): 1–10.

18. J. K. Burgoon, L. A. Stern, and L. Dillman, *Interpersonal Adaptation: Dyadic Interaction Patterns* (Cambridge, England: Cambridge University Press, 1995).

19. J. K Burgoon and A. E. Bacue, "Nonverbal Communication Skills," in *Handbook of Communication and Social Interaction Skills,* edited by J. O. Greene and B. R. Burleson (Mahwah, NJ: Erlbaum, 2003), 179–219.

20. B. M. DePaulo and H. S. Friedman, "Nonverbal Communication," in *The Handbook of Social Psychology*, edited by D. T. Gilbert, S. T. Fiske, and G. Lindzey (New York: McGraw-Hill, 1998).

21. M. Argyle, *Bodily Communication*, (New York: Methuen, 1988).

22. W. G. Woodal and J. K. Burgoon, "The Effects of Nonverbal Synchrony on Message Comprehension and Persuasiveness," *Journal of Nonverbal Behavior* 5 (1981): 207–23.

23. Argyle, *Bodily Communication*.

24. Woodal and Burgoon, "The Effects of Nonverbal Synchrony on Message Comprehension and Persuasiveness."

Chapter 8

1. S. A. Lloyd, "Conflict in Premarital Relationships: Differential Perceptions of Males and Females," *Family Relations*, 36 (1987): 290–294.

2. Our definition of conflict is adapted from W. Wilmot and J. Hocker, *Interpersonal Conflict* (New York: McGraw-Hill, 2007).

3. J. W. Keltner, *Mediation: Toward a Civilized System of Dispute Resolution* (Annandale, VA: Speech Communication Association, 1987); also see Wilmot and Hocker, *Interpersonal Conflict*.

4. D. J. Canary, W. R. Cupach, and R. T. Serpe, "A Competence-Based Approach to Examining Interpersonal Conflict: Test of a Longitudinal Model," *Communication Research* 29 (February 2001): 79–104; also see L. N. Olson and D. O. Braithwaite, "'If You Hit Me Again, I'll Hit You Back': Conflict Management Strategies of Individuals Experiencing Aggression During Conflicts," *Communication Studies* 55 (2004): 271–85; L. L. Marshall, "Physical and Psychological Abuse," in *The Dark Side of Interpersonal Communication,* edited by W. R. Cupach and B. H. Spitzberg (Hillsdale, NJ: Erlbaum, 1994), 281–311.

5. M. Sinha, "Family Violence in Canada: A Statistical Profile, 2010," *Juristat* (Ottawa: Statistics Canada; May 22, 2012): 20.

6. L. A. Kurdek, "Areas of Conflict for Gay, Lesbian, and Heterosexual Couples: What Couples Argue About Influences Relationship Satisfaction," *Journal of Marriage and the Family*, 56 (November 1994): 923–934; L. A. Kurdek, "Conflict Resolution Styles in Gay, Lesbian, Heterosexual Nonparent, and Heterosexual Parent Couples," *Journal of Marriage and the Family*, 56 (August 1994): 705–722.

7. R. J. Doolittle, *Orientations of Communication and Conflict* (Chicago: Science Research Associates, 1976), 7–9.

8. G. R. Miller and M. Steinberg, *Between People: A New Analysis of Interpersonal Communication* (Chicago: Science Research Associates, 1975), 264.

9. C. M. Hoppe, "Interpersonal Aggression as a Function of Subject's Sex Role Identification, Opponent's Sex, and Degree of Provocation," *Journal of Personality*, 47 (1979): 317–329.

10. K. Kellerman, "A Goal-Directed Approach to Gaining Compliance: Relating Differences Among Goals to Differences in Behaviors," *Communication Research*, 31 (2004): 397–445.

11. E. V. Wilson, "Perceived Effectiveness of Interpersonal Persuasion Strategies in Computer

-Mediated Communication," *Computers in Human Behavior* 19 (2003): 537–52.

12. R. Kilmann and K. Thomas, "Interpersonal Conflict-Handling Behavior as Reflections of Jungian Personality Dimensions," *Psychological Reports*, 37 (1975): 971–980.

13. A. Buysse, A. De Clercq, L. Verhofstadt, et al., "Dealing with Relational Conflict: A Picture in Milliseconds," *Journal of Social and Personal Relationships*, 17 (2000): 574–579.

14. J. P. Caughlin and R. S. Malis, "Demand/ Withdraw Communication Between Parents and Adolescents as a Correlate of Relational Satisfaction," *Communication Reports*, 17 (2004): 59–71.

15. R. Fisher and W. Ury, *Getting to Yes: Negotiating Agreement Without Giving In* (Boston: Houghton Mifflin, 1988). Also see D. Yankelovich, *The Magic of Dialogue: Transforming Conflict into Cooperation* (New York: Simon & Schuster, 1999).

16. D. Cramer, "Linking Conflict Management Behaviors and Relational Satisfaction: The Intervening Role of Conflict Outcome Satisfaction," *Journal of Social and Personal Relationships*, 19 (2000): 425–432.

17. S. R. Covey, *The Seven Habits of Highly Effective People* (New York: Simon & Schuster, 1989), 235.

18. S. G. Lakey and D. J. Canary, "Actor Goal Achievement and Sensitivity to Partner as Critical Factors in Understanding Interpersonal Communication Competence and Conflict Strategies." *Communication Monographs*, 69 (2002): 217–35.

19. W. Ury, *Getting Past No* (New York: Bantam Books, 1993); also see S. Hackley, "When Life Gives You Lemons: How to Deal with Difficult People," newsletter (Cambridge, MA: Harvard Business School Publishing Corporation, 2004.

Chapter 9

1. G. B. Ray and K. Floyd, "Nonverbal Expressions of Liking and Disliking in Initial Interaction: Encoding and Decoding Perspectives," *Southern Communication Journal*, 71 (2006): 45–65.

2. L. A. Baxter and C. Bullis, "Turning Points in Developing Romantic Relationships," *Communication Research*, 12 (1986): 469–493.

3. J. K. Kellas, D. Bean, C. Cunningham, and K. Y. Cheng, "The Ex-Files: Trajectories, Turning Points, and Adjustment in the Development of Post-dissolutional Relationships," *Journal of Social and Personal Relationships*, 25 (2008): 23–50.

4. S. Duck, "Interpersonal Communication in Developing Relationships," in *Explorations in Interpersonal Communication*, edited by G. R. Miller (Newbury Park, CA: Sage, 1976), 127–147.

5. J. W. Thibaut and H. H. Kelley, *The Social Psychology of Groups* (New York: Wiley, 1959).

6. L. A. Baxter, "Dialectical Contradictions in Relationship Development," in *Handbook of Personal Relationships*, edited by S. W. Duck (Chichester, UK: Wiley, 1988), 257–273; L. A. Baxter and B. M. Montgomery, "Rethinking Communication in Personal Relationships from a Dialectical Perspective," in *Handbook of Personal Relationships*, 2nd ed., edited by S. W. Duck (Chichester, UK: Wiley, 1997), 325–349.

7. D. R. Pawlowski, "Dialectical Tensions in Marital Partners' Accounts of Their Relationships," *Communication Quarterly*, 46 (1998): 396–416.

8. V. J. Derlega, B. A. Winstead, and K. Greene, "Self-Disclosure and Starting a Close Relationship," in *Handbook of Relationship Initiation*, edited by S. Sprecher, A. Wenzel, and J. Harvey (New York: Psychology Press, 2008), 153–194.

9. J. A. Bargh, K. Y. A. McKenna, and G. M. Fitzsimons, "Can You See the Real Me? Activation and Expression of the 'True Self' on the Internet," *Journal of Social Issues*, 58 (2002): 33–48.

10. A. M. Ledbetter, "Measuring Online Communication Attitude: Scale Development and Validation," *Communication Monographs Volume 76, Issue 4, 2009* (in press).

11. A. J. Johnson, E. Wittenberg, M. M. Villagran, M. Mazur, and P. Villagran, "Relational Progression as a Dialectic: Examining Turning Points in Communication Among Friends," *Communication Monographs*, 70 (2003): 230–249.

12. I. Altman and D. A. Taylor, *Social Penetration: The Development of Interpersonal Relationships* (New York: Holt, Rinehart, and Winston, 1973).

13. A. P. Bochner, "On the Efficacy of Openness in Close Relationships," in *Communication Yearbook 5*, edited by M. Burgoon (New Brunswick, NJ: Transaction Books, 1982), 109–24.

Chapter 10

1. P. Noller, "Bringing It All Together: A Theoretical Approach," in *The Cambridge Handbook of Personal Relationships*, edited by A. L. Vangelisti and D. Perlman (New York: Cambridge University Press, 2006), 769–789.

2. G. Makoul and M. E. Roloff, "The Role of Efficacy and Outcome Expectations in the Decision to Withhold Relational Complaints," *Communication Research*, 25 (1998): 25–30.

3. J. W. Younger, R. L. Piferi, R. L. Jobe, and K. A. Lawler, "Dimensions of Forgiveness: The Views of Laypersons," *Journal of Social and Personal Relationships*, 21 (2004): 837–855.

4. V. R. Waldron and D. L. Kelley, *Communicating Forgiveness* (Thousand Oaks, CA: Sage, 2008).

5. J. Lyndon, T. Pierce, and S. O'Regan, "Coping with Moral Commitment to Long-Distance Dating Relationships." Journal of Personality and Social Psychology 73 (1997): 104–13."

6. S. O. Gaines, Jr. and W. Ickes, "Perspectives on Interracial Relationships," in *The Social Psychology of Personal Relationships,* edited by W. Ickes and S. Duck (New York: Wiley, 2000), 55–78.

7. Statistics Canada. "2011 Census of Population: Families, households, marital status, structural type of dwelling, collectives," *The Daily*, Wednesday, September 19, 2012. http://www.statcan.gc.ca /daily-quotidien/120919/dq120919a-eng.htm

8. D. O'Hair and W. Cody, "Deception," in *The Dark Side of Interpersonal Communication,* edited by W. R. Cupach and B. H. Spitzberg (Hillsdale, NJ: Erlbaum, 1994), 181–213.

9. M. Knapp, "Lying and Deception in Close Relationships," in *The Cambridge Handbook of Personal Relationships*, edited by A. L. Vangelisti and D. Perlman (New York: Cambridge University Press, 2006), 517–32.

10. J. K. Burgoon and D. B. Buller, "Interpersonal Deception Theory: Purposive and Interdependent Behavior during Deception," in *Engaging Theories in Interpersonal Communication: Multiple Perspectives,* edited by L. A. Baxter and D. O. Braithwaite (Thousand Oaks, CA: Sage, 2008), 227–39.

11. A. E. Lucchetti, "Deception in Disclosing One's Sexual History: Safe-Sex Avoidance or Ignorance?" in *Communication Quarterly*, 47 (1999): 300–314.

12. O'Hair and Cody, "Deception."

13. T. R. Levine, K. J. K. Asada, and L. L. Massi Lindsey, "The Relative Impact of Violation Type and Lie Severity on Judgments of Message Deceitfulness," paper presented at the annual meeting of the National Communication Association (2002).

14. D. A. DePaulo and B. M. Kashy, "Everyday Lies in Close and Casual Relationships," *Journal of Personality and Social Psychology*, 74 (1998): 63–80.

15. O'Hair and Cody, "Deception."

16. A. L. Vangelisti and L. P. Crumley, "Reactions to Messages That Hurt: The Influence of Relational Contexts," *Communication Monographs*, 65 (1998): 173–196.

17. J. A. Feeney, "Hurt Feelings in Couple Relationships: Towards Integrative Models of the Negative Effects of Hurtful Events," *Journal of Social and Personal Relationships,* 21 (2004): 487–508.

18. Vangelisti and Crumley, "Reactions to Messages That Hurt."

19. S. Zhang and L. Stafford, "Perceived Face Threat of Honest but Hurtful Evaluative Messages in Romantic Relationships," *Western Journal of Communication,* 72 (2008): 19–39.

20. Zhang and Stafford, "Perceived Face Threat of Honest but Hurtful Evaluative Messages."

21. S. L. Young, "Factors That Influence Recipients' Appraisals of Hurtful Communication," *Journal of Social and Personal Relationships,* 21 (2004): 291–303.

22. L. K. Guerrero and P. A. Anderson, "Jealousy and Envy," in *The Dark Side of Close Relationships,* edited by W. R. Cupach and B. H. Spitzberg (Hillsdale, NJ: Erlbaum, 1994), 33–70.

23. L. K. Knobloch, "Evaluating a Contextual Model of Responses to Relational Uncertainty-Increasing Events: The Role of Intimacy, Appraisals, and Emotions," *Human Communication Research,* 31 (2005): 60–101.

24. L. K. Guerrero and P. A. Anderson, "Jealousy and Envy," in *The Dark Side of Close Relationships,* edited by W. R. Cupach and B. H. Spitzberg (Hillsdale, NJ: Erlbaum, 1994), 33–70.

25. Guerrero and Anderson, "Jealousy and Envy."

26. A. A. Fleishmann, B. H. Spitzberg, P. A. Anderson, and S. C. Roesch, "Tickling the Green Monster: Jealousy Induction in Relationships," *Journal of Social and Personal Relationships,* 22 (2005): 49–73.

27. Fleishmann, Spitzberg, Anderson, and Roesch, "Tickling the Green Monster."

28. S. M. Yoshimura, "Emotional and Behavioral Responses in Romantic Jealousy Expressions," *Communication Reports,* 17 (2004): 85–102.

29. Yoshimura, "Emotional and Behavioral Responses."

30. J. L. Bevan, "General Partner and Relational Uncertainty as Consequences of Another Jealousy Expression," *Western Journal of Communication,* 68 (2004): 195–218.

31. W. R. Cupach and B. H. Spitzberg, "Obsessive Relational Intrusion and Stalking," in *The Dark Side of Close Relationships,* edited by B. H. Spitzberg and W. R. Cupach (Mahwah, NJ: Erlbaum, 1998), 233–64.

32. W. R. Cupach and B. H. Spitzberg, *The Dark Side of Relationship Pursuit: From Attraction to Obsession and Stalking* (Mahwah, NJ: Erlbaum, 2004).

33. Cupach and Spitzberg, *The Dark Side of Relationship Pursuit,* 29–30.

34. B. H. Spitzberg and W. R. Cupach, "The Inappropriateness of Relational Intrusion," in *Inappropriate Relationships: The Unconventional, the Disapproved, and the Forbidden,* edited by R. Goodwin and D. Cramer (Mahwah, NJ: Erlbaum, 2002), 191–220.

35. Cupach and Spitzberg, "Obsessive Relational Intrusion and Stalking."

36. Cupach and Spitzberg, *The Dark Side of Relationship Pursuit*, 69–71.

37. V. Ravensberg and C. Miller, "Stalking Among Young Adults: A Review of the Preliminary Research," *Aggression and Violent Behavior*, 8 (2003): 455–469; B. H. Spitzberg, A. M. Nicastro, and A. V. Cousins, "Exploring the Interactional Phenomenon of Stalking and Obsessive Relational Intrusion," *Communication Reports*, 11 (1998): 33–48.

38. B. H. Spitzberg and W. R. Cupach, "Managing Unwanted Pursuit," in *Studies in Applied Interpersonal Communication*, edited by M. T. Motley (Thousand Oaks, CA: Sage, 2008), 3–26.

39. M. Madden, "Privacy Management on Social Media Sites," Pew Research Center's Internet & American Life Project, 2012.

40. Madden, "Privacy Management on Social Media Sites."

41. M. Philips and B. H. Spitzberg, "Speculating about Spying on MySpace and Beyond: Social Network Surveillance and Obsessive Relational Intrusion," in *Computer-Mediated Communication in Personal Relationships* edited by K. B. Wright and L. M. Webb (New York: Peter Lang, 2011): 344–67.

42. M. P. Johnson, "Violence and Abuse in Personal Relationships: Conflict, Terror, and Resistance in Intimate Partnerships," in *The Cambridge Handbook of Personal Relationships,* edited by A. L. Vangelisti and D. Perlman (New York: Cambridge University Press, 2006), 557–576.

43. Johnson, "Violence and Abuse in Personal Relationships."

44. Johnson, "Violence and Abuse in Personal Relationships."

45. Johnson, "Violence and Abuse in Personal Relationships."

46. C. M. Feldman and C. A. Ridley, "The Role of Conflict-Based Communication Responses and Outcomes in Male Domestic Violence Toward Female Partners," *Journal of Social and Personal Relationships,* 17 (2000): 552–573.

47. S. A. Jang, S. W. Smith, and T. R. Levine, "To Stay or to Leave? The Role of Attachment Styles in Communication Patterns and Potential Termination of Romantic Relationships Following Discovery of Deception," *Communication Monographs*, 69 (2002): 236–252.

48. G. R. Miller and M. R. Parks, "Communication in Dissolving Relationships," in *Personal Relationships 4: Dissolving Personal Relationships*, edited by S. W. Duck (London: Academic Press, 1982), 127–154.

49. J. Gottman with N. Silver, *Why Marriages Succeed or Fail* (New York: Simon and Schuster, 1994).

50. Gottman and Silver, *Why Marriages Succeed or Fail.*

51. W. W. Wilmot, "Relationship Rejuvenation," in *Communication and Relational Maintenance*, edited by D. J. Canary and L. Stafford (San Diego, CA: Elsevier, 1994), 255–274.

52. W. W. Wilmot and D. C. Stevens, "Relationship Rejuvenation: Arresting Decline in Personal Relationships," in *Uses of "Structure" in Communication Studies*, edited by R. L. Conville (Westport, CT: Praeger, 1994), 103–124.

53. G. R. Miller and M. R. Parks, "Communication in Dissolving Relationships."

54. S. W. Duck, in *Personal Relationships 4: Dissolving Personal Relationships*, edited by S.W. Duck (London: Academic Press,1982), 1–29.

55. M. J. Cody, "A Typology of Disengagement Strategies and an Examination of the Role Intimacy, Reactions to Inequity and Relational Problems Play in Strategy Selection," *Communication Monographs*, 49(3) (1982): 148–170.

56. M. Argyle and M. Henderson, *The Anatomy of Relationships* (New York: Guilford, 1991).

57. S. W. Duck, Understanding Relationships (New York: Guildford Press, 1991).

58. Duck, "A Topography of Relationship Disengagement and Dissolution."

59. Miller and Parks, "Communication in Dissolving Relationships."

60. L. A. Baxter, "Accomplishing Relationship Disengagement," in *Understanding Personal Relationships: An Interdisciplinary Approach*, edited by S. Duck and D. Perlman (Beverly Hills: Sage, 1984), 243–265.

61. D. DeStephen, "Integrating Relational Termination into a General Model of Communication Competence," paper presented at the annual meeting of the Speech Communication Association (1985).

62. Baxter, "Accomplishing Relationship Disengagement."

63. DeStephen, "Integrating Relational Termination into a General Model of Communication Competence."

64. Cody, "A Typology of Disengagement Strategies."

65. A. Weber, "Loving, Leaving, and Letting Go: Coping with Nonmarital Breakups," in *The Dark Side of Close Relationships*, edited by B. H. Spitzberg and W. R. Cupach (Mahwah, NJ: Erlbaum, 1998), 267–306.

Chapter 11

1. Maire Sinha, "Parenting and Child Support After Separation or Divorce," Spotlight on Canadians: Results from the General Social Survey. Statistics Canada, February 2014.

2. G. P. Murdock, *Social Structure* (New York: Free Press, 1965). Originally published in 1949.

3. 2011 Census Dictionary, Statistics Canada.

4. Vanier Institute of the Family, "About VIF," www.vifamily.ca/about/about.html

5. D. E. Beck and M. A. Jones, *Progress on Family Problems: A Nationwide Study of Clients' and Counselors' Views on Family Agency Services* (New York: Family Service Association of America, 1973).

6. H. J. Markman, "Prediction of Mental Distress: A 5-Year Follow-Up," *Journal of Consulting and Clinical Psychology*, 49 (1981): 760–762.

7. D. H. L. Olson, H. L. McCubbin, H. L. Barnes, et al., *Families: What Makes Them Work* (Beverly Hills, CA: Sage, 1983).

8. J. Koesten, "Family Communication Patterns, Sex of Subject, and Communication Competence," *Communication Monographs*, 71 (2004): 226–244.

9. W. Rawlins, *Friendship Matters: Communication, Dialectics, and the Life Course* (New York: DeGruyter, 1992), 157.

10. P. H. Wright, "Toward an Expanded Orientation to the Comparative Study of Women's and Men's Same-Sex Friendships," in *Sex Differences and Similarities in Communication,* 2nd ed., edited by K. Dindia and D. J. Canary (Mahwah, NJ: Erlbaum, 2006), 37–57.

11. Wright, "Toward an Expanded Orientation."

12. G. L. Greif, *Buddy System: Understanding Male Friendships* (New York: Oxford, 2009).

13. V. Satir, *The New Peoplemaking* (Mountain View, CA: Science & Behaviour Books, 1988), 4.

14. Satir, *Peoplemaking*, 13–14.

15. J. P. Caughlin, "Family Communication Standards: What Counts as Excellent Family Communication and How Are Such Standards Associated with Family Satisfaction?" *Human Communication Research*, 29 (January 2003): 5–40.

16. K. M. Galvin and B. J. Brommel, *Family Communication: Cohesion and Change*, 5th ed. (New York: Longman, 2000).

17. Satir, *The New Peoplemaking*.

18. P. Noller and M. A. Fitzpatrick, *Communication in Family Relationships* (Englewood Cliff, NJ: Prentice Hall, 1993), 202.

19. J. Howard, *Families* (New York: Simon & Schuster, 1978), 286–291.

20. "Family violence in Canada: A statistical profile, 2013," *Juristat*, Canadian Centre for Justice Statistics (January 15, 2015).

21. J. Gottman with N. Silver, *Why Marriages Succeed or Fail* (New York: Simon & Schuster, 1994).

22. S. H. Mathews, *Friendships Through the Life Course: Oral Biographies in Old Age* (Beverly Hills, CA: Sage, 1986).

23. S. J. Holladay and K. S. Kerns, "Do Age Differences Matter in Close and Casual Relationships? A Comparison of Age Discrepant and Age Peer Friendships," *Communication Reports*, 12 (1999): 101–114.

24. M. A. Fitzpatrick, "Family Communication Patterns Theory: Observations on its Development and Application," Journal of Family Communication 4 (2004): 167–80.

25. X. de Souza Briggs, "'Some of My Best Friends Are …': Interracial Friendships, Class, and Segregation in America," *City & Community*, 6 (2007): 263–290.

26. J. K. Rempel and C. T. Burris, "Let Me Count the Ways: An Integrative Theory of Love and Hate," *Personal Relationships*, 12 (2005): 297–313.

27. Z. Rubin, *Liking and Loving: An Invitation to Social Psychology* (New York: Holt, Rinehart and Winston, 1973).

28. P. M. Sias, R.G. Heath, T. Perry, D. Silva, and B. Fix, "Narratives of Workplace Friendship Deterioration," Journal of Social and Personal Relationships 21 (2004): 321–40.

29. J. Gabarro and J. Kotter, "Managing Your Boss," *Harvard Business Review*, 58 (1980): 92–100.

30. F. Japlin, "Superior's Upward Influence, Satisfaction, and Openness in Superior-Subordinate Communication: A Reexamination of the 'Pelz Effect'," *Human Communication Research*, 6 (1980): 210–220.

31. Japlin, "Superior's Upward Influence."

32. Newswire, "Female Firefighters Fight More Than Fires," *Lethbridge Herald*, April 9, 2004, 5.

33. Adapted from K. Kellerman, S. Broatzman, T. S. Lim, and K. Kitao, "The Conversation MOP: Scenes in the Stream of Discourse," *Discourse Processes*, 12 (1989): 27–61.

34. A. E. Lindsey and W. R. Zahaki, "Perceptions of Men and Women Departing from Conversational Sex Role Stereotypes During Initial Interaction," in *Sex Differences and Similarities in Communication*, edited by D. J. Canary and K. Dindia (Mahwah, NJ: Erlbaum, 1998), 393–412.